History's Peru

UNIVERSITY PRESS OF FLORIDA

Florida A&M University, Tallahassee
Florida Atlantic University, Boca Raton
Florida Gulf Coast University, Ft. Myers
Florida International University, Miami
Florida State University, Tallahassee
New College of Florida, Sarasota
University of Central Florida, Orlando
University of Florida, Gainesville
University of North Florida, Jacksonville
University of South Florida, Tampa
University of West Florida, Pensacola

D0920867

History's Peru

The Poetics of Colonial and Postcolonial Historiography

Mark Thurner

University Press of Florida
Gainesville
Tallahassee
Tampa
Boca Raton
Pensacola
Orlando
Miami
Jacksonville
Ft. Myers
Sarasota

First cloth printing, 2011
First paperback printing, 2012

Library of Congress Cataloging-in-Publication Data
Thurner, Mark.
History's Peru : the poetics of colonial and postcolonial historiography /
Mark Thurner.
p. cm.
Includes bibliographical references and index.
ISBN 978-0-8130-3538-3 (cloth: alk. paper)
ISBN 978-0-8130-4199-5 (pbk.)
1. Peru—Historiography. 2. Historiography—Peru—History. 3. Peru—
History—Philosophy. I. Title.
F3430.4.T48 2011
985—dc22   2010024732

The University Press of Florida is the scholarly publishing agency for the
State University System of Florida, comprising Florida A&M University,
Florida Atlantic University, Florida Gulf Coast University, Florida
International University, Florida State University, New College of Florida,
University of Central Florida, University of Florida, University of North
Florida, University of South Florida, and University of West Florida.

University Press of Florida
15 Northwest 15th Street
Gainesville, FL 32611-2079
http://www.upf.com

For Ana

La tarea verdadera consiste ante todo en examinar los orígenes, los perjuicios y los procesos de las verdades recibidas. En una palabra, hacer cuestión expresa de la historia de la historia.

Edmundo O'Gorman, *Crisis y porvenir de la ciencia histórica*

Contents

Figures

Preface

This book is a history of history. As such, it is a book about a world made by and in the words of history. The name of this world is Peru. And the history of that name is Peruvian.

The history of the Peruvian history of Peru is of unusual interest for the simple reason that "Peru" is one of the first colonial subjects of the modern historical imagination. "Born in an abyss of history" at "the edge of the world" in the early 1500s, Peru's colonial genesis as a historical subject dovetailed with the earth-shifting daybreak of the global or "modern" age. This age and Peru's genesis saw the revival of the classical "arts of history" both in Europe and beyond, and as a result Peru was soon fashioned as a marvelous subject of those high arts. Centuries later, Peru's enlightened rebirth as a postcolonial historical subject corresponded with the fiery dawn of the Age of Revolutions and with the rise of historicism in Europe and elsewhere. In words and things postcolonial, Peru was also a pioneer. In sum, the history of Peruvian historiography registers an intellectual history of the colonial and postcolonial world that runs, at an illuminating critical distance, zigzag to the better-known early modern, modern, and contemporary history of European historical thought. My contention in this book is that this colonial and post-colonial zigzag offers new critical insights into the history of history at large. If world history is something more than a European invention, then Peru is a good place to look for that "something more."

The chapters that follow consist of a series of critical meditations on the key turning points, authors or writing subjects, and texts that have shaped the long course of the history of Peruvian historical writing. I begin with the beginning, that is, with the early colonial poetic invention of "Peru" as a historical subject, which I argue was largely the work of Inca Garcilaso de la Vega, and I end with the end, that is, with the twentieth-century philosophical historicism of Jorge Basadre, who pushed the concept of a "Peruvian history of Peru" to its aporetic finale. In between I retrace the colonial history of a Peruvian "Book of Kings" or dynastic tradition in its Renaissance, Baroque, and ghtened naturalist inflections, and then I turn to the fertile death of that tradition, under the auspices of a postcolonial historicism, in the republican and democratic age of the Peruvian people. Throughout, I base my history of Peruvian history on a pointed reading of the most influential writings of Peru's most significant historians.

Chapter 1 is an inquiry into the series of events that named and configured Peru as a subject of empire and history and, in particular, into Inca Garcilaso de la Vega's (1539–1616) founding exegesis of "the origin and principle of the name of Peru." Chapter 2 explores the enduring complicities between the "arts of history" and the "arts of rule" in colonial Peru, again principally via the foundational texts of Inca Garcilaso. Chapter 3 is a meditation on the brilliant art and theory behind the early-eighteenth-century histories of Spain and Peru written by the Creole polymath Pedro de Peralta Barnuevo (1664–1743). Chapter 4 retraces the enlightened naturalist and historicist configuration of Peru, in the late eighteenth and early nineteenth centuries, as an ancient and universal "country" of prescient "genius," primarily through the texts of José Hipólito Unanue (1755–1833) and Mariano Eduardo de Rivero y Ustariz (1798–1857). Chapter 5 probes, principally via the pioneering pen of postcolonial Peru's "schoolmaster of history" Sebastián Lorente (1813–1884), the discursive means by which the rule of the Spanish monarchs and of the dynastic arts of history were displaced, under the republican sign of revolution, by the name of the people and the book of Peruvian civilization. Chapter 6 further examines the deep political and figurative significance of Lorente's philosophical history of the soul of Peruvian civilization. Chapter 7 is a meditation on the philosophical wagers and aporia of the historicist opus of Jorge Basadre (1903–1980), perhaps Peru's most brilliant historical thinker. In the epilogue I explore some of the at-large theoretical implications of the history of Peruvian historical discourse.

Several of these chapters draw upon and rework previously published pieces. Chapter 1 reworks my essay, "The Founding Abyss of Colonial History, or 'The Origin and Principle of the Name of Peru,'" first published in *History and Theory* 48 (February 2009), 44–62. Chapter 3 draws upon my piece, "The 'As If' of 'The Book of Kings': Pedro de Peralta Barnuevo's Colonial Poetics of History," from *Latin American Research Review* 44, n. 1 (2009), 32–52. Chapter 5 revisits material that appeared in my earlier chapter, "Peruvian Genealogies of History and Nation," in Mark Thurner and Andrés Guerrero, eds., *After Spanish Rule: Postcolonial Predicaments of the Americas*, (Durham: Duke University Press, 2003), 141–75, and in my article, "After Colonialism and the King: Notes on the Peruvian Birth of 'Contemporary

History,'" from *Postcolonial Studies* 9, n. 4 (2006), 393–420. Chapter 7 draws upon my article, "Jorge Basadre's 'Peruvian History of Peru' or the Poetic Aporia of Historicism," published in *Hispanic American Historical Review* 88, n. 2 (2008), 247–83. I thank the editors of these pieces for permission to use that material here. In addition, and with the exception of figures 8 and 9, all of the images in this book appear courtesy of the John Carter Brown Library at Brown University.

The research for this book in Peru, the United States, and Spain was supported by grants from the Social Science Research Council, the Fulbright-Hays programs, the Fulbright Program, the John Carter Brown Library, the Lilly Library, and the University of Florida. In Peru, my research was made possible by the Instituto de Estudios Peruanos, the Sala de Investigaciones of the Biblioteca Nacional, the Archivo General de la Nación, and the Instituto Riva-Agüero of the Pontificia Universidad Católica del Perú. The dedicated staff, colleagues, and friends at these venerable agencies and institutions are sincerely and gratefully acknowledged.

This book would not be what it is without the stimulating conversation and engagement of my dear friends, colleagues, and graduate students in Lima, Quito, Madrid, Mexico City, Buenos Aires, and Gainesville, Florida. Among these, Andrés Guerrero and Juan Carlos Callirgos deserve special recognition for debating, reading, and commenting upon the various incarnations of this manuscript. Elías Palti has also been an inspiration, and his conversation and critical insights have helped me articulate the questions I pose in this book, and for that I am grateful.

The publication of this book was made possible in part by a small grant from the Department of History at the University of Florida. Among my dear colleagues in the History Department, I wish to give special thanks to department chair Joseph Spillane for his support of this project. Among the dedicated, professional staff at the University Press of Florida, I especially wish to thank editors Amy Gorelick and Jacqueline Kinghorn Brown, and also my copy editor, Barbara Drake, for bringing this book to an afterlife in print.

1

The Founding Abyss

History is, in the final analysis, susceptible to only one type of architecture, always the same one—a series of events happens to such and such a subject. We may choose other subjects: royalty instead of kings; social classes, the Mediterranean, or the Atlantic rather than generals and captains. We are no less confronted by the leap into the void, against which no auxiliary discipline's rigors offer a guarantee: we must name subjects, we must attribute to them states, affections, events. And that is where the adherents of the chronicling tradition were already waiting . . . for the partisans of a revolution in history.

Jacques Rancière, *The Names of History: On the Poetics of Knowledge*

In the beginning there was the name. And in the end what remain are the effects of the name. This is so because history is "susceptible to only one type of architecture." A subject is properly named, a passage of events is invariably narrated and explained as so many affects and states of grace or being. The pinch is that behind or before any proper name of history there is always a gap, a void, a nameless abyss. Ergo: in the beginning there was the abyss. And in the end what remain are the effects of an absence. Rancière explains: "there is history because there is an absence of things in words, of the denominated in names." The words and names of history are always more (because they stand in for), and always less than (because they lack the substance of) the things they denominate. This "more and less" of history is the poetic ground of invention, variation, and contention, for "it is in relation to this absence that the positions of historical discourse are defined."[1]

There is a second sense, inherent in the first, in which history is founded on a void or absence. As Michel de Certeau argues, history is at one and the same time a "labor of death" and "a labor against death." Its "paradoxical procedure" is to posit a death that may live as the loss that founds a history. By placing "absence and production in the same area" or "field of vision," history both lays "the past" to rest and brings it to literary afterlife in the violent and compensatory acts of writing and reading.[2] Indeed, as Hayden White notes, "history as a discipline presupposes the idea that there is a divide or a gap between the past and the present that requires a special discipline to bridge it."[3] The trace of this gap of death in historical discourse—already present in such founding texts as the *Histories* of Herodotus—is the founding *topos* and justification of historiography, nearly always a variation on these words: "so that these worthy deeds not be lost in the mists of time." This patent, retrospective gesture of remembrance and revelation, operated on the particular words that recall the deeds and things of the past, now registered as the "more and less" of writing, and which has long been called "historics," is always already prospective and hopeful, that is to say, laden with "poetics." This is so, as Roland Barthes reminds us, because the historian already knows what has not yet been told. In effect, the poetic gesture of all historics is to send a message to posterity that will shape that posterity by configuring its future past. This is why, argues Barthes, historical knowledge works very much like mythology: it is always written and read from and for a posterity that is "us" or "ours," that is to say, from a future that already is or was.[4] As a historics that cannot help be poetic, then, the writing of history is always about what has been and is, but also about what should or will be.[5]

As historics and poetics, or a poetics of historics, history is founded on a double absence. On the one hand, its creative and contentious condition of possibility is the void between words and things, names and the denominated; on the other hand, this possibility is engendered by death, that is, by the abyss of oblivion and estrangement that threatens to separate the (words and things of the) past from the (words and things of the) present. In the face of this double absence, history performs a poetic "leap into the void." This leap traces and sutures the gash between words and things, past and present. This leap of history, Rancière notes, is always made "on the wings of the signature . . . the mark of its identity, the proper name"; since the leap is retrospective, it always reaffirms the "world of names" that already is, since that world is in effect the proper name's collective posterity.[6]

"Peru" is a proper name or signature of history. Before 1500 there was nothing in the world named "Peru." By the early 1600s, however, "Peru" was one of the most famous names in the world, thanks in part to the words and things engendered by the long reach of Spanish empire, and to the keen interest of rival European powers and readers in that empire. Peru's meteoric rise to fame was not a calm affair. Coined in a colonial mis-encounter "at the edge of the world," Peru "as a name and social fact" was, in Jorge Basadre's words, "born of blood and tears in an abyss of history, with a loud crash that shook the world."[7]

This "loud crash that shook the world" may now be heard as the distant echo of the colonial birthing of the modern age. Indeed, Peru's violent and resonant founding as a subject of history is of unusual interest precisely because it heralded the sudden birth of globality and its new, universal history. "This new country" of the global historical imagination, named Peru, Basadre continued, "found its expression in a work which, far from being clandestine or ignored, would acquire universal fame. Its title is *Los comentarios reales de los incas* (The Royal Commentaries of the Incas)." Its author was Inca Garcilaso de la Vega. "Something of the mythological figure of the Centaur inhabited his eminent and bifurcated soul. This dualism was proper to the auroral hour to which he belonged. And in this dualism lies the stamp of unity" of Peruvian history.[8]

Following Basadre's lead, in this opening chapter I propose a rereading of Inca Garcilaso de la Vega's founding exegesis of "the origin and principle of the name of Peru." My reading seeks to offer an approximate answer to a haunting question: What does it mean to be "born in an abyss of history" at "the edge of the world" at the colonial dawn of the global age of modernity?

Historical Truth

The Mexican philosopher Edmundo O'Gorman once pointed out that to uncover the meaning of distant historical events one should begin not by diving into the ocean of the archive but by questioning, in a hermeneutics of suspicion, the regnant topoi and received knowledge handed down by the historiography. This irony of historical knowledge—the cumulative operation by which the disciplinary procedures that produce hefty tomes and scholarly consensus obscure the more immediate meanings of past events—led O'Gorman into ever-deeper interrogations of the origins of such deafening commonplaces as "the conquest of Mexico" and "the discovery of America."

In the case of the latter commonplace, O'Gorman's critical rereading of the early chronicles revealed that the idea that "Columbus discovered America" was based on the contemporary "legend of the anonymous navigator." According to this legend, Columbus had been tipped off by an unknown seaman who knew a secret route to strange new lands to the west. This account, which had gained much favor among the unschooled and learned alike was on the surface apocryphal, for it was known that Columbus did not in fact seek to discover new lands. He had merely sought a direct route to the Orient, on the outer edges of which he apparently sighted land. Moreover, "America" did not yet exist. Why then did this apocryphal topos hold sway over so many learned minds, and what does the fact that it did tell us about the meaning of "discovery"? To merely dismiss the old legend as "fable" or "ignorance," as many modern historians then did and now do, would be to fall into the sterile methodological dogmas of a "historical science" that would admit only "one historical truth."[9]

Questioning this single measure of truth, O'Gorman argued that the Rankean professors of historical science had busily buried, under volumes of turgid prose, the "plural hermeneutical truths" of that world-historical event, in effect creating their own "fables."[10] First among these "fables" of science was the absolute measure of what constitutes "historical truth" (*verdad histórica*) and "historical fact" or "historical event" (*hecho histórico*).[11] For O'Gorman, the supreme justices of historiography who proclaimed an account to be "ignorant" and "false," or "wise" and "true," actually hindered "historical understanding" or "comprehension" (*comprensión histórica*). Such comprehension was, he argued, itself historical, and as a result could not be based on the "easy comprehension" and absolute contrasts of the judgment-passing professors of history. Instead "truth," being human and so historical, was based on a more elusive "recognition." Human or historical truths, he argued, may or may not be "recognized" (*reconocer*). That is, one may "prefer not to recognize" (*desconocer*) a certain truth (and not necessarily at one's peril) in lieu of another, and such preferences of truth shifted over time. Truth shifted, O'Gorman noted, because "truth was not an eternal and passive possession" but "a demanding lover that, in effect, requires of us a continuous effort of adherence so that she will remain ours; it requires not only an initial acknowledgment or recognition [*conocimiento*] but repeated acknowledgment or re-recognition [*re-conocimiento*]."[12]

O'Gorman argued that the historical comprehension of "the legend of the anonymous navigator"—or indeed of any past historical event or fact—lie in the crucial interpretive distinction between "ignorance" and "the preference not to acknowledge." Those early chroniclers who vouched for the legend were not ignorant—as modern historical scientists often claimed—of Columbus's "Asian objective." They simply preferred not to acknowledge it in favor of another truth that was the major consequence or "posterity" of his journey for them: the "discovery of new lands." The focus on this other truth, which was the consequence of a past future prior to O'Gorman and subsequent to Columbus, had made the "legend of the anonymous navigator" a "hermeneutical necessity." Over time, people adhered to this preferred or beloved truth, so that the "new lands" to which Columbus was secretly privy became the hermeneutical basis or the ontological truth of "our American being" (*nuestro ser americano*). Writing from the Creole "we" (*nosotros*) of America, "the discovery" could now be understood as an "invention," that is, as a projection of "man's destiny" to "create new worlds" in his own image.[13] In short, for O'Gorman the historical truth of "America" had first to be "recognized" within existing frames of reference as an "entity," whence her "being" could be lovingly sustained as a spiritual and corporeal or "continental" realization of the inventive desire, in O'Gorman's gendered language, of "man" to adhere to those things and beings that he creates in his own image.

O'Gorman's concept of "invention" was historicist and ontological or what he called, after José Ortega y Gasset and José Gaos (the latter translated Martin Heidegger's *Sein und Zeit* into a highly readable Spanish), "historiological." For O'Gorman, historiology was "true" history because it consisted of (here he follows Kant and anticipates Foucault) a reflexive historical ontology of ourselves, but also, and this most notably, because "things and events in themselves are nothing; their being depends upon the meaning that is ceded to them by the frame of reference of that image of reality that prevails in that moment."[14] I do not wish to address here the philosophical problems associated with "historiology." Instead, I wish to make use of O'Gorman's insistence upon the nothingness of events and things prior to "their being" and "meaning."

O'Gorman's ontological preoccupation with the "invention of America" as a process constitutive of "her being" points to the beckoning abyss of the historical subject. That is, it points to the seductive, siren call of the immediate nonbeing of things and events. This call is answered with names. The violent and loving meanings that, in time, will come to attach themselves to these empty proper names become the proper subjects of history. Behind this nominating, subject-generating operation, lies what may be called the *mise en abyme* of the colonial and postcolonial predicament. That is, the name of the master subject of the history (in our case "Peru," and in O'Gorman's, "America") which comes to absorb the historically truthful "recognitions" and "re-recognitions" of possession and belonging is in part a projection of the colonizer's desire to create in his own image; at the same time, however, that name must escape any definitive creation and possession since in effect it marks an absence, a void, a nothingness. In short, the colonial name is not only a mirror of desire but also the mark of a violent event of absence that voids any definitive projection of desire. This void both invites and eludes *dmphe*

the gaze of those who name and create. More pointedly—and in my reading this is the numinous implication of Inca Garcilaso's exegesis of the name of Peru—by gazing into the void those who name and invent may come to see themselves and their invention reflected in an abysmal or uncanny fashion. I am particularly interested here in the trace of this abysmal reflection.

O'Gorman's brilliant reading of the topos of "the discovery of America" may thus elicit another level of inquiry, which may be summarized as follows. What is the not-yet-named "it" that in its status as a void or abyss demands to be assigned a proper name ("America" or "Peru") and a gendered pronoun? To put it another way: What lies in a proper name that marks not only a projection of imperial desire, and not only the "hermeneutical necessity" of the truthful writing of history, but also, in time, the beloved object of "recognition" and "re-recognition" for the colonized or the so-named (that is, for "Americans" and "Peruvians")? This I submit is the founding question of colonial and postcolonial history.

The Name of Peru as Trace of the Abysmal Event

This question is both historical and theoretical in nature since, as it were, the proper name is both the trace of an event *and* the poetic means that enables the relation of events as a meaningful story with a possible future, without which no historian may perform the necessary "leap into the void" between names and the denominated. In my reading, the question of the colonial name points toward a strange kind of subject-generating event. This strange event or set of events was probed in illuminating ways by Inca Garcilaso in *Los comentarios reales*. This time-honored text is widely recognized as a Renaissance classic of "Hispanic literature" and it has long been read in Peru and beyond as the founding "Peruvian history." Nevertheless, the historical truth of the founding event of naming or, as I prefer, of the name-event that Peru is, has been rendered opaque by two formidable literary and historiographical topoi: "the discovery of Peru," and "the conquest of Peru."

In pursuit of the possible historical meanings of the founding event of the naming of "Peru" that lie buried under the topoi of "discovery" and "conquest," I turn to concepts proposed by Alain Badiou in *Theory of the Subject* and *Being and Event*. Badiou's theory of the subject begins with the "negative" philosophical and linguistic notion, traceable to Aristotle, that the proper name always names a void or abyss.[15] That is to say, proper names are, in theory, empty. Still, for Badiou there must also be an *événementiel* means by which the proper name comes to "mark the void" and thereby to "found" a singular historical subject.[16] That is, there must be a means by which the emptiness or abyss of the name may become an agent of history. Following, or rather twisting, Basadre's insight that the "name and social fact of Peru" was "born in an abyss of history," I will call this means by which a void is marked and becomes a colonial subject "the abysmal event."

As Elías José Palti has argued, abysmal experience or "disaster" is familiar to us. It may be seen to characterize, for example, the late-twentieth-century intellectual experience of the "crisis of Marxism." Such an experience, Palti continues, is clearly evident in the post-structuralist Marxist thought to which Badiou's theory belongs. The concept, Palti adds, may also be deployed to assist in the historical understanding of past "disasters" or abysmal events, such as the Aztec reception of what is so routinely called "the conquest of Mexico."[17] In theory, the abysmal event is not so much a "conquest" or "colonization" of the mind as a momentary disruption of the normal intelligibility of signs and self. In Badiou's theory, this disruption entails the opening of an "ontological fissure" or "destructure" in the structure of experience and meaning. This fissure is for Badiou precisely the site of "the mark" or the proper name.

This site of fissure, or the place of the name, is prior to what I will call, also after Basadre, "the baptism" or baptismal event. A baptismal event occurs after the subject is named in a fissure, and is thus a "secondary event." In the baptismal event, the named fissure may become a historical subject by virtue of an interpretive reception that, if positive, confirms its name and elicits an adherence to its "promise" or "possibility" as a being. In O'Gorman's hermeneutical scheme, such a secondary event would be described as a process of "invention" and "recognition." In Badiou's theoretical idiom, it would appear to qualify as an "event-to-come," or multiple "second event." Badiou argues that the second event consists of at least two, suturing "interventions of interpretation," wherein the second of the two interventions establishes the meaning of the first for that historical subject that is thereby constituted in the interval between the two successive "second events." In other words, in Badiou's scheme, if a historical subject is to "leave its mark on history" it must first await news of the reception of its proper name in a second event that involves two interpretive interventions. Modifying Badiou's scheme, I will call the second or confirming intervention of this "second event" the "tertiary event" since, in this case, it is historiographical. That is to say, the tertiary event emerges as a commentary on the "primary" and "secondary" sources that report the abysmal event. I will also suggest that this tertiary historiographical event is on the order of what Roland Barthes calls the "inaugural performance" of the historian, who thereby endows his history with a "mytho-poetic" structure.

My reading of the events of naming begins with the secondary, event-making news, that is to say, with the first intervention of Badiou's "second event" that, in effect, would confirm the abysmal event. In the case of our numinous four-letter name, the confirmation was resounding, even euphoric: "her name resonated universally as a fascinating announcement of riches and well-being."[18] In sixteenth-century Europe, the very utterance of "Peru" could easily evoke dizzying images of El Dorado. The proverbial phrase *poseer el Perú* ("to have Peru" or "he's got Peru") was quickly coined in Spain to denote extraordinarily wealthy and adventurous men of great influence, and it anticipated by more than two centuries that other famous and now more remembered Spanish proverb about the New World: *hacer la América* ("do America"), that is to say, get rich fast. Even more exhilarating was the exuberant exclamation, *¡Vale un Perú!* ("That's worth a Peru!"), which may still be heard in Peru and other South American countries such as Argentina. This phrase appears to have initially evoked an image of Captain Francisco Pizarro's fabulous "gift of Peru" to the Holy Roman Emperor Charles V, King of Spain and "Emperor of the Indies," and soon "Emperor of Peru" as well.

Notably, Pizarro's gift to the emperor was, according to the chronicles, made possible by an earlier, even more fabulous gift. This earlier gift was the "king's ransom" or "palace full of gold" reportedly rendered to the captains Pizarro and Almagro by the captive Inca Atahualpa circa 1533. In the second part of the *Comentarios reales* Inca Garcilaso goes to great pains to crosscheck and quantify the sums of Atahualpa's ransom. His estimate comes out slightly lower than that of the Peruvian Jesuit Padre Blas Valera, who estimated the treasure's worth at 4.8 million ducats. Inca Garcilaso compares Atahualpa's ransom to those kings' ransoms reported by Jean Bodin for the monarchs of Europe, and proudly concludes that the Inca's was the greatest ransom the world had ever seen.

Pointedly, the Inca's gold and silver were, for Inca Garcilaso, the principle material source of Spain's newfound greatness, for it was well established that prior to the conquest of Peru "Spain had little money." Writing 70 years after the event, Inca Garcilaso wryly noted that Atahualpa's unprecedented ransom now seemed like a paltry sum to his fabulously rich Spanish readers: "10 or 12 million ducats worth of gold and silver now sail up the Guadalquivir each year, sent by my land to all of Spain, and [from there] to all of the Old World." As it continued to flow in ever great quantities into Spain and Europe,

Peru's mineral wealth "revealed herself to be a cruel stepmother [*madrastra*] to her own sons and a passionate mother to foreigners."[19]

The tense resonance of riches with ransom thus strikes a dystopian chord of a world upside-down in which the mothering earth abandons her own sons and embraces others. The proud historical account of Atahualpa's record-breaking ransom becomes an exercise in the work of mourning, the announcement of an impending colonial critique. In the eyes and souls of many of the "Peruvian" reading subjects whom Inca Garcilaso's history founds, these lines will become a melancholy augury of a shared postcolonial misery. ¡*Vale un Perú!* would become "the measure of what we have lost" or "the distance we have fallen," if not "the curse of Peru." Ravaged by that storm of plunder that fills and tatters the bent-back wings of the angel of colonial history, Peruvian Jobs would wonder if Peru would not have been better off without Incas and without mountains of gold and silver.[20]

And yet Inca Garcilaso's *Comentarios reales* is itself a "king's ransom" of another kind, for it would purchase in the republic of letters eternal riches of the soul. These riches far surpassed the material losses inflicted by conquest and colonization, for this literary ransom of the soul delivered the sovereign "Incas, Kings of Peru that were" (*los Incas Reyes del Perú que fueron*) to all future Peruvians. As a ransom that returned an imagined, retrospective sovereignty to Peruvians, it recognized not only the loss and curse of the "riches of the body" remitted to Spain and Europe, but the extent to which those Peruvian gifts had made Spain and Europe "great." And so the literary purchase of the Peruvian kings would yield the ample historical compensation of the proudly worn scar. "Peru" would come to be about much more than the fame and curse of gold and silver. Henceforth, "Peru" would be borne on the torn but still airborne wings of colonial history—wings granted not by the "angel of progress" but by the mourning son who finds his literary home in metropolitan exile.

As it happened, colonial events had lent the not-yet historian his torn wings, too. At the prime age of 21, Gómez Suárez de Figueroa (1539–1616) sailed for Spain, in part because he had no future in war-torn Peru, in part to clear his father's name (he was accused of acting against the Crown in the conflict between rival conquistador bands), and in part to seek royal recognition of his noble Inca lineage. Gómez Suárez had been trained in the martial arts in Peru, and thus took up the heroic life of arms in the service of "His August Majesty," Philip II, "King of Kings" and "Defender of the Faith." After a failed bid to return to Peru, Gómez took up the religious life in the small parish of Montilla, near learned Cordoba. Taking advantage of an old Spanish patriarchal custom, in 1563 he adopted the new name and honorific title of "El Inca Garcilaso de la Vega" or "Garcilaso Inca de la Vega."[21]

The Andalusian exile (*destierro*) of the aging "Inca" in the land of his father produced a critical and persuasive work both of erudite scholarship and soulful mourning. The measure of what was lost and dead and in need of writing was both an exegetical challenge and the source of personal pain, for nearly all of his beloved royal kinsmen on his princess mother's side had been slain. But what is personal (exile) and royally familiar (death) is "translated as the collective lament of a people."[22] This erudite lament-in-exile founds a newly beloved loss with a future, a recognized subject of history.

As Freud saw, the work of mourning consists of "recovering from the loss of a love object by withdrawing libido from that object and restoring it to the subject, [that is] by withdrawing it from them, and restoring it to us."[23] Inca Garcilaso's writing will transfer the object of childhood love (an abandoned *patria*) from the past Incas to the new "Peruvian empire" and the "Peruvians," thereby restoring "to us," from that which is dead and left behind, a history with a brilliant future—even if its ultimate destination was the pearly gates of the final reckoning or Last Judgment.

This founding history of loss is marked by the trace of not just any exile, however. The exile from the colonial mother in the imperial home of the father is foundational, for it builds a colonial Renaissance bridge of words across the spatio-temporal abyss that separated the ancient from the modern, the Old World from the New, "Kings" from "Incas," father from mother, "Spain" and "Rome" from "the Indies" and "Peru." In this imaginative transit, the *Comentarios reales* inaugurated a hybrid genre of modern history that would be written in the wake of empire, and that we now call colonial (and postcolonial) history. As the founding "centaurian" history of Peru, however, it is perhaps more aptly called cosmopolitan and colonial, or cosmo-colonial.

That "Peru" should evoke riches, ransom, and loss is so not only because Pizarro's marvelous "gift" to the emperor promised an unparalleled flow of ships laden with gold and silver. More significant was the invented historical or hermeneutical truth to which future "Peruvians" would belong: that Pizarro's gift of "Peru" would come to signify the transfer of *imperium* or sovereignty from the Incas to Charles V.

This fictive sovereignty was the hermeneutical necessity of the early chroniclers and it was fully elaborated by the postconquest historians, chief among them Inca Garcilaso. The Incas were portrayed in the earliest accounts of "the conquest of Peru" as the sovereign "lords of the land," as the natural "kings" of otherwise barbarian subjects, and there is no doubt that Inca Garcilaso's dynastic history of the Incas confirmed this process of invention by which the Incas became history's utopian "Incas, Kings of Peru that were."[24] Nevertheless, this invention had at its heart the figure of the barbarian, and this barbarian was implicated in the "first" or "abysmal" event that named Peru. Pizarro's "gift" offered the fictive "throne" of "Peru" to the emperor of the world, but it was the historian's hermeneutical and narrative necessity to write a proper story of a sovereign subject, with which he could take the leap into the void between names and the denominated, that made it so. In making this leap of writing, the exiled Inca historian needed both the barbarian and the void.

The (so far) unending paper life of that void or "abyss of history," properly Peruvian by name, was inaugurated by the Inca historian with these memorable words:

One [of the ships sent from Panama by Vasco Núñez de Balboa] sailed farther than the others down past the equator, navigating along the coast, and as it went on its way it caught sight of an Indian fishing at the mouth of a river like those many rivers that enter into the Ocean there. . . . The ship passed before the Indian. . . . By way of signs and words the Spaniards . . . inquired of him: "What land was this and what was it called?" By their facial expressions and gestures the Indian understood that they were questioning him, but he did not understand what they were asking him, and to those whom he understood to be questioning him, responded he with haste (before they could do him harm) by naming his proper name, saying "Beru," and then he added another [name], saying "Pelu." What he meant to say was: "If you ask me what I am called, then I call myself Beru, and if you ask me where I was, then I say I was in the river. . . ." The Christians understood in accordance with their desire, imagining that the Indian had understood and so responded appropriately, as if he and they had spoken in Castilian [Spanish]. Ever since that time, which was in 1515 or 1516, the Spaniards—corrupting both names as they have almost all of the words they take from the language of the Indians of that land . . . have called that rich and grand Empire . . . that the Inca Kings . . . had conquered and subjected, "Peru." . . . That is the origin and principle of the name of

Peru, so famous in the world, and rightly so, for she has filled the world with gold and silver, pearls and precious stones.[25]

For the bicultural, cosmo-colonial Inca Garcilaso, the name of Peru was both obviously erroneous and manifestly true, for it was a predictable corruption of words made irresistibly true by the history of the usage of words. By the early 1600s the origin of the name of Peru had become confused by the corruptions of translation, the repetitions of error, and a deepening oblivion. Among the several early accounts of the origin of the name, the most notable and informed was that of the "ghost chronicler" and intrepid *mestizo* Jesuit, Father Blas Valera.[26] Blas Valera had argued that the name was not "proper" to Peru but was instead a Spanish corruption of the Quechua term *pirua* (granary). Despite his great admiration for Blas Valera's historical writings (the lost source of much of his own history), Inca Garcilaso rejected this view on historical and linguistic grounds. *Pirua* could not be the origin of "Peru" since at the moment of its coinage (1515 or 1516), the Spaniards had not yet penetrated into the Inca-ruled, Quechua-speaking interior and so could not possibly have encountered this word or the thing it named. The first boatloads of Spaniards, the Inca noted, had landed in the northern reaches (today southern Ecuador and northern Peru) of the "barbarian" Yunga-speaking coastal region.[27] Shifting the ground of the controversy to the linguistic probabilities at hand in the historical moment of the first act of utterance of the name, Inca Garcilaso offered an alternative account based, apparently, on his secondhand knowledge of the Mochica or Yunga language of the coastal lowlands. He observed that "it is known that in the language of that distant coastal province, Pelu is an appellative name that means river in general."[28] Given this usage and since historical accounts suggested that the Spaniards had come ashore near the mouth of one of these rivers, it was likely that this Yunga name for river was implicated in the event of Spanish discovery. But that was insufficient proof, for how could the Spaniards, unschooled in Yunga, have known that "river" was called "Pelu"? At the mouth of some such "Pelu" the Spaniards had therefore encountered a stunned, Yunga-speaking "Indian" barbarian and taken him aboard. The proper name of this barbarian was Beru. In short, "Peru" is, in the first instance, the *événementiel* conjuncture of the utterance of the words "Beru" and "Pelu" in the mouth of Beru (the barbarian) in the mouth of Pelu (the river's mouth at the sea) in the ears of wayward Spanish explorers. This conjuncture or event of naming was, as it were, retrospectively invented by the second and third or tertiary event. As we have seen, the second event was the enthusiastic reception of the name in Europe, and the third or tertiary event was the exegetical proof, offered by Inca Garcilaso, that the name made sense in historical and linguistic terms. It was this tertiary event that would found Peruvian history.

Now following Blas Valera and yet another giant of Jesuit New World scholarship, José de Acosta, Inca Garcilaso confirmed that "in Peru" the names "Peru" and "New Castile" (in the early sixteenth century these names were applied interchangeably, although the measurable dominion granted to Captain Pizarro as the emperor's *adelantado* and named "the province of New Castile" was rather less expansive than the imaginary Peru) were uttered only by Spaniards.[29] Although "Peru" was the preferred name in Europe, the name of Peru was 60 years after contact still uncommon among the provincial natives, "because in their language they did not have a generic name for the union of the kingdoms and provinces of the Natural Lords [*kurakas* or ethnic chiefs] that ruled over them, as when one says Spain, Italy, or France, which hold within themselves many provinces. They were accustomed to naming each province by its own proper name . . . and they did not possess a proper name that signified the entire realm."[30]

Things were different for the Quechua speakers at the high center of the Inca realm, however, and particularly for those high nobles, like Inca Garcilaso's kin, who were the privileged caste of that realm. In Inca Garcilaso's *lingua franca* or *lengua general del Inca* (Runa Simi or Quechua), that realm or "union" was called "Tawantinsuyu, which means the four quarters of the world" conquered and "united by the Inca kings."[31] Nevertheless, within or under each of the imperial *suyu* or "quarters" the many "provinces" retained their local names in so many languages, and these were all that were known to the provincial natives of the provinces. By an accident of geography and history, then, "Peru" had "resonated universally" well before the Spanish conquistadors had encountered Inca elites and granaries, or rather the appellative Quechua names of "Inca" and "granary."

But it was not just a question of mistaken identity. "Tawantinsuyu" was not, strictly speaking, a proper name for a land but instead a universal imperial gloss for the civilized or conquered world that, as Inca Garcilaso explained, resonated outward from the top and the center, for Cuzco, "the navel of the world," was the place where "the four quarters of the world" converged. But by the time he was writing his history from Andalusian exile, this was no longer true: Cuzco was no longer the world's navel. Lima, the new "City of Kings," was now the emerging center and lifeline of the Viceroyalty or "Kingdoms and Provinces of Peru." Via Lima, the "New World" to which "Peru" belonged was conjoined with the much vaster "Universe" known to

Christendom. This universe was ruled by the earthly representative of "The King of kings" and by "our Kings of Castile." The age of the limited or false universe named Tawantinsuyu had come to a providential close that, in turn, opened out onto the revealed, and truly universal age of "Peru."

Between (it was now revealed) the false universality of Tawantinsuyu and the true one of Christendom, a cosmo-colonial history would emerge. The historical subject named Peru was one of the first fruits of the new, cosmo-colonial universality. As in the ancient imperial age of Alexander the Great and the Hellenistic "universal historians," the known universe had suddenly expanded.[32] However, this time the expansion was truly global, particularly when seen from the predicament or subject position of colonial centers at "the edge of the earth," also called the "new lands." Inca Garcilaso was fully aware of his geopolitical predicament, and it is duly registered in the opening pages of his history. There, and before the author could proceed to discussing "the origin and principle of the name of Peru," he pronounces what might be called a cosmo-colonial manifesto. This manifesto serves to establish the author's knowing, trans-antipodal subject position. On the one hand, the author is a hearing and writing subject from the colony "at the edge of the earth," that is, a listening, "Indian Inca" (*Inca Yndio*) subject who had "suckled fables" at the knee of Incas as a youth. On the other hand, this same author is a "Spanish Inca" (the meaning of the pen name Inca Garcilaso) writing subject. This older writing subject now dialogues, in an erudite Spanish language, with his young aural self and thus with the Quechua "fables" or oral histories that constitute the primary sources of the text. In short, the subject position of the text is that of a listening and writing knowing subject who stands, head and ears up, feet and pen down, on either side of the globe. Inca Garcilaso thus gave a colonial twist to what was by then well known: the "antipodes" or upside-down people whom Aristotle had imagined were, as Saint Augustine had argued, patently absurd, since humans everywhere were ruled by an enveloping celestial sphere or "skin" toward which they raise their sights. The twist was that Inca Garcilaso spoke as an antipode in the metropolis, and his history would tattoo that universal skin with sovereign "Incas, Kings of Peru that were." In this trans-antipodal act, he founded the epistemics of a cosmopolitan mestizo history of the world.

The first part of Inca Garcilaso's two-part history is thus the story *not* of Tawantinsuyu but of "the Incas, Kings of Peru that were." How could it be otherwise? Since that anxious moment of riverine mis-encounter with the eponymous barbarian, the earthly world had doubled in size, riches, and glory, and "Peru" was now the marvelous name of "the better half" of those riches and glory.[33] Between that misty naming and the shining and cursed moment in which Inca Garcilaso wrote his history, Tawantinsuyu had become the fabled "Peru," and for that very reason (her famed name) was being bled of her mineral wealth, leaving her sons effectively motherless. Still, as a vast and rich "empire" ruled by "the greatest kings on earth," Peru was immensely repaid, for she had found her true voice in the universal "culture" or word of Christian history. As a properly named land endowed with "kingdoms and provinces," Peru was now, in the historical imagination at least, on equal semantic footing with "Spain, Italy, or France." Moreover, Peru's destiny was personally overseen by none other than the breathtaking "Spanish Mars," the celestial Virgin, "Queen of Heaven and Earth," and Mother of the King of kings, for she had appeared in all her glory in the skies above Cuzco to ensure the triumph of the Faith. In grateful reciprocity but also, as we shall see in the next chapter, in a subtle gesture of cosmo-colonial critique, Inca Garcilaso de la Vega dedicated the second part of his *Comentarios reales* not to the emperor but instead to the Virgin Mary. The Virgin was now the universal spiritual mother of the materially step-mothered Peruvians.

As Peruvians are fond of pointing out, even the eventual author of the unsurpassable *El ingenioso hidalgo Don Quixote de la Mancha* (1605) had responded to the marvelous call of Peru's name, though his application was turned down because he had lost an arm at the Battle of Lepanto. But here again history's loss was literature's gain. And yet this literary gain was also real, for, as Thomas Cummins notes, the creations of literature could also show up in the flesh of history. Leaving their author behind, Sancho Panza and Don Quixote made the Atlantic crossing in great style, arriving in Peru in 1607. They were soon pressed into action as theatrical figures in what surely must have been splendid reenactments of the Spanish conquest of the Incas.[34] All of this was no chivalric fable.

The Founding Trace Is Never a Misnomer

The name of Inca Garcilaso de la Vega's surprised Indian, caught fishing by errant Spaniards at the mouth of a river at the end of the world, would melt blissfully into the watery currents of the Renaissance literary imagination. And yet, thanks to Inca Garcilaso's literary and exegetical skills, the eponymous "Beru" has remained, under the literary and historiographical weight of the topoi of discovery and conquest, a curious trace that is both strange and revealing. The presentation of this hermeneutical figure in the opening pages of the *Comentarios reales* provides much more than a rehearsal of the author's exegetical method.[35] Indeed, "Beru" is the key to unlock the my-thopoetic treasure chest that lies sunken at the bottom of the ocean of the text. The figure and anxious utterance of Beru indexes not only the linguistic limit of Spanish understanding and the barbaric nature of first encounter; in Inca Garcilaso's hands it became the inaugural performance of "Peruvian history."

The mythohistorical conjoining of "Beru" and "Pelu" into "Peru" surely satisfied history's narrative requirement that its subject have a proper name with a future among a community of readers.[36] It did so by virtue not only of a deft mestizo exegesis but by taking literary recourse to the mythopoetic tra-dition of christening upon discovery, here informed by that ancient custom by which rivers and kings could "write their names on the land." For, as Inca Garcilaso lets on, the mouths of great rivers and "Indians" had echoed in the Spanish Renaissance imagination "in conformance with their desire."

It is quite clear that this "desire" was not a sign of the proverbial ignorance of early navigators. Instead, the source of ignorance about a historical truth lies much closer to home. From scholars to authoritative dictionaries to New Age nativists, knowledgeable and righteous voices are all too eager to inform us that "Indians" is a Columbian misnomer that under colonial rule became a prejudicial epithet. The problem with this view is that "Indias" and "Indians" became misnomers and signs of prejudice only very recently, and as such correspond to recent forms of historical "recognition." As a name of history, however, "Indias" was as true as "India." As Padre Acosta explained in his erudite *Historia natural y moral de las Indias* (1590):

Among us the word "Indias" is general since, in our tongue, when we say "Indias" we refer to far away and rich lands that are very different from ours. Thus we Spaniards call Peru and Mexico, China, Malaysia, and Brazil "Indias"; and if letters are sent from any part of these, even though said lands and dominions are very distant and diverse one from the other, we say that they are letters from the Indies. One can also not deny that the name "Indias" was taken from Oriental India, because among the ancients that other India was celebrated as a very remote and rich land so far away that it was taken to be the end of the earth. And so, those who reside at the ends of the earth are called "Indians."[37]

Padre Acosta's words reveal that the classical proper name of "India" had be-come the appellative colonial Renaissance name of "Indias." The name of "the end of the earth" was now plural, generic, repeating, worldwide, for Charles V had "pushed" the limits of Mediterranean empire beyond the "Pillars of

Hercules" to the "Indian" ends of the globe. The desire that led early modern Spanish speakers to name "the end of the world" was historically true in a most modern and imperial fashion, such that its name was everywhere the same.

That the inhabitants of "Peru" or "Mexico" or "China" were now named "Indians" was definitely not the mindless repetition of a misnomer coined by an errant navigator named Columbus. Instead, the dispersion of the appelative name "Indians" marked the repeating horizon of a global colonial modernity that has not yet reached its limit. As every edge of the world became the same colonial subject of a global history, the founding trace of that history was marked by the synecdochal figure of the "Indian." This repeating "Indian" who, thanks to colonial history, now falls under the national domain of this or that proper name (Peru, Mexico, India, et cetera) is the founding trace of colonial and postcolonial history.

However, to become the proper subjects of a proper history, that is, to become the "Peruvians" of "Peruvian history," the recipients of this modern colonial dispersion of the name "Indian" would require a founding speech act. In effect, this act was a modern repetition of an ancient historiographical "custom," and one whose history would later be traced by the brilliant Peruvian historian Pedro de Peralta Barnuevo. Father Acosta had written that "during the discovery of the New World it had been the custom to name lands and ports after the occasion of their discovery, and this is how the naming of Peru is commonly understood to have occurred. The opinion here is that, taking the name of the river where they first landed, called Piru by the natives, the Spaniards gave title to this entire land. This is confirmed by the fact that the native Indians of Peru do not use, nor do they know, the name of their land."[38] In his assumption that Peru took her name from a river that was the site of her discovery, Padre Acosta was following a historiographical convention of Neo-Platonist origin, and Inca Garcilaso would follow the same tradition. The name of Father Acosta's "other India" had been derived from the Indus River, that is, from the Sanskrit appellative name "Sindhu," which may be translated as "river in general." This "river in general" had written her name on the rich land of "India" and also on the wide sea to the south that swallowed her effluents. The same "ancient custom" and verisimilar truth had revealed itself in the case of the naming of Iberia, for that peninsula had taken her name from the Iberus (Ebro) River named by the Greeks and likely uttered (of hermeneutical necessity) by a native speaker of Basque.[39]

But the wise and learned *padre* was, according to Inca Garcilaso, mistaken on one small linguistic point. The original utterance could not have been

"Piru" since that was not the correct name for "river in general" in the language of the coast. Inca Garcilaso's exegesis revealed that the name uttered by "Beru" in the place of the Spaniard's first landing meant "river in general" in the Yunga tongue. The Inca's verisimilar or Neo-Platonist solution, which certainly agreed with what was known, was to put "Pelu" in the eponymous mouth of a native subject and to place that subject in "the river in general" at the founding historical moment of anxiety produced by "discovery."

As the hybrid and conjunctural offspring of Beru's anxious utterance of his own proper name and the appellative name for "river" in the Yunga tongue, Inca Garcilaso's "Peru" was both "imposed" and "natural." In *De lingua latina*, which was apparently known to Inca Garcilaso, Roman scholar Marcus Terentius Varro had "distinguished between names imposed on things by a person's fiat or will, and names arising from nature." Thus, Varro wrote, "there are only two kinds of origin of words, imposition and inflection; the first is like the fountain, the second like the river."[40] "Peru" was imposed by Spaniards, but only to the extent that it resonated with an authentic proper name inflected in an oracular, natural place in the original language and upon the "occasion of discovery." Resonant with such classical notions, Inca Garcilaso's account of the name became the canonical version.

In effect, Inca Garcilaso's exegesis and subtle literary turning of the words of the primal scene of contact returns authorship of the name of Peru to a paper conjuncture between the fictive proper name of a misspoken and misheard Indian barbarian and the name of the place in Yunga of Spanish discovery. The eponymous barbarian is the original eyewitness of this abysmal event. The universal place of this event is the oracular river-in-general at the end of the world, which was now that repeating colonial horizon of world history named "Indias." This ends-of-the-earth conjuncture was now "properly heard" and written by the cosmo-colonial historian. As the listening "receptor" of Beru's utterance and as writing "commentator" on imperial Spanish history, Inca Garcilaso's voice, ear, and eye moves between the time of Beru's utterance and the time of his own discourse. In tying these two times together he renders the name of Peru "verisimilar" in the idioms both of Renaissance "universal history" and a proper "Peruvian empire," which is now retrospectively reclaimed for a future "Peruvian history" as the exiled mestizo historian's true *patria*. Consequently, the eclipse of the name Tawantinsuyu was an enabling loss for Inca Garcilaso. His history accelerated that name's death by transferring that loss to the new and universal subject of history named Peru.[41] Peruvian history was born in this act.

Inca Garcilaso's textual baptizing of "Beru" as "Peru" in the river named

"Pelu" was, in Badiou's terms, a tertiary "intervention of interpretation" that only the cosmo-colonial historian could have performed, for this process shifted the tense of history from the retrospective "our Incas" to the futural "we Peruvians." Speaking in structural or formal terms, "Beru" responds to a grammatical rule in that narrative of identity that requires baptisms and eyewitnesses: proper history. The "river in general" speaks a natural truth, for she writes her irresistible name on the rich banks of the land. As the proper subject and object of history writing, "the land" with a proper name (Peru) thus became a "being," for "she" now embraces "kingdoms and provinces" just as "France" and "Spain" do. But to know the river's name Spaniards had first to hear that name uttered by a surprised "Indian" whose native tongue had also named the river, since in Neo-Platonist thought the original native name bore a special relation of "similitude" to the thing it named. Awed and stupefied by the sudden appearance of ships and bearded men, the ignoble "Beru" spoke his unreflective, natural, barbarian truth, but also what he imagined in a moment of anxiety to be what the Spaniards "desired" to hear. What the boatload of Spaniards heard was corrupted by their desiring ears, but in the grand scheme of things the audibility of "Peru" is inevitable given its rich resonances across the ocean in European ears. And so "Beru" is no longer any "Indian" of the modern imperial imagination. By virtue of the river of words in which the historian Inca Garcilaso baptizes him, he is now the founding name-giver of all future "Peruvians."

It is well known that the *Comentarios reales* is full of "fables" that are subjected to erudite "commentary," but the story of "Beru" is no fable. It is the founding mythopoetic gesture that, in effect, is performed in the very operation of commentary. Roland Barthes has analyzed the structure of this operation of commentary in historical discourse. Key to his reading is the concept of the strategic function of testimonial "shifters of listening," which was developed by the linguist Roman Jakobson. Shifters serve to "designate . . . the historian's listening, collecting testimony from elsewhere, and telling it in his own discourse." This prefigured manner of "anthropological" listening in the historical text is everywhere visible in the *Histories* of Herodotus, for example. The anthropological listening brings "fables" into the historian's field of commentary, and the conjuncture of commentary and primary speech in the text produces a mythopoetic, founding effect. Barthes explains:

> Historical discourse is familiar with two general types of inauguration.
> In the first place, there is what we might call the performative opening,
> for the words really perform a solemn act of foundation; the model for

this is poetic, the "I sing" of the poets. . . . Bearing in mind these different elements, we are likely to conclude that the entry of the "act of uttering" into the historical utterance, through these organizing shifters, is directed less towards offering the historian a chance of expressing his "subjectivity," as is commonly held, than to "complicating" the chronological time of history by bringing it up against another time, which is that of the discourse itself and could be termed, for short, the "paper-time." To sum up, the presence in historical narration of explicit signs of uttering would represent an attempt to "dechronologize" the "thread" of history and to restore, even though it may merely be a matter of reminiscence or nostalgia, a form of time that is complex, parametric, and not in the least linear: a form of time whose spatial depths recall the mythic time of the ancient cosmogonies, which was also linked, in its essence, to the words of the poet and the soothsayer. Organizing shifters bear witness, in effect—though they do so through indirect ploys which have the appearance of rationality—to the predictive function of the historian. It is to the extent that he knows what has not yet been told that the historian, like the actor of myth, needs to double up the chronological unwinding of events with references to the time of his own speech.[42]

Inca Garcilaso's dechronologizing inscription of "the origin and principle of the name of Peru" is surely a faithful and reflexive "finding" of a Renaissance humanist historical method that privileged "the highest" and diminished "the lowest" by bringing both into view in the historical text. The eyewitness account was highly valued by European readers both as a poetic resource and as firm evidential ground that could be marshaled as moral and political exemplaria in the narrative. As Margarita Zamora notes, "conflict between the accounts of those who traveled to America and the speculations of the revered authors of antiquity brought the authority of the eyewitness into a particularly privileged historiographical position."[43] And as Roberto González Echevarría argues, this same authority was highly valued by the legal system and notarial codes of Spanish empire. Indeed, Inca Garcilaso de la Vega's frequent recourse to the testimonies of eyewitnesses reflects the prescribed rhetorical procedures of the relación and his personal interests in clearing his father's name and his own for posterity.[44] The enduring historical and critical value of the Royal Commentaries lies precisely in this reflexive operation performed upon the eyewitness, who in turn is located in the writer's contemporary past. In modified form this same rhetorical device lives on in literature, history, and anthropology today. But we would be remiss to think of the Inca's history as grounded in ordinary "ethnographic" or "notarial" authority since in effect the text is doubly courtesan. That is, in this case the eyewitness authority is an intimate Inca ear united with a noble Spanish pen. The operation of shifters is a "social fact" that mirrors its own courtesan production, here encapsulated in a single authorizing phrase: "it will be better if this history is known through the Incas' own words rather than in those of foreign authors."[45] These original words are higher, more noble, and therefore more truthful than those of the foreign inspector or the scribe.

Inca Garcilaso's auto-ethnographic posture and use of shifters surely serve a courtly literary conceit of another kind, for his history and voice is at once proper and utterly foreign (after all, the text is composed in Spanish albeit in certain passages according to Quechua oral cadences), present and utterly distanced from those of his royal informants. His filial authority vis-à-vis Inca dynastic history is derived from his writing memory of a youthful hearing of his old Inca uncle's royal speech. By inscribing his own discourse in the time of the royally transmitted speech of familiar Incas from the past, Inca Garcilaso would achieve the improbable dream of all Renaissance courtesans, one that he failed to garner in life in Spain but which he abundantly enjoys in his Peruvian death. That dream, of course, is to become "eternal" by association with the aura of the king, who, in this case, is "the Incas, Kings of Peru that were." As a result of this retrospective courtly gesture of belonging—a performance enacted in the text and in the author's choice of his own proper name—the historian among the Incas will become the Inca among the historians. Notably, for this cosmo-colonial Inca among historians the retrospective courtly performance was also a critical move, for "we may say that the lack of good and faithful interpreters was the principal cause of the death" of the last "Inca kings of Peru."[46]

Founding Barbarians

In many ways Inca Garcilaso's history is a metatextual intervention of interpretation—an erudite commentary on primary discourse or speech by a privileged insider who transported himself in time and space to the primal scene—of those errors of translation that were "the principle cause" of the death of the last and tragic heirs to the Inca dynasty, "Prince Huascar" and the "Tyrant Atahualpa." In Inca Garcilaso's account, those crucial "errors" of the tongue that produced the fall of the Incas and the tragedy of conquest were committed by common, barbarian "Indians" of the Yunga lowlands. These barbarians of the tongue stood between the two empires and their languages, Cusqueña Quechua and Castilian Spanish, respectively. Other barbarians of the ear also stood in the way: wayward Spaniards who ignorantly assumed the transparency of language, and who were filled with a "desire" to "name upon discovery." Inca Garcilaso corrected those predictable errors of history by revisiting the names, and so produced a verisimilar "translation of empires," one in which the spoken word was rescued by the firmer, more noble written word. The noble word of history would make right in paper time what common acts of speech had made wrong in real time.

This cosmo-colonial history lesson, in which the speech of the barbarian plays a founding role, required the deployment of a high or noble mestizo knowledge of both languages of empire. The necessarily high founding of "Peruvian history" is enabled by the constitutive errors of barbarian orality and aurality, useful errors that may only be transacted in a retrospective "intervention of interpretation" that endows this history with a durable structure. This tertiary event of historiography may be thought of as that enabling displacement that, for de Certeau, "causes the production of an exchange" among dead, living, and future souls. What arises from this death-in-translation is the subject and soul of a history named "Peru" and "Peruvian."

Like all founding histories, Inca Garcilaso's presupposes a "rapport" with "a lost object," an interdiction in the "death that makes it possible." Here that lost object is the speech that it would "resuscitate" but that may only be brought back in a paper afterlife that is, in effect, history's lease on life. The "lost object" is the exegetical finding of a work of mourning, and as a result Inca Garcilaso's "history is a labor of death and a labor against death." As de Certeau has argued, any such labor against death always leaves "the forever-remnant trace of a beginning that is as impossible to recover as [it is] to forget."[47] Inca Garcilaso's history leaves such a trace largely because "by etching his text in the discourse of commentary, he allowed the original [oral] text to surface and endure as [its] ultimate authority," since it was good notarial and historiographical practice to summon witnesses.[48] As a consequence of this evidential surfacing, "Beru" will assume an inaugural place as the signature trace of "Peruvian history." But Beru's trace is surely a strangely telling authority, for it beckons from "the abyss of history" whose mark is the voice and name of the interstitial barbarian who inhabits the "contact zone" between two empires.

If all history is founded and refounded on the twofold absence of things in words and of the dead among the living, then "Beru" is the trace of that "abyss of history" that gave birth not only to "Peru," but to the modern world that made "Peru" a universal subject of history. And if all history writing presupposes a certain exile from the present, and a certain absence of the things of the past in that present, then the condition of exile and absence that made Peruvian history possible was at once colonial and metropolitan. The proper name of that condition was "Peruvian," and its history was penned, in a post-conquest, trans-antipodal, retrospective work of mourning and memory made in Andalusian exile, so that "the Incas, kings of Peru that were" could be "made known to the universe" and live "in eternity." This founding *cantar de gesta* left its trace on all subsequent Peruvian histories of Peru, including those of Basadre.

Another minor character figures large in Inca Garcilaso's account of "the conquest of Peru." This figure is a barbarian "Indian" who is christened "Felipillo" (Little Philip). In the Inca's account, this curious figure is an ignorant and uncouth barbarian from an island (Puna) off the north Peruvian coast (that is, from Beru's whereabouts) who accompanies the Spanish conquistadors as translator and guide. Apparently Pizarro picked up this isle-bound Indian in 1527 and carried him back to Spain to become a good Christian, to learn Spanish, and to meet the emperor. Returning as "Felipillo" or "Felipe Huallpa" in 1530, he was now Pizarro's translator and guide in the epic campaign known to history as "the conquest of Peru." In *Los comentarios reales* Felipillo's botched translations are held partially responsible for the massacre at Cajamarca that culminated in the bloody and tearful extinction of the Inca dynasty, that is, in Basadre's "loud crash that shook the world." Like the much abused La Malinche or Malintzin of Mexican history—the infamous concubine and translator who served Hernán Cortés in "the conquest of Mexico"—the name of Felipillo has lived on as a curse. Today a *felipillo* is a traitor, a servant of imperial interests, a smooth-talking sneak, and in Peru the epithet is usually reserved for politicians deemed to be too close to the United States or Chile. We may be permitted to imagine, however, that Little Philip displayed keen qualities of mimicry and perhaps a sly civility, and that he was christened in honor (in another poetic error of the tongue and the ear?) of the *infante* or only son and heir of Charles V—that is, the future King Philip II—born in the very same year that Pizarro picked up "Felipillo" off the coast of "Peru."[49] In Inca Garcilaso's "anti-Felipillo" history, which was written and published under the reigns of Philip II and Philip III, it was by virtue of the "stupidity of the translator" (*torpeza del intérprete*) that Atahualpa had misunderstood the Spanish (and possibly Latin) words of Fray Valverde's rendition of the Requirement. The Requirement demanded recognition of the emperor's legitimate dominion, which had been granted by the Pope. In the

Inca's account, the Spaniards misinterpreted Atahualpa's gestures, triggering a righteous Christian "just war" that came suddenly down upon his head.[50] But it was not just a question of Felipillo's linguistic incompetence or the paucity of cognates among Yunga, Quechua, and Spanish. In Inca Garcilaso's account, Felipillo's uncouth desire for one of Atahualpa's royal wives led him to conspire with the Spaniards against the Inca. In short, a caste-trespassing, barbarian "desire" was also at work in Inca Garcilaso's configuration of "the conquest of Peru."

Inca Garcilaso's portrayal of Felipillo suggests an obvious question. Was the transgressive native barbarian whose desiring tongue "got it wrong" not among the "founding fathers" of Peru? Curiously, and as literary devices that enable the narrative of encounter and conquest to proceed as a linguistic event marked by confusion and desire, "Beru" and "Felipillo" are the hermeneutical necessities of historical truth. As the eponymous barbarian "king" of Peru, "Beru" may be read as the founding father of the Peruvians. Notably, Beru and Felipillo are the first *cholos* (transgressive natives) of Peruvian history, that is, the first uncouth "Indians" or "inappropriate others." And yet it is the anxious speech and desire of these inappropriate others that provide a narrative bridge across the abyss that separated the Spanish and Inca empires and their languages, Castilian and Quechua. Another question is thus raised: How may empires connect if not for the interstitial or border zone inhabited by the barbarian who makes translation and "naming upon discovery" hermeneutically possible? How, in short, may colonial and postcolonial history be written if not for the stained page upon which the native barbarian offers to write?

Although Inca Garcilaso's founding inscription of the speech of the barbarian is an exegetical and hermeneutical necessity à la O'Gorman, it is also tinged with critical irony, for barbarism is a universal condition that may be shared by the "shipwrecked Spaniard." At the close of the eighth chapter of book 1 of the first part of the *Royal Commentaries*, Inca Garcilaso thus inserts the parable of "Pedro Serrano." The parable functions as a literary device that makes the anxious emotional state of Beru available to European readers. Slyly inserted as filler ("por que este capítulo no sea tan corto"), the tale of Serrano notably appears in the chapter entitled "The Description of Peru." Zamora finds that the "hermeneutical key" to this parable lies in its harmonious finale, when Serrano and the other shipwrecked European embrace "their common faith in Christ."[51] Zamora's reading makes perfect sense, but here I wish to propose a slightly different interpretation of its meaning.

In Inca Garcilaso's telling, the shipwrecked Pedro Serrano swam ashore to an "unnamed" and unpopulated island without vegetation or water. Serrano the discoverer etched his surname on the island, which as a result came to be known as Isla Serrana. How did he achieve the fame that permitted the etching of his name on the face of the island? Naked and armed only with a knife, Serrano survived for three years by eating turtles and gathering rainwater in their upturned shells. Meanwhile, his skin turned into "pellejo de animal, y no cualquiera, sino el de un jabalí" (the pelt of an animal, and not just any animal, but that of a wild boar) and his hair and beard grew down past his waist. The discoverer was now a barbarian. In the fourth year another shipwrecked Spaniard arrived on "his" island. Startled by the appearance of this man, Pedro Serrano took him to be the devil. Crying "Jesus, Jesus, save me from the Devil!" he ran away from the Spaniard. But hearing Serrano's Christian words, the newly arrived Spaniard shouted back: "Do not flee, my brother, for like you I too am a Christian!" After some days of Christian peace the two began to quarrel over the menial tasks that each should perform, namely, keeping the fire from going out, and procuring food and water. Eventually, though, they came to embrace their common "misadventure" (*desventura*) and so survived four more years. By now both of the men sported "the fur of beasts" (*pellejo de animal*).

So that passing navigators should not shun them as savages ("porque no tenían figura de hombres humanos"), the men cried out the creed and "the name of Our Redeemer" to those ships that passed. Both men were eventually picked up, but Pedro Serrano's companion expired en route to Spain. Pedro arrived safely in Spain and from there continued on to Germany, "where the Emperor [Charles V] then was." Pedro decided not to alter his beastly appearance, however, "as proof of his being shipwrecked and of what had happened during that time." The emperor was duly impressed and rewarded the beastly Pedro with 4,000 pesos in rents from Peru. After his imperial interview in Germany, Pedro had his hair and beard cut, but only just above the waist, evidently having grown fond of it, in part it seems because "some lords and noble gentlemen took pleasure in his figure and aided him in his travels." The long-haired, furry Pedro set sail back to Peru to assume the management of his rents, but died in steamy Panama before he could enjoy them.

In my reading, the tale of Serrano resonates with the tale of Beru and "the origin and principle of the name of Peru." Barbarism was the ignoble condition of the shipwrecked, the unlettered, the kingless, the deserted, but this universal condition could remedy itself by canting "the name of Our

Redeemer." The *Comentarios reales* gives berth to "barbarian speech" as that universal "abyss of history" that, by virtue of the contrast between its bottom-less state and the noble "name of Our Redeemer," enables history to be told as a story of uplift and redemption. Pedro Serrano is the discoverer-become-barbarian who by virtue of the telling of the tale becomes the name-giver of the island (Isla Serrano). The name-giver is rescued by Christians who respond precisely to Pedro's utterance of the name of the Devil, since this ut-terance reveals the common name of Their Redeemer. Similarly, albeit in the inverse, Beru is the lost barbarian who, in a like moment of anxiety utters not the name of "the Devil" but his own, and in so doing is taken aboard. In turn, Beru's proper name and the abysmal moment of its utterance is rescued from oblivion and ignorance by the "Indian-Inca" historian who, in effect, hears the name of his redemption in Beru's "human" utterance. By virtue of the Inca's intervention of interpretation, the humanity of that utterance is restored to its rightful place as the founding speech act of Peruvian history.

For the European-turned-barbarian named Pedro, salvation lies not only in the Christian word but in the long hair that pays for his travels and brings him before the curious gaze of the emperor of the world; for the barbar-ian-turned-Peruvian named Beru, a posthumous salvation lies in the Inca's founding exegesis. It is not unreasonable to speculate that in the Inca's his-torical imagination "Beru" stood before him as "Pedro Serrano" had before Charles V. Named "Beru" or "Pedro," the figure of the barbarian is that abyss to which any man may fall; that abyss which serves as a telling mirror for kings and historians; that abyss which connects empires and founds histories. But what the Inca among the historians gave to his barbarian was not the passing gift of uncollected colonial rents in Peru but instead a proper lease on an eternal afterlife as the founding name-giver of Peru and Peruvian history. It has been the purpose of this opening chapter to re-recognize (*re-conocer*) the historical truth of this literary "ransom," the dividends of which continue to be collected.

2

The Arts of History and the Arts of Rule

Lord: Venerable Antiquity called Histories Books of Kings, in part because they are composed of the actions and events of kings, and in part because its principal teachings point directly to the Arts of Rule, since one may collate from the variety of Examples what Providence may reveal and what Imitation should embrace. It follows from this principle that the noble temerity of Writers who dedicate their Works to Great Kings is less presumptuous, and more generous among Historians who, without disputing the estimation of the other disciplines, must assume the Education of the grandest of Auditors.

Antonio de Solís, *Historia de la conquista de México, población, y progresos de la América septentrional conocida por el nombre de Nueva España*

Sacred, Catholic, Royal Majesty, Defender of the Faith. . . . Unless I am mistaken, these first fruits of the imagination are the first to be offered by the natives of the New World, and in particular those of Peru . . . in this genre of tribute which is owed to Your Royal Majesty . . . King of Kings.

Inca Garcilaso de la Vega, *La traducción del indio de los tres diálogos de amor de León Hebreo*

If a portion of [*Comentarios reales de los incas*] enters into the dominion of Art, it would be that Art which we may call, with Aristotle, 'truer than History.'

José de la Riva-Agüero, *La historia en el Perú*

In this chapter and the next I continue to probe the ways in which the arts of rule and the arts of history conspired in the invention of words and things Peruvian. If the subject of history named "Peru" was born in a colonial abyss of history that shook the world, Inca Garcilaso's arts of history would equip that subject with a numinous past in that world which it had only recently joined. For the greater glory of God and as a humble "tribute" to the "King of Kings" on earth (Philip II), that written past or "culture" and its future not only rivaled but in key respects exceeded and was truer than Rome's. If, as Petrarch boasted, "all history is but the praise of Rome," that history was now put to the work of praising Peru.

At the same time, the playful and dialogical heterogeneity of the *Comentarios reales*—its erudite exegesis and commentary on Inca oral traditions and Spanish chronicles, the Herodotean meanders in the fields of Andean "rites and customs," the Thucydidean narration of the misfortunes of war, and the overriding poetic fact that the opus is addressed not only to "the Grandest of Auditors" but to a compatriot posterity of its own making—purchased for its author eternal *fama* as the Inca-king of historians. Rudolf Agricola's high praise for Petrarch (for his having rescued Cicero from oblivion) may thus apply just as well to Inca Garcilaso's colonial Renaissance rescue of the Incas: "All ages owe him a debt of gratitude—antiquity for having rescued its treasures from oblivion, and modern times for having with their own strength founded and revived culture, which he has left as a precious legacy to future ages."[1] What made Inca Garcilaso so different from Petrarch, however, was the abysmal historical fact that the "Peruvian" had oral access to (a New World) "antiquity." That intimate antiquity had only just expired in a colonial spectacle of blood and miracles, and the work of Inca Garcilaso's history was to lay it to rest for a modern posterity that was his to write. This posterity of colonial modernity lay far beyond Petrarch's "modern" horizons. The history of the Inca would thus live a brilliant afterlife of its own, both as councilor to the Spanish empire's "arts of rule" in Peru and the Indies, and as mestizo muse to "the arts of history" in the colonial and postcolonial imaginations of generations of Peruvians to come.

Writing the Incas into the Book of Kings

Comentarios reales belongs to that ancient and modern genre of history aptly called the "Book of Kings." As a mestizo or hybrid "New World" variation on that Old World dynastic genre, Inca Garcilaso's cosmopolitan and colonial, or cosmo-colonial, history was both derivative and foundational. As the

Spanish court historian of the Indies, Antonio de Solís, noted in his prologue to *History of the Conquest of Mexico*, such Books of Kings were, among other things, about the words and deeds or *res gestae* of kings, and they were usually addressed to kings or soon-to-be kings. Dedications to kings or princes thus open countless secular history books printed in Europe and Spanish America between the sixteenth and nineteenth centuries, and many of these include impressive, allegorical frontispieces that feature the figure of the king or prince, as Solis' did (see fig. 1). In the early modern period, kingly history in Europe and the Americas was often called "the noble science of princes," in part because history lessons were princely, that is, principled discourses full of examples of virtue and heroism that should be imitated. "The noble science" thus guarded the venerable Ciceronian topos of *historia magistra vitae*. Exemplary deeds and kings were contrasted with admonishing instances of malice and tyranny, the latter frequently embodied in the figure of the Oriental despot.

The Renaissance humanist poetics of imitation (writing history of and for the noble) that characterized the Book of Kings could sometimes be a high road to employment at court and scholarly fame.[2] In the colonial case it seems just as often to have led not to high places but into the deep woods of exile and the book, and from there—if access to the pearly gates could be had—"eternity in heaven." As a result, the noble aspirations of the historian could be altogether dreamy, if not critical. Failed bids to make it at court (such as Inca Garcilaso's) were common, so that the success of any history came to be another, more eternal measure, sufficient reward in itself for lonely labors. Perhaps in part for this reason, in the colonial Hispanic world histories were addressed not only to the king, the prince, and the viceroy, but also to the abstract subjects of the political and religious imagination: the nation, the *patria*, the country, the political orb, the universe, even the Virgin Mary.

The political and poetic process by which the Incas were inscribed in the Book of Kings tradition may be traced to the early postconquest "relations" and chronicles. The impulse to "chronicle" the events of conquest and "relate" the "customs, rights, and ancient things" of the fabled land of "Peru" was from the beginning driven by the need to legitimize Spanish rule in faraway but "regimented" lands, that is, to name, claim sovereignty or *imperium*, and then rule over vast lands and peoples already graced with "republics," "lords," and "mosques." Hispanic historiography was well positioned to meet this imperial task.

Since the conquest of Toledo in 1085 by King Alphonso VI of Castile and the imperial coronation of King Alphonso VII in León in 1135, where Pope

VTRAQVE VNVM
HISPANIA
NOVA HISPANIA
RENOVABITUR
RENASCETUR
HISTORIA
de la
NUEVA ESPAÑA
Por
D. ANTONIO DE SOLIS
AL
REY, N.ro SEÑOR
Por mano del
Exc.o Sen.r
CONDE DE
OROPESA
Theod. Ardeman inv.
I F Leonardo sculp.

1. Frontispiece, Antonio de Solís, *Historia de la conquista de México, población, y progresos de la América septentrional conocida por el nombre de Nueva España* (Madrid, 1684).

Innocent II granted him the extraordinary title of "King of Kings," Castile's kings had demonstrated imperial and crusading pretensions that rivaled those of the "German" Holy Roman Emperors. A century later, Alphonso X, "the Wise" (r. 1252–84), made an unsuccessful bid for election as Holy Roman Emperor. His bid for universal rule stimulated the writing of a "history of Spain." Although unfinished, the *Estoria de Espanna* would leave its mark on subsequent Hispanic historiography. The *Estoria* emphasized the history of Roman Empire in the Iberian Peninsula, and it sang the epic story of the heroic military campaigns to expand Christian "Spain." Notably, this vernacular history of Castilian kings and knights engaged in Christian *Reconquista* (Reconquest) helped establish in historical discourse the imagined, unitary subject of history named "Spain" anticipated by the Roman "Hispania" of Isidore of Seville (c. 560–636).[3] "Spain" was configured here as an imperial desire for realm that evoked Roman "Hispania" in the name of a crusading Christian mission led and written by the Wise King. This history was addressed to notables, the church, allied lords, and other European courts, and it was written "in the name of Spaniards." Action and words or sword and pen were united in a militant and studious humanism that made strong poetic use of the *cantares de gesta*, or poetic recitation of heroic deeds.

Two centuries later, Charles I of Spain realized Alphonso's dream when, in 1519, he was elected Holy Roman Emperor. Taking the title of Charles V, his reign as "King of Rome and Emperor of the World" represented the early modern apex of Christian universal empire. Notably, Charles V's universal reign coincided with the conquests of the "monarchies" of "Mexico" and "Peru." Charles V's historical claims to world dominion were duly promoted in Miguel de Ulzurrum's *Catholicum opus imperiale regiminis mundi* (1525).[4] The heirs of Charles I continued this imperial, Book of Kings tradition. Under kings Philip II, the original "Sun King" and "Emperor of the Indies," Philip III, and Philip IV, the famous "Planet King," the imperial "history of Spain" begun by the Alphonsine historians was expanded to include civic or moral and natural histories of the "conquests" and "new lands" of the Indies.[5]

In the earliest relations or brief chronicles of the "conquest of Peru," published in Seville in 1534, the Inca "Atabaliba" or "Atabalipa" ("Atahuallpa" or "Atahualpa" in later accounts) is represented as a "Lord" (*Señor*) carried, in Oriental style, on a litter and with a parasol. As art historian Thomas Cummins notes, the woodcut image of the Inca that graced the first page of this history strongly resembles a 1506 engraving of the "King of Cochin of India" (see fig. 2).[6] This Orientalized Andean "Lord" is said to have rejected the ultimatum or Christian "Requirement" read to him, which demanded that he

☙Uerdadera relacion de la conquista del Peru
y prouincia del Cuzco llamada la nueua Castilla:Conquistada por el magnifico
y esforçado cauallero Francisco piçarro hijo del capitan Gonçalo piçarro caua
llero de la ciudad de Trugillo: como capitan general de la cesarea y catholica
magestad dl emperador y rey nõ señor:Embiada a su magestad por Francisco
de Xerez natural de la muy noble y muy leal ciudad de Seuilla secretario del
sobredicho señor:en todas las puincias y conquista de la nueua Castilla y vno
de los primeros conquistadores della.☙☙☙☙☙☙☙☙☙
☙fue vista y examinada esta obra por mandado de los señores inquidores
del arçobispado de Seuilla:z impressa en casa de Bartholome perez en el mes
de Julio. Año del parto virginal mil z quinientos y treynta y quatro.☙☙
✳   ✠   ✠

2. Frontispiece, Francisco de Xerez, *Verdadera relación de la conquista del Perú* (Seville, 1534).

submit or be subdued.[7] Consequently, he is justly attacked and captured by the intrepid Spaniards (see fig. 3). Later, the captive lord offers, or is obliged to pay, a king's ransom (a palace full of gold) for his release. At his trial, Atabalipa is found guilty of having captured and killed his half-brother, the legitimate Prince Huascar (called *Cuzco hijo del Cuzco viejo*) and his royal kin. Sentence is passed, and he is executed, ostensibly for regicide and tyranny.[8] Atabalipa appears in this and other early chronicles as a paramount "Lord of the land" (*Señor de la tierra*) with sovereign dominion over lesser native lords, called *señores naturales* or *caciques* (the latter term is of Caribbean origin). As in the Mexican case of "Moctezuma," the representation of the Inca as "Lord of the land" would permit a transfer of dominion to the Castilian Crown, for only a "Lord of the land" could "transfer" his realm, vassals, and riches to the emperor. The political theory behind "transfer of *imperium*" was supported by a venerable topos or commonplace of historical discourse, traceable to the *logoi* of Herodotus, that "barbarian" peoples "could never live without a king."[9] This notion in turn rested in part on the mythological and patriarchal postulate that the misty origins of "nations" could be traced to founding kings or sages.[10]

In Francisco de Xerez's foundational *Verdadera relación de la conquista del Perú* (*Truthful Relation of the Conquest of Peru*), the rites and customs of the peoples of Peru are represented as horrifying spectacles (*suciedades de sacrificios y mesquitas*). Moreover, relates the narrator, in the course of these idolatrous rites "all the best products of their lands" were offered to "false gods" worshipped in "mosques."[11] Despite the strong criticisms and revisions of this story emanating from ecclesiastical quarters, Xerez's 1534 history justified the conquest and transfer of *imperium* to the kings of "Spain."[12]

The capture and just execution of the tyrannical "Lord of the land" of Peru was soon followed by "civil wars" among the rival conquistador bands of the captains Francisco Pizarro and Diego de Almagro, who clashed over the extent of their respective grants in Peru. These wars concluded not only with the triumph of the Crown and the establishment of the Viceroyalty of Peru (1542) but also, as Sabine MacCormack notes, with the writing of a "classical" historiography about them.[13] In the wake of the wars, the Crown's triumph at Cuzco against "Manco Inca" and other rebel elements of the Pizarro band were attributed not only to the "invincibility of Spanish arms" but to the miraculous interventions of Santiago (initially as an avenging specter of the slain Francisco Pizarro) and the "Spanish Mars" or the Virgin Mary. It would be the histories of the Jesuit Padre José de Acosta and Inca Garcilaso

Nter deß drang ein Prediger Münch mit namen Vincentius de valle viridi mitten durch die Indianer hindurch/kompt für den König Atabaliba/hielt ein Crucifix vnd sein Breviarium in der Hand/ließ dem König Atabaliba durch einen Dolmetscher anzeigen/ daß er von Römischer Kay. May. auß Befelch deß Bapsts zu Rom/ als Statthalters Jesu Christi/vnd der dem Römischen Kayser dieselbe vnbekannte Landen vbergeben vnd geschenckt hab/mit dem gedinge/daß er Wolgelärte/ vnd zu solchem Ampt würdige Personen/dahin schicken solte/welche das heylsame Euangelium alda predigten/ꝛc. zu ihm Atabaliba gesandt sey. Darauff zeigte er ihm sein Breviarium/sagte darinnen stehe verfast das Gesetz des ewigen Allmächtigen Gottes/ꝛc. König Atabaliba fraget den Münch/ woher er solches wüste. Der Münch antwortet/ daß Buch welches er in den Händen hab/sagte ihm solches. Als nun der König dasselbige Buch vom Münch empfing/vnd hin vnd her vmbschlug/lächelt er etwas darzu / vnd sprach/ wil es mir doch nichts dergleichen sagen/warff damit das Buch von sich hinweg. Der Münch hub es wiederumb auff/ruffet den Pizarrum vmb Hülff an/ermanet ihn diß er solches nicht wolle vngerochen lassen. Darauff Pizarrus so bald befihlt/daß man daß groß Geschütz loßbrennen solt/vnd daß sein Bruder Ferdinandus sampt den andern Reutern die Indianer anfallen solten. Als nun die Wilden das grausam blitzen vnd donnern deß Geschützes/vnd daß vngewöhnliche gerassel vnd Geleut der Schellen/so an dem Zeuge der Pferd hiengen/vernamen/wurden sie alle erstarret/vnd flogen darvon. Franciscus Pizarrus fiel selbst mit den Fußknechten an den König Atabalibam/ erlegt der Feinde ein grosse Anzahl/risse den König Atabalibam auß dem Sessel/darauff er getragen worden/vnd nam ihn also gefangen.

3. "Atabalipa Rex Peruanus a Franciscus Pizarrus capitur," Teodoro De Bry, *Americae Pars VI* (Frankfurt, 1596).

de la Vega that would secure these "spiritual" interpretations of the battle for Peru.

As Juan Carlos Estenssoro Fuchs argues, these post-civil-war, miraculous readings of the events of Spanish conquest would serve to resolve the tensions between the Crown, the conquistadors and their heirs, and the church. For those churchmen in Peru who were inspired by the polemical defense of the Indians led by Bartolomé de Las Casas (he called for the return of sovereignty to the Incas), the Requirement was no longer sufficient grounds for a legitimate transfer of imperium, particularly given the advanced nature of Inca civilization, law, and religion, and the peaceful, innocent nature of the Inca's common Indian subjects. For a civilization that was increasingly seen in providential terms, and which was favorably compared to pagan Rome, nothing short of miracles was required. The revisionist historiography of miraculous interventions gave the church grounds to insert itself as the crucial mediator of the "colonial pact" between conquerors and conquered.

During the reigns of Philip II and Philip III, the early "relations" and chronicles of the conquest campaigns and civil wars gave way to more detailed and erudite investigations into the "royal genealogy" of the Incas. The "Lords of the land" or Incas would now be written as genuine "kings" with a dynastic history. The genealogical inquiries responded both to practical and mythopoetic demands. Of significance too was the symbolic fact that, after Charles V, no Castilian monarch would hold the universal title of Holy Roman Emperor. Under the three Philips (II–III–IV), the genealogies of Inca and Aztec dynasties would assume more central roles in the elaboration of a mythic genealogical tree for the Spanish monarchy. This tree now included the tributary trunks of the extinguished "monarchies" (those of Mexico and Peru) of "the Empire of the Indies." In addition, a firmer knowledge of royal genealogies in the Indies was needed to resolve claims to compensation and nobility among the many "native lords" who had "served His Majesty" in the conquest campaigns or who had otherwise pledged loyalty to the Crown.

In part to lay such disputes to rest, in 1571 the Spanish viceroy of Peru commissioned Pedro Sarmiento de Gamboa to write his *History of the Incas*. This official history, which formed the second part of the *Historia Índica*, compared the Incas to the treacherous Carthaginians; Spaniards, meanwhile, were portrayed as the legitimate successors to Rome.[14] Moreover, in Gamboa's account the Incas were belligerent newcomers to the Cuzco region who had violently dispossessed the "native lords" from their rightful dominions. Sarmiento de Gamboa's history, as well as the *Government of Peru* (1567) penned by Juan Ortiz de Matienzo, would help justify a colonial project of indirect rule. This project, whose most vigorous champion was the viceroy Francisco Toledo, sought to eliminate the royal lineages of Cuzco's dynastic houses or *panacas* and to "restore" the ethnic chiefs or *kurakas*, who would function as colonial chiefs or "principal *caciques*" subject to the jurisdiction of the *Corregidor de indios* or Spanish magistrate. The dominion of the colonial chiefs over Indian peasants and laborers was also checked by elected, native *alcalde* or village authorities. In the long run, the Toledan project of indirect rule would triumph, albeit in Andean form. With some notable exceptions, the Incas became "the Kings of Peru that were," that is, the useable, sovereign past of imperial dynastic history, art, ritual, and memory.

The Toledan project required not only a revisionist official history but also a new archive of images and words. To this end, Viceroy Toledo commissioned indigenous artists trained in European techniques to paint "portraits" of dead Inca rulers. He created an archive for official papers, which was intended to supplant the oral, artifactual, mummified, woven, and *quipu* (mnemonic devices of colored and knotted cord) forms of Inca dynastic memory that he sought to destroy or abolish. The official portraits were sent to Philip II, and they soon found a place on the walls of the Alcazar or Hapsburg Palace, in Madrid. As Cummins notes, the portraits of the Incas appear to have been of great symbolic value to Philip II and the Spanish monarchy, for they were hung in the royal chamber alongside Titian's equestrian and allegorical masterpieces of Charles V and Philip II, now on display in the Prado Museum, in Madrid.[15] Another set of portraits, arranged as a genealogical tree and with far many more heirs, was apparently sent to the Spanish court via Inca Garcilaso de la Vega in 1603 but has since been lost. The remarkable but unpublished dynastic histories of Martín de Murúa (1590 and 1614) and Felipe Guamán Poma de Ayala (1615) were notable contributions to this new archive of royal portraits of the imagined "Inca kings."[16]

The official culmination of the imperial translation of "Incas" into "kings" was registered in Antonio de Herrera's monumental *Historia general de los hechos de los castellanos en las islas y tierra firme del mar océano* (General History of the Deeds of the Castilians on the Islands and Spanish Main of the Ocean Sea), published in 1615. This official history relied on the early Spanish relations and chronicles, on the first part of the *Comentarios reales*, and on the royal archive of manuscripts and portraits housed at Simancas.[17] Notably, the cover of the fifth "decade" or volume of Herrera's *Historia general* sports the portraits of 12 supreme Incas, from Manco Capac to Huayna Capac and Prince Huascar (see fig. 4). In short, the Incas had assumed their colonial

4. Frontispiece, Antonio de Herrera, *Historia general de los hechos de los castellanos en las islas y tierra firme del mar océano, V década* (Madrid, 1615).

place in the Tacitean annals and Livean decades of "the deeds" and "things" of Spanish empire.

The Incas as Mirrors

Much of the discourse in the *Comentarios reales* is driven by dynastic questions that are also theological inquiries into the nature of the Inca's law: "Who was the first of our Incas? What was his name? What was the origin of his lineage? How did his rule begin? With what people and what arms did he conquer this great empire?"[18] These questions are not just rhetorical ones. We are told that these queries were in fact posed orally to his sagely uncle, himself an Inca of the royal blood, when Gómez Suárez (Inca Garcilaso) was a youth growing up in postconquest Cuzco. The elder historian transcribes his youthful memory of his beloved uncle's wise responses into his text, and these passages are always marked by "the Inca said" (*el Inca dijo*).

"The Inca said" device serves to confirm and authorize what "the Inca writes." This dialogical strategy, by no means unknown to the Renaissance's "science of princes," places the historian Inca Garcilaso in the close company of Inca royalty, thereby purchasing his own *fama* and "eternity in Heaven." Moreover, the courtly aural source and device allows Inca Garcilaso to assume a "proper" position of "Inca-Indian" critique vis-à-vis those "foreign authors" whose access to native oral tradition was mediated by language and social distance. Thus, Inca Garcilaso will insist, in characteristically modest fashion, that "we say nothing new except insofar that, as a native Indian of that land, we may amplify and extend with our own proper history the account of the Spaniards which, being foreigners, they cut short because they could not grasp the properties of the language, and because they did not suckle the milk of fables and truths as I did."[19] The effect of such devices and claims was anything but modest. In the *Comentarios reales,* the Old World's noble written word was marvelously assisted by the New World's proper royal ear and voice. The result was that the historian among the Incas would become an Inca among the historians.

As a modest eyewitness and native-born historian, Inca Garcilaso takes an exegetical approach to the orally transmitted deeds and achievements of the 12 Inca dynasts, from the founder Manco Capac to the last great Inca, Huayna Capac. In general terms, his aim is to show "how the Incas performed their divinely ordained historical role" as the "apostles of reason" in Peru and how the pagan civilization they created and ruled was in fact a *Praeparatio evangelica* in the Eusebian mode.[20] The approach is Neo-Platonist in the sense that its method presumes a truthful correspondence between words (signi-fiers) and things (signified) via what Michel Foucault has called "similitude" but which during the period in question was simply called "verisimilitude."[21] This approach is applied to the Quechua names and epithets associated with the Inca dynasts. In short, and as Zamora notes, Inca Garcilaso's history of the Incas is a philological commentary that is both a modest critique of the limits of European understanding and an authoritative interpretation of the true essence of Inca dynastic rule.[22] Written in the topical idiom of Cicero's *historia magistra vitae*, Inca Garcilaso's discourse "both represents the exem-plary and impels the reader to action [by] imitating [or avoiding] the ex-ample," observes Zamora.[23]

The prosaic "portraits" that Inca Garcilaso paints of the 12 Incas are moral "mirrors of princes." The true meaning of these mirrors is revealed through a Quechua exegesis of each Inca's name. Although "fabulous," the first Inca, named Manco, and whose Quechua epithet is *Capac* (splendid founder), Inca Garcilaso tells his readers, is the "morning star of reason" who brings the natural light of the sun to a dark, pre-Inca world of barbarous idolatry and error. In Inca Garcilaso's account, Manco Capac's founding virtues in-clude his decisive promotion of "human life" or civilization, associated in the Renaissance historical imagination with cultivation, urbanity, and individual land holdings. Thus:

> The Inca Manco Capac, having populated his villages at the same time as he taught his vassals to cultivate the land, and to build houses and irrigation canals and all the other things necessary for human life, also instructed them in urbanity, good company, and fraternity, in accor-dance with what reason and natural law taught them. . . . [He] ordered that the fruits harvested in each village be stockpiled so that each might receive what he needs, until it was disposed that each Indian in particu-lar be given lands.[24]

Margarita Zamora suggests that Sir Thomas More's *Utopia* (which may have drawn upon early reports from Peru) may have been a model for the *Comentarios reales*. Like Inca Garcilaso's Manco Capac, More's fictional founder-king, Utopus, lifted his kingdom's "rude and uncouth inhabitants to such a high level of culture and humanity that they now excel in that regard almost every other people."[25] Zamora is right to suggest that More's *Utopia* and Inca Garcilaso's *Comentarios reales* are "not simply a celebration of the achievements of a pagan civilization [but] a statement in support of the complementary nature ... of reason and revelation."[26] Despite these similarities, it is clear that Inca Garcilaso did not need *Utopia* as a model.

Sir Thomas drank of the same classical and patristic historiographical canon as did Inca Garcilaso. In this tradition, wise kings or great men gave their names to lands, founded cities, and introduced civilization. In *De inventione,* Cicero had speculated that the first age of primitive men had ended with the appearance of a "great and wise man."[27] Earlier debates on the primacy of Moses and Mosaic Law between Origen and Celsus, and the histories of Diodorus and Clement of Alexandria, established a clear precedent to the Roman topos of the founder king. The historical genre of "the life of great kings" was made famous by Plutarch's *Life of Alexander the Great* and by Eusebius' *Life of Constantine* (wherein Constantine is likened to Moses), and these histories embraced the myths surrounding these great men.[28] Closer to home, and as previously noted, the Alphonsine historians had established the imperial dynastic history of "Spain" and the topos of the wise founder king.[29] By the late sixteenth century, a significant number of prestigious Spanish chroniclers, including Oviedo, Cieza, Zarate, and Diego Fernández, had framed the events and personages of the conquest of Peru in terms analogous to those of Roman antiquity as described by Sallust, Livy, Cicero, and Tacitus. Finally, the narrative or mythopoetic imperative of a kingly founder may have found an echo, in Inca Garcilaso's ears, at least, in the "life history" oral tradition of the pre-Hispanic Capac dynasty.[30]

The story told in the *Comentarios reales* of each of the succeeding Inca dynasts is one of conquests and the advance of civilization on the Roman model, although, as David Lupher notes, the Incas generally exceed the achievements of the "ancient" Roman emperors. Indeed, for Inca Garcilaso the only "advantage" that ancient Rome had over Cuzco was that she had "come upon the word" and so was better equipped to "immortalize the deeds" of her sons. Inca Garcilaso would now balance the history books, and for the most part "Peru" would come out on top.[31]

Two Beginnings and Two Endings without End

Histories have beginnings because they have ends. The first part of Inca Garcilaso's two-part history has two endings, both of which are openings that will take some two centuries, if then, to reach closure. Similarly, the first part has two beginnings: the first, as we saw in the last chapter, involves the eponymous Beru, while the "cornerstone" of the second beginning is Manco Capac. Let us begin with the first ending.

The first ending is a remembered conversation with the author's "old Inca" uncle, and it transpires in his mother's house on the day after the death of "Don Francisco, son of Atahualpa." Although Don Francisco has not yet been buried, the atmosphere at his mother's house is festive. Inca Garcilaso's puzzled, youthful self asks the "old Inca" why they are celebrating a kinsmen's death. Was Don Francisco not the cousin of the deceased? The "old Inca" responds with visible anger, saying:

> Are you to be the relative of the son of the Auca [Tyrant] who destroyed our Empire? Of he who killed our Inca? Of he who consumed our blood and extinguished our lineage? Of he who committed cruelties completely foreign to the tradition of our Inca forefathers? Give him to me dead, like this [cape], and [biting his cape] I will eat him raw without salt and pepper! His father the traitor Atahualpa was no son of Huayna Capac our Inca, but rather the son of some Indian from Quito who together with his mother [also an Indian princess from Quito] betrayed our King. If he really was the Inca not only would he not have committed the cruelties and abominations he had, he could not even have imagined them. . . . Therefore, do not say that he who turned against all of our ancestors is our relative; by doing so you insult them, all of us, and yourself by calling us the relatives of a cruel tyrant.[32]

Notably, Atahualpa is a "cruel tyrant" not only because "the Inca said" so, but because he is comparable to the vile Ottoman ruler who by a "barbarous custom" took all of his many brothers with him to the grave. In Inca Garcilaso's account, the "Ottoman" Atahualpa accompanied his father, the last great Inca, named Huayna Capac, on the epic campaign of conquest in the northern, barbarian lands of "Chinchaysuyu," earning the great Inca's affection in battle. He is thus the favored son, the brilliant and daring military chief who will "return to Rome" (Cuzco) to claim or, as it were, lay waste to his father's realm. It is an archetypal story of dynastic decline and devastation, with an insinuated East-West architecture, repeated (as Inca Garcilaso points out) again and again in ancient and modern times. But just as the Incas were greater than Romans, so was Atahualpa viler than the Ottomans. Atahualpa had ordered the slaughter of all of his father's royal kin, women and children included, among them Inca Garcilaso's own mother, who miraculously escaped his bloodlust. Atahualpa is thus given the appellative *Auca*, Quechua for "demon." In short, Atahualpa is not Inca Atahualpa but Auca Atahualpa, the wicked tyrant who serves as a horrifying mirror for princely readers, that is, as an example of Oriental despotism to be avoided at all costs by those Spaniards who would govern Peru. The Andean Ottoman, however, is also the source of a horrifying river of blood that stained Inca Garcilaso's youth.

Inca Garcilaso tells us that his second ending to the first part of the *Comentarios reales* was appended in response to an elaborate and illustrated petition from the Inca heirs of Cuzco, "some days after having finished this book." The intent of said petition (*recaudo*) was to gain recognition of royal titles and exemption from tributes. The documents had been sent to Inca Garcilaso in March of 1603 with the request that he present them before the Spanish court at Valladolid. Inca Garcilaso informs his readers that since he was duly occupied in writing his book, he passed the petition on to Don Melchor Carlos Inca. Don Melchor had arrived in Spain in 1602 and gone to court in search of his own royal title as the legitimate Inca heir and son of Paullu. In a decision much lamented by historians, Inca Garcilaso chose not to transcribe the lengthy petition into his history or to include the painted genealogical tree, which has since been lost, although some scholars believe that it may have influenced the drawing of the portraits that appear on the frontispiece of Antonio de Herrera's official history. Instead, Inca Garcilaso adds a brief final chapter that summarizes the post-Atahualpa history of Inca heirs and the genealogical claims of the "survivors of Atahaulpa's cruelties and tyranny." In this chapter Inca Garcilaso relates that the petition contains the claims of all 11 royal houses (*panacas*) of Cuzco, each of which corresponds to a past supreme Inca. The petition is signed by 11 Inca heirs, one from each panaca. However, the total number of surviving patrilineal panaca royalty is listed as 567 persons.

Inca Garcilaso closes the first part (and the ninth book) for the second and last time with a courtly note on Don Melchor Carlos Inca, the nephew of Paullu and the great-nephew of Huayna Capac. Don Melchor, he has learned, has had some success at Valladolid. It seems that his own claim to be of royal blood was recognized and that he has been assigned substantial rents in Lima, although he will not be allowed to return to Peru. His princess wife was ordered brought to Spain, and he is given reason to hope that the royal Inca couple will be assigned "a place in the Royal House" (*esperanzas de plaza de asiento en la casa Real*).

This second ending leaves open two possibilities, each of which could conceivably extend the dynastic history of the Incas into the future. The first possibility is that many Inca heirs survived in Peru, while the second suggests that at least one Inca heir survived and was officially recognized in Spain. With the hanging suspicion of these possible survivals, various prophecies and rumors of Inca restoration would find fertile ground.

The first ending won out and appears to have been Inca Garcilaso's preference. That ending squelches any such rumors of the survival of legitimate Inca heirs and it seals the providential narrative of the transfer of sovereignty. It also makes Inca Garcilaso's personal history the definitive history as a "labor of death" that lays the real Incas to rest as dignified, Neo-Platonic mirrors of princes. The first ending, which is bloodied by the spectacle of the rage and death of the "Tyrant" Atahualpa, enables a providential *translatio imperii* from the Incas to the "Roman Emperor" and "King of Spain" Charles V. Both endings are openings for two, alternative modes of dynastic history, the first providential and universal, the second restorationist and utopian. In part, they represent Inca Garcilaso's personal negotiation and exculpation of moral debts to his maternal and paternal lineages. Notably, these two endings to the first part are repeated at the close of the second and final part of the *Comentarios reales.*[33]

The first ending was also canonical because it was the result of the epic, fratricidal struggle of succession between Inca Huayna Capac's two sons and half-brothers, Atahualpa and Huascar. In the *Comentarios reales,* Huayna Capac is great not only because he is Inca Garcilaso's mother's brother but because he extended the Inca empire far to the north, spreading the unifying lingua franca of Quechua, which Inca Garcilaso, following the Quechua linguist Fray Domingo Santo Tomas, associates with *policía* or the well-ordered polity and with the polished and noble properties of Latin.[34] Atahualpa is the favored but bastard son (in Inca Garcilaso's account his mother was queen of the "Kingdom of Quito" and his real father was actually an Indian from Quito, although the Inca Huayna Capac apparently did not know this) and a military hero who has accompanied "his father" in the conquests of the northern region of Chinchaysuyo (today northern Peru, Ecuador, and southern Colombia) but who upon his return to "Rome" becomes the plotting and bloodthirsty "Auca" or "Tyrant" Atahualpa. Prince Huascar is the legitimate heir who resides in the imperial center at Cuzco. At first Huascar accepts Huayna Capac's division of the realm, wherein Atahualpa is granted the Kingdom of Quito in Chinchaysuyu and any additional conquests, while Huascar is the Supreme Inca of the other three *suyus* or "quarters of the world." Huascar then realizes that this division of the empire is a bad idea, for he sees that Atahualpa will soon grow militarily powerful with his new conquests of the rude barbarians of the north who now come under his command, and so he demands that Atahualpa cede his dominion. Atahualpa agrees but in a deceitful way, for he plots to eliminate Huascar and claim the empire for himself. Atahualpa marches to Cuzco, ostensibly to celebrate Prince Huascar's coronation, and when the prince goes out to receive him, he is captured by Atahualpa's superior forces. Atahualpa then declares that he only desires a dual coronation and so invites all the other Inca royalty to the festivities, at which time he massacres them in cold blood. The tragic struggle between the half-brothers thus destroys the Inca dynasty of Tawantinsuyu and so opens the way for Spanish "deeds" and the "incorporation" or conquest of Peru, the subject of the second part of the *Comentarios reales*.

The tragic story of Huayna Capac, the last great Inca and the progenitor of the unfortunate heirs Atahualpa and Huascar, thus closes Inca Garcilaso's dynastic history of the Incas in an apostolic dozen. His fall and that of Tawantinsuyu resonate in their outlines with the Eusebian story of the Christianization of Rome under the Emperor Constantine I and with the paradigmatic struggles among his sons and heirs. As all good Renaissance historians knew, dynasties collapsed and empires were divided (or gave way to new and more powerful and righteous ones) under the weight of tyranny and vice and/or the quarrels of heirs. It was the way of Providence, and Greco-Roman histories were full of such lessons.

The canonical narrative of providential Inca decline that leads inexorably to the first ending of the *Comentarios reales* bears a family resemblance to the modular story of Constantius I, the father of the first Christian emperor of the Roman empire, Constantine I (Constantine the Great or, for the Eastern Orthodox, Saint Constantine), and of Constantine's three sons, Constantine II, Constantius II, and Constans. Not entirely unlike Tawantinsuyu (which had four lords, one for each *suyu* or province, and also two Incas, one high or *hanan* and one low or *hurin*), late Rome since Diocletian, who recognized Maximianus as co-emperor in 286 AD, was a tetrarchy. The tetrachic system was apparently designed to resolve the endemic military conflicts that surrounded imperial succession in Rome, for it was common for successful generals to return home to assert claims to the throne. Under Diocletian's system there would be two emperors, or *augusti*, and two appointed crown princes, or *caesars*. Constantius I was the caesar of Maximianus, while Diocletian chose Galerius as his caesar. In turn, Constantius chose Severus as his caesar, while Galerius fingered Maximinus Daia. However, Constantius soon died. The troops of Severus declared Constantius' son Constantine to be augustus. Meanwhile, the son of Maximianus named Maxentius claimed that he should have been named caesar. The Roman Senate upheld his claim, and Severus was removed. A conference was held to resolve the situation, and Constantine was named caesar of the west and Licinius, augustus of the west. Maxentius' claim was not recognized, and so he was considered a usurper. In the east, Galerius and Maximinus Daia remained as augustus and caesar. However, with the death of Galerius Maximinus, Daia was challenged by Licinius, who had remained in the east. Licinius struck an alliance with Constantine against Maximinus Daia and Maxentius. The two camps came to battle in 312, when Constantine converted to Christianity. In 313 Licinius's forces defeated those of Maximinius Daia, bringing an end to the tetrarchy. In 324 Constantine defeated Licinius (who he had previously recognized as co-Emperor) and became sole emperor. After Constantine's death, the empire was distributed among his sons, who also struggled for succession. Constantius II had many of the rival imperial kin murdered, an act that anticipated Atahualpa's fury against Prince Huascar's kin.[35]

The storied successions of Roman emperors were not exact parallels but, rather, moral exempla that were well known to Inca Garcilaso and his readers. That the glorious Inca dynasty of Tawantinsuyu, founded by the great Manco Capac, could consume itself in a violent struggle among brother heirs to the throne was not at all strange but instead an archetypal and even providential story, as Inca Garcilaso's narrative reveals: "Showing great mercy for [our] gentility, the Lord Our God permitted the discord among the two brothers so that the predicators of His Doctrine and Catholic Faith could enter into this land with greater facility, and less resistance."[36] Subsequent tragic errors of violence committed by the conquistadors were also familiar events. Likewise, the *Comentarios reales* depicts malice in the Spanish camps in Roman terms. (Inca Garcilaso's father was a member of Pizarro's band, and the author sides, with a certain amount of deft maneuvering, with the controversial Pizarro brothers and condemns the Almagro camp, blaming them for the execution of Atahualpa.)[37]

The second part of the *Comentarios reales*, or *Historia general del Perú*, is appropriately dedicated not to the Catholic king but to the mother of the King of kings, for the Virgin Mary or "Spanish Mars" was the decisive agent at the battle of Cuzco.[38] Inca Garcilaso writes that it was "with her celestial favor that the strong arms of noble Spain . . . had opened [the doors of] sea and land to the conquest and conversion of the opulent provinces of Peru." Such celestial favor was required, for the glorious conquests and deeds of the Inca dynasts "could compete with the Dariens of Persia, the Ptolemies of Egypt, the Alexanders of Greece, and the Cyprians of Rome," the dedication notes, adding that "Peruvian arms are more worthy of praise than those of the

Greeks and Trojans."[39] Given the military prowess of the Incas, Spanish arms were truly "invincible."[40] The Spaniards had the greatest army the world had ever seen, at the service of the greatest emperors and kings (Charles V and I), who, with the favor of Jesus Christ, the King of kings, had "conquered both worlds." Inca Garcilaso also credits the Spanish captain Francisco Pizarro for just punishment of the tyrannical Auca Atahualpa, thereby "conserving" the "Peruvian Empire" from the Auca's impending reign of devastation. Pizarro's execution of Atahualpa at Cajamarca, then, is not regicide but the administration of royal justice in the interests both of the Cusqueño and Castilian "thrones" and the larger interests of the Faith. Indeed, Pizarro's intervention makes possible the perpetuation of the "Peruvian Throne," since Atahualpa's sovereignty passes via his hands to Charles V. Thus, the second part of the *Comentarios reales* effectively translates the glorious past of the Incas into the Peruvian future, at which point it becomes a forward-looking narrative, predominantly of divine intercessions and Spanish deeds.[41] Part 2 explains that the "Peruvian Empire" is presently "no less rich" than it was when "possessed and governed by her ancient Princes, the Incas, Peruvian Caesars in happiness and strength," for she is now blessed "with the treasures of wisdom and knowledge of God, whose Faith and Evangelical Law" reigned in the world. Also, notes the prologue, there is "no shame in being subjected to the strong, valiant, and noble Spaniards, or to our Catholic Kings, Monarchs over most and the best of the World."[42]

While Inca Garcilaso's providential narrative of conquest as a translation of empire conjoined by the continuous dynastic narrative of sovereigns would endure, so would the coda about the 567 Inca heirs. José Eusebio Llano Zapata's unpublished *Epítome cronológico o idea general del Perú* (1776) and the first part of his *Memorias histórico, físicas, crítico, apologéticas de la América Meridional* (1757) would reproduce Inca Garcilaso's courtly, Janus-faced narrative of the Incas and conquest, albeit there distributed in two works. The *Epítome cronológico* of Llano Zapata would place Atahualpa as the last or fourteenth Inca who enables a succession, via the sovereignty of the kings of Castile, to the governors and viceroys of Peru. In long footnotes to the *Memorias*, however, and as in Inca Garcilaso's appended ending to the first part of the *Comentarios reales*, Llano Zapata would emphasize the legitimacy of the post-Atahualpa Cuzco heirs.[43]

Two Beginnings and "the Arts of Rule"

The *Comentarios reales* also has two beginnings. Inca Garcilaso presents the "fabulous" Manco Capac as "the cornerstone of the edifice" of his history. This is surely true if we hold that the first part of the *Comentarios reales* is primarily a Eusebian and Ciceronian history of the Inca dynasty, which, by virtue of Pizarro's "gift of Peru" to the Holy Roman Emperor and Spanish king Charles, will continue as "the Peruvian empire" of the Hapsburg dynasty. As Basadre notes, "in binding together the names in a single narrative" of the first Inca Manco Capac and the founding Spanish conquistador Francisco Pizarro and his king, Charles V, "Peru as a continuity in time becomes visible." And it is in this sense that the *Comentarios reales* are the *cantar de gesta* of the nationality" of Peru, Basadre notes.[44] However, if we consider the founding place in the Inca Garcilaso's history of the eponymous Beru, we must also admit that the Indian barbarian is a "cornerstone of the edifice" of the arts of history and rule that invented "Peruvian nationality." Indeed, in the *Comentarios reales* the brief description of life in Peru before the appearance of the Inca kings foregrounds "the age of the Incas." As noted in chapter 1, the description of this age of barbarism follows directly upon the telling of the tale of Pedro Serrano. That age reflects a universal condition of history and as such need not be read as a failure on Inca Garcilaso's part to register the cultural significance of the pre-Inca age, as more than one critic has suggested.[45]

Inca Garcilaso's history is consequently divided into two ages or stages of religious life. The author tells the reader that "so that the idolatry, life, and customs of the Indians of Peru may be better understood, it will be necessary to divide those centuries into two ages: we will tell of how they lived before the Incas, and later we will tell of how those [Inca] Kings governed, so that . . . the customs and gods of one age are not confused with those of the next." Nevertheless, Inca Garcilaso's ethnographic commentary on living barbarians does just that: It confuses "the ages" as traces in the present colonial order of Peru. During the first or primal age, he continues, "some Indians were little better than domesticated animals while others were much worse than wild beasts." They had a "great variety of gods" and they also adored an array of wild beasts. But for the cosmopolitan historian, these practices were "not surprising for people without letters or education," since "it was notorious that the Greeks and the Romans, who thought they had so much science, had at least thirty thousand gods during the flowering of their Empire."[46] This "great variety of gods" existed only because "the doctrine and teaching of the Inca Kings had not reached them."[47] We then learn that some of those same Indians who had not been reached by the Inca's teachings are alive and well, "as barbarous and brutish today as they were then."[48] The "Indians of the First Age," Inca Garcilaso notes, "dressed like animals, since they only wore the skin that nature had given them." But en route to Spain in 1560, the historian notes, "I met five Indians without clothes in the streets of Cartagena, but they did not walk together but in a row like cranes, for having been around Spaniards for so many years."[49] These Indians still live "in an antique rusticity," are "irrational and barely have enough language to understand one another within their own nation, and live like animals of different species, alone, without gathering together or communicating."

The clear message of this "confusing" sketch of the "First Age of Gentility" and its colonial presence was that an antique barbarism still existed, and perhaps was accentuated, under Spanish rule. Its colonial existence was proof of what the Incas had accomplished and what the Spaniards had yet to do.

Inca Garcilaso's second beginning or Eusebian emplotment of Manco Capac as the "morning star" of natural reason in a "age of gentility full of errors" had some unintended consequences for "the arts of rule" and the "rule of history" in colonial Peru. In theory, at least, many of the founding Inca's "policies" and "deeds" described in the *Comentarios reales* were later pursued by Crown officials in Peru. Ironically perhaps, this was particularly true under the regime of Viceroy Toledo, whom Inca Garcilaso had criticized. The Toledan administration began to implement, in a *res gesta* reminiscent of the great Manco Capac, a vast resettlement or "reduction" of the Indian population into modern, planned villages, arrayed with individual plots and commons. As a colonial Manco Capac, Viceroy Toledo would bring a violent end to the "Capac" Inca lineage. Notably, its "reason of state" would remain, now augmented by Christian revelation and the archive-informed minds and plans of Spanish magistrates.

These colonial arts of rule followed from Inca Garcilaso's dynastic arts of history in part because the theoretical basis of the myth of the founder king lie in the Janus concept of the "great simplicity" of untutored barbarians. This commonplace of the Renaissance historical and colonial imagination had ancient roots in the notion, noted earlier, that barbarian nations could not live without a king and when without were ripe for the picking. A notable passage from the *Comentarios reales* sums up Inca Garcilaso's reflection on the matter:

> What I may conjecture, in accordance with what I witnessed of the condition and nature of those peoples, with respect to the origin of this

Prince Manco Inca whom his vassals called, in honor of his greatness, Manco Capac, is that he was probably an Indian of good mind, prudence, and council; and that he well understood the great simplicity of those nations, and saw their need for doctrine and teaching [so as to achieve] the natural life, and with astuteness and sagacity, and to earn esteem, he fabricated the fable, saying that he and his wife were children of the Sun, that they had come from the heavens and that their father had sent them to indoctrinate and make good among them. And to make them believe, he wore [a gold emblem of the sun] on his body and clothing, particularly in his ear lobe which, as the Incas had elongated them, were incredibly huge for anyone who had not actually seen them, as I have.[50]

But it was not just a question of deception. As politics, it was also a matter of results. Noting that "the benefits and honors that accrued onto his vassals confirmed the fable of his genealogy," the naïve Indians "firmly believed that he was the son of the Sun come from heaven, and they adored him as such, like the ancient Gentiles who, although less brutish, had adored others who brought similar benefits."[51]

There was more to the Indian's "great simplicity" than the natural tendency to accept the agrarian benefits associated with solar rule. The Inca's solar cult was not the "pure" form of religion among the peoples of Peru. Indian simplicity was also the pure sign of an innate, primitive religiosity, particularly dear to early missionaries, the basis also of a new and expanded ecumene that would herald the Second Coming of Christ. The concept had been firmly established in Fray Bartolomé de las Casas' scathing *Brief Relation of the Destruction of the Indies* and other writings, in which Christian notions of a noble, primal purity serve as an impetus to a utopian missionary enterprise.

This pure simplicity of the Peruvian Indian's soul was also dear to the "Inca Yndio" who, as a priest of a small parish in Andalusia, penned his providential history. The Peruvian Indian's innate religiosity could serve as an inner resource to be drawn upon in the author's noble quest to conquer his own barbarism. In their wide-eyed spirituality, and under the wise political rule of the Incas, the docile Indians had developed an inner appreciation of the supreme and invisible creator, called Pachacamac (World-maker) in the Quechua language. Even the Inca kings were aware of Pachacamac's omnipresent power. Nor was the Inca historian making it all up so that his people would look good in the eyes of Europe's Christian readers. It was the reliable Spanish soldier and chronicler Pedro Cieza de León who had "told the truth when he said that the God of the Christians and Pachacamac were one and the same" and that "Pachacamac" was the word Indians used "to name the Christian God who gives life and being to the Universe, which is what the name means."[52] Indeed, the Peruvians under the Incas were more innocent and pure than the primitive Christians had been in the age of Rome. In this spiritual domain, Peruvian Indians held a clear historical "advantage" (*ventaja*) over contemporary Spaniards.

As an example of this *ventaja*, Inca Garcilaso cited the cloistered virgins (*aclla*) dedicated to the Inca's houses of worship. These were not the Oriental harems of filth and debauchery reported by early Spanish chroniclers but rather were the Peruvian equivalent of chaste Christian convents. The only elements that Peruvians lacked were the "culture" of the pen and its firm "science and knowledge of God." That lack was now being remedied by the Jesuit fathers, however. Now revelation would complement an exemplary natural reason that had surpassed that of pagan Rome. And with the historical *ventaja* of a pure form of monotheistic religiosity, Peruvians would outnumber Europeans at the gates of heaven.

The notion of the "great simplicity" or childlike innocence of Indians underwrote an enduring colonial discourse of rule among functionaries, conveniently resumed in the topos of the "miserable Indian."[53] Throughout the colonial period, Inca Garcilaso's exemplary Manco Capac was incessantly cited by Spanish and Creole magistrates, as well as by mestizo and native governors or *kurakas*, as historical justification for a paternal and disciplinary regime of Indian tutelage and tributary labor. This colonial "reason of state" found a high place in Spanish political theology and law.

As Jorge Cañizares-Esguerra notes, Juan Solórzano y Pereyra's monumental *Política indiana* (1647) argued that "the Crown should follow the example of the Aztec and Inca rulers [like Manco Capac] who had forced their subjects to do things as absurd as to collect and fill bags with fleas to combat their innate idleness." Solórzano's Aristotelian and historicist approach to law, which was based in part on the writings of Father Acosta and on the aphorisms of Cicero ("the customs of each region are no less different than the air that bathes them," and "the good legislator . . . should always tailor his precepts to the regions and the disposition and capacities of the people to whom they are addressed"), anticipated by a century some of the main arguments put forth in Montesquieu's unoriginal *Spirit of the Laws* (1748) and it gave Spaniards and Creoles alike a "contextual" and "climatic" understanding of the colonial arts of rule.

The Jesuit chronicler Bernabé Cobo had argued along similar lines, noting that the Indians "are phlegmatic by nature" and so should be ruled with a
harsh regime of discipline, as the Incas reportedly had. As Cañizares-Esguerra
argues, the discourse of the lazy "phlegmatic Indian" carried the "assumption,
implicit in Hippocratic and Galenic theory of humors and constitutions, that
negative bodily temperaments were caused by negative climatic and astral
influences affecting everybody" in the antipodal New World south and not
only Indians. So that Aristotelian distinctions could be drawn between "natural" indolents and "accidental" ones, Creoles and Spaniards invented the "racialized body." Under this scheme, Spaniards and Creoles in the New World
suffered only the "accidental" affects of the "humid clime" on their constitutions, which were as a result generally more "sanguine" than the "phlegmatic"
nature of Indians.[54]

Nevertheless, Cañizares-Esguerra's brilliant reading of the Spanish American invention of the racialized body does not consider the logical problem
that the founding *res gestae* of Inca rulers posed to this paradigm. How could
Manco Capac have performed so vigorously if his bodily temperament was
naturally phlegmatic? As we shall see in chapters 3 and 4, such questions
would lead later European scholars to speculate that the Incas were likely to
have been of foreign origin, that is, members of a "superior race" distinct from
that of the phlegmatic Indians or "naturals" over whom they ruled. It was Inca
Garcilaso's "second beginning" or kingly narrative of the abrupt transition
from barbarism to civilization that invited this speculation.

The Inca's Addressees

In his *Rerum familiarum,* Petrarch noted that "writing entails a double labor:
first to consider to whom you have undertaken to write, and then what his
state of mind will be when he undertakes to read what you propose to write."
Inca Garcilaso gracefully engaged in this double labor, and as a result his legacy for Peruvian historiography went far beyond the "arts of rule." Another,
deeper legacy, this one for the "arts of history," lived long and true in the Inca's
addressees, auditors, and anticipated readers.

Inca Garcilaso's first success in the life of the pen was a Spanish translation
from the Italian of the Neo-Platonist poet León de Hebreo's *Three Dialogues
of Love* (1586). An excerpt from the book's dedication to Philip II, which
was reprinted in the prologue to the second part of the *Royal Commentaries,*
serves as the second epigraph to this chapter. As the New World's first native

interpreter and historian, Inca Garcilaso pays a "genre of tribute" to Philip II, "King of Kings," in the form of the "first fruits of the imagination." In this dedication Inca Garcilaso announces and asks royal favor for two works in progress, later published as *La Florida del Inca*, and the two-part *Comentarios reales*.

The first part of the *Royal Commentaries* was published in Lisbon more than a decade after Philip II's death and it is dedicated to Princess Catalina of Portugal, Duchess of the House of Braganza. Inca Garcilaso had procured her favor to have his book published, and at the time Portugal was united with Spain. This brief dedication to the princess—one of several heirs to the Portuguese throne before it was assumed by Philip II in 1581, passed on to Philip III in 1598, and then to Philip IV in 1621—opens with a gesture to the Book of Kings rhetorical tradition resumed in the first epigraph to this chapter. Inca Garcilaso begins:

> The custom of ancient and modern writers who always strive to dedicate their works, which are the first fruits of their imaginations, to generous monarchs and powerful Kings and Princes, so that with their help and protection they be more favored by the virtuous, and more free of the calumnies of mordacious critics, inspired me, most Serene Princess, to imitate their example and take the risk of dedicating these Commentaries to Your Highness.

But in the next line Inca Garcilaso turns this flattering dedication to the princess toward his own historical arguments:

> Your Highness ... is known not only in Europe but in the most remote parts [of the globe] East, West, North, and South, where the glorious Princes progenitors of Your Highness have planted the standard of our health and of your glory at the cost, as is well known, of their blood and lives. How high the generosity of Your Highness reaches is well known to all, since you are the daughter and descendent of the illustrious Kings and Princes of Portugal, although this in itself is not what makes Your Highness so estimable, but rather the shine of heroic virtues that envelops the gold of so much highness ... [and] the state of grace with which The Lord Our God has enriched the soul of Your Highness.

We may read in this passage an oblique reference to the Incas, "glorious Princes and Caesars of Peru," whom Inca Garcilaso portrays as "progenitors" of Spain's (and Portugal's) glory. There is also planted here a recognition of the "blood and lives" (Inca and Spanish) that were sacrificed for "our health and your glory." Moreover, it is the great virtues of such heroic deeds that make the gold of the princess's illustrious lineage "shine."

The second part of the *Comentarios reales*, also titled *Historia general del Perú*, which is primarily concerned with the deeds and consequences of Spanish conquest, was published in Cordoba one year after the author's death. It is duly dedicated to the Virgin Mary, who is the decisive "historical agent" in Inca Garcilaso's narrative of conquest (see fig. 5). The historian justifies his dedication to the Virgin, in good humanist style, by referencing an ancient Greek tradition:

> Antiquity consecrated its arms and letters to the goddess Palas, to whom they thought it was due. I, with maximum devotion and veneration, consecrate Spanish arms and my miserable letters to the Virgin of Virgins, Bellona of the militant Church, Minerva of the triumphant, because I believe that for a thousand reasons they are due, since it was with her celestial favor that the strong arms of noble Spain, putting Plus Ultra to the Columns of Hercules, opened by sea and land the doors and roads [that led] to the conquest and conversion of the opulent provinces of Peru, so that the victorious lions of Castile owe much to such a sovereign lady, since she made them lords over the principal part of the New World, the fourth and greatest of the orb, with deeds and valor greater and more heroic than those of Alexander of Greece and the Caesars of Rome.

Once again, Inca Garcilaso turns the lofty dedication to his own purposes, which is to sing the compensating spiritual story of the "vanquished Peruvians" and to make known to the world his own Inca pedigree:

> No less indebted are the vanquished Peruvians who, with the favor of heaven, emerged [from the Conquest] victorious over the devil, sin, and hell, receiving a God, a faith, and a baptism. I, your devoted Indian, although unworthy, should also dedicate my historical letters and these arms, given their author and argument, to . . . my most estimable tutor. I am obliged to do this for three reasons and causes. First, the plenitude of gifts and talents of nature and of grace which, as the mother of God, is an almost infinite advantage over all of the saints combined. . . . Second, the insuperable benefits and mercy that beyond all estimation and appreciation are received from your royal hand, among these the conversion to our faith of my mother, made more illustrious and excellent by the waters of holy baptism than by the royal blood of so

HISTORIA
GENERAL DEL
PERV

TRATA EL DESCVBRIMIENTO DEL,
y como lo ganaron los Españoles. Las guerras ciuiles
que huuo entre Piçarros, y Almagros, sobre la partija
de la tierra. Castigo y leuantamiēto de tiranos: y
otros sucessos particulares que en la Historia se contienē.

ESCRITA POR EL YNCA GARCILASSO DE LA
Vega, Capitan de su magestad, &c.

DIRIGIDA A LA LIMPISSIMA VIRGEN
Maria Madre de Dios, y Señora nuestra.

CON PRIVILEGIO REAL.

¶ En Cordoua, *Por la Viuda de Andres Barrera, y à su costa.* Año, M. DC. XVII.

5. Frontispiece, Inca Garcilaso de la Vega, *Segunda parte de Los comentarios reales
de los incas o historia general del Perú* (Cordova, 1617).

many Peruvian Kings and Incas. Finally, the paternal devotion, inherited from the nobility and name of the famous Garcilaso, commander of the Ave Maria, the Spanish Mars, whose triumph is more than Roman, and whose trophy is greater than that of Romulus. . . . And so for these reasons and motives I humbly offer this Second Part of my *Royal Commentaries* to Your Sacred Majesty, August Empress of Heaven and Earth, made more noble by virtue of being dedicated to the Queen of angels and men, since it treats the rich realm of Peru and her powerful Kings as much as the glorious battles and victories of the heroic Spaniards . . . who, with superhuman force and valor, subjected and subjugated that Empire of the New World to the Crown of the Catholic Kings in the temporal, and in the spiritual to the King of Kings, Jesus Christ, and to his Vicar the Pope.[55]

The appropriately posthumous dedication to the literate "Empress of Heaven and Earth" places the Inca and his *General History* in the company of angels. Back on earth, the Inca continues with an upbeat prologue addressed to "los Yndios Mestizos y Criollos de los Reynos y Provincias del grande y riquisimo Ymperio del Perú" (Indians, mestizos, and Creoles of the kingdoms and provinces of this great and very rich empire of Peru). He now explains that his purpose in the first part of *Comentarios reales* had been "to make known to the universe our homeland, people, and nation" (*patria, gente y nación*). Inca Garcilaso's "our" is here foundational for "national history," more so because it speaks, as a posthumous call, from beyond the tomb. It is from this proud trinitarian "we" that the Inca historian now addresses "Peruvians" as "brothers and countrymen" (*hermanos y paisanos*). Here the Inca historian humbly presents himself as a native "Indian Inca" (*Inca Yndio*), for the vices ascribed to those Indians also run through his veins. He confesses that among his motivations for writing his history was his personal desire to conquer his own "vices of idleness" with the "honest and noble" occupation of historical study and so set an example for the "Peruvians" whom he encourages to follow in his footsteps. Sounding the humanist hymnal of sword and pen that was his personal coat of arms, he exclaims that virtuous study in the "pastures of genius" could pay far "more dividends to the soul" than all the "pearls of the Orient, or the silver of our Potosi, to the body."[56]

The study of history was more precious than the spoils of treasure hunting, for it raised men to noble heights more surely than did the acquisition of material riches. Although Peru had been won by the sword, it was the scholarly pen of history that would open the gates onto a heavenly future, Inca

Garcilaso argued. He thus exhorts his "Indian, mestizo, and Creole" countrymen to follow his example by "advancing yourselves in the exercise of virtue,
study, and the martial arts, for your own sake and for our good name, with
which you will become famous in your own soil, and eternal in heaven. Along
the way, the political and Old World will understand that the New, which
appears barbarous to them, is not so, nor has it ever been, except insofar as it
has lacked culture."[57] This appeal to posterity and bookish learning as gates
to the future—by "culture" the Inca meant the written word and its "firmer
knowledge" of history and God—purchased a founding-father position in
Peruvian historiography.

Brilliant eighteenth-century Peruvian historians such as Pedro de Peralta Barnuevo would heed the Inca's call to "study . . . for your own sake and
for our good name," and so too would Peru's postcolonial historians. In this
sense, the legacy of Inca Garcilaso's Book of Incas is found not only in the
colonial "arts of rule" but also in the long rule of the historical arts in Peru.

3

The *As If* of the Book of Kings

Among all the illustrious Works that men undertake, History is
among those that are at once the most glorious and the most useful,
since all is directed toward Honor and Example. It is an enterprise
formed by two beams of immortality: that which shines on the past
with its name; and that which predicts the future with its rules. Indeed, History does more than actual heroism, and it extends beyond
all great deeds, because it is itself a fecund heroism, it is itself the
sum of all immortal deeds.

Ángel Ventura Calderón y Cevallos, "Al Príncipe Nuestro Señor," in Pedro de
Peralta Barnuevo, *Historia de España vindicada*

Inca Garcilaso de la Vega's "Arts of History" wrote the providential Incas into the venerable Book of Kings tradition. As we have seen,
that tradition was dedicated to the sovereign's Arts of Rule. Inca Garcilaso's
books were thus dedicated to the Spanish "king of kings," Philip II, to the
princess of Portugal, and to the "Spanish Mars" or Virgin Mary. As we have
seen, these royal dedications could harbor critical and pro-Peruvian insinu-
ations, however. By addressing their histories to what Spanish historian of
the Indies Antonio de Solís so eloquently called the "Grandest of Auditors,"
historians might do more than merely genuflect before all-powerful patrons
and censors. Indeed, such dedications are as characteristic of unofficial or
noncommissioned histories as they are of official ones. Moreover, it is prob-
able that most history books in the Book of Kings or "Mirror of Princes"
genre were not read or commissioned by kings, princes, or their courts. What
may we learn from the royal earwax?

In this chapter I suggest that colonial dynastic history was a "letter to the
king" that was written not so much as a *libellus* (a legal petition to an absent
person) but *as if* the ear of the distant king was within its acoustical range.

Composed within imaginary royal earshot, dynastic histories would not only require the prescribed forms of a respectful appeal but also a bright-eyed, noble, and sweet poetics worthy of the educated king or prince whom it "imitated" in word. In short, history would acquire the noble aura of the sovereign subject to whom it was addressed. This aura was "majestic" and humanistic, and is not to be confused with the legal robe and skeptical reason of the judge promoted by Jean Bodin (himself a jurist) and his modern followers.[1] It was not merely a question of following numinous classical examples; moreover, it was not merely a picaresque *carte d'identité*.[2] Instead, colonial dynastic histories imitated or "copied" the imagined and real dynastic addressees and subjects they recreated in discourse, thereby fashioning themselves as the imagined prince's presence or bookish double, that is to say, as his simulacrum (a copy that has no original).

As the exemplary, *as if* presence in words of the imaginary prince, history was, in the words of Pedro de Peralta Barnuevo, an "animated reason" that was "truer than life." As animated reason, history could stand in a sovereign, critical and futural position vis-à-vis the past of the empire, the distant king, and the imagined prince it tutored. The princely *as if* aura of dynastic history lent itself to a characteristically ambivalent form of colonial (and postcolonial) critique in which, as the imagined prince's tutor and double, a history was not merely an unseen "mirror of princes" and an undelivered "letter to the king" but instead the true sender and the addressee of "the answer" to the prince's eager "question" of "how to rule." In short, as the truer-than-life example that the imagined prince should follow, history ruled. History thus founded in the simulacrum of its "animated reason" its own sovereign authority, thereby making itself available to political and aesthetic projects, including those revolutionary ones that would later decapitate the imperial body politic in the name of a "history" or "destiny" that history itself had made imaginable. Stated another way, this kingly decapitation in the realm of discourse could only proceed efficaciously whence the "royal head" of "the nation" could be imagined to be not the prince but his textual "copy," history itself. In a word, history would come to mirror not the prince but itself. As a mirror of its own production history could speak as the sovereign "head" of the nation.

The most brilliant Peruvian example of the truer-than-life colonial "arts of history" is to be found in the lesser known, and when known often disparaged, texts of the Creole "Cosmographer and Engineer of the Realm," Pedro de Peralta Barnuevo (1664–1743). A late Baroque/early Enlightenment polymath, Peralta was an accomplished mathematician, astrologer, poet, historian, and rector of Lima's first university. Unfortunately, Peralta and his baroque style of historical discourse have been frequently mishandled if not abused by professional historians. Beginning with the Peruvian iconoclast José de la Riva-Agüero (1885–1944), Peralta has been depicted as backward, scholasticist, and fond of Empire; as lacking national consciousness, and as failing to apply modern empirical methods.[3] But as Peralta scholar Jerry Williams has recently argued, Peralta's work consciously exhibits the colonial marks of Creole hybridity and ambiguity, his epistemics were fully modern by the measures of his time, and any shortcomings of his scholarly research are largely the product of a limited colonial library and a lack of funds.[4] An admirer of Antonio de Solís's theory of discourse, Peralta wrote parallel histories in prose and verse of Spain and Peru dedicated to the Spanish prince and the Peruvian viceroy, respectively, but not sponsored directly by either of them: *Historia de España vindicada* (History of Spain Vindicated), the first part of which was published in Lima in 1730, and *Lima fundada o la conquista del Perú*, (The Founding of Lima, or the Conquest of Peru), published two years later.[5] These two histories will serve as the primary subject matter of this chapter.

Peralta's *Historia de España vindicada* is an explicit historicist defense of a Spanish empire in crisis and under attack by upstart European powers, pirates, and intellectuals, but it is also an ingenious and unprecedented colonial Creole critique of that empire. It appears to be the only history of Spain ever written by a colonial subject, and the text's rhetorical strategies reveal that Peralta is acutely aware of his provincial place within the empire and thus of the boldness of his intellectual enterprise. What is immediately noteworthy about this history is that it is only an *as if* or allegorical dynastic history. That is, it is a history not of the royal houses of the Goths, the Hapsburgs, or the Bourbons but of "Spain" *as if* "she" were a noble "lineage" and a "Queen." The political and imperial subject of history named Spain had been fashioned much earlier by the Alphonsine historians, but Peralta gave "Spain" a new colonial twist that would resonate with Peru's history of Inca and viceregal culture-heroes. Peralta achieves this allegorical effect of Spain as queen of history by uniting in a single mythic chain or political genealogy the several dynastic houses and culture-heroes, human and divine, that at one time or another guided the "Political Ship of Spain." Peralta's chain links the early "Hispanic" kings to the Roman caesars, to Jesus Christ, the King of kings, to the Virgin Mary, to various archangels and martyrs, to the Gothic kings, and, had the second part or volume been completed, to the dynasts of "Modern Spain," from Alphonso the Wise to Ferdinand and Isabella, to the Hapsburgs, and, finally, to the Bourbons. Despite the long and providential passage of worldly and otherworldly *dramatis personae*, the master subjects of Peralta's history are actually the "Political Ship of the Name of Spain" and the "country" named "Iberia." These master subjects are notably interpolated from a "Peru" that is in many ways both Spain's double and its future.

The dedication to Prince Ferdinand (proclaimed Ferdinand VI) that precedes and introduces *History of Spain Vindicated* was penned by Peralta's local sponsor and academic colleague Ángel Ventura Calderón y Cevallos. The content of such princely dedications, including those of official chroniclers such as Solís, was normally much more than a stylistic genuflection before the majesty and power of the monarch. Instead, such dedications were seized as golden opportunities to reflect upon the philosophical nature and political utility of the history that ensued. Don Ángel's eloquent discourse, a passage from which serves as the epigraph to this chapter, takes full advantage of that opportunity. History, writes Calderón y Cevallos, "completes with memory what was unclear in life." Not only does history "compensate for the lack of events, it improves upon them, since the reality of its lights exceeds the evidence of the cases." History is not merely a "mirror" of all that is great in life; history is "greater than life" because it is nothing less than the "sum of all immortal deeds." And what is the king? He is the "improved sum of all the immortal deeds of his ancestors," that is, of the "kings" and "heroes" of his lineage, "such that he is a supremely animated History of their deeds." In a word, history's cognitive objects (all of the immortal deeds of the past, incarnate in the writing of history) imitate the lineage of history's sovereign subject (all of the immortal deeds of the king's lineage, incarnate in the figure of the prince), such that "history" and "the Prince" are "improved copies" of one another. Like virtuous princes, writes Calderón y Cevallos, each new history book should "improve" upon past history books or "ancestors." According to this model, the stuff of histories is kingly and dynastic, but histories are more than the king and his dynasty because, like the prince, every new history is itself a "fecund heroism" that should improve upon previous histories. Histories thus acquired a dynastic or heroic model of progress or advance and as such became the "improved" bookish doubles of the prince in the realm of learned discourse.

As the bookish double or improved "copy" of the prince, history was endowed with a cumulative dynastic temporality and renewable authority, and as such it embodied a mythopoetic and critical power that exceeded that of the *relación*, of the notarial archive, or of simple "rustic annals." In his brilliant reading of the repeating origins in "myth and archive" of Latin American narrative, Roberto González Echevarría argues that novels and histories constantly return to that origin of writing which is "the founding of cities and punishment" and "the control of the State, which determines its mimetic penchant." This repressive return to origins is done "through the figure of the Archive, the legal repository of knowledge and power from which it sprung."[6] In the critical hands of González Echevarría, Inca Garcilaso de la Vega's *Comentarios reales*—an urtext for Peralta—is quickly reduced to a legalistic appeal to authority set in a high Renaissance and autobiographical mode so as to exonerate his father's questionable actions during the conquest of Peru. But what both Inca Garcilaso de la Vega's *Comentarios reales* and Peralta's *Historia de España vindicada* amply demonstrate is that colonial history's legal "appeal to authority" and "return to the archive" is never sufficient, since the "truth-bearing power" that their histories claim may only be made manifest in the *as if* or allegorical status of the text as the truer-than-life "imitation" of the prince and his lineage. In the case of Inca Garcilaso de la Vega, and also in Peralta's *Lima fundada*, this poetic operation of sovereign imitation turns the historian's text into an outsized "copy" of the Incas, "kings of Peru that were." Moreover, it is precisely this *as if* poetics that establishes history's more "regulative," futural subject-position of critique and authority vis-à-vis the archive or, as Peralta puts it, the "sum of all immortal deeds" that is also the "Prince's lineage." For dynastic history then, the "return to the archive" remitted not only to the dusty papers and memories of distant foundations, in themselves insufficient since all they may produce is "rustic annals," but instead to all of the notable events that, having become life in the body and blood of the prince's lineage, constituted history's "intellectual map of all the ages." In short, the return to the archive was both insufficient and excessive since as the double of the imaginary or allegorical prince (and, as we shall see, of the imaginary queen as country), history would have the all-hearing ear of the king and in this sense was a child and mistress of power and grace born of the historian's pen. This, Calderón y Cevallos sagely observed, was the "theory" of Peralta's *History of Spain Vindicated*.

Calderón y Cevallos' dedication makes it quite clear that Peralta's history is "not merely the repayment of a debt that corresponds to Your Highness' dominion" but is instead:

A Copy dedicated to Your Highness by Virtue, since Y. H. is an improved compendium of her Kings and Heroes; such that one could say that from this moment forward Y. H. is a supremely animated History of your deeds, and that History is the inheritable mental Reign of your royal seals. In this History Y. H. will see all that your August Blood has been, and all that shall exceed your immortal Name. Your Sovereign Progenitors have not formed, but rather entered Y. H.'s Greatness as communicating Oceans, such that the Circulation of Regal honor that Y. H. receives makes perennial your glory. These are registered in this History not only for the pleasure of Y. H., but as a stimulus. . . . Read them not to learn what you desire, but to imitate with respect, since Y. H. was born Parallel, and so only need live as excess. . . . Y. H. need only imitate that which deserves an ardent cult, erecting your Royal Veins like the animated Altars of the August Saints they contain. Thus Y. H. will adore your own Royal Lineage, rendering your qualities as offerings.[7]

The language here may be mistaken today for an exaggerated colonial flattery but at the time it was surely nothing of the sort. Calderón y Cevallos' discourse summons an erudite philosophy and a poetics of history that do not so much flatter and inflate as they exalt and challenge the mind. The prince is informed that "one could say that from this point forward Your Highness is a supremely animated History of your deeds" and that "History is the inheritable mental Reign of your royal seals." This is heady stuff. Calderón y Cevallos fully equates history with the prince in the subjunctive (each is the "one could say" or *as if* double or copy of the other) via the concepts of "animated reason" and "inheritable mental reign." Both history and the prince are greater than "the communicating Oceans" that flow into them precisely because they actively "imitate" only that which "deserves an ardent cult," since the prince (and thus history) "is born Parallel, and so only need live as excess."

It is precisely as "parallel" and "excess" that Peralta's *History of Spain* is a truly animated colonial "copy" of the Spanish prince. In Peralta's own prologue, the Peruvian historian "consecrates" his own historical efforts to "Our August Prince," not only so that the prince should "find within a lesson from your Royal Ancestors, of that excess which I will leave as an example to their descendents" but, more importantly, "so that the fruit of this History should in a single stroke (*en una sola atención*) extend to the two Worlds, since Royal heads are the seat of the soul of Realms, and it is from [those heads] that the spirits of instruction should be diffused in wise choices and good deeds." Peralta admits that he hopes his history will "render a singular service to the Nation and to the Orb." The nature of this "singular service" is twofold. First, what Peralta as a colonial subject has to offer the "Nation and the Orb" is a "history vindicated of the offenses [against truth] committed by [Spanish self-] love and emulation." As a colonial subject of Spanish empire, Peralta presents his history as the most credible response to the recent attacks of anti-Spanish French and Protestant intellectuals, who had set out to defame and orientalize Spain and her Indies as "despotic" and backward.[8] Second, Peralta's history of Spain is in many ways actually about Peru; writing the history of the metropolis is the preamble to writing the history of the province.

Peralta's twofold agenda has not always been evident to his critics. Concolorcorvo's oft-cited travel narrative, *Lazarillo de ciegos caminantes desde Buenos Aires hasta Lima* (1775) anticipated twentieth-century critics of "dependency" when its pseudonymous author lamented that, in Williams' words, Peralta "idled away his time pursuing a defense of the Monarchy" and writing about Europe when he should have been writing "our history."[9] According to the alias Concolorcorvo, Peralta's history of Spain reflected "an inclination to follow events in faraway lands at the expense of what goes on in his own."[10] Although Peralta had since the early 1700s written a great deal about Peru, the Creole historian's desire to publish his history of Spain prior to his history of Peru made perfect political and intellectual sense. To understand this sense, however, requires an appreciation both of Peralta's art and of the discourses within which it operated.

Unfortunately, such an understanding has not been readily forthcoming from modern professional historians, Peruvian or otherwise. Two examples will suffice to illustrate this lack of understanding and the reasons for it. In his widely influential 1910 doctoral thesis on the history of Peruvian historiography, the young José de la Riva-Agüero (considered by many in Peru to be the "father of modern Peruvian history") found some notable things to admire in Peralta but more to lament, ridicule, and reject. Most objectionable was Peralta's "submissive and flattering" courtesan style, which for Riva-Agüero was the regrettable product of his "frivolous veneration of the principle of authority." Riva-Agüero thus asks: "Is it not sad that a genius like don Pedro Peralta should deny the right to criticize and council rulers, or even to resist tyranny, arriving at a point [of adulation] that very few absolutists did in Spain, and write these words: 'Even the tyrant deserves the veneration of the justice of Majesty. . . . The Prince is a visible deity, with whom the word has no other office than that of the hymn or the request'?"[11] What Riva-Agüero misses here is that Peralta's defense of the "tyrant" could be an oblique reference to Auca Atahualpa and that the "visible deity" of the prince evoked the invisible deity of history. For Riva-Agüero, Peralta's style of writing history is "normally very bad and detestable because overblown, extremely affected, and very pedantic." What is even sadder for the impatient Riva-Agüero, however, is that "in confirmation of the irremediable blindness and perversity of the taste of that epoch, there were those who proclaimed that [Peralta] was an example of clarity and straightforwardness, and an antidote to affected pomposity!"[12]

Following the insights of Juan María Gutiérrez, Riva-Agüero concedes that what appears to be "flattery" and "submission" in Peralta could have been the "rhetorical affectation" or dissimulation of court culture. But such a concession—which in any case appears to be insincere since Riva-Agüero judges Peralta's entire epoch to have suffered from "terrible style" and "frivolous veneration"—misses the point. Riva-Agüero's concession here responds to the fact that he was engaged in a project to "extract and recover" what was "wise and useful" in past Peruvian histories, understood as "historical sources" (*fuentes históricos*). Beneath the sycophantic style, the modern historian of history could uncover useful "historical facts" (*noticias*) and, on rare occasions, evidence of wise and true "political" thought—that is, of a "precursor" to "our" own manner of thinking and writing history. Unfortunately, of course, what was "wise and truly useful" in Peralta's histories was nearly always "damaged" by "the deplorable literary taste in which he was immersed, and the loud, panacolor garments of his style."[13] In a predictable rhetorical move, Riva-Agüero positions his own voice as steering a sober middle course between those who condemn and those who celebrate Peralta, but the criteria of what is positive in his assessment is always "evidence of good judgment," that is, of what is "correct" and "useful" in the histories, and never the poetics or theory of the writing itself, which is rejected or simply passed over. Finally, the only way Riva-Agüero can save something of Peralta is by saying that "if only he had been born in another age and place, he could have become a very distinguished economist."[14]

To his credit, Riva-Agüero admits that Peralta himself had a contrary perception of his own writing style. As evidence of this point, however, Riva-Agüero distorts a passage taken from the prologue to *Historia de España vindicada*. In the passage in question, Peralta actually writes that "in terms of style, I naturally reject the affected and only follow the proper, which I hope imitates those original [historians] whose work has been so amenable to the tastes of all nations in all the ages, that is, Sallust, Livy, Tacitus, and Florus." Riva-Agüero's quote of this passage reads: "in terms of style, I [Peralta] naturally reject affectation." The difference between the two versions here is critical since, in effect, Peralta's point about his own style makes it very clear that the historian of "frivolous veneration" fully anticipated Riva-Agüero's criticism. That is, what is really sad about all of this is that Riva-Agüero did not know how to avoid falling into the kinds of errors of reading that Peralta had predicted two centuries prior in his text. Peralta's point was not that he did not seek to create poetic "affect" in his writing—all of the classical historians, he noted, did precisely that—but that his style was his own, that is, a "proper" or self-styled "imitation" or truer-than-history "copy" of the original style of the great classical historians. By "copy" Peralta did not mean "aping." The "apes" were those who doggedly followed the sterile conventions of those "modern" historians who naively held that history should be an unadorned recounting of facts and events stripped of poetry. Those moderns had failed to learn from the rhetorical "arts of history" of the "original" or ancient historians. It is this very same failure to appreciate the arts of history of the ancient historians that leads Riva-Agüero to repeat the error of the moderns and in the process to miss the meaning of Peralta's style.

More recently David Brading, a noted British historian of the idea of Creole patriotism, has dismissed Peralta's work in similar if more punctual fashion.[15] For Brading, Peralta's talent is outrun by his ambition, and "the entire project is vitiated by the incongruity between his elevated style and his often banal subject matter." Brading adds that "the often inane exuberance of his classical comparisons soon prov[es] more wearisome than amusing." These very same points were made by Riva-Agüero in 1910 when he wrote that "from an artistic perspective, what most mars [the text *Lima fundada*] and produces a grotesque effect is the strange mixture of classical mythology, the Christian miraculous, and the indigenous names and idols: the angel of America asking Jupiter to send Christians to convert the natives of Peru."[16] Brading identifies Peralta's ostensibly incongruous style with an equally ostensible "narrowly Limeño patriotism" diagnostic of a colonial aristocracy that defended Spanish empire. For Brading, this colonial aristocracy defended the interests "of a social class rather than a possible nation."

In short, Riva-Agüero and Brading alike dismissed Peralta's "affectatious" and "inane" style because it did not meet the conventional stylistic demands of truth in history writing as they understood them. Both historians also insinuate that Peralta's style was consonant with the "frivolous veneration" of a colonial elite enthralled with Spanish empire. Against these readings, I take the poetics and politics of Peralta's writing seriously as a discourse of historical truth. I will argue that the style and content of his writing is not only coherent but indivisible. More: I suggest that Peralta's writing constitutes a serious contribution to the theory and history of history.

Peralta's poetics of history were informed by the Neoclassical "arts of history" and the Neo-Platonist imaginary of the colonial Hispanic Baroque. In this artful imaginary of truth, enigmatic icons and heraldic emblems were carefully read and rendered in an eloquent writing not only as enduring aids to historical interpretation but as powerful embodiments of the truth or providential design of history. Peralta demonstrates his art and its imaginary in the opening pages of his history of Spain. As in Giambattista Vico's *New Science,* which also begins with an "Explication of the Frontispiece," Peralta begins with a demonstration of his own powers as an interpretive historian and in so doing he repeats a gesture made famous by Erasmus: "Although the preceding engraving has been rendered so clearly that it pronounces its own spirit in the syllables of images, its harmonious execution of a large number of these symbols could form more of an enigma than an enterprise; for this reason it seems to me that, since the engraver's chisel was the interpreter of thought, it would not be disagreeable if here the pen should be [the interpreter] of the plate."[17] The hermeneutic gesture here is clear: Since with the passage of time the key to the engraver's symbolic images might become an enigma for thought, the historian's pen could provide enduring clues for its interpretation. Unfortunately, Peralta's faith in the pen appears to have been unwarranted, for professional historians today seem unable to read those clues.

Peralta's pen wants to tell us that in the engraver's symbolic art, "Spain" is "interpreted" in the "elegant and august figure of a beautiful Queen fitted in her Triumphant Crown" and "sublimely occupying a heroic Throne." The throne's three steps of Virtue (Valor, Constancy, and Religion) take the queen named Spain "to the heights of Eternity" since in those steps we may divine "the three spheres of her glory." Spain, the bountiful queen, "holds in graceful elevation the Image of Our Lord the Prince." The prince's image is framed by the inscriptions of the four royal houses that have ruled "Spain" across the ages: the Gothic, the Hispanic, the Hapsburg, and the Bourbon dynasties. Meanwhile, under Spain's heavy throne groan the historical trophies of her invincible arms: barbarians, Romans, and Muslims (see fig. 6).

Peralta's pen tells us that at the base of Spain's throne stands an "elegant Nymph who represents History"; crowned with laurels, History "insists on the Globe" that is turned to "the New Orb, the point from which this work is offered." The nymph or History is a symbol of the intellectual virtues of Peru, for she (as Peralta) offers a "History of Spain" to "Spain." This Peruvian Nymph of History is accompanied by "three beautiful genies that signify the three qualities that History should have: Truth, Elegance, and Instruction." Represented by the mirror, a "symbol of a clear disillusion," and glossed in Saint Augustine's motto, *Veritas pateat,* Peralta reminds us that the "first Genie represents clarity." The second, notes Peralta, wields a torch that indicates "brilliant splendor" and her motto is *Veritas luceat,* while the third, with

6. Frontispiece, Pedro de Peralta Barnuevo, *Historia de España vindicada* (Lima, 1730).

"some gold chains that, flowing from his lips, attract hearts," expresses persuasion and is clearly identified by the motto *Veritas moveat*. Although Saint Augustine's sublime trinity of *Veritas pateat, Veritas luceat, Veritas moveat* was intended to teach Christian doctrine, Peralta explains that the same rules may "easily be adapted to the causes of reflection and judgment with which History moves [its readers] to imitate the virtues and deeds to which it refers."

Peralta's exegesis of his own frontispiece is an ingenious hermeneutical move, a copy of a copy, or an interpretation of an interpretation, of the "thought" of "Spain." The true source of this interpretation is not the "Prince" but the Nymph or "Pen" of History that is none other than a symbol for the interpretive and rhetorical powers of Peralta himself. Central to the poetic imagery of the literary frontispiece that Peralta writes is the symbolic trinity of the Queen, the Prince, and the Nymph. The Queen represents or "interprets" "Spain." "Spain" holds aloft the Prince, who represents "the Royal head of the Nation," while the Nymph or History addresses that Prince from Lima, Peru. Notable too is the symbolic fact that no "Indian" lies crushed under Spain's throne. The absence of the Indian there anticipates a central theme in *Lima fundada*, in which Peralta will present "the conquest of Peru" not as the vanquishing of "Indians" by Spaniards but as the "union of two empires into one." What makes those two empires one is neither Madrid nor Cuzco but, rather, Lima, the "City of Kings of Peru" and the point from which the Nymph offers to the Prince her history of Spain.

In the discussion that follows the interpretation of the frontispiece, Peralta distinguishes "true history" from crude and simple annals. History, he writes, is an elegant and precise "poem of truth" whose ultimate task is "to instruct." Like the prince himself, true history is an "animated being of reason," whereas annals, like the royal lineage, are lifeless "statues of narration." Here Peralta turns to the classical historians (Tacitus, Livy, Salustius, and Florus) for ammunition. He notes that in their great works of history the classical historians frequently deployed "metaphor, hyperbole, and antithesis" to achieve an effect of "living reason." These classical stylistic devices and "thought-images" were, Peralta writes, "the savings of discourse, by means of which an idea is made manifest, since these are at once reason and example, thought and object." Nevertheless, history was not to be confused with the affectatious play of words. "History," Peralta now insists, "only has the form and not the content of Poetry." History possesses a "style of thought, not a style of speech," for "pleasure and devout affection are the doors of perception and understanding." It was precisely the pleasure and affection or aesthetics of an elegant discourse of "animated reason" that distinguished "true history" from the "humble huts of memory" recorded in primitive annals. True history "instructed" and the most persuasive way to do so was in a precise and exemplary style that illuminated the events and personages of history "with a majesty that authorizes." Cicero had said that "History was the light of reason." Peralta now adds: "Why should we take away that which makes it shine?" And if history was the "science of princes," Peralta wonders, "why should it not have rules to govern" its reception? Peralta concludes that "these have been the conclusions of the best critics who have written about the art and style of History."

In his history of Spain Peralta applies the classical and Christian rhetorical arts of style to the history of Spain's mythic genealogy. He examines the verisimilitude of heroic figures, human and divine, who at one point or another captained, across the "Ocean of the Ages," the sturdy "Political Ship" that is the "Name of Spain." As in the enlightened historicist thought of Peralta's contemporary Vico—for a time an equally obscure provincial subject of Spanish empire—history is guided by "Divine Providence" and assisted by heroic *dramatis personae*.[18] In this case, these heroes ensure not only the perpetuity of Spain's name, but in that name the universal development and spread of Christian "civil" or "human" institutions. Despite periods of darkness in which events were inhospitable to the keeping of records, Peralta's history would seek to prove that "Spain" had existed in unbroken perpetuity since the time of Hercules.

As an unbroken chain and vessel of universal civilization, the "Name of Spain," despite threats from pirates, armchair philosophers, and the British and French empires, was unlikely to soon disappear from history. In addition to possessing its most ancient and glorious name, which summed up the entire history of world civilization, Spain could claim what no other empire could: that she "had added another World to the World." The best and most glorious part of that "New World" or "Orb" was none other than the "Empire and Name of Peru," whose viceregal capital was Peralta's glorious city of Lima.

In the "intellectual Map of all the Ages," the "Name of Spain" was the most glorious and famed "of all the Empires," exclaimed Peralta. Like the good prince, the Peruvian historian of Spain now carried that glory and fame forward. In accordance with the poetic rules outlined in its prologue, Peralta's history seeks to "improve" upon the great tradition of "mythic" Spanish dynastic history.[19] Not only does Peralta employ more rigorous methods than the Spanish historians did; the Peruvian will also engage in a critique of the errors of "love and emulation" that led some of those historians astray and he will do so by virtue of the critical but "generous" distance that his provincial or colonial subject position affords.

As if Empire Were Generative

Not surprisingly, the first substantial chapter of Peralta's *History of Spain Vindicated* is dedicated to "the country and clime" of Iberia. The convention or topos of including a background chapter on the "land" or "geography" was as old as history. The "geohistorical" convention is traceable to Herodotus and Tacitus; it comes back with a vengeance in the early modern and enlightened French geohistoricisms of Bodin and Montesquieu; and it reaches its apogee perhaps in the Annales School of social history and in the geographical "background" chapter once so common to modern ethnographies. The geohistorical gesture has always provided the indispensable "setting" for the historical actors or subjects of the narrative. This device actually prefigures or "sets the stage" for the historical actors or agents introduced in subsequent chapters, creating the literary effect of belonging and "context."

In truth, the literary topos of the geographical prologue functions in much the same way as does the dedication to the prince. That is, the union of "land and clime" is configured as a sovereign historical force that exercises "influence" over its subjects. In Peralta's case, the effect of geohistorical sovereignty is established by recourse to an *as if* (*como si*) dynastic rhetoric and lexicon that anticipates the geohistorical idiom of postcolonial republican Peru's "history of the people and the *patria*," discussed in chapters 5 and 6 of this book. Peralta's geohistorical sketch establishes not only the "stage" of Spanish history but, more fundamentally, the "character" of her people, since an "intimate relation" obtains between the "country" and its "inhabitants." Peralta launches the chapter with a lyrical and detailed description of Iberia's idyllic clime and celestial glow, her fertile soil and the "fruits of the land." The intimate relation between this fertile and blessed country and its inhabitants is configured in a dynastic lexicon:

> The nobility of the soil where one is born has always been the first honor of mortals, as if the temperament of the clime were an influence on virtue, and as if the properties of the terrain were privileges of the blood. These things provide the universal stock of the Nation, which shares a common Lineage [*Estirpe*] in the same *Patria*. Lands are like manly minerals which in accordance with the actions of their spirits produce the wealth of genius; and since the purity of metals may hardly

lie about the quality of the rock, the generosity of the soul rarely contradicts the excellence of the Country [*Pays*]. It thus follows that by
the accident of the region one may judge the quality of her inhabitants.
Now it is true that the same inhabitants form their nature by the lights
of their own customs, making a virtue of their origin in the sympathy
of imitation. But there is no doubt that as in the luminous bodies of the
Sky where there are Constellations or Stars of more pure composition
or more benign light, so too on Earth by virtue of the special constitution of the Celestial Sphere are there exhaled more favorable spirits and
influences on the immediate terrestrial sphere, and which men receive
at their birth. And so it would appear that, as if Spain had been chosen
to be the gate and throne of Europe, she was adorned with illustrious
gifts by the Supreme Author of Nature . . . and this nobility is the first
fortune of her native sons. Situated at the edge of Africa, it appears as if
she takes [that continent's] valor without her barbarity since she enjoys
the softening effects of the Temperate Boreal Zone, and has an entailed
Estate [*Mayorazgo*] of happy influences.[20]

This passage is typical of Peralta's use of *as if* phrasing. Here the use of *as if*
signals both the common knowledge of the naïve, who think that the clime
produces "virtue" and the soil "privileges of the blood," and the learned voice
of Peralta, who knows better. But we soon see that the *as if* may not be so far
from the truth of the matter, since it appears to be confirmed by the course
of events. Spain's privileged position between the Mediterranean Sea and the
Atlantic Ocean, as well as between Africa and Europe, has made her the "gate
and throne of Europe" (a reference to the pillars or columns of Hercules that,
since Charles V, have adorned the royal seal of Spain). It is *as if* Spain had
been adorned with "illustrious gifts" from the "Supreme Author of Nature"
Himself. It is *as if* history confirmed what had always been geographically
true by the grace of God.

The poetic confirmation of this historical truth is manifested in Peralta's
dynastic language. The soil is "noble" and is man's "first honor," while the
clime appears to instill "virtue," and the "terrain" flows in the "blood." The
patria is a "lineage" or "stock" that establishes the "nation." The dynastic metaphors common to biblical discourse merge with an Aristotelian lexicon of
"exhalations" of minerals and the sublunary sphere and "inhalations" of the
terrestrial. As a "country" blessed with the best of African and European climatic influences (a condition which may be confirmed in retrospect only by
history), she has inherited an "Estate" of happy influences.

"The country" in Peralta's work is an *as if* noble lineage and inheritance that founds itself not in climate and soil but in the dynastic language of history in which these imaginary things are prefigured. In subsequent chapters, this noble lineage of the country is made to "harmonize" with the noble lineage of culture-heroes. Peralta will apply similar language and concepts to Peruvian history, in some cases recycling well-established topoi drawn from the *Comentarios reales,* in which, for example, the mineral riches of Peru are said to produce "generous faculties" and "mines of understanding" among her native sons. Given the extraordinary richness of Peruvian mines, for Inca Garcilaso these Peruvian faculties clearly exceeded those of the Europeans.

Peralta was a talented and rigorous reader of texts who understood that toponyms could result from error or wishful thinking. After all, he noted, to a "Florentine usurper" had been assigned "title to a whole world." Following Inca Garcilaso's canonical tale of the eponymous Beru, Peralta noted that Peru's name "was imposed by the accident of an utterance repeated by her barbarous owner, a mere inhabitant of a village encountered by a ship which, reconnoitering the coast, had been sent to discover the Pacific Ocean."[21] In his critical discussion of the origin of the name Iberia, Peralta notes with satire that "there are those who will have no River without her King and who, sistering [*hermanando*] that river with the region, pretend that the name [of the country] was born of the same Ibero." Those credulous seekers of eponymous kings had argued that "Ibero" was the name of an ancient wandering king. However, Peralta insists that in the case of Ibero this claim was an "absolute conjecture . . . founded on the custom by which men have made the first kings into the descendents of their own kingdoms, as if Empire were generative, and to whom, in a species of political genealogy, they have left their name as lineage, as has been seen in the cases of the Assyrians, the Medes, the Trojans, the Latins, and the Romans."[22]

Here again Peralta enlists the same kind of language and argument as in the passages about the "clime and soil" of Spain examined earlier. By "custom" men believe what is manifestly contrary to reason, that is, they talk about the past as if it were descended from the present, as if origins could be divined from consequences. But unlike certain of the more strictly rational Enlightenment historians of the late eighteenth century, Peralta, like Vico, does not reject such "custom" out of hand. There was strong precedence for exercising caution here. The political genealogy of eponymous kings that reached from Assyrians to Romans traced the old Four Monarchies theory or periodization of the westward march of "universal empire" and world history. The theory was based on Daniel's famous interpretation of King Nebuchadnezzar's dream, in which the king's body was read "as a cryptogram for the Four Ages of the world." The succession of the Four Monarchies was to end, after the plague of the Antichrist, in Saint Augustine's final Age of Christ, and many held that this last age was that of the Holy Roman Empire centered in "Germany." Although the Four Monarchies design was famously criticized by Jean Bodin in *Method for the Easy Comprehension of History* (1566), it appears to have garnered the favor of at least some of the court historians of Charles V and Philip II, and Peralta was quite familiar with their histories.[23] Williams interprets Peralta's tolerance for such unscientific thinking as a "negotiation" of his censored milieu, but I suggest there are good reasons for reading it as a faithful reflection of his *as if* idiom of writing history.

Notably, Peralta's disapproval of a generative "political genealogy" did not keep him from conceding that the customary idea that "a river must have her king" was in the case of "Ibero" and Iberia "not a weak idea." It was "constant" for Peralta that the name Iberia was in fact borrowed from that of the Ibero River (Ebro, Latin *Iberus*). The problem was not so much that no eponymous king named Ibero could be found in the annals of history but that the river itself, understood as a "communicating" geographical subject, seemed to historically confirm its own geohistorical claim or course, etched in the land, to "unite the Peninsula." The riverine hypothesis "was not so weak" precisely because in Peralta's mind it confirmed what appeared to be an empirically observable fact: the Ibero River "communicated the country."

Of course, the argument for the river is no more convincing than the argument against the king, since it is not on empirical, geographical grounds that "Ibero" makes its stand in the history of an imagined "country" that did not yet exist. Ibero's stand is made on the poetic grounds of the ancient Greek custom of naming peoples after rivers, and this is the same ground on which the king stands. In a word, the "intimate relation" of riverine and kingly lines in Peralta's work is effectively realized by means of the time-honored poetic and political gold of homonymy. Homonymy creates *as if* effects by virtue of the multiple semantic domains referenced by a single name. "History" is one such homonymy.[24] In Peralta's history, place names (Hispania, Iberia, Spain) harmonize with the names of kings (Hispania), rivers (Ibero), and peoples (Iberians, Spaniards) in source-critical, *as if* plays of association. The truth of his historical discourse lies in these poetic plays.

These plays are as old as history and truth. Greek colonists who came ashore at the mouth of the so-called Iberus in the sixth century BC are said to have named the inhabitants of the region "Iberians." Historians suggested that the name was derived from the Basque words for river (*ibai*) and valley (*ibar*).

This Greek custom of naming peoples after rivers is found in abundance in the *Histories* of Herodotus, for example. Herodotus spilled literary rivers of ink on both eyewitness and hearsay descriptions of other rivers, lands, and peoples, which he then "baptized" for Greek history under a plethora of corresponding *logoi* and toponyms.[25] A related topos is also traceable to Herodotus and, more precisely, to the Greek belief that "barbarian" peoples "could never live without a king."[26] More fatal or useful (depending on your epistemics) to Peralta's reasoning, however, is that no "river" or "king" may give its name to a "country" that does not yet exist as such except in the sense that the one is the double or "echo" of the other. In other words, "country" and "river" and "king" are all *as if* poetic plays of language, or images of thought, that may only name one another. In sum, what makes the riverine hypothesis "verisimilar" for Peralta is precisely the poetics of "political genealogy" that on the surface he rejects in the case of the king named Ibero. This is so because Peralta's idiom of history has already prefigured "the country" not as a rich realm that "influences" her inhabitants but as an "animated reason" or *as if* dynastic subject that corresponds to the language of those who write her.

Peralta is thus quite willing to accept the idea that Hispania or Spain has her eponymous king. "Hispania," which for Peralta is the origin of the name "España" or Spain, and so of the "Political Ship that is the Name of Spain," presented similar problems of etymology, association, and historical interpretation as "Ibero." After considering the alternatives, however, Peralta settles on the "verisimilar" idea that Hispania took her name from "Hispano, partner of Hercules of Egypt." For Peralta, then, Hispano is the first king and eponymous founder of Hispania. Peralta's "finding" aligns "Spain" with those ancient universal empires of the Four Monarchies, whose names were also derived, in a species of "political genealogy," from eponymous kings. By granting to "Ibero" another origin, and one moreover that is not dissimilar to the origin of the name Peru (also named after a river and a native in a barbarian tongue), Ibero was differentiated as a "country" (which included Portugal) from the "Political Ship" of empire named Hispania and later Spain.

I now wish to suggest that it was Peralta's own *as if* subject position as a colonial historian of Spain—that is, his Creole status as an *as if* Spaniard writing the "political genealogy" of the name of Spain from the "country" of Peru *as if* the "Peruvian empire" were a future Spain—that best explains or, better, and to use Peralta's language, "interprets" his imaginary enterprise. Although the Limeño historian has never set foot on "Iberian soil," he is a provincial vassal of the "Empire of Spain." Consequently, he reads her history with a colonial "generosity" that is not based on *amor propio* but instead on a certain *amor ajeno*, that is, from a critical hermeneutics of empathy and affinity that lives in customs, names, and books. Following the great armchair examples of Tacitus and Livy, and of the official Spanish court historians of the Indies, Antonio de Herrera and Antonio de Solís,[27] Peralta waves aside the eighteenth-century mania for eyewitnesses and travel accounts and instead insists on that hermeneutic intimacy available to those patient souls who tread along the grain of the archive.[28] This move is patriotic, for in the same gesture Peralta deflects contemporary European dismissals of Inca Garcilaso's *Royal Commentaries*, now routinely accused of those "gross exaggerations" that supposedly ensued from the new historiographical sin known as *amor propio*.

This waving aside of the eighteenth-century fashion for ethnographic authority was (and is) condemned by professional historians and anthropologists but it was surely amenable to Peralta's deeper political and poetic cause. This cause was not only to offer "Peru" via her "illustrious sons" as a "Tribute" to Spain's "Virtue" and "Empire," nor was it merely to suggest that the relationship of Peru to Spanish empire was now the same as that which had once obtained between Hispania and the Roman empire when the former was the latter's "most noble Province." Those points had been made earlier by Inca Garcilaso de la Vega. To be sure, they needed remaking now that Peru had matured and, in certain respects, Spain had declined, but precisely for that reason a second edition of the *Comentarios reales* had been recently reprinted in Madrid (in 1723). Like the good prince of history that he was, Peralta would go further. "Hispania" had become "Spain" and she, a modern Rome, spreading the humanist "virtues" of "the pen and the sword" to her most favored province on the other side of the "Political Orb." Despite the lack of libraries and sponsors of the kind that abounded in Europe, "Peru" could now offer to "Spain" a virtue she did not possess but now desperately needed: a critical yet "generous" history of her name. "Spain" was, like the prince, an "animated reason" greater than the dynastic chain of culture-heroes that had steered the "Political Ship" across the "Oceans of the Centuries." The future of this "animated reason" lay in Peru, the place from which the "history" of Spain is offered. In a word, Peralta's history of Spain executes a *translatio studii* or the geographical movement of learning from the old imperial metropole to the new colonial center.

The Seat of Historical Knowledge and Empire

Having prepared the ground, Peralta was now ready to pen an epic history of Peru in verse. Appropriately dedicated to the Marquis de Castelfuerte, viceroy of Peru, *Lima fundada* is a "heroic poem of truth" that sings the founding *res gestae* of the Viceroyalty of Peru and her "City of Kings of Peru." However, this is no ordinary poem. *Lima fundada* is an updated transposition in verse of Inca Garcilaso's prosaic *Comentarios reales*. Notably, Peralta's history in verse has only the "form" and not the "content" of a poem, for its "animated reason" is supported not only by Inca Garcilaso's recently republished history but by an ant army of footnotes that reveal a vast erudition.

Peralta's princely dedication of *Lima fundada* is addressed to the viceroy of Peru. Not unlike the Spanish prince who is the "immortal sum" of all the deeds and blood of his ancestors, the viceroy is "immortalized" via the "geometry of honor" that aligns him with the conqueror of Peru and founder of Lima, the agile and Aeneas-like Francisco Pizarro. Both the founder and the viceroy are "heroes" of the "Peruvian empire" (*peruano imperio*, a term used by Inca Garcilaso) and the "Peruvian orb." The *orbe peruano* glossed that vast reach of Lima's viceregal power that stretched beyond the limits of the old Inca empire, reaching north to Panama and south to Patagonia. Peralta's "geometry of honor" includes Peru's "viceroys, archbishops, saints, and illustrious men" and it reaches all the way back to the founding Inca dynast himself, Manco Capac. Like others before and after him, Peralta connects the "Inca" and "Ultramarine" or Spanish dynasties in a single chain of "Peruvian emperors." What links the two royal dynasties of Cuzco and Castile is the historical act of the transfer of imperium or "union of empires" performed by Pizarro. Singing Inca Garcilaso's account, Peralta notes that Pizarro passed the *borla colorada* (*maskaypacha* in Quechua) or Inca royal seal from the executed Inca "Tyrant" Atahualpa to the next legitimate heir, Manco Inca (since Prince Huascar had been slain), but that Manco returned it to Pizarro.[29] Pizarro then tells Manco that before accepting the Inca royal seal he must first consult with the emperor. In the end, and after the celestial interventions of the Archangel Michael and the Virgin Mary, the royal seal of the Incas is passed to Charles V.

> Y con asombro de ambos Hemispherios,
> Un Imperio formar de dos Imperios.
> [And to the wonder of both Hemispheres,
> One Empire was formed of Two.]

Peralta's heroic poem relates that Pizarro's next move is to march to the coast to found Lima, "City of Kings that forms one Empire." Significantly, Peralta refers to Lima as "City of the Kings of Peru" (*Ciudad de los Reyes del Perú*). In Spanish the meaning of this titular phrase is ambiguous and in Peralta it seems purposively so, since it may be translated to English as the "City of Kings in Peru" or, which is quite another thing, as "City of the Kings of Peru," that is to say, the city of the Inca and Spanish kings of Peru.

As the author relates in the prologue, the models of *Lima fundada* are Homer, Horace, and Virgil, although the latter's writing is "the most admirable for its prognostics." Like Vico, Peralta argues that verse lies at the origin of civilized or "political" life: "if men were subdued to the political life, their first settlements were the conquests of Verse." The historical point is immediately driven home: Pizarro's deeds are comparable to those of Achilles, Ulysses, and Aeneas, but such great deeds "do not count for much unless there is a voice of genius that intones them." This is why Virgil is the "Prince of the Epic," for he

> united the illumination of the Patria with that of the Heroes via the memory of the great men that she had produced after him and up to Augustus Caesar (in whose time he wrote) so as to exalt the future lineage with that of posterity and celebrate example with imitation. But since that could not be done without breaking the Law of the Unity of Action and going beyond the Catastrophe or the Conclusion [of history] he decided to present those great men as a prediction, doing them homage ahead of time and addressing them in a song of the future. ... The same zeal for the Patria could not help but burn in me just as actively as in that famous poet. ... And so desiring that the thread of glory of this famed City not be allowed to fall out of hand, I aspired to make manifest that virtue with which, having become a Political Phoenix, she has been wise enough ... to be her own heir by uniting her high Origins with [her own] learning and competing [in the world], thus making that [origin] pay what it owes her, to give her that which will enrich her.[30]

In this remarkable passage Peralta reveals his poetics and politics of history. His purpose is to make the sung heroes of the past pay for the "future lineage" that the historian's pen of genius has announced. Pace Riva-Agüero and Brading, a more "political" and "national" approach to Peru and her history is scarcely imaginable. In Peralta's history, Lima "harmonizes" the Inca and Spanish dynasties as that "Political Phoenix" that in its brilliant rise traces a future lineage from the glory of the heroic past to the greatness yet to come. Peralta's interest in Lima is no more narrowly "aristocratic" or "urban" than most of Peru's nineteenth- and twentieth-century national histories, including those of Lorente and Basadre. On the contrary, Lima is sung because, and like the prince, she is the "royal head" and the "seat of learning" that unites the empires of "Spain" and "Peru." Aided by the "genius" of the historian, that unity may write, and so come to inhabit, its own glorious future.

A striking graphic representation that approximates the imagery of Peralta's dynastic poem was printed for Antonio de Ulloa and Jorge Juan's *Relación histórica del viaje a la América meridional* (1748) and inserted in the appendix entitled "Resumen histórico del origen, y sucesión de los Incas, y demás soberanos del Perú, con noticias de los sucesos más notables en el reynado de cada uno" (Historical Summary of the Origin and Succession of the Incas and other Sovereigns of Peru, with Notes on the Most Notable Events in the Reign of Each One).[31] The plate captures the classical and majestic style of Peralta's histories and the spirit of the times (see fig. 7). It was made for the royal occasion of Prince Ferdinand VI's proclamation ceremony. The engraving was the work of Juan Bernabé Palomino and was based on a drawing by Diego Villanueva. In turn, Villanueva's drawing was based on the pictorial art of Alonso de la Cueva, a Creole churchman working in Lima. Like Peralta's *Lima fundada*, the "Resumen histórico" (compiled by Ulloa) was an abridged and updated rendition of Inca Garcilaso's account of the Inca dynasty, albeit in a dry annals style much admired by Enlightenment historians but which Peralta would likely have found tedious and primitive.

Like the allegorical frontispiece to Peralta's *Historia de España vindicada*, Palomino and Villanueva's image is an "offering" to Prince Ferdinand VI.[32] It represents his *as if* or allegorical succession to a "Peruvian throne" constituted by virtue of a retrospective and "generative political genealogy." This imaginary Peruvian throne is identified as the prince's "inheritable mental Reign," since the *borla colorada* of the Incas is one "of [Ferdinand's] royal seals." Indeed, this plate serves as a paper "mirror of the prince" (*espejo del príncipe*), a bookish double of those ephemeral arches erected for the ceremonial entries of viceroys in Mexico and Peru.[33] In addition, the processional imagery of royal succession that it presents appears to have been performed in the plazas of Lima.[34] Unfortunately lacking an erudite "interpretation of the plate" of the kind Peralta performs in *History of Spain Vindicated*, the "Peruvian Emperors" are framed by what appears to be an allegorical representation of the *Teatro Político* or Political Stage, a Spanish Golden Age topos that glossed the notion of "Political Orb" and which here appears to represent the "Peruvian Orb." Hovering angels suspend the gold "chain of honor" that links the pendants of Peru's Inca and Spanish dynasts, from the founding Inca Manco Capac to the newly proclaimed Ferdinand VI. In this "majestic" representation of Peru as a sovereign lineage of kings, the "last" Inca, Atahualpa, appears

7. Insert, Antonio de Ulloa and Jorge Juan, *Relación histórica del viaje a la América meridional* (Madrid, 1748).

as the "fourteenth Peruvian Emperor." Atahualpa offers his royal scepter to the sword-wielding Holy Roman Emperor Charles V, here named "fifteenth Emperor of Peru," and whose pendant exhibits the Holy cross, which absorbs the pagan light of Manco Capac's sun, from which the first Inca himself is descended (depicted in the first royal pendant on the lower left-hand side of the plate). The maker of this "Peruvian dynasty" appears to be *Fides* or *La Fe* (Faith). Faith prepares the pendant of Ferdinand VI, to be hung as the latest link in the "thread of glory" of "Peruvian Emperors."

Significantly, Faith occupies the symbolic place of the Queen in Peralta's frontispiece to *History of Spain Vindicated* (compare figs. 6 and 7). There the Queen holds aloft the image of the very same Prince Ferdinand whom the Nymph or History (Peralta) "instructs." Here Faith installs that same prince as the next king of Spain and emperor of Peru. The centrality of *La Fe* in this dynastic image of Peru marks it as quite distinct from Alonso de la Cueva's schema and others like it made in Peru in the 1720s. As noted, these images served as models for Villanueva and Palomino, and Peralta was undoubtedly familiar with them. In Cueva's pictorial representation of the imperial succession of "the Kings of Peru" and in other Peruvian versions of the same, Jesus Christ, "the King of kings," sits on his celestial throne at the top of the

8. Oil painting, attributed to Alonso de la Cueva, *Efigies de los ingas o reyes del Perú* (c. 1725). Museo de la Catedral de Lima.

composition, flanked on either side by the royal seals of (Spanish) Castile and (Inca) Peru, respectively (see fig. 8). Unlike Palomino's engraving, in which the royal seal of Castile adorns the cornice of the imperial arch and the *borla colorada* or *maskaypacha* of the Inca is strewn on the lower-left foreground, in the earlier Peruvian versions the dynastic seals of "Spain" and "Peru" are placed on equal footing on the same high plane. In addition, the Inca queen Mama Ocllo (or Mama Huaco) appears opposite Manco Capac, as the ur-mother or progenitor of all of the "Kings of Peru." Villanueva and Palomino's plate skillfully displaces Mama Ocllo with Faith, perhaps to avoid any suggestion of an "Indian" or pagan "bloodline" from a lofty lineage that included living Hapsburgs and Bourbons.[35]

Rather than dismiss Peralta's arts of history, in this chapter I have proposed instead that his histories of "Spain" and "Peru" offer brilliant insights into the nature and theory of history in the early modern colonial Hispanic world. Peralta's poetics of "imitation" configured the prince and history *as if* both were truer-than-life "animated reasons" and prognostic "heads" of the "nation" and the *patria*. This was precisely the mimetic position of Lima and of Peralta vis-à-vis "Spain" and "Peru." "Peru" was to "Spain" what "Hispania" was to "Rome." "Lima" made that futural conjugation possible, since, thanks to Peralta's *History of Spain Vindicated*, the "City of Kings of Peru" was now the enlightened site of an ingenious *translatio studii* that followed upon that great *translatio imperii* that had "formed of two empires one." Peralta's *Lima fundada* wrote Lima's glorious past as her own "inheritance" or future. It is in his colonial Limeño capacity as prognostic "Nymph of History" that Peralta offered to "Spain" a glorious past so that "Peru" might have her brilliant future. Peralta's prognostics or poetics of history thus formulated a bold answer to the prince's eternal question of how to rule. History's advice to the prince of its own making is: Rule "as if you were a copy of my future self."

The future of Peruvian history after Peralta suggests that the name of Peru could have "generative" political effects even as the Book of Kings or dynastic history found a place to rest first in the enlightened natural history of "the country" and then in the republican history of "the people and the *patria*." The rule of the arts of history would thereby outlive the princely arts of rule.

4

The Proper Name of
El País de los Incas

In the instant in which we name Peru the towns and cities begin to disappear from our view and even the opulent spires of Lima are annihilated. . . . Penetrating the dark centuries that have ceased to exist, in search of the fragments of the edifices of the Incas so as to contemplate the history of their Monuments, we have come to rest upon those days when the human imprint has not yet irrigated the sands of this favored region, nor had the farmer cultivated his fertile fields. Only Nature appears, surrounded in a mysterious silence.

José Hipólito Unanue, "Geografía física del Perú"

I'm not sure if it was a poetic movement, in which the nation was taken to be the soil, or if it was one of those truly insane ideas that were never lacking during the epoch of emancipation, but the fact is that the independence of Peru and the reconquest of the empire of the Incas were proclaimed as one and the same thing.

Bartolomé Herrera, *Sermón pronunciado el día 28 de julio de 1846, aniversario de la independencia del Perú*

In the middle to late decades of the eighteenth century, an enlightened Bourbon and Creole project of imperial revival set out to recover the fading grandeur and prestige of "Spain" and "Peru." To use the naturalistic metaphors of that project, it provided fertile soil for the erudite cultivation of a verdant patriotism rooted in a historical, scientific, and practical discourse on the *país* or country. As in Europe, the ancient theological and dynastic language and topoi of the "three kingdoms" of "Nature"—mineral, vegetal, animal—and the "Great Chain of Being" remained key to this discourse.

However, and as Arthur Lovejoy argued for Europe, the Neo-Platonist and Aristotelian notions of plenitude and continuity inherent to those ancient topoi were now notably temporalized, scientized, and romanticized.[1] The old "optical" language and topos of the "eyes of history"—from Tacitus to Vico and, in Peru, Peralta—now became the romantico-scientific gaze of the "observer." The result of these shifts was a more measured and "practical" historical discourse on "nature" and "man." In Peru, the proper "Peruvianization" of two ancient topoi contributed strongly to the naturalization and temporalization in historical discourse of Peru as a country: "clime" and "soil." Investigations into the circum-equatorial Andean clime would be the basis of the Neo-Platonist and Enlightened notion that Peru contained within itself all of the world's climes and was thus a complete microcosm of the entire universe. Lacking nothing, Peru was the most universal of lands on earth. "Soil" was a key metaphor in the romantico-scientific notion that Peru was an ancient land of native "genius." Taken together, "clime" and "soil" provided natural historical grounds for imagining Peru as an independent and sovereign entity. The eighteenth-century vision of the "land of the Incas" as a universal "country" of "nature" properly named Peru would lay the epistemological and poetic foundation for the republican history of the people.

Clime and Soil

The concept of clime and the tradition of the theory of climes had ancient roots and may be traced in the Greco-Roman writings of Plato, Aristotle, Polybius, Plinio, Tito Livio, Tacitus, and Cicero. That tradition had been passed on by the medieval and early modern writings of Thomas Aquinas and Jean Bodin, among many others. Early modern Spanish and Spanish American historians also produced a rich literature on the natural history of the New World. The writings on Peru of Gonzalo Fernández de Oviedo (1478–1557), the Jesuit scholar José de Acosta (1539–1600), and Antonio León Pinelo (1590–1660) established a remarkable and erudite tradition that conjoined theological, philosophical, and natural historical reflection. Acosta had suggested that the Peruvian interior was the closest thing to Paradise on earth, and León Pinelo went further to argue that Peru was the original site of the Garden of Eden. Among Peruvian Creoles who contributed to this tradition, the "Creole patriotic astrology" of the Augustinian friar and historian Antonio de la Calancha (1584–1684) was also remarkable. Calancha had confirmed Acosta's appreciation for Peru in Creole patriotic style, adding favorable astrological readings.[2] Calancha was convinced that Peru's stars, clime, and abundant natural resources far surpassed those of Europe, and indeed that Peru (for the Chuquisaca-based Calancha, "Peru" embraced more or less all of South America) was the most blessed and universal land on Earth. Indeed, deep in the mines of Cailloma, Peru, an Indian had unearthed three crosses, this on the eve of the discovery in Jerusalem of Emperor Constantine's cross of Christ. Moreover, Peru herself was positioned directly under the five-starred Southern Cross. For Calancha these were providential signs of Peru's unequaled "advantages," which "all the world envied."[3]

The natural investigations, writings, diagrams, and maps of the prolific Prussian natural scientist Alexander von Humboldt (1769–1859) were clearly significant in the shaping of the Spanish American imagination in the early nineteenth century. Nevertheless, a natural historical vision of America and in particular of Peru as a verdant microcosm of unparalleled natural diversity was established before Humboldt's arrival on American shores. In a revisionist critique, Jorge Cañizares-Esguerra has recently argued for the derivative nature of Humboldt's work.[4] To support this argument, Cañizares-Esguerra points in particular to the pioneering investigations of the "Colombian" naturalist Francisco José de Caldas (1768–1816).[5] Like Caldas, José Hipólito Unanue (1755–1833) anticipated and in other ways went far beyond Humboldt's speculations on the diversity of tropical American nature and the origins and nature of ancient American civilization. Although many of Unanue's unpublished manuscripts and statistical tracts were lost when his house in Lima caught fire during the unrest of independence, his earlier publications in the 1790s and early 1800s established the foundations of Peruvian historical discourse on the "country" named Peru.

Creole naturalist discourse and knowledge had provided much of the basis for Humboldt's unoriginal view that Spanish America was "naturally" fit for home rule. Unanue's researches went further, leading the Peruvian doctor to theorize that the particular "genius" of the American imagination, burning under the equatorial sun but sweetened by an unparalleled diversity of altitudinal climes, had since the age of Manco Capac guided the development of Peruvian civilization with unparalleled brilliance. Manco Capac's laws had been wisely adopted and modified by the Spaniards.[6] The clear implication was that Peru's "clime" had generated its own "genius," and in turn that genius had created sagacious and beneficent social laws of indigenous origin. There was nothing that Peru lacked. Her natural bounty was unparalleled, for she contained all of the world's climes within her territory. Likewise, her human diversity defied and exceeded European classification schemes that attempted to fix civilizational potential based on the predominance of one racial type and one clime, since all manner of humanity (every race and every possible mixture of races) inhabited her all manner of climes. Peru was not only a natural and human "microcosm" of the globe.[7] In Unanue's mind, Peru was more universal than any land in the world, and this universality revealed the provincialism of Europe and the European mind.

Although Unanue was an accomplished statistician who would later serve as independent Peru's first minister of the Public Trust (*ministro de hacienda*) under José de San Martín and then Simón Bolívar, his historical thought is more patriotic and physiological than republican and revolutionary. For much of his productive life, Unanue served under the Bourbon viceroys of Peru. His historicist and naturalist vision of Peru was informed by antiquarianism, medicine, and the experimental sciences, and by what Cañizares-Esguerra has called "Creole patriotic epistemology."[8] Patriotic epistemology in the eighteenth-century Americas was a scientific historical discourse that privileged first-hand observations of material or cultural artifacts (native glyphs, codices, and mnemonic devices such as *quipus*, monuments, and customs) and the eyewitness accounts of native noblemen and sages with access to native languages. These native sources were judged to be superior to the passing impressions of non-Hispanic European travelers and the armchair speculations of European philosophers and naturalists. Most of Peru's and Spanish America's better-known "patriotic epistemologists" were exiled Creole Jesuits (the Company of Jesus was expelled from the Spanish realm in 1768). The most famous Peruvian among these was Juan Pablo Viscardo y Guzmán, who called for American independence from Spain in 1792. However, secular scholars also contributed strongly to the historical defense of American nature and civilization.[9]

Unanue was a weighty contributor to Peru's stellar historical, literary, and commercial review, *El Mercurio Peruano de Historia, Literatura y Noticias Públicas* (1791–94). Although some historians and social scientists have considered *El Mercurio Peruano* as a "newspaper" incubator of Creole nationalism and the Peruvian "public sphere," and although it was later read in Peru as a "precursor of Peruvianness," the periodical was not a significant incubator of republican nationalism.[10] Instead, it was the cultured review of a learned network of associations fomented by the Bourbons throughout the empire named Amantes del País (literally, "Lovers of the Country"), although the local branch in Lima was first called La Sociedad Académica de Amantes de Lima, and the publication itself was addressed to the enlightened courtly, university, clerical, and mercantile elite, and was sponsored by the Spanish viceroy in Lima.[11] Dependent as it was on the viceroy's patronage, the periodical's life was phoenix-like. The pages of *El Mercurio Peruano* registered wider trends in enlightened historical discourse, and in certain ways this discourse did lay the poetic and scientific ground that would later be occupied by republican history.

The banner and first charge of the editors of *El Mercurio Peruano* was the historical, literary, and scientific enterprise of reviving the empires of "Peru" and "Spain." In the inaugural prospectus of the journal, editor Jacinto Calero y Moreira declared that the review's purpose was to rectify the worrisome fact that "the Peruvian kingdom, so favored by nature with a benign climate and opulent soil, occupies only a diminutive place in the portrait of the Universe painted by Historians. . . . History—not understood as general principles or bare annals of events that may be altered, but as the elucidation and practical knowledge of our principle achievements—that kind of History will be the first cause of this periodical."[12] The beloved *país y Reyno* (country and realm) imagined and embraced in the pages of *El Mercurio Peruano* was considerably larger than the still unimaginable, undesirable, and rather diminutive Peruvian Republic of post-1821, and, despite the journal's name, its readership or "universe" was rather tiny. In the pages of *El Mercurio Peruano, país* is not synonymous with the future "nation" or territory of Peru. Rather, the "country" glosses not only the "natural" expanse of the Viceroyalty of Peru as it was in 1791 but also, and more as a historicist dream of return, the "greatness" of that "Grand Peru" whose real historical manifestation was not Tawantinsuyu (the precolonial Inca Realm) but the vast viceroyalty or "Kingdoms and Provinces of Peru" that had once claimed as its dominion nearly all of Spanish South America. After this imagined Peruvian *país* (the natural and cultural realm of the kingly realm) came the *patria* of America or the New World. The historical turn of *El Mercurio Peruano* thus betrayed a piquant sense of decline among Lima's elite and a desire to recover, via historical, statistical, and geographical study, the glorious Peruvian past that had been invented in the sixteenth and seventeenth centuries. As *El Mercurio*'s editor would lament in the inaugural issue, albeit with some inaccuracy in regard to dates, "this great Empire, whose foundation by the Incas remains shrouded in the darkness and uncertain tradition established by a handful of fables, has lost much of its greatness since the dismemberment of the northern provinces of the Kingdom of Quito (1718) [sic] and then of those to the east, which now constitute the Viceroyalty of Buenos Aires (1778) [sic]." (The correct dates are 1717 and 1776, respectively.) In short, the revival of Peruvian historiography in the pages of *El Mercurio Peruano* responded to a Lima-centric revindication of the dismembered "Peruvian empire." Such a project would surely have pleased Peralta.

What is most notable in the late-eighteenth-century historical discourse of Peru is that the concepts of *país* (country) and *patria* (homeland) were now being historicized apart from, or in addition to, *nación* (nation). In the 1790s and up until San Martín's declaration of independence in Lima in 1821, usage of "nation" or "nationals" among Peruvian Creoles almost always glossed the global or imperial "Spanish Nation." Among Creoles, "Spain" was often referred to as the *Madre patria* and "Peru" (great or small) as the *país*, while "America" was the *patria*. That is, *país* and *patria* had not yet displaced *Madre patria* or *nación* but instead were added to these concepts as legitimate, scientific domains of research and historical discourse. In many ways this shift was an intended and logical consequence of Bourbon colonial administrative reforms, which had sought to scientifically chart and exploit the natural and historical resources of its respective dominions. The notion of the *Madre patria* would not be displaced until circa 1824, which in part explains why the rhetorical wars of independence in Peru pitted *patria* and its *patriotas* against *nación* and *el ejército nacional* (the national army or forces loyal to Spanish empire). The rhetorical war between *patria* and *nación* was another reason why independence would be described in political and historical discourse as the triumph of "the *patria* and the people" over "the King" (see chapters 5 and 6). The revolutionary association of American *patria* with "our history" had been announced in 1792 by the exiled Peruvian Jesuit Juan Pablo Viscardo y Guzmán, who, writing on the third centennial of Columbus's maiden voyage, proclaimed: "The New World is our Patria. Her history is our history."[13] Still, Viscardo y Guzmán's Americanist declaration was not republican and it did not hail the imminent arrival of the Republic of Peru. What made it possible to imagine not an American but a Peruvian "*patria* and people" was the unifying concept of *país*.

As the first issue makes clear, *El Mercurio Peruano*'s approach to history was patriotic, practical, and naturalist in the Creole-Hispanic sense described by Cañizares-Esguerra, that is, it would be a reliable source of self-knowledge and at the same time a strong critique of "foreign," that is, non-Hispanic, lies, for Spain was still the "motherland" of the "nation." The critical task of Peruvian history was to correct the errors and distortions of northwestern European (mainly English, Dutch, and French) historiography and travel writing, and to disseminate true and practical historical knowledge of Peru.[14] This task involved the renovation or scientific updating of the worthy accounts of the most notable "national authors," that is, Inca Garcilaso de la Vega, the Spanish court historian of the Indies Antonio de Herrera, and the Spanish chronicler Agustín de Zárate, among others.

Notably, for the editor of *El Mercurio Peruano*, the new model "national historian" was not a "Peruvian" by birth but rather the Spanish "moral and natural" scientist Antonio de Ulloa, praised as the "national pride" of enlightened Lima for "writing about the inhabitants of these lands [and elevating] his pen to the contemplation of Man in his moral and physiological system."[15] Peruvian Creoles admired Ulloa as well for his nuanced defense of the indigenous origins of the first Inca, Manco Capac. Speculations that Manco Capac might be of foreign origin were in some cases linked to a general assault by European rivals on the legitimacy of Spain's empire in the Indies. Defending the Spanish empire against the rising tide of European critics, Ulloa had argued that Manco Capac must have been a "prince" from the pre-existing patrilineage of a "small nation" near Cuzco. Subsequently, this small nation had expanded. Maintaining a respectable critical distance from Inca Garcilaso and noting that "all historians today agree that the origin of the Incas is a fable," Ulloa noted that the achievements ascribed to Manco Capac by Inca Garcilaso were simply too tall to believe.[16] But that did not mean that Manco Capac had hailed from some foreign land. There must have been a longer, indigenous development of an ascendant "nation" within Peru that had conquered the rest. This nation had undoubtedly hailed from the Cuzco or Tiahuanaco regions. Of course, Ulloa's defense of the "Peruvian" origins of the Inca confirmed the providential narrative of the legitimate transfer of imperium from the Incas to the Spanish kings.

Ulloa's abridged dynastic history of Peru examines in some detail the ongoing insurrection in eastern Peru of Juan Santos Atahualpa, although he does not refer to the leader of that rebellion by that name. Ulloa dismisses the hereditary claims of this pretender and his movement as the "novelty" of "modern Indians" whose "rusticity and torpidity does not offer sufficient lights to understand such things." Ulloa reasoned that the followers of this quack Inca "merely applaud whatever they are told," for, among these "Chunchos Indians, whose Pueblos are modern mission towns," there is "a stronger disposition than in other peoples to embrace novelty."[17] Ulloa's account was broadly consonant with Inca Garcilaso's history, as well as with the colonial discourse of the "miserable Indian" typical of the pronouncements of viceroys, magistrates, and inspectors in Peru (and Mexico) and described in chapter 2.[18] In this discourse, commoner "modern" Indians were routinely described as phlegmatic of mind and body and thus easily seduced by the seditious claims of demagogic imposters who presented themselves as avenging heirs to the Inca dynasty. In Ulloa's history, as in the discourse of colonial magistrates, there is a temporal and moral abyss or schism between the reasoned and "glorious" ancient Inca past, which leads in providential fashion to Spanish sovereignty, and the "miserable" and modern Indian present, whose "novel" presence and ignorance challenges the order of that sovereignty.

This abyss between the glorious and ancient Inca past and the miserable and modern Indian present was anticipated in the structure and method of Inca Garcilaso's two-part history, which generally traces an arc from primitive barbarism to reason, from tyranny to revelation, and finally to the "culture" of the word. In the *Comentarios Reales,* the founding schism would correspond to the privilege granted to the accounts of informed Inca nobles and the corresponding distrust that fell upon the anxious utterances of ignorant and linguistically incompetent Indian commoners. More broadly, Inca Garcilaso's method reflected the division of the social (and linguistic) body into nobles and commoners. By the eighteenth century of Ulloa, however, that old social and linguistic abyss was temporalized and narrativized. Wise Incas were a thing of the ancient past who bore no true relation to modern colonial Indians or to the rebel imposters who called themselves "Incas."

On the critical question of the relation between "ancient" and "modern" Peruvians, Unanue's approach would differ notably from Ulloa's. Closer to home than Ulloa, it was the Arica-born Unanue who would become an inspiration for future Peruvian historians and scientists, whose nation would no longer include Spain and the rest of her Indies.[19]

Unanue's programmatic essay, "Idea general de los monumentos del antiguo Perú, e introducción a su estudio" (General Idea of the Monuments of Ancient Peru, and Introduction to their Study) appeared in the March 17, 1791, edition of *El Mercurio Peruano.* "Idea general" was extended and complemented in Unanue's "Geografía física del Perú" (Physical Geography of Peru), published on January 5, 1792. About a decade prior to Humboldt's arrival in Peru, then, Unanue's essays announced not only the scientific study of "ancient monuments" but also the existence of a natural and statistical image of "Peru" as *país*.[20] "Idea general" opens with perhaps the most common topos of Creole patriotic epistemology: the colonial historian's lament over the archive destroyed by the avaricious greed and ignorance of the Spanish conquistador.[21] The *quipu* (mnemonic devices of knotted and colored strings) records of the Incas believed to be deposited in "the archives of Cuzco, Cajamarca, and Quito" had been "reduced to dust," Unanue notes. Given the reliance on oral memory, the "traditions of the memorable events of that Realm had been altered." And so "to complete the imperfect portrait," based on oral sources and "drawn for us by [Inca] Garcilaso of his ancient empire," the modern "observer is obliged to turn to the collation, or rather the interpretation, of the fragments and ancient ruins."[22] As in Egypt and other ancient nations, Unanue notes, the remains of the great monuments of the Incas had survived "the ravages of time," asserting that in "the study of those works, monumental or functional, that they erected, we may cast a new light, capable of penetrating the obscure depths in which lie the historical and civil aspects of the Peruvian Monarchy in the times before conquest."[23] In the glow of this new light, Unanue invites the readers of *El Mercurio Peruano* to join him in the "climb to the heroic age of Peru."[24]

This climb is itself heroic. Overcoming the colonial destruction of the archive and the historical fallibility of orally transmitted memory, the postcolonial antiquarian must become an "observer" of fragments and ruins. This observer is also an ethnographer, since "the traditions and relics of their ancient customs still persist among the modern Indians who conserve and cling tenaciously to their ancestral ways."[25] For Unanue, the most notable among these ancient customs are the techniques of irrigation, collective agricultural labor, and weaving. Modern Peruvian pastoralists, he notes, still use primitive quipus to keep track of their herds, while dances, songs and, above all the Quechua language are living evidence of "the stage of civilization to which they ascended, and indeed of the durability of their empire." Unanue is Peru's first postcolonial ethnohistorian: He formulates the still current practice of "observing" ancient ruins and critically reading fragments of conquest-era texts as if these could be read as so many "silent witnesses" to an enduring cultural truth that could be confirmed with ethnographic observations. Unanue thereby constitutes in the scientific imagination the living museum of Indian "customs" as a true source of historical knowledge. Notably, what links the "monuments of the Incas" with the living "customs" of Indians is the "soil" with a proper name.

"Soil" was an agrarian metaphor as old as history, but like "clime" it now acquired an updated, romantico-scientific hue, and at the same time a "Peruvian" identity. In "Physical Geography of Peru," Unanue announced the arrival of the image and study of a "soil" with a proper name:

> The first object that presents itself to the contemplation of the Philosopher of the History of the Monuments of ancient Peru is the portrait of the organization and diverse disposition of her vast territory. His pen is destined to trace, among the ravages of time and men, the level

of culture to which that famous Nation had ascended; [that Nation] which, without the assistance of [ancient] Egypt, Phoenicia, or Greece, knew how to establish wise laws, and to excel, in certain aspects, in the Arts and Sciences; it thus appears indispensable to study the soil upon which stand the ruins. . . .

Unanue asserts that it was indispensable to study the soil "since the qualities of a region influence the spirit of those who populate it." Consequently, he adds, "without physical knowledge of Peru it will never be possible to draw the eminent advantages enjoyed by her past or present inhabitants."[26] Unanue's contemplation is fixed upon the ruins' soil and its inhabitants in much the same way that, as we saw in chapter 3, Peralta's was centered on the noble soil and clime of Spain. The "eminent advantages" of Spain or Peru will favorably "influence" her inhabitants past and present. Despite Unanue's language, there is nothing necessarily "observable" here, for Peralta could make the same claims for a distant land via his reading of Spanish texts and his application of the Aristotelian theory of climes.

Here, however, the optical language and romantic poetics of Unanue's enlightened vision penetrate deeper to a sublime "Peru" of "Nature" before monuments and men: "In the instant in which we name Peru the towns and cities begin to disappear from our view and even the opulent spires of Lima are annihilated. . . . Only Nature appears, surrounded in a mysterious silence."[27] Wondrously, this primal, geological vision finds in pristine "Nature" the proper name of "Peru." And it is in the proper naming of the timeless natural land that Unanue strikes that inexhaustible vein of national gold. This vein of gold is mythopoetic. For it is not "Nature" but the rich and eternal subsoil of the name that is the foundation upon which all "national maps," "national museums," and "national monuments" are erected. After Unanue, "Peru" becomes "our" timeless "soil" and "country," the treadable poetic ground upon which Peruvian history still stands.

This ground was universal in a Neo-Platonist way. That is, the diversity of climes, which was the product of its equatorial altitudinal gradations, was the sure sign of the "plenitude" of Peru.[28] Unanue provides moving and scientific descriptions of the rich diversity of Peruvian regions, arguing that Peru contains within itself African, Asian, and European climes and is thus the most blessed and universal of lands. Indeed, the theme of climatic or ecological diversity along altitudinal gradients will become a trademark of Andean historical and anthropological thought from Humboldt to John V. Murra, and although this theme was sounded early by the Spanish chroniclers Acosta and Herrera, Unanue is foundational because his gaze is scientific, his measurements exact, his name and ground Peruvian.

In his remarkable *Observaciones sobre el clima de Lima y sus influencias en los seres organizados, en especial el hombre,* (Observations on the Climate of Lima and Its Influence on Organized Beings, and in particular Man) first published in 1805, Unanue satirizes European theories of aesthetics, the gradation of races, skin color, and environmental determinism. Sketching an alternative world history of "genius," Unanue argues that these European "ideas may be combated with victory, thereby restoring to three-quarters of humankind the hope that they may ascend to the glory that man is capable of." Unanue elaborates an ingenious "physiological" theory of perception based ironically but unsurprisingly both on European racialist and environmentalist theories of history and civilization (those of Charles Louis de Secondat, Baron de Montesquieu, Cornelius de Pauw, and Georges-Louis Leclerc, Comte de Buffon) and on Leibniz's Neo-Platonist "monadology" or theory of the universe as the sum of complex singularities, or monads. Turning the tables on the likes of Montesquieu, who had argued that "temperate" climes like those of France produced more energetic, rigorous, and intelligent men, while hotter, southern climes produced men who were servile, passionate, and unthinking, Unanue argued that the circumequatorial South American climate actually exercised the paradoxically positive effect of sharpening the social and political imagination. Unanue did this by accepting, at least on the surface, the mechanics behind the European contention that those who dwelled in tropical climes were "indolent" and "weak-willed" and thus inclined to inactivity. It was precisely the debilitating effects of the equatorial sun on the physical body, argued Unanue, that heightened the nervous sensibilities, such that Peruvians were endowed by nature with special powers of perception that exceeded those of Europeans. The hypersensitivity of the nerve endings of circumequatorial Americans was an "influence" of the environment upon the neural sensors, which, in turn, pulsate rapid repetitions of the images of observed objects to the brain, thus endowing Peruvians with extraordinary powers of imagination unknown among Europeans.

Unanue's sensorial theory of the South American circumequatorial imagination constituted a critique of the new northwestern European racial certainties of the eighteenth century and it had clear implications for the recent flurry of speculation on the origins of Manco Capac and Inca civilization. Judging Inca Garcilaso de la Vega's tall claims to have been colored by that cardinal sin of enlightened historical thought known as *amor propio*, prestigious northwestern European scholars such as William Robertson, Abbé

Guillaume Raynal, and Alexander von Humboldt now speculated that Manco Capac had probably not been "Peruvian" at all. Peralta's brilliant contemporary and fellow subject of Spanish empire, Giambattista Vico (1668–1744), had argued in his *New Science* that "Western" or European "nations" were nearly always founded by "Herculean heroes." Furthermore, these giant heroes were not necessarily "sons of the land," that is, not local noblemen (the original meaning, Vico tells us, of the word "indigene"). Although Peralta appears not to have read Vico (few did at the time since Vico's texts did not circulate), the Peruvian Creole entertained similar notions. In his history of Spain, Peralta argues that in ancient times "Hercules of Egypt" had founded "Hispania" or "Spain," thus laying the western foundations for her first native "king," appropriately named "Hispano." Vico's "critical" reading of the "poetics" of ancient annals had suggested that "Eastern" or Asian "nations" were most often founded not by Herculean heroes but by "Zoroastrian" sages.[29] Renaissance and Enlightened historical thought on cultural origins—including that of Inca Garcilaso and Peralta—was derived in part from such classical, East/West formulations. What kind of founder did the "Peruvian nation" have? Was he a Western hero or an Eastern sage? Or was he perhaps both? Was he born in "Peru" or was he a wanderer from some "foreign" land of another name? If foreign, from what great "mother civilization" did he hail?

Influenced by eighteenth-century British and German Orientalism, the cosmopolitan Humboldt had speculated that Manco Capac and his Quechua language were Oriental "in spirit" and so likely to be of Oriental origin. Humboldt suggested that Manco Capac brought benign, well adapted, but despotic "Asiatic laws" to Peru.[30] Gathering the traditions and interpretations registered in the *Comentarios reales* and other early chronicles, the Baron of Prussia would write that "men with beards, and with clearer complexions than the natives of Anahuac [Mexico], Cundinamarca [Colombia], and the elevated plain of Cuzco [Peru], make their appearance without any indication of the place of their birth; and, bearing the title of high-priests, legislators, and friends of peace and the arts which flourish under their auspices, they operate a sudden change in the policy of these nations, who hail their arrival with veneration. Quetzalcoatl, Bochica, and Manco Capac are the sacred names of these mysterious beings." For Humboldt, "the history of these legislators, which I have endeavored to unfold in this work, is intermixed with miracles, religious fictions, and with those characters that imply an allegorical meaning." In a reference to Raynal, Humboldt notes that "some learned men have pretended to discover that these strangers were shipwrecked Europeans," but, he concludes, "a slight reflection on the period of the Toltec migrations, on the monastic institutions, the symbols of worship, the calendar, and the form of the monuments of Cholula, of Sogamozo, and of Cuzco leads us to conclude that it was not in the north of Europe that Quetzalcoatl, Bochica, and Manco Capac framed their code of laws. Every consideration leads us rather towards Eastern Asia, to those nations who have been in contact with the inhabitants of Tibet, to the Shamanist Tartars, and the bearded Ainos of the isles of Jesso and Sachalin."

Humboldt then notes that "nothing is more difficult than a comparison between nations who have followed different roads in their progress towards social perfection. The Mexicans and Peruvians must not be judged according to the principles laid down in the history of those [Western] nations, which are the unceasing object of our studies." Notably, Humboldt refuses to make this comparison not because he is a relativist but because he considers ancient Peru to be essential "Oriental." Thus: the Peruvians and Mexicans "are as remote from the Greeks and the Romans as they bear a near affinity to the Etruscans and the people of Tibet."

Notably, this remoteness was that distance which European Orientalism had erected between itself—the refined and secular West—and the despotic and theocratic Orient. Thus, the Prussian writes, "among the Peruvians, a theocratic government, while it favored the growth of industry, the construction of public works, and whatever might be called general civilization, presented obstacles to the display of the faculties of the individual." It was precisely the contrary case "among the Greeks," among whom "liberal and rapid progress of individual talents outstripped the tardy steps of general civilization." In short, "the empire of the Incas may be compared to some great monastic establishment, in which each member of the congregation was prescribed the duties he had to perform for the general good." Moreover, these Oriental traits could be observed in the contemporary faces of Peruvians, since "when on the spot we study those Peruvians who, through the lapse of ages, have preserved their national physiognomy, we learn to estimate, at its true value, the code of laws framed by Manco Capac, and the effects produced on morals and public happiness." In those faces Humboldt discerns "a more submissive resignation to the decrees of the sovereign than patriotic love for the country; passive obedience, without courage for bold enterprises; a spirit of order, which regulated with minute precision the most indifferent actions, while no general views enlarged the mind, and no elevation of thought ennobled the character." In short, "the most complicated political institutions recorded in the history of mankind had crushed the germ of personal liberty, and the founder of the empire of Cuzco, in flattering himself with the power

of forcing men to be happy, reduced them to the state of mere machines."
Humboldt concludes that "the Peruvian theocracy was, no doubt, less op-
pressive than the government of the Mexican kings" but both "contributed
to give the monuments, the rites, and the mythology of the two nations that
dark and melancholy aspect which forms a striking contrast with the elegant
arts and soothing fictions of the people of Greece."[31]

Cañizares-Esguerra argues that Humboldt's foundational Orientalist hypothesis of Inca origins was a relatively positive development in Americanist
historical discourse, not so much because it broke with the Renaissance tradition that had compared Incas and Aztecs to Romans and Greeks but because
it constituted an anthropological critique of the disparaging views of such
influential European historians as Raynal, Robertson, and de Pauw.[32] Those
historians had found American cultures and climates to be inferior to those
of the Old World in nearly every aspect. The influential Raynal had opined
that Manco Capac and Mama Ocllo were "whiter than the natives of the land"
and that they were likely "descendants de quelques navigateurs d'Europe ou
des Canaries, jetés par la tempête sur les côtes du Brésil."[33] In a word, the
Incas probably were, like the Creoles of the day, immigrant (and perhaps de-
generate) whites who lorded over darker, more primitive natives. If derived
from the great ur-civilizations of the ancient Orient, however, American civilization might appear in a more favorable light, and this light would attract
scientific investigation. This may have been so, but the fact is that Peruvian
Creoles often criticized and even blasted Humboldt's Orientalist interpretation of the origins and character of Peruvian civilization.[34] Unanue was first
among them.

The two illustrious men of science met briefly in Lima. Undoubtedly they
found that they had many things in common, but a theory of the origin of the
Incas was not one of them. Humboldt and the other European diffusionists
were mistaken, for Manco Capac was clearly "Peruvian" for scientific reasons
that had to do with the supposed influence of the equatorial American clime
on the human nervous system. Unanue had observed that "to those who are
born in this New World is granted the privilege of exercising a superior imagination and of discovering all that flows from comparison." By "imagination"
Unanue did not mean "those strong and tumultuous impressions, excited by
objects analogous or contrary to our passions, and profoundly engraved upon
our sensory organs, recurring perpetually and involuntarily, almost forcing
us to act like brutes, without deliberation or reflection," but, instead, "the
power to rapidly perceive the images of objects, their proportions and qualities, from which arises a facility to compare and energetically exploit those

images." In this manner, Unanue continued, are "our thoughts illuminated, our sensations augmented, and our sentiments painted with vigor." This accelerated and acute tropical imagination was "the source of that astonishing eloquence with which the savages of America often express themselves: the natural and strong comparisons of their discourse, and the vitality of their sentiments. After hearing the stirring speeches of Araucanian warriors, we are convinced that Colocolo was no less deserving of the consideration of Ercilla than was Nestor of Homer. . . . From this same precious source flows skill and dexterity in sculpture and painting, without any other master than one's own genius."

In clear contrast to Humboldt's racialist thinking, for Unanue the supposed aesthetic "distance" between Europe and South America was simply a question of training. Thus, in the art of "expressing our images and ideas, there is in Mexico, Quito, and Cuzco a multitude of artists capable of competing with and surpassing—if given the training the [Europeans] receive—the best of Europe." In Prince College in Lima, Unanue adds, "one often sees Indian boys learning to read while, at the same time, and with pencil in hand, they make perfect copies of Klauver prints." He concludes: "I am thus persuaded that the imagination, that precious gift of nature in America, shines with special brilliance in circum-equatorial regions. There have been few legislators who could perceive, as Manco Capac did, the inclinations of his vassals, compare them with their needs, and translate these into such a beneficent and sagacious constitution."[35] The clear implication of Unanue's neural theory of the tropical imagination was that Manco Capac's law could not have been a mere extension of Oriental despotism but only the sagacious product of the keen imagination and comparative powers of reason of a native-born "legislator" who was, therefore, neither Eastern nor Western.

The Historicist Critique of European Reason

Unanue's differences with Humboldt's Orientalist vision of ancient America ran deeper and wider than the repeating question of Manco Capac's origins. As may be discerned from the previously quoted passage, Humboldt's thinking was based in part on the presumption that ancient Greek or Western civilization was far more refined than ancient Oriental civilization. Unanue did not share this view. For Unanue, the Orient and North Africa and not Greece were the fountainheads of refinement, beauty, genius, and civilization, and these cultural gifts had come down to Peru via the Arabs and Spain. It was Spain who had transmitted these gifts of civilization to northern Europe.

The northern European claim to a "monopoly on genius" was therefore spurious. Instead, all history was subject to "the vicissitudes of human affairs," which, when properly considered in their historical dimension, offered hope to "the other three-quarters of the globe." Unanue would demonstrate that the other three-quarters shared in "the genius of man" and he would do so by turning both to the old and sacred notion of the "Great Chain of Being" and to the comparative science of world or universal history. Unanue was also fond of the satirical turn of phrase, and this he employed to great effect in his portrayal of Europe's pretentious position as the self-appointed "Tribunal" of History and Man. He writes that "all the nations on earth dispute the favor of genius, that precious gift that distinguishes man from beast; but the Europeans—who today triumph over the other three-fourths of the globe, not less by the energy of their pens than by the force of their victorious arms—have erected themselves as Tribunal, and have passed sentence in their own favor." This upstart European tribunal now proclaims "that the external features of the body are a certain sign of the excellence of the soul that inhabits it" and that "all the world's beings are linked together in a single chain tied to the foot of God's throne, descending from angels to man, who loses the beautiful dispositions of his body in accordance with the degradation of the privileges of his soul, until he meets with the beasts." The principle indicator of talent for this tribunal is "the raised brow, such that, even among irrationals, for having this distinction the elephant is the wisest; at the same time, the raised brow that is proportionate to the rest of the facial features constitutes beauty."[36]

In short, Europe's self-appointed "Tribunal" on intellect and beauty had reduced the gradations of being to the curvature of the brow. European scientists now claimed that the "ancient statuaries of Greece, which have left us the models of beauty, measure the most perfect angle of 100 degrees" and that "any wider angle supposes an imperfect face." The statuaries of Rome were a close second, with an angle of 95 degrees. Under this European scheme, if these two models are applied to the "faces of nations," they "will reveal that the Europeans occupy the first slot, with a facial measurement of around 90 to 80 degrees; the Asians are in second place, with angles of from 80 to 75 degrees.... The Americans ... with facial angles of 75 to 70 degrees are third. Finally, these proportions decrease in Africans, among whose Blacks the facial angles are only 70 to 60 degrees, which is arriving at the measurement of quadrupeds." Of course, it is "for that reason the Negro is the last on the chain, the one who links man with beast." With the same scheme of degradation, "the talents" are said to "descend from the celestial and sublime of the European to the stupid and rude of the Negro. That is why men born in that happy part of the globe are thoughtful men, and only among them may laws, arts, sciences, and valour flower." Under this plan, "the Asian is without talent to reform his pleasures and despotism"; the American "cannot leave his ignorance behind"; and "the Negro" is incapable of conquering "his brutality." Thus, the "other three quarters of the globe" may not present "any other advantage relative to the European except that of their bodily senses, supposing that the acuity of those senses increases in proportion to the decrease in the privileges of the spirit."[37]

It was precisely this inverse relation between "bodily senses" and "privileges of the spirit" that Unanue's tropical theory of the South American imagination undercut. Moreover, these follies of the modern European mind were contradicted by "the vicissitudes of human affairs" and the global history of genius and beauty. For Unanue, Asia and Africa and not Europe were the cradle of the arts and sciences, and "since to found sciences takes more talent than it does to advance them, I am not at all sure whether the souls that animate the bodies of those with high brows have any clear advantage over those with low ones."[38] Moreover, northwestern Europeans were simply ingrates: "Empires fall under the weight of their own splendor and culture, leaving behind only imperfect traces of their existence; at the same time others arise in the midst of rustic nations and, in their newfound felicity, forget the origins of their lights, and like ungrateful children destroy the breast that suckled them."

Unanue's appreciation of the vicissitudes of ancient and modern world history enabled a critical reading of modern European history that granted the Arabs and the Spaniards key roles in the conservation and dissemination of beauty, science, and law. In effect, it was in the sixth century that "the lights that Asia and Africa had carried to Greece and in Europe to Spain, were eclipsed." During this eclipse, "two peoples emerged to subjugate the lovely provinces of the Roman Empire. One came from the North of Europe, the other from Arabia. The first introduced extreme barbarism; the second began to dissipate that barbarism and to elevate Europe by degrees to the heights in which it now basks." Paris was not the center of learning and culture. Instead, asserted Unanue, "Baghdad was then the center of politics and culture, and also Cordova and Seville, colonies which had acquired victorious arms." The French, Italians, and Germans found it "necessary to come [to Spain] to obtain any knowledge of the natural sciences." After imbibing the knowledge imparted by the celebrated Spanish and Arab schools and returning to their homelands, Unanue noted sardonically, "they were taken for witches and magicians." Finally, Unanue asked in typical rhetorical style: "What do you think they would have made of that comparison of faces as an indicator that, in the pursuit of the sciences, certain souls were more capable than others?"[39]

Unanue then turns the tables on Europe's new tribunal, deploying its own measures against its very claims to an innate intellectual and aesthetic superiority. Fine, he writes, "let us congratulate the Europeans for their scheme, in which handsome features are the most certain sign of the nobility of spirit; for if such is the case, then . . . there are many peoples capable of competing with, and even exceeding Venus."[40] Unanue's sources on the stunning beauty of men and women in Asia and Africa are, of course, the very accounts of European travel writers. "There is no place, says Mr. Bougainville, where one may encounter models more bizarre than Hercules or Mars than in Tahiti. The women have features no less gratifying than those of European women, and in the symmetry and fine proportions of their members they compete with the well-endowed."[41] But Unanue is also an eyewitness to beauty and genius: "Here in South America big black eyes animated with fire are common. The Greek artists paid much homage to this aspect of beauty in both sexes, so that in their busts and medals the eyes are always larger than in those of the ancient Romans."[42] Unanue remarks with pride that the eyes of Andean llamas are perhaps bigger, wider lashed, and at least as beautiful as those of the fabled antelope to whom beautiful African women were often compared. Who could deny the famed beauty of the *limeña*? Did not this irresistible beauty also beckon from her big, dark, llama-sized eyes?

Unanue's global history of the cultural routes of genius and beauty grants Asia and Africa (particularly the Arabs) primal roles in the cultivation of the arts and sciences of civilization in the post-Roman Mediterranean world and in Europe, and his theory of a compensatory sensory perception in Andean equatorials restores Manco Capac and Inca civilization to its indigenous American roots. Reclamations of the role of the Arab world as conduit of modern civilization were not uncommon in eighteenth-century Spanish and Spanish American historical discourse, when Hispanic intellectuals battled to fend off "the ever-louder northern European criticism of the Spanish mind" and empire.[43] From Montesquieu in the 1740s to Hegel in the 1820s, "Europe" had been diminished to Francocentric and Germanocentric dimensions and made into a "fortress of reason" with ancient Hellenic roots, in effect marginalizing the south and east of Europe.[44] "Spain" or the "Peninsula" of Iberia was semantically dislodged and set adrift, as "Europe" was now imagined to end at the Pyrenees (and the Italian Alps), as indeed it does in Hegel's *Philosophy of History*. In response, "Spain" and her colonial worlds, considered by northwestern European critics (Montesquieu was especially influential) to be in decisive ways "Oriental" and "African"—the Spanish empire was now readily compared with the Ottoman—now became sites of critique from which to provincialize the pompous historical claims of the newly ascendant northwestern corner of the continent that now claimed to speak for Europe.

The defense of Spain as an idyllic and hybrid civilization situated midway between Europe and Africa and as heir to the ancient Mediterranean and Near Eastern empires found an echo in cities like Lima where Creoles, who fancied themselves to be heirs to the great Inca empire, had long commingled with peoples of African and Asian origin. Lima and Peru were diverse and universal (indeed more universal than any Old World land, including Spain), with rich and deep histories that revealed "the glory of man" and the beauty of big eyes, classical markers of high civilization and intrinsic worth that were not the sole property of those ancient Greeks whom modern northwestern Europeans now imagined to be theirs.

An Ancient Future for Republican Peru

José Hipólito Unanue's historicist and scientific critique of European theories about Inca origins and American civilization would find a resounding echo in postcolonial republican Peru. The study of "ancient monuments" and artifacts would remain a bulwark both of national defense and of critiques of Europe. The monuments provided Peruvian historians and antiquarians with a firm ground from which to attack the prestigious views of such European philosophical historians as Amédée François Frézier, Cornelius de Pauw, the Abbé Raynal, or William Robertson. To make America fit their armchair theories, all of these famous European scholars had in their writings foolishly denied or diminished the existence and significance of monumental architectural structures in ancient Peru.[45] Inevitably, however, the new naturalist and archaeological critique would be turned against "our" Inca Garcilaso de la Vega. For Mariano Eduardo de Rivero and other Creole scholars of the independence-era generation, Inca Garcilaso had been insufficiently severe but not misguided. Echoing the eighteenth-century opinion of the French explorer Charles-Marie de La Condamine, for example, Rivero noted that Inca Garcilaso's history of the Incas was surely distorted by a blinding "pride of *patria*."[46] Spanish chroniclers who claimed great feats for Spanish arms could be even worse in this regard, however—for example, inflating the nature and numbers of the Inca enemy so as to make the Spanish appear more invincible than the Romans of classical antiquity—so that a vexing confusion

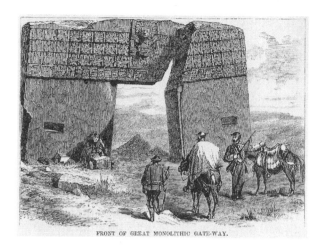

FRONT OF GREAT MONOLITHIC GATE-WAY.

9. "Front of Great Monolithic Gate-Way," Ephraim George Squier, *Peru: Incidents of Travel and Exploration in the Land of the Incas* (New York, 1877).

of conflicting and exaggerated accounts plagued the modern "observer" of Peruvian history. Still, the "critical examination" of monuments, artifacts, and skeletal materials; the pursuit of linguistic or lexicographic researches; and the critical rereading of chronicles would eventually set things straight.[47] Unanue's faith in ruins and fragments would be upheld.

In the nineteenth century, the altiplano region around Lake Titicaca became the South American Mecca of wandering savants, romantics, and prospecting scientists in search of the origins of "Peruvian civilization" and its fabled founder, Manco Capac. Notably, it was the conquest-era *Crónica del Perú* (1575) of Pedro Cieza de León that had pointed them there. In *Vue des Cordilleres*, Humboldt updated Cieza's call, with the plea for "some learned traveler [to] visit the borders of Lake Titicaca, in the district of Collao, and the high plains of Tiahuanaco, the theatre of the ancient American civilization" to verify Cieza's chronicle.[48] Léonce Angrand, Alcide d'Orbigny, Jacob von Tschudi, and Ephraim George Squier were among those who heeded the call. Each of these explorers published travel accounts or scientific reports with line drawings of the ruins. In all of these drawings, one monument stands out: the Puerta del Sol or Sungate at Tiahuanaco. Squier appears to have taken the first photographs of the Sungate, which served as the basis for the drawing that appeared as an illustration in his *Peru: Incidents of Travel and Exploration in the Land of the Incas* (1877) (see fig. 9).

Squier had been an aspiring student of the Yankee historian of Spanish empire William Prescott, and the author of notable books on Mississippian Indian mounds and Nicaraguan antiquities. For Squier, Tiahuanaco was nothing less than "the Baalbec of the New World."[49] Baalbec was, of course, Phoenician, and Squier's classical analogy suggested the foreign and pre-Inca origins of "Peruvian civilization."

Many savants suspected that Tiahuanaco had been the center of a very ancient, pre-Inca civilization that may have given birth to the Inca dynasty and its famed solar cult. The Sungate drew so much attention in part because it was thought to have been an early monument to this ancient cult. The Sungate was inscribed with what appeared to be a relief figure of a solar deity with serpent-staffs in either hand and flanked by condor-like figures. The stonework at the site was monumental and generally considered superior to the heralded masonry of the Incas at Cuzco. Nearby shaft tombs contained ancient burial remains, and some of these were dug up and examined. Lending dynastic oral confirmation to the archaeological suspicion, Inca Garcilaso had noted that native oral traditions indicated that Manco Capac had hailed from this region.

Prestigious European philosophical travelers, natural scientists, historians, and early ethnographers—from Walter Raleigh to Alcide d'Orbigny—had all questioned the "Peruvian" credentials of Manco Capac.[50] As late as 1901, these questions were still hotly debated, as is made clear in the following passage written by W. Golden Mortimer of the American Museum of Natural History. Mortimer's summary betrays not only the late-nineteenth-century preoccupation of Anglo American anthropology with questions of race but the persistence of the origin question among historians. Were the first Incas white, yellow, or red? Were they of the same race or "trunk" as that mass of "Peruvians" over whom they ruled? Sounding the old speculations of the chroniclers, of Humboldt, and of Prescott, Mortimer writes that "who these people were before they settled in Peru, where they came from and how they got there, or whether, as has been suggested, Peru was the cradle of the human race from which was peopled other continents, is an enigma, the solution of which is locked in the impenetrable mystery of the past." Frustratingly, "antiquarians, ethnologists and archaeologists have delved in vain toward unearthing this hidden past, for these people had no written language." Among the old chroniclers, "Montesinos declares that they came from Armenia about five hundred years after the deluge," while the more modern "theorists connect them with the Egyptians, with the early Hebrews, and with the Chinese." Still others "have supposed that the Incas may have come from what is presumed to have been an earlier civilization in Mexico and Yucatan, which with Peru had certain resemblances to the Eastern nations." Citing yet another old theme from the chronicles, Mortimer notes that "Gregorio Garcia, a Spanish

Dominican author, alludes to a tradition, according to which the Peruvians proceeded from the nine and a half tribes of Israel, whom Shalmaneses, King of Assyria, carried away captive." Among the modern Orientalists, he notes, "Humboldt has traced the origin of the Toltecs to the Huns, while Paravey, in 1844, attempted to prove that Fu-Sang, described in the Chinese annals, is the Mexican empire which was known to the Chinese in the fifth century, and showed that at Uxmal in Yucatan, there had been found sculptured the Buddha of Java seated under the head of a Shiva." In short, the revised consensus of scholarly opinion was that "these people in some prehistoric time found their way to the shores of South America from China and other parts of Eastern Asia." And finally, "whatever opinions and traditions there may be on the early origin of the Peruvians, all coincide on one point: that the first appearance of the progenitors of the Incan race was in the Titicaca region." The most frequently cited legend of Inca origins "describes a pair of white people—Manco Capac and Mama Ocllo—as mysteriously appearing on the shore of Lake Titicaca."[51]

Most of the positions described by Mortimer had been taken up or challenged by Peruvian historians and natural scientists during the nineteenth century. José María de Córdova y Urrutia addressed the question of origins in his pathbreaking *Las tres épocas del Perú o compendio de su historia* (1843). *Las tres épocas* was deeply indebted to the *Royal Commentaries* of Inca Garcilaso and also to the derivative *Resumen histórico* of Antonio de Ulloa, and possibly also to Llano Zapata's unpublished manuscript on the Incas. In Córdova y Urrutia's neodynastic annals, physical "Peru" is the work of giants who had separated the land from the water, extracting the Andes from the Asiatic archipelagos sometime after the mighty Hercules had opened up the Mediterranean Sea to Atlantic waters. *Las tres épocas* also confirms the providential mission of the Incas and affirms that the apostles Thomas and Bartholomew had "announced the Gospel in these regions" centuries prior to the arrival of the Spaniards in Peru. Blazing the path of *historia patria*, Córdova y Urrutia rejected the rude speculations of those European savants who had suggested that the founder of the Inca dynasty was not "Peruvian" at all. Noting that "this [speculation] has reached the extreme of depriving us of the glory of Manco Capac's being born in our country, persuading [us] instead [to believe] that he came from some foreign land," the Peruvian historian rejects Humboldt's view that Manco Capac's laws were "Asian" and he finds John Ranking's claim that Manco had been a "son of the Gran Kublai Khan" equally absurd. Instead, Córdova y Urrutia cites Inca Garcilaso's version of the Ayar Brothers myth and insists that both Manco Capac and Mama Ocllo (the original Inca Queen Mother) undoubtedly "came from a small island in Lake Titicaca."[52]

Las tres épocas reveals that the question of Manco Capac's origins was not just a question of "race," although over the course of the nineteenth century it increasingly became one. The question of origins was raised first by the obvious schism (discussed in chapter 2) that Inca Garcilaso's providential narrative had opened between the brilliant civilization of Manco Capac and the dark, barbarian past and colonial present of common Indians.[53] As the nineteenth century advanced, however, that kingly schism between barbarism and civilization and the origin question it raised were increasingly probed and answered in the racialist language of the new sciences of comparative lexicography, phrenology, and anthropology. This new language flourished as physicians and scholars raced to publish new evidence that argued for the Aryan, Chinese, Japanese, Hindi, or Peruvian origins of Manco Capac.

The pursuit of and scientific debate surrounding Inca origins produced curious "finds" in Peru. "Buddhas" were dug up not only in Uxmal, Mexico, but in Ica, Peru, as well. In 1890 M. García y Merino and T. Olaechea published a collection of previously published archeological field reports under the title *Antigüedades nacionales* (National Antiquities). Among these is an 1866 report on a dig in the south-central coastal region of Ica. The Ica report sported a crude drawing of an unearthed *huaca* or figurine evidently inscribed with Chinese characters. The character inscriptions on the Buddha-like figurine could be and were read to support the theory that Manco Capac had been Chinese. The faulty Chinese inscription on the Buddha of Ica evoked a notion of Oriental despotism then associated in the Western imagination with the centralized control of irrigation works. This fabulous artifact attracted the attention of serious foreign scientists, including the Spaniard Marcos Jiménez de la Espada (1831–1898). His archive in Madrid contains several photographs taken by J. Laurent of the very same artifact, and there is also a good drawing by Diaz Carreno.[54] The piece existed.

Whatever their scientific or historical standing, such reports and "artifacts" duly resonated with current events and national debates in Peru. Peru's coastal planters were then engaged in a raging national debate over immigration. One faction of the urban elite based in Lima wanted to restrict immigration to white Europeans, so as to "improve the race" and foster "civilization" in the frontier regions of the republic. Facing the decline of slavery, Peru's coastal sugar planters needed *brazos* or field hands to cut cane, and that meant importing Chinese "coolies" or bonded laborers. Ica was the first plantation region in Peru to import Chinese bonded laborers on a large scale (and, one may presume, to import Buddha figurines). Although further research is required to resolve the suspicion, the supposed archaeological discovery of the Buddha of Ica may well have been intended to lend support to planter arguments that the Chinese were not the "undesirable" immigrants that many among the urban elite of Lima supposed. No dusty pamphlet emblazoned "Manco Capac, First Chinese Immigrant" has yet emerged in Peru's archives, but my surprise will be mild when it does.

Archaeological evidence of blonde mummies in the cloud forests of northern Peru in the 1840s provided fuel for the liberal side of the policy debate on immigration, which would restrict entry to white European settlers. A report by Chachapoyas judge Juan Crisóstomos Nieto, dated January 31, 1843, was printed in the official daily, *El Peruano*, and reprinted in the highly respected *Bulletin of the Geographical Society of Lima* in 1892. The report described seven mummies with fine, blonde hair "unlike that of today's indigenes." Crisóstomos Nieto speculated that the fortress of Quelap was a "Tower of Babel in Peru" and its finely crafted artifacts had been "transferred by an enlightened and great nation that occupied this territory, but that later came into decadence . . . until it was encountered, in a state of isolation, by the great Manco [Capac]." It is quite possible that Crisóstomos Nieto had in mind the legends about Manco Capac and Mama Ocllo being "white." The dark age of barbarism that Manco encountered had been preceded, it now seemed, by an earlier age of white civilization in Peru. Consequently, the judge concluded that the ruins of the ancient Tower of Babel at Quelap demonstrated that "America is the Old World with respect to the other four parts of the globe." The editors of the *Boletín de la Sociedad Geográfica de Lima*, who sought to attract German immigrants to the region, published a learned commentary by Modesto Basadre Chocano on Nieto's report. Although admitting that more thorough scientific expeditions were required, Basadre Chocano confirmed Crisóstomos Nieto's view that "the crania covered with fine, trim blonde hair proved, without need of additional evidence, that the men who built that edifice [at Quelap], and who have long since disappeared, were of a completely distinct race . . . indeed, a very ancient and very superior race, compared to that of the Indians."[55]

In a more serious but equally imaginative racialist line of investigation, the Philadelphian phrenologist Samuel G. Morton in *Crania Americana* (1838–39) described the "American Family" of races, which was one of six such "families" in the world. Morton argued that "the most natural division of the American race is into two families, one of which, the Toltecan family, bears evidence of centuries of demi-civilization, while the other, under the collective title of the American family, embraces all the barbarous nations of the New World excepting the Polar tribes or Mongol-Americans."[56] The "Toltecan family" included "the civilised nations of Mexico, Peru and Bogota."[57] In the chapter dedicated to the "Ancient Peruvians," Morton claims to have examined "nearly one hundred Peruvian crania: and the result is, that Peru appears to have been at different times peopled by two nations of differently formed crania, one of which is perhaps extinct, or at least exist only as blended by adventitious circumstances, in various remote and scattered tribes of the present Indian race." Of these two "nations" or "families," that which predated the appearance of the Incas was designated the "Ancient Peruvian, the remains of which have hitherto been found only in Peru, and especially in that division of it now called Bolivia." These tombs "abound on the shores and islands of the great Lake Titicaca, in the inter-alpine valley of the Desaguadera, and in the elevated valleys of the Peruvian Andes. . . . The country around this inland sea was called Collao, and the site of what appears to have been their chief city, bears the name of Tiaguanaco."[58] Like everyone else, Morton cites Cieza de León's observations at Tiahuanaco, to the effect that the buildings were pre-Inca and that the first Incas had held court there and indeed had modeled the walls of Cuzco upon the structures at Tiahuanaco. Morton also cites Inca Garcilaso and "an unnamed author of an article appearing in the *Mercurio Peruano*" (e.g., Unanue), to support this affirmation. However, on the point of the "Ancient Peruvians" Morton relies finally on the recently published observations of the Englishman Mr. Pentland, "who has recently visited the upper provinces of Peru. This gentlemen states that in the vicinity of Titicaca he has discovered innumerable tombs, hundreds of which he entered and examined. These monuments are of a grand species of design and architecture, resembling Cyclopean remains, and not unworthy of the arts of ancient Greece or Rome. They therefore betokened a high condition of civilization."[59] But for Morton "the most extraordinary fact belonging to them is their invariably containing the mortal remains of . . . an extinct race of natives who inhabited Peru above a thousand years ago, and differing from any mortals now inhabiting our globe."[60] Morton thus divides the Peruvians into the "Ancient Peruvians" (the Collas) and the "Inca or Modern Peruvians." This "modern" family is also divided in two races, however, one "Toltecan" and the other "American." The founders of the Inca dynasty were "Toltecans" who had migrated south from Mexico in the twelfth century.

In words that anticipate those of Mortimer, Morton notes that "the origin of the Incas of Peru is shrouded in fable." These origins "are represented in their traditions as two celestial personages, a son and daughter of the sun himself, who were sent from heaven to instruct and civilize a favored people . . . Manco Capac, the first Inca, and Coya Mama, who was both his sister and his wife. They appeared first on an island in the Lake Titicaca, and taking the people under their jurisdiction, began at once a reform of all the institutions of the country." Not unlike his predecessors Inca Garcilaso and Ulloa, Morton then proceeds to characterize this tradition as an incredible "fable." He concludes that "this preference for [an origin in two rulers] was calculated to render the account more marvelous, and the descendents of the individuals more respected." Doubting this account, Morton asks: "Can it be credited that this total revolution in social and civil government was the result of moral causes, operating on nations who were as strongly devoted to their own institutions as any other people? Certainly not." Given the impasse, Morton turns to a foreign origin hypothesis of a racialist nature. Thus he writes: "On the contrary we are compelled to attribute this change to an influx of foreigners, whose number and intelligence enabled them to overcome every obstacle that arose in their path. Who could these strangers be?" For Morton, the likely candidates were "the Toltecans, the most civilized nation of ancient Mexico." After governing that country for four centuries, he noted, they "suddenly abandoned it about the year 1050 of our era." There is, he continued, "a coincidence in the squared and conical form of the head in the Toltecans and Peruvians that is very striking, and which will be more particularly adverted to in a future part of this work." Morton concludes: "whether the preceding inference, which is by no means new, be correct of not, there can be little doubt that the Inca family was an intruding nation, led perhaps by a few individuals of the sacerdotal class; and having conquered Peru, much the same political relations appear to have subsisted between them and the pre-existing inhabitants, as we at present observe between the modern Greeks and the Turks."[61]

Morton's phrenological investigations furthered two notions: first, that the Incas were a "superior race" not native to Peru, but also that an "ancient" and now "extinct" race probably founded Tiahuanaco, and that the "Toltecan" Incas drew on this ancient civilization when they founded their own. These findings would hardly quell debate or hinder new exploration, for Morton had not resolved the question of origins or race in a definitive manner. Notably, Morton was also something of a "patriotic epistemologist" himself who defended "American civilization" against European cynics. Although "origins" were still in question, what was not in question was the existence of ancient civilization in Peru, and it is perhaps for this reason that Morton was read in Peru. After "a review of the preceding facts," Morton exclaims: "How idle is the assertion of Dr. Robertson, that America contained no monuments older than the conquest! How replete with ignorance are also the aspersions of Pinkerton and de Pauw! Two of these authors, who wrote expressly on American history, are unpardonable for such gross misrepresentation. They appear to have veiled the truth in order to support a hypothesis." Sustained by his American "patriotic epistemology," Morton declares that "it is in vain any longer to contend against facts; for however difficult it may be to explain them, they are nevertheless incontrovertible. Whence the Peruvians derived their civilization, may long remain a mooted question; that they possessed it, cannot be denied."[62]

Nevertheless, Peruvian Creoles like Rivero favored the views of the versatile Swiss anthropologist Jacob von Tschudi. An early Peruvianist in the round sense of the term, von Tschudi had carried out extensive field and linguistic researches in Peru (having a command of Quechua) and he had visited the site of the Sungate at Tiahuanaco as well. In contrast to Morton, von Tschudi argued that skeletal and lexicographic evidence suggested that three more or less equally endowed "races" (which, being the linguist of the German school that he was, he named "Aymara," "Quechua," and "Chincha") had populated Peru. Von Tschudi's analysis suggested that "race" in Peru was the product of cultural phenomena and geography and that it had nothing to do with "civilization" per se, since all three of these Peruvian "races" achieved civilizations in different regions of Peru.[63]

In his summary of the various speculations about the origins of the Incas, Mortimer claims that Rivero had followed Humboldt. The Peruvian, he says, "considers that there is no doubt but Quetzalcoatl, Bochica, and Manco Capac were Buddhist priests, and that the Peruvian gods Con, Pachacamac, and Viracocha corresponded to Brahma, Vishnu and Shiva."[64] This characterization of Rivero's view is not entirely accurate, however. In *Antigüedades peruanas* (1851), Rivero had guardedly accepted Humboldt's speculation that Manco Capac was most likely an Oriental sage and that he could have been a Brahmin or a Buddhist priest who, by virtue of his "superior and civilizing doctrine" was "able to dominate the animus of the indigenous peoples and elevate them to political supremacy."[65] Yet Rivero arrives at this confirmation of Humboldt's hypothesis in part because, like the intrepid Jesuit missionaries of centuries past, the Peruvian Creole considered Buddhism and Christianity to be analogous religious traditions.[66] Moreover, Rivero's inclination toward Humboldt's thesis did not stop him from asserting that the glory of the Inca dynasty was still "indigenous" to Peru. Rivero surmised that Manco Capac had merely been a sagacious, priestly "reformer" and therefore could not have been an actual "Inca" of the royal bloodline of the Sun. Rather, the enterprising Manco had placed Inca-Rocca (in Inca Garcilaso's account Inca-Rocca or "Sinchi-Rocca" is the second Inca dynast), an able member of an illustrious local family, on the Peruvian throne. Rivero reasoned that his name of "Inca" was strong lexical evidence that he was the likely founder of the lineage.[67] Here Rivero followed the lexicographic and archaeological methods of the British antiquarian and Orientalist John Ranking, who had observed that the name "Manco" was likely to be of Oriental origin.[68] Thus, for Rivero, Inca-Rocca was "the first Indian autocrat, the stump of the tree of the Peruvian Monarchs."[69] Although Rivero did not take Manco Capac to be the founding dynast, he is still, by virtue of his having placed "Inca-Rocca" on the throne of Peruvian civilization, the founder of "our Inca dynasty." Rivero's reading is also in keeping with classical traditions and indeed it parallels Pedro de Peralta Barnuevo's dynastic history of Spain (discussed in chapter 3), in which Hercules of Egypt is the foreign founder but the native Hispano is the first king.

In some contrast to Prescott and Squier, however, Rivero was not coolly removed from the study of ancient Peru, in large part because that study contained deep and positive lessons for the country's future. In the concluding chapter to *Antigüedades peruanas,* Rivero momentarily shifts from the scientific "we" (which he shares with his coauthor, Jacob von Tschudi) to the auto-ethnographic "I" more characteristic of colonial Renaissance chronicles, including, as we saw in chapter 2, Inca Garcilaso de la Vega's *Comentarios reales.*[70] Here this "I" speaks for the national "we" that makes the Incas "ours." Anecdotal reflection on ruins in the first-person singular was an established tradition in travel writing but somewhat out of place in scientific reports like this one. Rivero's text straddles the genres as it speaks to alternative readerships: the republic of scientific letters abroad and the republic of the lettered people at home. At the oracular pre-Inca archaeological ruin known as Chavín de Huántar, Rivero takes romantic flight across the ages of violence and returns with the lesson and national duty of memory's preservation in monuments, without which the nation's future generations would surely condemn his own time. Ironically, in this moment of illumination Rivero accurately peers into the future, for Jorge Basadre's postwar generation will do precisely that, as we shall see in chapter 7 of this book.

"Fatigued and at the same time satisfied with my arduous investigations," Rivero writes, "I took rest upon a slab of granite some three meters long, engraved with certain signs or designs that I could not decipher, and which I had stumbled upon as I emerged from a subterranean passage near the river." In that moment of repose, and in seeming exercise of those powers of imagination that Unanue had theorized, "my imagination took flight with the speed of lightning, ranging over all the ancient sites I had visited and all the great events that had taken place in the time of the conquest. Saddened, I raised my eyes toward the ruins of this silent site and saw the deplorable images of destruction committed by our ancient oppressors." Three centuries of pillage, he notes, "had not been enough to erase from memory those infinite maladies suffered by the pacific and simple inhabitants of the Andes, and I thought I saw in the narrow current water stained with the blood of victims, and that the rubble along the bank was a mountain of cadavers upon which fanaticism had erected its throne of tyranny, and from which it had given thanks to Heaven for having achieved its work of destruction." Absorbed by such melancholy meditations and "sympathizing with the unhappy luck of such a laborious and sagacious nation," Rivero records that "I thought I heard a voice from the depths of the subterranean passageway, a voice that spoke to me thus: 'what motives have you to wander in these places of eternal rest, to remove rubble and tread on the ashes that time has respected, now that men are content to deprecate them? Are the data of histories not sufficient proof of our greatness, our simplicity, our hospitality and love of work? Perchance are the monumental remains that escaped the bloody sword of the inhuman conqueror better testimonies of the opulence of our ancestors? Better than the robbery of our treasures, the sacking of our cities, the treacheries, the death of our adored Inca, of our wise men [*amautas*] and of our nobility?'"

Rivero's lonely meditations registered that loss to which ruins speak. For those who would listen rather than deprecate, these speaking ruins ask if the "data of histories" is not enough. Like Unanue, Rivero finds that given the destruction of the archive, those histories must "pass in silence over many notable things." The truth of this destruction was self-evident, for "he who denies what we were, who denies the persecutions and torments, the bad that was done to our Patria, to the arts and to humanity, will first have to confess that the Sun, our father, does not contribute with vivifying warmth to the development of animate beings, or that the high and majestic Cordillera does not hold rich veins of precious metals," and now sounding that dystopian chord and colonial clamor first sounded by Inca Garcilaso, "the primary cause of our ruin." The history of the conquest of Peru "presents us with sad portraits of vengeance, petty passions, and the obsession to destroy all that might serve to enlighten subsequent generations. Thus, no matter how much we consult the authors of various epochs, they repeat what others have said, or pass in silence over many notable things." And since soon after the arrival of the Spaniards the Inca Huascar and nearly all of the nobility perished at the hands of Atahualpa, and since they were the only ones who were instructed in the history of the country and the reading of quipus, "we have remained in complete ignorance concerning the origins of these nations and of that great conqueror and legislator Manco Capac." Finally, Rivero exclaims, "May this serve as an example: we must strive to preserve the precious relics of our ancestors so that future generations do not accuse us of being destructive and ignorant."[71]

Rivero and Tschudi's *Antigüedades peruanas* was more than a scientific report. To begin with, the book was dedicated not to princes or royal academies of science. Breaking with the imperial Book of Kings tradition of princely dedications, the first republican book of "Peruvian Antiquities" was dedicated to the "Congress of Peru" and the "cause of National Sovereignty." Rivero sought funding from Congress to publish the plates to his book, but his gesture was more than a bid for favors. The cause of national sovereignty is the "cause of memory against ruin." The book's epigraph, quoted from Jean Casimir Perrier, reads: "Monuments are like History, and like her, inviolable. They should preserve the memory of great national events, and cede only to the ravages of time."[72]

Rivero was founding director of independent Peru's first national museum (notably, he was also founding director of Colombia's national museum) and he had secured funding from Congress to subsidize the printing of lithographic plates in imperial Vienna, thanks to his Swiss colleague von Tschudi, a member of Vienna's Royal Academy of Sciences. In the preface, Rivero repeats Unanue's refrain, lamenting the sorry colonial legacy of destruction and neglect for, he writes, "centuries have passed before Peru possessed a collection [of artifacts] drawn from her ancient archaeological monuments." Today, however, "these mute yet eloquent witnesses reveal the history of past events and they demonstrate to us the intelligence, power and greatness of the nation ruled by our Incas." This material demonstration was of the utmost importance, for the "history of nations . . . is not of interest merely to know what stage of power and culture was attained . . . but rather to instruct us in their progress . . . and to prepare the people for the enjoyment of national lib-

10. Frontispiece, Mariano de Rivero and Jacob von Tschudi, *Antigüedades peruanas,* vol. 2 (Vienna, 1851).

erty. . . . Babylon, Egypt, Greece and Rome are not the only empires worthy to serve as nourishment for a generous imagination."[73]

The frontispiece to the second volume of *Antigüedades peruanas* offered as "nourishment" for the "generous imagination" of the Peruvian people and their Congress (and European readers, too) an iconographic representation of Peru's deeply promising history (see fig. 10). The ancient ruin of the Sungate (Puerta del Sol) at Tiahuanaco now appears transformed as the triumphant arch of the republic, the ancient threshold of the Peruvian national future. The pastoral Indian family and the native flora and fauna "animate" the bounty of the landscaped native soil, while the ancient glory of Inca kings and the monumental stone portend the even greater glories to come.

And yet Rivero's republican Sungate is also a "mirror" that would soon become a logo, serving as an architectural motif for the façade of Peru's national museum of archaeology or turning up in reproduction in museums in Bolivia and Argentina.[74] In the same manner in which the ephemeral viceregal and imperial arches constructed for royal ceremonies in the seventeenth and eighteenth centuries served as majestic "mirrors of the prince," Rivero's imaginary republican arch is a "mirror of the people."[75] It assembles all the key optical elements of the new natural historical and romantic vision of Peru. The "country" is represented in the signature volcanoes and native flora and fauna that landscape the generously reconstructed Sungate; the portraits of entombed Inca Kings represent the solid foundations of "Peruvian Civilization," ringing the threshold of Peru's republican future. Now, however, the diminutive, common Indian in "national costume" points up to Peru's sovereign future, here emblematized by the title of the work which is held aloft by the mighty condor, "sovereign of the avian kingdom" and also "sovereign of these regions."

This generous mirror of the republican historical imagination carries the trace of the old imperial dynastic history and its colonial discourse, however. The images of the 12 Inca kings and the two heirs of Huayna Capac (Huascar and Atahualpa) on the frontispiece of *Antigüedades peruanas* are copies of the engraving of Juan Palomino drawn by Diego Villanueva (and based on drawings by Alonso de la Cueva) that had adorned Antonio de Ulloa's 1748 plate of the "Peruvian Emperors" (see fig. 7, chap. 3). The imagery of Rivero's republican and scientific arch of "Ancient Peru" constitutes an instructive contrast with the architecture of imperial dynastic history's heavenly Teatro Político and its providential *translatio imperii* from Inca to Spanish dynasts. In effect, River's arch is a graphic image of the republican succession to the Book of Kings and its dynastic imaginary. Here in the "country," the Inca dynasts are carved in the ancient stone of the "soil" from which their civilization arose. They are now "our Incas" because they are entombed in "our land." Etched in monumental stone, the Incas who animated the pages and imaginary of the dynastic Book of Kings and its "Peruvian empire" now find a monolithic afterlife as the ancient threshold of the republican future.

This threshold was largely invisible to foreign historians and critics. Following the condescending views of many "armchair" European historians, the influential William Prescott, for example, held that Manco Capac was a mere "figment of the vain imagination of Peruvian monarchs."[76] Although the Yankee historian never visited Cusco, and if he had could not have seen it, he nevertheless could not resist speculating on the meaning of the Inca ruins at Sacsayhuamán, outside Cuzco. The ruins were material proof of a grinding "despotism" that was ultimately of Oriental origin. Transporting himself in prose to the site, Prescott wrote that "we are filled with astonishment when we consider that these enormous masses were hewn from their native bed and fashioned into shape by people ignorant of the use of iron ... without the knowledge of tools and machinery familiar to the European. Twenty thousand men are said to have been employed in this great structure, and fifty years consumed in the building." The Yankee historian now continued in a more somber tone: "we see in it the workings of a despotism which had the lives and fortunes of its vassals at its absolute disposal, and which, however mild in its general character, esteemed these vassals, when employed in its service, as lightly as the brute animals for which they served as a substitute."[77]

In making this argument Prescott thought he was wielding the authoritative phrenological evidence of Morton. Prescott claimed that the Incas were a "superior race" that lorded over primitive tribal natives, but, as we have seen, this was not Morton's argument. Prescott added that he was uninterested in the origins of this "superior race," since that was a matter for "speculative antiquarians," not real historians. In the end, for the document-bound and blind Yankee historian, Inca origins lay in a "land of darkness ... far beyond the domain of history."[78] But readers of Morton and Prescott in republican Peru took this "land of darkness" very seriously. For them the Manco Capac question was a national question. Prescott's "land of darkness" fell very much within the optical spectrum of national history, and indeed was foundational and necessary to its full elaboration.[79]

In contrast to Prescott's "darkness" and "figment of the vain imagination," Sebastián Lorente's Manco Capac bore the bright light of the "national spirit." Lorente's account would also differ from Inca Garcilaso's providential dynastic history, wherein Manco Capac is the unprecedented hero-king who founds Peruvian civilization. In Lorente's republican history of "Ancient Peru," Manco is not a dynast but an enlightened "reformer" imbued with the national spirit, who "in his native wisdom knew how to amalgamate all those elements of civilization that already existed in Peru."[80] Lorente's view of Manco Capac drew upon the Creole "patriotic epistemology" and "physiology" of Unanue.

Trained in more modern medicine, Lorente did not share Unanue's physiological theory of the circum-equatorial sensory imagination, but his argument that Manco Capac must have been "Peruvian" is likewise inspired by an apprehension of and identification with "the national spirit." For Lorente, "anyone who impartially interrogates history" will find that the "origin of Manco Capac" is "not in doubt." That man "who so perfectly knew the lay of the land and its people—who was so inundated with the national spirit that with its knowledge he could amalgamate all of the elements of the anterior civilization—that man was without doubt born in Peru," asserts Lorente. Manco Capac's works "bear the seal of the national race and that of the land; it is the expression of his epoch as a man of genius would comprehend it."[81]

To support his view, Lorente turned, much as eighteenth-century patriotic epistemologists had, to nonliterate native forms of memory and to the Inca oral testimony registered in early colonial reports. However, Lorente treats these sources not as mere "fables," as did the Anglo American and European theorists, but rather, in the fashion of Vico, as cultural evidence. Thus, he finds that the "nationality of Manco [Capac] is deduced from other conclusive evidence, and is also revealed to a certain point by legends and direct oral testimonies." The *quipocamayoc* or record-keepers "of Pacariqtambo, where the mission of the first Inca appears to have commenced, supposed that Manco had been engendered there by a ray of sunlight," he explains.

Although in Lorente's view Manco Capac was not a dynast but "only a reformer of institutions," this does not diminish the leader's glory, since he had "secured the unity of Peru, the basis of its future greatness."[82] Lorente's reading of Manco Capac was a critical step in the republican rewriting of Peruvian history. Peruvian civilization would now be refounded not on "the Incas, kings of Peru that were" of the Book of Kings but on the primitive "soul" and living "communal spirit" of indigenous villagers, that is, by the Peruvian people.

We may now appreciate the significance of Bartolomé Herrera's twenty-fifth anniversary remarks of 1846, quoted in the second epigraph to this chapter. Before, during, and after "the epoch of independence" the "Empire of the Incas" was properly reconfigured as the numinous "country of the Incas." This was not then an "insane" idea, although it might appear so in retrospect. This poetic movement of the soil was initiated in historical discourse under Bourbon imperial auspices precisely as an intellectual "reconquest of the empire of the Incas" by Unanue and other "patriotic epistemologists" of his generation. As Unanue argued, it was upon the soil of the *país* that the ruins of ancient Peru stood and it was from the Peruvian clime that the genius of Manco Capac and the Incas sprang. Moreover, this clime and its genius were universally available to all those born in Peru. In the decade following Herrera's sermon, Rivero's republican arch would fully execute that "poetic movement, in which the nation is taken to be the soil." The frontispiece of Rivero and Tschudi's *Antigüedades peruanas* offers a "symbolic space that gives the kings a good death" in the republican historical imagination of Peruvians.[83] Rivero's nationalist Sungate lays the Incas of Peru to rest as the entombed threshold of a republican history whose future lies not in the continuation of the Inca dynasty but in the generous imagination of the Peruvian people. Rivero's arch is precisely an allegory of and for that generous imagination.

That arch and threshold would now open onto the national campus of Peru, where the new "schoolmaster of history," Sebastián Lorente, would deliver his history lessons. Those republican history lessons would begin not with Manco Capac but instead with Manco Capac's "Peruvian" cultural origins.

5

The Postcolonial Death of the Book of Kings

The new Government is aware of the power that names have over ideas, and it also knows that the dignity of things is born of the words that are adopted to characterize them; for these reasons the denominations of the new functionaries and the principle public establishments have been altered. It is imperative to destroy everything that may be used to sustain the old institutions, and to remember the abuses and crimes of the Spanish regime by virtue of the contrast with the advantages of the new order.

Bernardo Monteagudo, *Exposición de las tareas administrativas del gobierno desde su instalación hasta el 15 de julio de 1822*

"History," wrote an author whose name we don't recall, "is the Book of Kings; but it must be written by free and truth-loving men." That author must have been a courtier since if he was not he would have said: "History is a schoolmaster who teaches modern societies to read in the book in which ancient societies learned to spell."

Juan Espinosa, *Diccionario para el pueblo*

In Peru's first college textbook of "contemporary history," published in Lima in 1876, Sebastián Lorente noted that it was not the crowd at the Bastille but rather the fiery and eloquent Bishop de Blois who had delivered history's death sentence to the French king. Speaking before France's National Convention, the republican bishop noted that the "Name of the King" had been upheld by the "Book of Kings." And "the history of Kings," he proclaimed, "is the martyrdom of nations!"[1] The time of that book and its king was about to end. For Lorente, de Blois' public sentencing of the

Book of Kings announced the arrival of a worldwide "Contemporary Age of Revolutions." Peru was at the forefront of this new age. The words and acts of this age were not specific to the revolutions of France; instead, they were the people's untutored answer to the rule of the king. As Bernardo Monteagudo declared at Peru's independence, "the name of King has become hateful for those who love liberty."[2] And as Santiago Távara would write four decades after the event, "the [Peruvian people] felt the torment of the whip, they hated the pain, and [they hated] the Governor with that whip; he was called the King; his antagonist was Democracy and the Republic: That was enough! To arrive at this conclusion the people did not need complicated syllogisms, nor studies of the revolutions of France."[3]

In Peru, the colonial regime of the Spanish king would be abolished not by repeating the refrains or actions of the French but by erasing and writing over the imperial Name of the King. Reviewing the evidence decades later, Lorente would write that in Peru "an intimate but secret union . . . existed between the cause of independence and the cause of the republic. . . . The end of colonialism and the abolition of the monarchy blended together; the cause of the King was diametrically opposed to the cause of the Patria; the People inclined instinctively to the Republic, and the most illustrious patriots were in general enthusiastic republicans."[4] For Lorente, the foundational republican acts of negation and nomination were also history, because these acts revealed a deeper, genetic logic etched in the "soul" of the Peruvian people's civilization. This deep history of the soul would displace the old history of kings, for the death of the king in politics signified "that kings are dead as the centers and forces of history."[5]

In Peru, as in France, the new task of writing a "headless history" of and for the people fell to "the second generation."[6] In France the Revolution of 1830 proved to be an impetus to the writing of a "contemporary history" of "Civilization," "the Revolution," and "France," with such historians as François Guizot and Jules Michelet leading the way, albeit in different political directions. In Peru a similar impetus came from the Liberal Revolution of 1854. Although he is largely forgotten today, Lorente was by far the most prolific and influential historian of Peru in the post-1854 period. His philosophical vision and narrative of the history of Peruvian civilization would give the Book of Kings or dynastic history a good, postcolonial death as the political froth "under" which ran a deeper current of Peruvian cultural history. This deeper history of civilization charted Peru's long national development, from primitive communal origins to independent republican nationhood, and from there to a boundless future of universal liberty.

Event Narrative: Death to the Name of the King!

In colonial South America no Spanish king's body was available to be seized and beheaded. Territorially and symbolically speaking, however, His Majesty's composite "Indian" body was severed from its sovereign, Hispanic, metropolitan head, and in the bloodied soil of patriotic martyrs (and in the bloody pages of history) its colonial members reemerged as the sovereign "countries" of so many postcolonial South American republics. In Peru, the death or displacement of the king would operate not on his body proper but on his simulacra (His Royal Portrait, His Royal Seal, His Royal Banner, His Royal Ceremony) and so was fittingly figurative, poetic, spatial. In short, the king's death was enacted at a colonial distance.[7] In Lima, for example, the semisacred and lifelike portrait of the king (*retrato del Rey*) appears to have been defiled and it along with other "signs of His dominion" were effectively defaced or retired from public spaces. The revolution of independence would ban the Name of the King by writing old "Peruvian" names over it; collective acts of forgetting and rewriting would seal the republican future.

Preparing the stage for Peru's Declaration of Independence in Lima (July 28, 1821), the Rioplatense ("Argentina" had not yet assumed its life as a properly named historical subject)[8] "Protector of Peru" José de San Martín decreed that all "Coats of Arms of the King of Spain be removed from the public buildings of the state," since as "signs of vassalage" they were inconsistent with independence.[9] The Protector of Peru then personally seized the "Standard of Pizarro." For many patriots, this banner symbolized the Spanish conquest of the "empire of the Incas" 300 years before. Lima was known famously as the "City of the Kings of Peru."[10] Now it was declared that the capital should henceforth be named the "Heroic and Valiant City of the Free."[11] In a similar gesture, San Martín abolished the royal tribute (*Real tributo*) paid by Indian commoners to the king of Spain and emperor of the Indies, declaring that "the name of Indian" was a "humiliating sign of His dominion." Although Monteagudo's declarations had anticipated San Martín's, it was now declared that henceforth the "Indians or Naturals" would be officially named "Peruvians."

Contrary to Benedict Anderson's fruitful but misinformed assertion, "Peruvians" was not a "neological" name for "half-obliterated" Indians coined by a "Creole pioneer" who sought fraternal communion with newly imagined nationals. Although both men had gone to university in the ex-Peruvian colonial town of Chuquisaca (then part of the new Viceroyalty of the Río de la Plata), Monteagudo and San Martín were not Peruvians in the limited territorial sense that the name would soon take on, and in the early days after independence many Peruvian-born Creole elites did not identify themselves as Peruvians either.[12] Moreover, "Peruvian" was an old colonial term coined, as we saw in chapter 1, prior to the Spanish conquest, and by the early sixteenth century it was widely used in Europe to refer to the past and present native inhabitants of Peru. In addition, the *Real tributo* and the term *indio* (Indian) had in fact already been abolished by the Cortes de Cádiz or Parliament of the Spanish Commonwealth in 1812. Subsequently, the term *Real tributo* was changed to *contribución* (contribution) for precisely the same reason that would be cited by San Martín nearly a decade later. At the same time, the commonwealth had rechristened all *indios* as *españoles* (Spaniards). In short, the Quixotic liberator from Río de la Plata appears to have shared something with Benedict Anderson and John Lynch (the Latin Americanist historian upon whom Anderson had relied): He was not up on his Peruvian history.[13] Still more: the title of "Peruvian" was not necessarily desired by those "Spaniards" or "ex-Indians" upon whom it was now so righteously bestowed. In a word, the name was not San Martín's to give nor was it the Indians' to receive but, nevertheless, from that gift "something came to be."[14] That "something" was born more of forgetting than of memory.

In effect, San Martín's act of christening was a gesture of oblivion that served as a strategic semantic wedge against those numerous Creole reformists who now called only for autonomy (and not independent nationhood) as "American Spaniards" under the Spanish commonwealth's remarkably progressive Constitution of 1812. For the constitutionalists and autonomists, the Indians were "Spaniards." At the same time, however, the name of "Peruvians" recalled the fabled "Peruvian empire" of Inca Garcilaso de la Vega's *Comentarios reales de los incas*, reprinted in 1723 as part of a concerted cultural offensive intended to restore the grandeur both of Peruvian and Spanish empire. That evocation would prove to be deeply moving for a host of learned patriots, for, as Bartolomé Herrera noted 25 years later, patriot rhetoric had, in "a poetic movement in which the nation was taken to be the soil," sung the cause of independence as "a reconquest of the Empire of the Incas."[15] This "poetic movement of the soil" was not about restoring the Inca empire, however. Instead, and as we saw in the previous chapter, it was about installing in the historical imagination the natural sovereignty of "the soil" and "the clime." It was this movement that had made it possible to imagine the "Realm of Peru" as an independent and ingenious "Country of the Incas." Lorente would now give that country a primitive and enduring "soul."

In another symbolic displacement of the Name and Book of Kings, the Colegio del Príncipe (Prince College)—under the viceregal regime dedicated

to the education of the talented sons of native noblemen, many of whom became royal scribes—was rechristened "Liberty College." In 1822 the Colegio
de la Libertad housed the new National Library of Peru, ex-Jesuit bookish
cradle of national history, also created by decree of San Martín at the behest
of Monteagudo.[16] As Monteagudo explained, the National Library would
"offer superabundant means for the enrichment of the intelligence of Peruvian youth, thereby expanding its exquisite sensibility." The National Library
would, he continued, foment "contact between the People and those men
who live or have lived in order to enlighten their fellow men."[17] At the same
time, San Martín and Monteagudo declared the creation of an honorary order of enlightened patriots that would displace the old colonial nobility and
which was called, after the Incas, the "Order of the Sun." The Order of the Sun
was "the historical expression of the Land of the Incas, an evocation both of
the glorious times before [Spanish] enslavement and of the present happiness that Independence has recovered."[18]

First Minister Monteagudo understood that his revolutionary task was
foundational and therefore nominal. As a South American counterpoint to
the gesture of Napoleon Bonaparte, who had ordered the erection of a French
version of Trajan's Column in the Place Vendôme of Paris, Monteagudo now
proposed that a "Pillar of Time" be erected in the center of Lima's old Plaza of
the Inquisition, the new home of the people's Peruvian Congress. (The pillar
was never built, and today this spot is occupied by an equestrian statue of
Simón Bolívar, who gives his name to the plaza itself.) The Peruvian version
of Trajan's Column would not be the measure of glorious deeds of French empire, insisted Monteagudo, but rather would stand as the historicist tower of
the new Peruvian nation. It would consist of commemorative rings inscribed
with key events in the "independent life" of the Peruvian Republic, beginning
with 1821 or "Year One."[19] Monteagudo's earlier work, published in 1809, *El
diálogo entre Atahualpa y Fernando VII en los Campos Eliseos* (Dialogue between the Inca Atahualpa and King Ferdinand VII in the Champs-Élysées),
had compared Ferdinand VII's unjust exile under the despotic Napoleon to
the cruel fate of Atahualpa at the hands of the "barbarous" Pizarro. Published
in the midst of autonomist cries of Spanish American support for Ferdinand
VII, *El diálogo* suggested that the sixteenth-century transfer of sovereignty
from the Inca dynasty to the Crown of Castile was illegitimate and that as
a result Peru had never relinquished its ancient sovereignty. Notably, in the
patriot ranks of the armies both of San Martín and Bolívar, the "avengeance
of Atahualpa" was a rallying cry to arms.

In similar gestures of violent renewal, Peru's First Constitutional Congress renamed the Spanish fortress at Lima's port of Callao, known as the Castillo del Real Felipe (King Philip's Fortress) and at the time still occupied by hold-out loyalist forces, as the Castillo de la Independencia (Fortress of Independence). Its five bastions or towers were renamed as well: the King's Tower became the Tower of Manco Capac (ancient founder of the Inca dynasty); the Queen's Tower was now the Tower of the Patria, an allegorical mistress or female figure who represented the native land.[20] Even the official paper headed by Ferdinand VII's royal seal—and upon which many of the patriotic decrees would now circulate—was restamped or written over with the new national emblem of Peru, bearing these words: "Year One of Independent Life" (*Año primero de la Vida Independiente*).

While San Martín, Monteagudo, and the Congress were resetting the names and clock of independent Peru in Lima, the last viceroy and royal military commander of Spanish Peru, José de la Serna, marched upward and southward across the Andes with a significant loyalist force (notably named the "National Army"), which by all accounts garnered considerable support from the Andean populations of the interior.[21] Enter Simón Bolívar. Following an exit interview with San Martín at the port of Guayaquil, the general from Venezuela assumed command of the cause: End Spain's rule on "American soil." In the once vast Viceroyalty of Peru, the revolution of independence was prolonged, intermittent, ambiguous, and violent, but with Bolívar's entrance it became definitively republican and Spartan, thanks in large measure to the decisive military and political campaign of the Liberator and Dictator (a title which at the time did not carry the negative associations it does today) of Venezuela, Colombia, Peru and Bolivia. Having soundly defeated the royalist forces of the viceroy in 1824 at the Battle of Ayacucho, Bolívar's field marshal Antonio José de Sucre marched triumphantly into Cuzco, the ancient capital of the Incas. Bolívar, who had strategically occupied Lima to take political control of the precarious new state, was not present. Notably, however, his image was. The local newspaper, *El Sol del Cuzco*, reported that on the afternoon of February 3, 1825, "the bust of our Dictator was placed in the ancient Temple of the Sun. The Inca-Kings that lie there lifted up their heads from their sepulchers and, beholding the Liberator of their land, blessed him; covered with glory, they returned satisfied to their frigid tombs."[22]

The classical republican from Caracas would have been pleased to read that the Incas had returned to the tombs where they belonged! Arriving months later in Cuzco, Bolívar—himself a planter of noble Spanish descent and now officially bestowed with dictatorial powers by the Peruvian Congress—declared the abolition of all titles of nobility in Peru, including "the title and

authority of the *caciques*" or native and mestizo governors of the Indian communities, many of whom were lesser nobles and a few of whom could and
did claim to be distant descendents of Inca royalty.[23] Bolívar also undid San
Martín's Order of the Sun (it was later restored), which the Venezuelan republican considered too reminiscent of Spanish titles of nobility. Peruvian
congressman and later Supreme Court justice Benito Laso confirmed the
new, more rigorously republican "name of Peru" in his notable address to the
Second Constitutional Congress. "Peruvians," Laso declared, "you owe your
life, your liberty, and your name to Bolívar . . . He is the enemy of the Name
of Kings and the angel of the regime of representation."[24]

These military and political acts of war and speech were the founding dis-
placements of the Republic of Peru and its new "contemporary history." Following the independence wars and a subsequent series of border disputes
between contentious new states and patriot armies with wages to collect, the
territorial claim of the República Peruana was now a much reduced but still
central segment of the once-vast sixteenth-century viceroyalty known as the
"Kingdoms and Provinces of Peru." Of great significance for a new republican
historical discourse, the territory of the Peruvian Republic encompassed the
old highland Inca center at Cuzco and the viceregal court or colonial capital
at coastal Lima, with the latter becoming, in a metamorphosis of "the King"
into "the Free," the capital of the new republic. Peru's successive political mu-
tations from precolonial Inca realm to Spanish viceroyalty and finally postcolonial republican fragment lent a particular political urgency to the task
of rewriting the Book of Kings as the republican and "national" history of
civilization.[25] Nevertheless, this task was not easy or readily forthcoming, in
part because the postindependence milieu was marked by the resurgence of
the old, local sovereignties of town and province, and in part because further
strife both civil and international would riddle the new republic for the next
two or three decades. The definitive writing of republican history would require a repetition, that is, a second revolutionary event: the Liberal Revolution of 1854.[26]

Narrative Event: Death of the Book of Kings

Inspired by the same historicist visions—namely, those associated with the illustrious names of Montesquieu and Rousseau—that had informed Bolívar's
thought, independence war veteran Juan Espinosa (yet another Rioplatense)
declared in his *Dictionary for the People* (1855) that "History" was no longer
the Book of Kings but rather, in a play on the venerable Ciceronian topos

of *historia magistra vitae*, a "schoolmaster" (*maestro de escuela*) who "teaches modern societies to read in the book in which ancient societies learned to spell." This schoolmasterly history of the people's civilization would be critical and true, and in the face of all horrors and setbacks it would tell the history of the "eminence of man's soul." For Espinosa, the brilliant future of the "soul of man" was not the birthright of any race; on the contrary, it revealed an ancient and universal history laden with "practical" lessons. The historical essence of man was not ethnic or racial but soulful and philosophical, and for this reason all men formed but one multicolored family of history:

> The pretension of belonging to one or another race is Quixotic, and even more ridiculous in the Americas where, in a single family, one finds very white and very black brothers, with straight or curly hair, with long or blunt noses, with intelligence or stupidity . . . where a black woman has a child by a European, and a white woman a child by an African, and where from the mix we get colors and features as ill-defined as those on a painter's palette. The only rational distinction one can make among this Babel of Castes is that of morality, intelligence, and bearing . . . the rest is absurd. Man is nothing more than this: a soul with a heart for feeling and brains for discourse. The eminence of these two constituent elements makes him eminently good or eminently wise . . . nothing else matters.[27]

The premier embodiment of history as "schoolmaster of the people" in postcolonial republican Peru was not the enlightened soldier Juan Espinosa but instead the Spanish-born philosophical historicist Sebastián Lorente (1813–1884). For Lorente, the French Enlightenment's notion of the eminence of the soul of "man in general" was surely true but insufficiently historical to be of "practical" use. Although the "logic" of history was universal (since all that was false withered with time, leaving only the true), "Peruvian civilization" exhibited a particular "history of national development." In *Historia antigua del Peru* (1860), Lorente makes it clear why "the ancient history of Peru" was now required reading for contemporary Peruvian society: "Although the ancient civilization of Peru . . . offers something of general interest to men of all countries, for us it is of special interest for the present and future. This ancient civilization is personified in monuments which still stand, it lives in our customs, and it influences the march of our daily social and political life; whoever ignores it cannot comprehend our situation, nor can they lead our society with confidence."[28] The history of Peru was "of special interest to us" because Peru harbored an ancient and singular "soul" and a "national spirit" that could serve as sure guides to "our" republican future. Lorente would draw out the "practical" lessons of that "soul" and "spirit" for the young republic. As director of Peru's leading liberal college, holder of chairs in Natural History at the Medical College and in the History of Peruvian Civilization at its first university, San Marcos, where he was the founding Dean of Letters, Lorente almost single-handedly wrote postcolonial Peru's first generation of republican history textbooks and along the way he founded and institutionalized the new "contemporary history" in Peru's colleges and universities.

Lorente did for historical discourse what San Martín and Bolívar had done for political discourse, only more so and to greater and lasting effect.[29] In Lorente's histories, "Peruvians" became not the politically correct and strategic name for ex-Indians and ex-Spaniards (as in San Martín's decree), but the timeless name of an ancient people who carried a deep history of civilization etched in its soul. Lorente's synthetic, epoch-ordered, narrative "critical history" of "Peruvian civilization" contemplated "national development" as the sublime "harmony among all of the civilizing elements," from the immemorial past to the limitless future. His truly "Peruvian history of Peru" established the main lines of contemporary Peruvian historical discourse down to the present. Although in certain ways closer to Guizot, Lorente shared Jules Michelet's "conception of history as a unified whole that realized itself in the people, from an original moment to a destiny, manifested in the harmonious identity of the national soul."[30] Also like Michelet, Lorente gave "the King" a good republican death by burying his name and his book in the deep "unity" or "harmony" of the native land and the people with a proper name.[31]

Peru's republican "schoolmaster of history" was born not in Peru but in the small town of Alcantarilla near Murcia, Spain, in 1813.[32] There he studied the customary triumvirate of theology, medicine, and law, after which he pursued the study of philosophy at university. In 1835 he was awarded the chair in philosophy at the prestigious Royal College of San Isidro, in Madrid. But the 1830s and 1840s were turbulent years in Spain; republicans battled monarchists, constitutionalists engaged absolutists, and generals intervened in the fray, and many illustrious Spaniards found their careers interrupted. In 1842 Lorente was approached by the powerful Peruvian merchant, planter, and liberal politician Domingo Elías and by Elías' Spanish business associate Nicolás Rodríguez. Elías and Rodríguez offered Lorente passage to Peru and the directorship of a new liberal *colegio* (primary and secondary school) in Lima. Lorente arrived in Lima in early 1843 and in 1844 assumed the post of director of Our Lady of Guadalupe College. He soon introduced a liberal curriculum previously unknown in Peru. With Lorente and then Pedro Gálvez at the helm, the Colegio de Nuestra Señora de Guadalupe became the bastion of liberal education in Lima and the ideological springboard of the Revolution of 1854.[33] Fomented by Elías and later commanded by the popular *caudillo* Ramón Castilla, a group of notable intellectuals including Lorente, Galvez, Carlos Lisson, Santiago Távara, and Juan Espinosa lent their pens, guns, and students to the Liberal Revolution that abolished slavery, the Indian tribute or contribution (once again), and capital punishment, and whose National Convention (1855–1857) briefly made effective—for the first time in the republic's history—the universal (popular adult-male) suffrage that independence had promised 30 years before.[34] Lorente's sacrifice and his commitment to the cause were notable for a man not born in Peru. He joined the revolutionary *montoneros* (mounted irregular fighters) in battle against the incumbent regime, and in an unrelated but tragic incident Lorente lost his Peruvian wife, pregnant with child, in the same year of 1854. Lorente now fully committed himself to the cause as editor in chief of the voice of the revolution, *La Voz del Pueblo*. In its pages, or rather at the bottom of the front page, ran in every issue his "Pensamientos sobre el Perú" (Thoughts on Peru), in which Lorente spoke poetically of the downtrodden but hardworking Indian peasant in the mountain valley of Mantaro, of his festive customs and tragic sorrows, and of the moral imperative for uplifting change. Lorente was not a newcomer to the highland world. He had carried his liberal pen to the Andean highlands during an extended leave from Colegio de Nuestra Señora de Guadalupe (1850–1855) to recover his health in the clear mountain air. During this time he founded the Colegio Santa Isabel in Huancayo, still the most important school in Peru's central highlands. He also published in Ayacucho his *Course in Philosophy for the Colleges of Peru*.

Thanks to revenues derived from the lucrative guano (bird-dung nitrogen fertilizer) and coolie trades in which Elías was invested, Peru under Castilla experienced unprecedented growth of the state sector.[35] State patronage extended to education and the humanities. President Castilla created the National Archive (Archivo General de la Nación), and funds were made available through the Ministry of Education for the publication of colonial documents, the founding of journals, and the writing and printing of new textbooks for the schools and colleges. As inspector of education, Lorente was instrumental in the systematization of a new liberal curriculum in Peru's growing number of public institutions of learning and he authored slim and inexpensive textbooks or "primers" on a score of subjects, including philosophy, aesthetics, historical geography, literature, style, hygiene, Catholic catechism, economics, universal history, and Peruvian history.[36] With guano-rich state patronage (Elías was now Peru's deep-pocketed minister of the trea-sury) and aided by an opportune appointment as secretary on a Peruvian diplomatic mission to Central America and Europe (1856–1864), Lorente emerged as Peru's most prolific and philosophically minded historian. In Spain he pored over archives and read histories and upon his return from Paris (where his *Historia antigua del Perú* was published in 1860), Lorente as-sumed an active profile as a public intellectual. As secretary of Peru's Society of Friends of the Indian, he took part in debates on how best to address the plight of the indigenous people of Peru. Lorente served presidents Balta and Pardo as a special advisor on educational reform, traveling again to Europe on government commission to study the most recent advances in liberal peda-gogy. In 1868 he was elected the first dean of the College of Letters at San Marcos, Peru's oldest and leading university. Returning from Europe in 1872, Lorente was reelected again and again by the faculty, such that he served as dean of letters until his death in Lima in 1884. His successor at San Marcos was Carlos Lisson, the founder of Peruvian sociology. Lisson memorialized Lorente in these terms: "In this year [1884] and in all of the preceding years since its foundation, the history of the College of Letters is manifested in one name: Lorente. Everything is his creation: plan of study, the establishment of chairs, textbooks, methods, discipline, everything; I repeat, everything is his creation, in everything we see his hand."[37]

During his founding tenure as dean of letters, Lorente established the chair in the History of Peruvian Civilization, which was the pedagogical inspira-tion for his landmark history by that name, published in 1879. According to legend, his lectures at San Marcos "attracted so many auditors that even the President of the Republic, Don Manuel Pardo, was among them."[38] The his-torical significance of this republican rhetorical act was not lost on Lorente. The schoolmaster now instructed the "Grandest of Auditors" of Peru—that is, the president of the republic and not the prince or viceroy as in the colonial tradition of the Book of Kings. However, Lorente's histories also addressed and reached the lettered people and the promising young pupil. That pupil was no longer the soon-to-be-king prince but instead the soon-to-be-citizen schoolboy of the republic. Lorente had his hand in the drafting of the new Code of Public Instruction of 1876, and in the same year published his pocket-sized *Historia del Perú: Compendiada para el uso de los colegios y de las personas ilustradas del Perú* (History of Peru: Abridged for the Colleges and Enlight-ened Persons of Peru). In 1945 historian Raúl Porras Barrenechea would characterize this precise little book as "one of the best manuals of Peruvian history to date. . . . Events are well documented and at the same time it offers a general philosophical vision that clarifies and coordinates events."[39] This slim and affordable tome abridged Lorente's hefty, six-volume *Historia general del Perú* (General History of Peru), published between 1860 and 1876, and whose title carried on the venerable tradition begun for Peru by Inca Garcilaso de la Vega in the second part of the *Comentarios reales*. In the same year Lorente published his *Compendio de historia universal* (Compendium of World History), a set of six pocketsize volumes whose subjects range from the history of the ancient Orient to that of the contemporary world. The war with Chile and the occupation of Lima interrupted his production, but Lorente carried on with his lectures, collaborating, it is said, with the resistance. He died of heart failure in 1884, and his colleagues at San Marcos offered him profuse homage.

Lorente was the only historian working in nineteenth-century Peru to complete and see published a series of histories covering the entire sweep of "Peruvian history," from the "primitive epoch" to the "contemporary age." His indispensable textbooks and histories circulated widely in Peru's colleges, bookstores, and parlors. For this reason alone, his work constitutes the best map of the general drift of nineteenth-century historical thought in Peru. But it was not just a question of chronological sweep and course adoptions: it was a question of philosophy.

Lorente stands out among the Peruvian historians of his time. Most of Peru's historians during this period are perhaps better characterized as erudites, annalists, bibliographers, biographers, folklorists (*costumbristas*) and essayists. His closest competitors in Lima's republic of historical letters were Manuel Mendiburu, Mariano Felipe Paz Soldán, and Ricardo Palma. General Mendiburu compiled an invaluable "biographical-historical dictionary" of great men and the events and times that surrounded them, but it was not history. Paz Soldán, honored by professional historians for introducing the systematic use of the footnote and for editing Peru's first history journal, *La Revista Peruana* (to which Lorente was a star contributor), compiled copious sources for the history of independent Peru, but by his own admission (modest but true) his truncated *Historia del Perú independiente* (1868) was no more than an incomplete "annals or chronicle" of events, crude even by the lowest of Rankean standards.[40] Palma was an influential and erudite literary historian or *tradicionalista*, director of Peru's National Library and author of the notable *Anales de la Inquisición en Lima*. Notably, Palma himself did not consider most of his own writings to be history proper. His understanding of history was similar to that of Paz Soldán. He took history to be a true Rankean account of "how it really was," based upon profuse documentation of political events and personages. Perhaps by temperament uninclined to that kind of writing, Palma churned out lively and entertaining vignettes, often in the picaresque mode, many of which were based on, and sometimes transcribed, colonial documents. In the process, Palma fashioned a hugely popular genre for Lima's liberal literates.[41] In contrast, Lorente's histories were not biographies, annals, or fictionalized vignettes. Temperamentally republican, the schoolmaster of history did not flaunt erudition or style, and in part for this very reason his histories were unquestionably worthy of the name of history in the contemporary age. Lorente understood that contemporary history was not primarily about the encyclopedic accumulation of data, nor was it about picaresque anecdotes relative to great events and personages. Far from being the science of chroniclers and genealogists and removed from the anecdotal ironies and conceits of fiction, history was philosophy by example—that is, historicism. History was the "critical" inquiry and "philosophical" story of the "lives" or "development" of humanity's "souls" and "spirits," and these were to be found in the cultural "evolution" of civilizations. In this regard, Lorente's key concepts were historicist in the sense described by the German scholar Friedrich Meinecke in the 1930s.[42]

Lorente's history combined Enlightenment philosophical concepts with historicist understandings of the spirit of peoples and the life of the soul. History writ large was the universal philosophical history of freedom, albeit via the diverse or particular careers of "national spirits." The world history of spirit was not the erudite encyclopedist's cunning compilation of "brute and disconsolate facts." Rather, Lorente argued, it was a "philosophical" and "faithful relation of the memorable events of humankind, organized by peoples, times, and places."[43] Its method, called "historical critique" or "critical history," was akin to the "correct judgment" of Kantian "ideas," only that in history writing it is "historical critique" that "determines the truth value of the data" and suppresses all that is untrue or vain.[44] Although inspired by such "generalizing spirits" as Raleigh and "the Italian Vico," who "sought to trace the philosophy of history," Lorente noted that "Universal History in our century" had "renovated the history of the ancient world" by employing a new set of critical methods.[45] No longer an exemplary "mirror of princes," universal or world history, Lorente noted, was now a multidisciplinary enterprise in inquiry. It employed archaeology to study antiquities; genealogy to unravel lineages; heraldry to decode emblems; ethnography to investigate the races; numismatics to know coins and medals; and philology to trace the origins and connections among languages.[46] However, returning to Vico,

Lorente insists that "the true eyes of history are geography and chronology, which allow one to see events in their time and place."[47] It is through the eyes of historical geography "that one should study the country, since it significantly influences the destiny of peoples; one should also study the historical locations, which may clarify events."[48] In this Lorente was following the time-honored tradition that ran from Tacitus to Bodin and, in Peru, from Peralta Barnuevo to Unanue (discussed in chapters 3 and 4), and those eyes led him to peer into the obscure depths of "national history."

Lorente's proposal to write the "critical history" of Peruvian civilization implied both the renovation of classical sources by virtue of the new methods and the Creole patriotic critique of such "systematic" European thinkers and "cynics" as William Robertson, Cornelius de Pauw, Thomas Buckle, Guillaume Raynal, Georges-Louis Leclerc, Compte de Buffon, and, to a lesser extent, the North American historian William Prescott.[49] Applied to the ancient history of Peru, the new critical methods would "dispel those novelistic fictions that, gathered by the insufficiently severe historians of the sixteenth century, have come down to us as well-reasoned truths," asserted Lorente. At the same time, the new methods would "confirm the advances made both before and after the Spanish Conquest—progress that is roundly negated by skeptics and superficial thinkers, or placed in doubt by the systematic spirit," and in the process "illuminate unexpected and copious sources" for writing the history of Peruvian civilization.[50] Moreover, he added, "only the application of philosophy to history may serve to unite, in a vast synthesis, the necessary kinds of knowledge now made available to analysis. And only a philosophical spirit, in possession of ample and well-meditated data, is capable of undertaking the task of writing an orderly and luminous exposition of the history of Peruvian civilization."[51]

Like his more prolific and influential post-Enlightenment European contemporaries (Michelet and Ranke come to mind, each in his own way), Lorente rejected the ironical "systematic spirit" identified, rightly or not, with certain writings of Descartes, Voltaire, Raynal and other French "skeptics"; however, he also wasted no time in shrewdly turning their best methods toward the poetic and political work of writing history in a "philosophical spirit."[52] That is, post-Enlightenment historicists employed rational-empirical methods but they also reached back to the rich narrative and poetic traditions of the Renaissance. They argued that world history should be based on sound, scientific proofs but it should be written in an uplifting, philosophical, and vernacular fashion; the historian's prose should be as luminous and instructive as human history itself. Lorente believed strongly in the power of narrative unfettered by the "pompous vice of footnotes" or the "invasions of statistical tables." The narrative also should be free of "anecdotal digressions" and the turgid and "extended reflections" of a pretentious "high philosophy." Instead, the philosophical design of history should be figuratively intimated to the reader via the narrative so that "the events speak for themselves and history administers its eloquent teachings with only the aid of common sense."[53]

Lorente's appeal to an eloquent common sense was deeply republican. Indeed, clean narrative for the people was the new literary regime of truth that, aided by the instructive poetics of the "science of princes" (as, for example, in Peralta's late colonial histories, discussed in chapter 3), would fend off the destructive "skeptics" who questioned not only the validity of the entire historical enterprise but also, in particular, that America could have an ancient history of civilization that was both knowable and worth knowing. What Hayden White recognized as "explanation by emplotment" was, in this case, the strategy best suited to the schoolmaster's task, which was to write the history of the nation's deep progression toward unity and liberty in such a way that its ancient "practical" lessons could be readily grasped by the people.[54] This simple strategy or technique of Lorente follows not from a lack of erudition (as some of his Peruvian critics maintained) but is instead the logical expression in writing of his philosophy of history. Since for Lorente historical change is never capricious or chaotic but rather the luminous history of man's soul, the anecdotal sketches of events compiled by sophists, annalists, and bibliophiles only distract thought and "feed vain curiosity." Events are always expressions of the "evolutions of humanity under the double agency of Providence and Liberty" and, as such, are subject to the deep "physical and moral laws" of humanity. The historian's representation of events should likewise be ordered and harmonious, "an animated and faithful painting of reality" in consonance with Vico's geography and chronology but answering ultimately to the higher callings of "Truth and Liberty."[55] In short, histories should "harmonize" with history (the succession of events and epochs) itself. For Lorente, then, there was only one true manner of history, for "only the methodical history of civilization, the true history that presents events in their vital and luminous unity, may be called, in the words of Cicero, the light of truth and the mistress of life."[56]

Lorente turned to the ancient history of Peru's "national civilization" not only because Cicero had revealed to him the "true path of history." Like

Michelet, Lorente was driven by the demands of his revolutionary age and by a soulful search for meaning in the past. In his introduction to *Historia antigua del Peru*, Lorente explains that

> Having decided to write the history of Peru, which for many years had become my constant object of study, I could no longer ignore the significance of such an important period, without which national civilization would have been for me an enigma impossible to decipher. Wanting to embrace the life of Peru in her progressive evolution—record her events, link causes with consequences, present a clear idea of the whole, and a living image of the great events, and also to give practical lessons—I could not help but take up her first origins. It was clear that I could not comprehend the situation of the Republic without having studied the colonial epoch, colonial rule without studying the Conquest, or the Conquest if I ignored the Empire of the Incas, nor the Empire if I did not have knowledge of the primitive culture of Peru.[57]

The desire to unravel the enigma of Peru and present its "practical lessons" thus led Lorente to an ever-deeper inquiry into the "national civilization." This search through the ages brought into view the "permanent and harmonious elements" of Peruvian civilization that could not be denied for the sake of political convenience or the adherence to dogma. Lorente's pursuit of the enigma of Peru would mean that "it was necessary to go back to the first origins" of Peruvian civilization and from there to "descend the torrent of the centuries so as to contemplate national development." It was the historian's philosophical and poetic task to organize and write this descent from origins in a clear and orderly fashion, "without jumping around" or "confusing the epochs."[58]

The Epochal Structure of Peruvian History

The principal divisions of Universal History as it was written in Europe in Lorente's time corresponded to the four major "epochs" of the Old World (ancient, medieval, modern, contemporary). But these epochs differed in the New World. For Lorente, ancient history in the Old World "extends from the origin of peoples to the dissolution of Roman society" and it has "three divisions": Oriental, Greek, and Roman. In contrast, "ancient history" in the New World runs right up to "conquest" in the early sixteenth century. In Europe, "medieval history" (*historia media* or *historia de la Edad Media*) concerns events from the end of ancient history to the discovery of America by Spain. Notably, America has no "Middle Ages." In both the Old and New Worlds, however, "modern history" runs from "this transcendental discovery [of America by the Spanish] to the French revolution." Finally, world "contemporary history" extends "from that great revolution down to our day."[59] In sum, for Lorente Universal History begins in the Orient and runs through Rome, but it is Spain—for she made that "transcendental discovery" that ushered in modern world history—that initiates the "Modern Age" (*la Edad Moderna*), and it is France with her revolution that sounds the music of the "Contemporary Age" (*la Edad Contemporánea*) of the people. This contemporary age meant the "death of colonialism and the King." This career of world history differs notably from the standard northwestern European and Anglo American "rise of the West" narrative, which, as Thomas Abercrombie has pointed out, usually "bypasses Iberia in its march from Mesopotamia to Greece, Jerusalem, Rome, and from Paris to London and New York."[60] In Lorente's narrative of world history, modernity is Spanish and American first, and there is a crucial distinction between the "modern" and the "contemporary." The contemporary is born of the "age of revolutions," while modernity is the product of colonialism.

Lorente periodized Peruvian history in evolutionary fashion, as is evident in his *Historia del Perú compendiada*. Here Lorente notes that the history of Peru may be distributed in six epochs, as follows: Epoch of Chiefs, Epoch of the Incas, Epoch of the Conquest, Epoch of the Viceroyalty, Epoch of Emancipation, and Epoch of the Republic. But he further reasons that the epochs of conquest and emancipation were not really epochs but instead "momentary and rapid epic campaigns" (*epopeyas rápidas y momentáneas*), brief but providential political events that initiated new epochs, such that "Peruvian civilization should be considered in four phases: primitive, Incan, colonial, and contemporary."[61] A third major epic event derived, albeit with notable modifications, from the dynastic narrative of Inca Garcilaso de la Vega's *Comentarios reales* is also evident in Lorente's epochal emplotment. This "epic campaign" was the founding civilizing gesture of the mysterious Inca culture-hero Manco Capac. For Lorente, this "epic campaign" marked the passage from "primitive civilization" under local chiefs (*la Época de los Curacas*) to the "civilization of Peru under the Incas." Inca Garcilaso had recognized a primitive stage of incipient civilization under the *kuracas* or local ethnic chiefs, but, as we saw in chapter 2, his Cuzco-centric dynastic history necessarily underplayed the significance of pre-Inca culture since his providential narrative required a founder king (Manco Capac) who brought civilization to barbarians. In contrast, for Lorente Manco is not a founder king but instead an "enlightened reformer" imbued with "national spirit" who "in his native wisdom knew how to amalgamate all those elements of civilization that already existed in Peru."[62] Manco Capac was thus a mirror of Lorente the historian, who now likewise "harmonized" all those "elements of civilization" in a unified philosophical history of Peru.

Lorente thus proposed the pre-Inca and sub-Inca existence of civilization "in Peru," and that is why he called it "Peruvian civilization" rather than "Inca civilization." Lorente's evolutionary view of "Peruvian civilization" as primitive and enduring was new, but his notion that Manco Capac was imbued with the "national spirit" or "genius" had been previously argued, as we saw in chapter 4, by Unanue.[63] Peru's ancient history then, like that of the Orient, exhibited two broad "phases" of civilization: the primitive or disperse and the centralized. Unlike Europe, Peru had no feudal "Middle Ages" however, so that "Peruvian civilization" passed directly from the "ancient phase" to the "colonial phase" of the "Modern Age" under Spain, which was then the "vanguard of Europe." At independence, for which she had been well prepared by history, Peru boldly entered the "Contemporary Age."

To write an "animated" narrative and philosophical history of the four evolutionary "phases" or "epochs" of "Peruvian civilization," Lorente had little choice but to turn to the "insufficiently severe" but poetically rich and politically deep Book of Kings or imperial dynastic history. It was a matter of uniting, under republican auspices, the various dynastic elements developed by previous historians of Peru, albeit now subject to "historical critique." In this sense Lorente's postcolonial historical discourse was necessarily "Peruvianized" by the imperial and colonial tradition that enveloped not only past writers, but present and future readers as well. Although Lorente was well read in the voluminous body of early colonial chronicles, official histories, and memoirs, the content of his narrative of the epochs of "Peruvian civilization" largely rested upon four foundational chronicles: Pedro Cieza de León's *Crónica del Perú* (1553); José de Acosta's *Historia natural y moral de las Indias* (1590); Inca Garcilaso de la Vega's two-part *Comentarios reales* (1609 and 1617); and Antonio de Herrera's *Historia general de los hechos de los castellanos en las islas y tierra firme del mar océano* (1601–1615). However, Lorente's history was no mere "neodynastic" annals in the style of Justo Apu Sahuaraura Inca.[64] Nor did it resemble the work of José María de Córdova y Urrutia.[65] Lorente did much more than merely assemble the dynastic structure of Peru's political history in an extended chain. He gave the received dynastic history of Peru a "preformist" or genetic narrative of the progressive, subdynastic permanence of its civilization, and he set it in the "historical geography" of the native land. Lorente's history was also *historia íntegra*, since his subject was the whole book of civilization. Cañizares-Esguerra notes that, in accordance with Renaissance and Baroque rules of evidence, the late-colonial historical discourse of Creole "patriotic epistemology" nearly always favored aristocratic native knowledge and the eyewitness accounts of wise nobles and was quick to de-authorize the vulgar opinions of native commoners. As a result, most late colonial historical writing was, despite its American patriotism, still laboring under the aristocratic structure and language of dynastic history. Although it necessarily incorporated elements of colonial patriotic epistemology, Lorente's republican history of civilization subtly displaced the royal subject and its language of history and country. What distinguishes Lorente's republican philosophy of history from that of most eighteenth-century Creole historians is the centrality of the enduring subject of "Peruvian civilization" *bajo* (under) this or that dynasty. In a word, Lorente produced the first narrative of Peruvian history "from below" or, more precisely, "from under." It was the "primitive civilization" in its "general movement" that captured Lorente's republican historical imagination and established the epochal thread of Peruvian history. In that movement, dynasts could be the political instruments of unity and order, and the organizing devices of memory and narrative. In the long evolutionary embrace of the "genetic" progress of the people's civilization, however, Hapsburg or Bourbon dynasts "from abroad" were imposing but ultimately passing figures who united or hindered its movement, but they were not its enduring and luminous "soul." "Under" those dynasties lay a long, spirited, and progressive history of "national development."

The Sun Also Rises in Peru

As was common among European philosophical historians from Leibniz to Voltaire and Hegel, Lorente regarded the "ancient history of the Orient" as being "of the highest interest" because that vast and populous region—defined as Asia, its archipelagos, and North Africa—was "the cradle of humanity and of civilization." Moreover, its study fully confirms "the great advantages of the historical perspective, that is, to compensate for our lack of experience and to guide us, via the great examples, to truth, beauty, and the good, and to quicken our desire to pursue all the principle branches of knowledge."[66] The ancient history of the Orient then was both a sublime teacher and a privileged object of contemplation, and for these reasons Lorente wrote a precise history of the ancient Orient for Peru's classrooms, titled *Compendio de la historia antigua de Oriente para los colegios del Perú* (1876).

The ancient history of the Orient is a "teacher" because it is the story of the forgetting of origins. In contrast, the dual history of the West and Christianity is one of remembering, and returning to, the purity of origins. "In the Orient," Lorente relates, "the family quickly degenerated from the pure primitive state to which it has been returned by Christianity." Moreover, the fall of the Orient from God's grace is confirmed by the modern disciplines of universal or world history, namely archaeology, ethnography, and philology. "Judging by the ancient names with which the first tribes designated mother and siblings, they had preserved the sanctified union of one man with one wife," writes Lorente. The "pure, primitive, and universal" practice of monogamy was eclipsed when polygamy was introduced under the despotic rule of patriarchs and expanding states, thereby "degrading the fairer sex" and "distancing the family from pure affections," producing a "fundamental degeneration of society."[67] The ultimate consequence of the Oriental "caste system" was that man's "original and universal fraternity" was "forgotten." Meanwhile, the upper classes, dominated by the "priestly caste," slid into "egoism." The "social injustice" of the caste system was a consequence of the false priest's predilection for idolatry. Among Oriental peoples only the Hebrews avoided this fatal mistake. Idolatry was also the cause of barbarous wars, and despotism was the consequence of idolatry. It was "sustained by the upper classes and authorized by false religions, and it strapped the peoples to the yoke so that they lost their sense of primitive liberty. As a result generations are born, they vegetate, and are then extinguished in eternal servitude. The dominant classes surround themselves in dazzling luxury; they rule by caprice, are the owners of lives and estates, and look on the miserable people as simple instruments of power and pleasure."[68] Nevertheless, Oriental civilization had at its disposal "powerful elements" of fraternity and unity that would serve as the basis for future progress, that is, the development of pure and universal origins, once the "obstacles" of despotism, idolatry, and caste were destroyed.

Any pocketsize history for schoolboys must make memorable generalizations. Still, Lorente's *Ancient History of the Orient for the Colleges of Peru* is not so far from the main lines of British and French Orientalist scholarship during this period.[69] Lorente's compact history offered Peruvian students the usual Christian equation: polygamy + idolatry + caste = despotism = historical immobility. The Orient offered the panorama of a "great and brilliant" civilization struggling to overcome "major obstacles" to her progress. Her "immobility" followed from the forgetting or eclipse of what the contemporary West and, more precisely, the epoch-founding French Revolution had recovered: "the solid bases of liberty, of fraternity, of religious truth, and of moral family." For Lorente "religious truth" and the "moral family" were the primitive foundations of "equality" among the sexes and the classes. Without these elements, the "mysterious and brilliant but fragile" civilization of the Orient would remain subject to tyranny, which would keep it from achieving the "sustained progress" that was otherwise its birthright.[70]

For Lorente the sun also rises in Peru, but its light is of another hue. To be sure, Lorente's narrative of the ancient Orient resembles his "history of ancient Peru." The history of Peruvian civilization is like that of the Orient, "mysterious, brilliant, and fragile," and it is marked both by "enviable splendors and unimaginable catastrophes." Like the Orient, Peru exhibits all the "civilizational elements of an indestructible progress" as long as she will "fully value liberty" and "follow the plan of Providence."[71] But what distinguishes Lorente's history of ancient Peruvian civilization is that it is both Occidentalist and Orientalist. *Historia antigua del Perú* was both derivative and foundational in this regard. It was derivative because it relied upon the established narratives of Peruvian dynastic history and the chronicle. It was foundational because it cast these received traditions in the new republican framework wherein the universal history of civilizations progressed under the providential guide of liberty and wherein the primitive and ancient "phases" of civilization were of critical importance to the unity, grandeur, and future progress of the contemporary nation.

Historia de la civilización peruana (1879) was Lorente's crowning achievement.[72] All but forgotten, this concise history anticipates by several decades many of the central concerns of twentieth-century Peruvian historical thought. The book's thesis is that the permanent element of ancient and modern Peruvian civilization is to be found in an enduring yet flexible "communal spirit." This Andean Volksgeist is previous to and more durable than the Inca state. Orchestrated on a grand scale and without violence by the "reformer" Manco Capac and the Inca dynasts that centralized his law, Peru's communal spirit had achieved what only ancient Greece had accomplished, albeit on the lesser scale of Sparta, and what contemporary communists never could since, in Lorente's view, large-scale communism had been relegated by history to the marginal status of a "dangerous utopia."[73] In ancient Peru, however, that utopia was historically real because it struck a balance between the "spirit of the Orient" and the "spirit of the Occident." In addition, what distinguished ancient Peruvian civilization both from the "more despotic" Oriental states and the extinct Western example of Sparta was the unusual intersection of the communal spirit of the villages and the "communist architecture" of the Inca state.

Why did this unique, East-West socialist concert of communal spirit and communist architecture fail to endure? Incan "socialism on a grand scale could not endure because it contradicted the more powerful sentiments of liberty, property, and family; thus it grew weaker and corrupt as it extended its domain, always exposed to any sudden blow, because its social hierarchy deposited the destiny of all in a single leader."[74] The problem was that the "interests of the *patria* were confused with that of authority."[75] It was the over-extended scale and excessively centralized monarchical structure of Incan socialism that condemned it to the republican dustbin of history. Lorente's "communal spirit" was thus to be distinguished from the "monarchy" and "communism" of the Incas. Here Lorente departs from the pessimistic views of such grand savants as Alexander von Humboldt and William Prescott, each of whom saw in Peru's indigenous past only fetters. In contrast, Lorente's hybrid Orientalist-Occidentalist narrative granted a deeper, more generous "spirit" to Peruvians, one which "was not an obstacle to progress." This was because, in Lorente's view, "Peruvian civilization" is previous to, more local, and more durable than the centralizing rule of Incan or Spanish dynasts. In short, local communities were the building blocks of the state in all epochs of Peruvian history.[76] This is why the communities of Peru survived long after the fall of the Inca dynasty and long after the ousting of the Spanish dynasty by those patriotic forces that had founded the Peruvian Republic.

Lorente thus gave Peruvian villagers a proper and ancient history "under" the rule of Incas that was highly readable and "contemporary." Peruvian schoolboys and literate persons now learned that "Peruvian civilization" was based on a primitive and enduring communal spirit that had animated the village life of "Peruvians" down to the present. Modern Peruvians now possessed an ancient history that augured well for the future. Moreover, the deep genealogical or epochal structure of Lorente's communal history of civilization and "national development" gave colonial dynastic history a good post-colonial death. Incas and kings of the past still stood as notable markers of the progress of civilization but they were no longer the central forces of history. The real currents of history were deeper. The ultimate source and resource of Peru's sovereignty as a state, and of her contemporaneity as a ancient civilization and a modern nation, lay not in the heroic rulers of the past nor in the ideas of foreigners but in the common people's enduring communal spirit.

Like Pedro de Peralta Barnuevo's Baroque notion, discussed in chapter 3, that history was a truer-than-life "copy" of the prince and his glorious lineage, Lorente's republican history of the soul now mirrored the people and its "national development" in evolutionary epochs. Here the mirror effect was clinched by the name of the people that is also the proper name of the *patria*, the *país*, and the Inca empire, for the name "Peruvian" now united in a "communal spirit" and a "national soul" the epochs of primitive, Inca, colonial, and republican Peru, in effect rendering them all "contemporary" in the minds of Peruvian readers. In a word, Lorente "Peruvianized" Peru. Fulfilling Juan Espinosa's republican charge for a new history, Peruvian history now began with primitive "spelling lessons" that made the words "Peruvian civilization" readable as a "practical" guide to a Peruvian future that, since the events of independence, already was "contemporary." This contemporary spelling lesson in Peruvian civilization was grounded in the communal spirit of native villagers. The contemplation of the broad cultural and political "harmonies" of Peruvian history were now within every literate citizen's grasp. In Lorente's hands the Book of Kings thus found a good postcolonial death as the means to an ancient future of liberty that had always already belonged to the Peruvian people.

6

Popular Sovereignty and the History of the Soul

> Today no one doubts that those who would propose solid bases for social doctrines, and who would lift themselves up to God, must depart from the phenomena of the soul.
>
> Sebastián Lorente, *Curso elemental de filosofía para los colegios del Perú: Sicología*

Was Peru ready for a republican independence? This most historicist of political questions gave occasion to spirited debate in postcolonial republican Peru. Here the "republican question" was raised in response both to domestic and European critics. These critics argued that the republic was foreign to Peruvian history, if not to modern history at large, and that an errant and ungovernable postcolonial Peru should return to the European breast of imperial monarchy and to the long arms of the Vatican or, failing that, follow the independent example of the neo-European constitutional monarchy of the empire of Brazil. Because any "return" to monarchy raised the specter of European rule, in Peru the "republican question" of the historical suitability or viability of the republican form of government was always a "postcolonial question." It is in part for this reason that "the national question" was raised in postcolonial Peru (and Mexico) decades before that question was articulated in Europe.[1] In this regard at least, postcolonial Latin American Creoles were true "pioneers" of the contemporary national historical imagination.[2] That the republican question should be a postcolonial-national question meant that the answers proffered to that question were usually historicist or historical, that they nearly always presupposed concepts or theories of sovereignty, civilization, and national development, and that they frequently harkened

back to the precolonial Incas or beyond. In short, and as Elías Palti has argued, here the national question was always political in postcolonial ways.[3]

What is significant about the various historical or historicist answers to
that repeating postcolonial political question, however, is not that they are
true or false, but that they preconfigure perceptions of what is possible and
what is timely. Thus, the historicist question of whether the Peruvian nation
was ready or "mature" enough to shoulder the responsibilities of the republican form of government, or to withstand the anarchic pressures of popular
democracy, easily shaded over into deeper questions about "the nature" of
Peru: Was Peru modern? Was Peru western? These questions, in turn, implied comparisons: Was Peru like France or England? Was the Inca state Oriental in origin or spirit? Was "the indigenous race" indolent and infantile,
and therefore incapable or not yet capable of exercising the "virtues" of patriotism and republican citizenship supposedly found, for example, among
Anglo America's yeoman pioneers, or France's peasantry? Looking ahead to
the next chapter, Peru's twentieth-century Hegelians would repeat the same
political question albeit in an updated historicist idiom: Was Peru's history
guided by a progressive capitalist spirit, or did a colonial "feudal spirit" still
reign? Or was it that, in an unfinished dialectical process, these competing
"spirits" struggled the one against the other? Or could it be that Peru was
governed, on a more profound level, by an "ancient communist law?" The
correct answer to these doctrinal questions would reveal whether or not Peru
was ready for socialist revolution. Notably, most of the historicist answers—
Peruvian or otherwise—to the question of Peru's political modernity—or, as
I prefer, Peru's political contemporaneity as a historical subject—have been
and continue to be negative. Indeed, historicist arguments to the effect that
Peru is not yet a democracy, that Peru is not yet a nation, or that Peru is not
yet modern remain commonplace today in nearly every sphere of Peruvian
discourse.

In this chapter I will nevertheless argue that Sebastián Lorente's postcolonial philosophical history of the Peruvian "soul" provided the political community of Peru with a positive and persuasive historicist narrative of its own
modernity and contemporaneity as a sovereign historical subject. In contrast
to the standard negative or "not yet" plots of most narratives of Peru then
and now, Lorente's account maintained that Peru was ready for the popular
sovereignty of the contemporary age of democratic revolutions not only because she was blessed with a primitive "communal" and "national spirit" that
had guided her progressively through "turbulent" epochs, but because "those

who would propose solid bases for social doctrines ... must depart from the phenomena of the soul." That is to say, Lorente's narrative discourse would confirm, both on historical and theoretical or philosophical grounds, that Peru was inherently ready to partake in the contemporary age of democracy.

Working within historicist concepts, Lorente's philosophical narrative of the soul is for the most part notably immune to today's postcolonial critique of historicism. According to this critique, the Enlightened historicist idea that singular entities unfold along universal lines of development in effect guarantees the subaltern position of "nascent" postcolonial polities, who always seem to come up short when compared to more "mature" European nations. Indeed, for Dipesh Chakrabarty this idea of "historicism ... came to non-European peoples in the nineteenth century as somebody's way of saying 'not yet' to somebody else."[4] Lorente's narrative suggests instead that historicist concepts such as "soul" and even "progress" could underwrite a discourse of colonial and postcolonial political modernity that ran contemporaneous and parallel rather than behind and subordinate to "Europe." Perhaps unfortunately, Lorente's critical achievement was lost on twentieth-century Peruvian professional historiography. In spite or perhaps because of that neglect, Lorente's underlying narrative or "figurative historicism" would leave a profound and lasting mark on Peruvian historical discourse.

Although Lorente was born and schooled in Spain, the significant thing about his histories is not only that they were—as we saw in chapter 5—inscribed in the collective Peruvian "we" but that, indeed, they contributed decisively to the temporal and democratic expansion of the horizons of that "we" across "the ages of Peruvian history." Most notably, Lorente's histories also squarely addressed Peruvian political concerns and debates, and they were written for and read by "enlightened" Peruvian citizens and schoolboys. Moreover, Lorente's philosophical approach to the history of "the phenomena of the soul" bridged diverse and sometimes mutually hostile positions in Peru's highly politicized nineteenth-century debates on the nature of the Inca past, the colonial regime, and the meaning of independence. Among these heated postcolonial debates on Peruvian history none were hotter than the ongoing polemics surrounding the republican "social doctrine" of popular sovereignty. The polemics around the doctrine of popular sovereignty went to the heart of all of the major competing historical narratives of Peru, and it was Lorente who provided the most cogent and persuasive solution.

These polemics were manifested in the press, the colleges, the national congress, the courts, and the church, and although the debate peaked in the 1840s the partisan exchanges among intellectuals spanned nearly a half-century of republican life, from the 1820s to the 1870s. Although many other authors could be cited, my summary or heuristic reading of the debates focuses on select writings of the more influential public intellectuals, officials, and clergy who framed their arguments in historical or historicist terms, including Benito Laso, Bartolomé Herrera, José Mariano de la Riva Agüero, Santiago Távara, Juan Espinosa, Francisco Paula Vigil, Carlos Lisson, and Félix Cipriano Zegarra. A review of the central concepts and arguments of their historical writings will allow us to place in relief the extent to which Lorente's philosophical historicism, at the heart of which lay a Leibnitian and Kantian appreciation of "the phenomena of the soul," embraced these contradictory positions in a higher synthesis that sought to transcend the aporia inherent to the concept of popular sovereignty.

History and the Semi-God

Benito Laso (1783–1862) was the voice of Simón Bolívar in Peru. It has even been suggested that Bolívar drafted Laso's famous 1826 *Exposition to Congress*. The *Exposition* is notable for its ontogenical vision of the nation and for its summary judgments of the Inca and Spanish heritages. It is clearly also a call for the Peruvian Congress to appoint Bolívar as President for Life.[5] A footnote suggests that Bolívar's just completed draft of the Bolivian Constitution be studied and adapted to Peru, since it "throws up dikes against ambition and anarchy, and reconciles political stability with the most ample enjoyment of national liberty."[6] The text represents, then, the historical vision of Bolivarian republicanism, that is, a patrician, postrevolutionary blueprint for the South American republics that emphasized a strong, military-political executive and a hereditary or pseudo-hereditary senate of enlightened elites, both of which were intended to "throw up dikes" against the extremist and divisive tendencies of a popularly elected congress of representatives and of a populace deemed to be prone to anarchy. There was much resistance to the proposal in Peru's Congress, and in the end Bolívar would respond to the call of his sinking, chaos-ridden Gran Colombia. Leaving Peru may have been Bolívar's biggest mistake, however, for once back in Colombia his enemies saw to it that his political capital and health rapidly dissipated. Deathly ill, the politically defeated Liberator of the Andes would at the dark end of his days reflect that making revolution in South America was akin to "ploughing the sea." Notwithstanding, the Peruvian Congress of 1826–28 ploughed ahead, adopting into law a number of Bolivarian proposals on property, citizenship, and taxation, and in general the Peruvian Constitution that emerged was more conservative and historicist than that of Peru's first Constitutional Congress (1822–23).[7] Bolívar had left his mark on the land, after all.

In the unapproving eyes of the Peruvian Bolivarians, the first Peruvian Congress had been dominated by the "theorists" and fiery orators of "the doctrine of popular sovereignty," among them Francisco Xavier de Luna Pizarro and José Sánchez Carrión. In contrast, the Bolivarians elaborated an early historicist or developmentalist critique of what they took to be the blind "theory of general maxims" of those fiery orators who, in their view, had conjured up republics in the Andes based on little more than their "exalted imaginations" and the thin air of "foreign doctrines." These doctrines might be "perfect" in theory but they were not suited to the societies of Spanish America, they argued. The Bolivarian critique of blind "theory" was informed by the pedagogical historicisms of Rousseau and Montesquieu, both of whom are frequently cited as authorities in their texts. In sober contrast to the exalted demagogues, Laso argued that the nation in its "epoch of political infancy" would require an enlightened and firm rule that could "protect liberty" and "guide the people" toward their destiny. The *Exposition* argued that

> Nations, like individuals, pass through all the stages of life, from cradle to grave. Weak in their infancy, active in their youth, vigorous in their virility, and rotten in old age, they can never alter nor advance the order in which they march toward their destiny. It would be impossible for an infant state to possess the activity and vigor of youth, or the maturity and prudence proper to states with constitutions sustained by centuries of custom that in themselves lend firm strength to its institutions. Thus, all those who propose to establish the form and legislation of a land will never succeed unless they adapt their plan to the precise epoch of her existence. In the same manner, poorly fitted clothes that are not cut in proportion to a man's figure are most ungraceful. It is from this perspective that Peru should be considered by those who are charged with fabricating the costume in which he will present himself and figure in the grand theater of the political world. If the clothes are too tight they will restrain his movements, if too long and baggy he will trip and fall in the precipices. These maxims should be kept in mind when we form our Constitution, lest we expose ourselves [to ridicule], retard our prosperity, or submit ourselves to the horrors of a damaging liberty.[8]

A footnote to this passage cites chapter 8 of Rousseau's *Social Contract*, adding that "just as the architect observes and surveys the soil to determine if it will support the weight, so too the wise legislator may not formulate good laws without first examining whether or not the people to whom they will be applied are capable of supporting them." Laso was of course a legislator, and later he would become a Supreme Court Justice. Faithful to the official definition of nation inscribed in the new Peruvian Constitution,[9] Laso equates "nation" (nación) and "Peru" with the new "political State" (Estado político). This political state was born on December 9, 1824—the date of the decisive Battle of Ayacucho and the capitulation of the Viceroy to Bolívar's Field Marshal, Antonio José de Sucre—and not July 28, 1821 since San Martín's declaration of independence was precarious and limited to Lima and because San Martín himself apparently harbored suspicious, possibly constitutional monarchist sympathies. In contrast, Bolívar was the true founder of Peru because he was the uncompromising "enemy of the name of kings," the "angel of the regime of representation," and thus the first author of the "political state" or "nation" of "free Peruvians." Given this new 1824 birth date, Peru was the latest of the new American republics to join "the great revolution of the New World." In its fragile, two-year-old infancy, Peru on its own could do little more than "cry like a baby about past misfortunes" and "feel his own present weakness." This babe needed a strong, guiding hand for that "dangerous march" ahead toward "perfection," and that hand was Bolívar's.[10]

Peru's "pre-political" history, that is, Peru before December 9, 1824, was characterized by a colonial "diversity of castes" diagnostic of "a species of gangrene that augured dissolution" unless urgent measures were taken to "neutralize the ignorant and gross ideas of some, the false knowledge of others, and the conflicts of interest among all."[11] Notably, Laso's summary of the "blind and apathetic submission" of the "indigenous caste" placed emphasis on the legacy of a "theocratic" Inca rule. His was a historicist critique aimed at the delusions of exalted pedants and "theorists" who, blaming Spanish colonial rule for all of Peru's problems, had imagined in 1821 "that Indians had the necessary virtues and wits to be republicans!" Under the "theocratic" Incas, Laso explained, the "indigenous caste was the most innocent race that the world has ever seen," whence it "acquired that blind and apathetic submission that has been, and for a very long time will continue to be, fatal for the progress of their civilization." Here Laso followed the summary judgments of Alexander von Humboldt (see chapter 4) but he also anticipated by two decades the prejudices of the Anglo American historian William Prescott, who in his History of the Conquest of Peru (1847) would depict the Inca state as a totalitarian despotism that had smothered the "individual energies of progress." For Laso, Spain's "colonial domination" had only made things worse. Spain had "annihilated the instinct, common even among savages, to preserve the dignity of the species." Following Montesquieu, Laso distinguished "between the passive virtues cultivated by . . . theocratic and despotic states, and the active virtues that are the soul of a democratic regime." Theocratic and despotic regimes were based on "obedience, respect, or fear." The "republican system," on the other hand, required the active virtues of "national love, public spirit, the normative desire for equality, dedication to work" and "in short that deep reservoir of virtues that is called patriotism."[12] Was it possible to "suddenly uproot the common ignorance of our peoples, and form among them virtues, such that they could immediately receive without setbacks the laws of a republican state" and thus magically make of them virtuous republican citizens?

> That would be the greatest of miracles . . . History shows how long the road of civilization is . . . Savages in a state of nature, barbarous and sometimes ferocious in their first civil associations, and weak and volatile when they receive a few rays of wisdom must, to call themselves civilized, pass through thousands of years of criminal errors and sufferings. If a few nations have made rapid leaps of progress it is because of a few men of heroic genius, or the extraordinary circumstances that gave rise to them. Katherine and Peter the Great are the only ones who could give Russia the impulse it needed in the career of civilization; only semi-gods may work in such marvelous ways.[13]

For Laso and the Bolivarians, San Martín's newly baptized "Peruvians" (that is, the "ex-Indians") were completely unaware of the true meaning of their name. They now cheered "the Patria" rather than "King Ferdinand," but that was all: a simple substitution of names. "National spirit is unknown among our people." Given their historical passivity and ignorance, "Peruvians" were unmoved by "the name of citizen" and they had no idea what "popular sovereignty" meant because they could not grasp the scope of "such an extraordinary metamorphosis."[14] The Bolivarians thus recycled the old colonial discourse, founded, as we saw in chapter 2, on Inca Garcilaso de la Vega's history, that asserted the "certified simplicity" of Indians, and their call for lifelong presidencies and hereditary senates recalled elements of imperial dynastic history. In short, Peru needed a great man or "semi-god" of history to guarantee and oversee "such an extraordinary metamorphosis," and Bolívar was that semi-god. Still, even Bolívar could not make this miracle happen in a single stroke. Only "History" could do it, and this is perhaps why in Bolívar's constitution for Bolivia—now proposed for Peru—the President-for-Life (the Liberator intended this post for his Field Marshall Sucre) was a "Prince without a Head." As Peralta had anticipated nearly a century before, as a "Copy" and simulacrum of the Prince, "History" was at least in theory the true legislating "Head" of the nation (see chapter 3); in Bolívar's constitutional vision, the legislating, historically-minded "Head" would reside not in the princely president but in a hereditary senate of enlightened patriots modeled after ancient Greece and resembling, with certain necessary modifications, the British House of Lords. Laso declared that

> it was not our task to violate the epoch of [our native people's] enlightenment, because that will be the fruit of indirect, wise and prudent measures which, by steps, will diffuse the prerequisite social knowledges, thereby awakening among them those noble passions that are the wellsprings of civic virtues. Meanwhile, and without compromising the nature of the state, it is the task of our legislators to indicate, with circumspection, the means by which to prepare their advancement, and so elevate the natives to the same rank as cultured men, so that they may exercise with utility the functions of citizenship.[15]

Thus, for Laso, the epochal "not yet" of a proper historicist reading, in this case modeled after Montesquieu, provided the most apt mode of reasoning in which to judge whether or not Peruvians were ready for the "extraordinary metamorphosis" that republican self-rule implied. In contrast, the "exalted theorists" did not "study impartially and with care the homemade history book of our own country."[16] It would take a long time to turn Indians into republican citizens. Still, the "indirect" means for achieving that historical readiness might very well be found in Bolívar's draft constitution for the new state of Bolivia. Moreover, Laso, as representative of the border province of Puno in southern highland Peru, wished to see Bolivia (the former Upper Peru) reunited with Peru, and Bolívar was the means to that reunification.

History and God

The sermon by Curate Bartolomé Herrera (1808–1864), delivered in Lima on the twenty-fifth anniversary of San Martín's Declaration of Independence and subsequently revised and expanded for publication, stimulated a heated round of debate on popular sovereignty and history in independent Peru.[17] Herrera was appointed director of the National Library in 1839 and a decade later was elected to Congress as representative (*diputado*) for Lima. He taught at Colegio de San Carlos and the University of San Marcos, and in 1851 became Peru's director general of education under President José Rufino

Echenique. In the 1860s he was appointed bishop of Arequipa. Twenty years after the *Exposition,* Herrera's principle opponent in this debate was still Benito Laso, now a Supreme Court justice. In the 1850s, Bartolomé Herrera's new rival would be the congressman and educator Pedro Gálvez, a comrade-in-arms of Sebastián Lorente and Lorente's successor as director of Colegio Guadalupe. But Herrera now took center stage, in part because after 25 years of "political life" Peru's founding republicans did not have much to show for their efforts. Herrera's preamble to his sermon set the tone:

> Thanks be to God that after so many calamities He concedes to us this 25th anniversary of our political life! *Severely has He castigated us; but He has not delivered us onto death* (Psalm 117, verse 18). Although those punishments, this tormenting convulsion, and these harsh pains that Peru has suffered since it proclaimed its independence—which God may not express in his sublime idiom, but without which he to whom that idiom is directed may feel the anguish of destruction and the vertigo of falling into nothingness—are actually the work of our own perennial imprudence. . . . The ruin of nations, like that of individuals, is of their own making. The work of God is to see to their welfare. . . . Any government that claims to have its origin in law and to live by and for that law procures to slowly repair the ravages of the past. That law and a soil richer and more blessed by God than that of Canaan are the gifts of the Lord, in the midst of which we come to adore Him as the author of our political existence. . . . What, oh Lord, would you have me say in Your Name to this people?

Bartolomé Herrera's twenty-fifth anniversary sermon was more than the ideological confession of an "authoritarian reactionary" (as Jorge Basadre would characterize him 100 years later) who rejected the new doctrine of popular sovereignty. His discourse was a civilizing, historicist critique of the naturalist and Incanist "patriotism of soil" that characterized late colonial and early republican discourse, and in certain ways it actually anticipates Basadre's own historicist vision of Peru. Indeed, Basadre would half-recognize this fact when he noted that the only thing that he could agree with in Herrera's otherwise reactionary sermon was his "integral Peruvianness" (*peruanidad integral*).[18] What Basadre did not say is that this "only thing" was in fact the main thing. As in Lorente, the erudite preacher's discourse strongly resembled that of Vico's *New Science*, in which the arts of civilization follow universal laws of development and the history of Christianity is consonant with the world history of civilization.

By "tilling the land" and adopting God's universal civil laws, Herrera's precolonial Incas had "prepared the soil" to receive Jesus Christ's "grain" of Truth, and it was Columbus who had carried that "grain" or "seed" to the New World:

> Given their isolation, the Empire of the Inca dynasts—who God sent to unite and prepare these peoples so that they could receive the high doctrine of Jesus—had achieved the highest possible stage of prosperity and progress. The fundamental principles with which God has established the moral order of the world are found in [the Incas'] legislation. The land was plowed and disposed to receive the gospel. But how could the mysterious grain reach that soil? That was God's secret. The union of the kingdoms of Ferdinand and Isabella and the reconquest of Granada had formed a great power that, free of the Muslim shadow, beamed with the faith of Christ in all of its splendor, and whose power grew with each new day. Those Kings whose religious zeal had earned them the title of Catholic Monarchs were at the time the most propitious to carry the complete, that is to say Christian, civilization to the vassals of the Incas. Peru was thirsty for divine truth, and in Spain "the fountain of life" was brimming over. In Peru the seeds of a war of succession threatened to destroy the Empire.... Peru now needed its baptismal; Spain extended her vigorous arms and embraced peoples to offer to the Church.... A Columbus was lacking, and so God sent Columbus.... The valor and Catholicism of Spain were mobilized.... A fistful of brave men were sufficient to incorporate in the formidable Monarchy of Charles V the powerful kingdoms of America.... They destroyed the altars of the idols but left untouched the true Pachacamac, sovereign of the cult that had been disputed by vile creatures. They formed the new Peru, the *Spanish and Christian Peru* that we celebrate today.[19]

There is almost nothing in Bartolomé Herrera's sermon that may not be found in the writings of Inca Garcilaso de la Vega or Bartolomé de las Casas. What is new here is not the content but its repetition as a gesture of remembrance, which now serves as a critique of the republic. Herrera's critique consists, as it were, in reminding Peruvian Creoles that they had forgotten what their Spanish ancestors had so wishfully wanted to forget after conquest. Anticipating Ernest Renan's arguments by half a century, Herrera argued that the forgiving forgetting of conflict was the true basis of nationhood. In the case of Peru, that forgetting-based nationhood was carried forward by the "Spanish spirit." But republican Creoles had forgotten this spiritual fact and so they stupidly or deceitfully declared their new nation to be heir to the "Empire of the Incas." The independent Peruvian nation was not heir to the "Empire of the Incas" because that empire had been absorbed long ago by the "Spanish spirit." The "new Peru" forged under Spanish rule was based on sublime Catholic reason and a transcendental forgiving. Following Inca Garcilaso de la Vega, Herrera argued that the empire of the Incas had been brought down not by Spanish injustices but by Atahualpa's bloody tyranny and the good celestial offices of the Virgin Mary. Indeed, Spain's "conquest" of Peru was not a conquest at all but a divinely ordained "incorporation." In an extended footnote to the published version of the *Sermon*, Herrera exclaimed that "anyone with eyes will see that the Peru of today is not the Peru of the Incas." This state of affairs was so because miscegenation had created "an entirely new people" and because "the new social body was created by the Spaniards and is imbued with the Spanish spirit." All of this was so obvious "that it was not worth the effort of saying it." Nevertheless, it was now necessary, in a footnote, to remind "those who had forgotten it."[20]

And, yet, in this postcolonial context Bartolomé Herrera's historicist critique and admonishing reminder could undermine itself, for Herrera himself was guilty of condemning a fertile form of patriotic forgetting cultivated by his republican political enemies. To wit, Herrera's critique was inspired by the more immediate memory of the bloody Tupac Amaru II insurrection (1780–84). For Herrera and many of his Creole contemporaries, this insurrection had been a barbarous "race war" led by bloodthirsty and avenging modern "Incas" like Tupac Amaru, and it had made manifest the absurdity and anachronism of any political return to the "empire of the Incas." Herrera's sermon implied that Creole patriots had actively forgotten that they in fact were the sons of those same "Spaniards" who had fallen under the knife of Tupac Amaru's "Indian rabble." To declare independence in the name of the Incas was pure hypocrisy, and for a Peruvian Creole to identify himself as an "Indian" heir to the "Inca empire" was "truly insane."[21] Republican writers, however, had attempted to resignify the blood spilled by "the Inca's hordes" as patriotic martyrdom for the cause of independence. It was in fact this sublime, patriotic form of fertile forgetting that Herrera now attacked, and veteran republicans would, as we shall see, lash back in defense of their forgetting. Herrera sermonized:

> I'm not sure if it was a poetic movement, in which the nation was taken to be the soil, or if it was one of those truly insane ideas that were never lacking during the epoch of emancipation, but the fact is that the

independence of Peru and the reconquest of the Empire of the Incas
were proclaimed as one and the same thing. And many of these Peruvian Spaniards were so convinced of this that even today they remain
persuaded that they belong to the Empire of the Incas, that they are
Indians, and that the European Spaniards had conquered them, and
had visited great harm upon them. But the Indians were not in a state
in which they could take active and intelligent part in that revolution
[of independence]. And if they had been, they would have taken quite
positively and literally the absurd idea of recovering the independence
of the Empire of the Incas. . . . In the midst of their revolutionary fervor they would have included in their hate the Spaniards of any time
and any place, including Peruvian [Creoles], and indeed anything that
was not perfectly indigenous. Would Peru not have suffered the fate
that Tupac Amaru had prepared for her? The civilized men would have
perished at the hands of a ferocious savagery, and merrily the survivors would have been expulsed like the Moors of Spain, Christianity
would have disappeared and with it all the habits and culture that had
formed Spanish reason. Happily, the mental retardation of the majority
of Indians and the good sense of a few guerrilla leaders preserved the
[patriots] from this awkward error.[22]

Apart from the venom of "truly insane ideas," Herrera's *Sermon* correctly recognized the patriotic "poetic movement, in which the nation was taken to
be the soil." As we saw in chapters 4 and 5, this movement to entomb the
"genius" of the Incas in the soil of the "Country of the Incas" had enabled in
the realm of historical discourse the birth of the Peruvian Republic. It is also
notable that, for Herrera, what had saved Creole patriots from this grave error was the "mental retardation" of Indians. Ironically, for the Bolivarians this
same retardation would explain why most Indians had in fact supported the
Royalist cause. In short, early Bolivarian republicans like Laso and conservative defenders of divine sovereignty like Herrera enlisted a similar historicist
discourse that effectively kept Indians outside of the political sphere as the
unwitting pedagogical objects of laws and sermons. Moreover, the political
and ideological enemy of both was one and the same: the blind "theorists" of
popular sovereignty or "the men of 1821."

In yet another extended footnote that, in this case, appeared to contradict
the suggestion made in the sermon proper that Spain had not really "conquered" Peru, Herrera now argued that the most powerful nations ancient
and modern, including the Inca empire, were in fact the fruits of conquest.

Both the Inca and Spanish conquests were justified by "the opinion of their respective ages," since there had been "no problem in taking away the sovereignty of a government that blocked the moral and religious development of its subjects." Moreover, such conquests responded to the designs of Providence. Following Inca Garcilaso de la Vega, Herrera noted that in assuming sovereignty over Peru, Spain did little injury to the Incas. Huascar, the prince regent, was killed by his bastard brother and usurper Atahualpa, who had no right to rule.

Although he dismissed the concept in the sermon, Herrera summoned the notion of "conquest" in this footnote because he had a contemporary political agenda to forward. The footnotes are clearly addressed to the lettered republican elite, and this one was directly aimed at the current policy debate over what to do with the vast lowland frontier of Amazonia that lay to the east of the Andes, where, since independence, Spanish colonial missions had been abandoned and "savages ran wild." Peru, argued Herrera, should have no scruples about conquering these savages of the Peruvian jungle, thereby civilizing them and aggrandizing the nation. "It would be out of the natural order of things if a civilized man, strong and truth-loving, should stand before a savage with his arms crossed without feeling the impulse to dominate him and enlighten him." Moreover, "this instinct of domination and proselytism, just and to a certain extent necessary, serves the designs of Providence. . . . This is something that will never be understood as long as we remain slaves to the errors left to us by the men of 1821."[23] Those slavish errors of independence should be corrected by the lessons of history, and these in turn should be applied to the nation's own frontiers.

As noted, in the text of the sermon Herrera argued that Peru had not been "conquered" and that, contrary to the discourse of the republicans (and here he included Bolivarians like Laso), Spanish rule was not a "tyranny." Rather, the rule of the Spanish monarchy in Peru was a legitimate "incorporation" that had been "spontaneously" accepted and approved for 300 years "by all the towns and villages [pueblos] of Peru." The "men of 1821" had propagated the lie that they had been "conquered" illegitimately and then rapaciously exploited and degraded by "tyranny," when in reality they owed everything to Spain including the "Patria" named Peru. The republican patriot thesis that Spanish rule was an "usurpation" of the "Empire of the Incas," based on the notion that conquest was illegitimate (Pizarro's execution of Inca Atahualpa was, in this view, regicide) was an absurdity that if fomented could lead to anarchy and the dismemberment of the Peruvian Republic. By this twisted patriot logic, argued Herrera, "Peru" itself would be nothing but a "usurpation," for "to destroy every usurpation they should have [had to] establish independent republics in [the Peruvian provinces of] Chimú, another in Lima, another in Cañete, etc." In short, "Peru" was only sovereign because Spain had made it so, and Spain was merely carrying out its role in the design of Divine Providence.

Herrera's argument was in some ways similar to that advanced by his more well-known Mexican contemporary, the historian and statesman Lucas Alamán. This argument was persuasive given the still precarious nature of the new postcolonial republics of Spanish America and the lingering appeal of the notions of divine sovereignty, monarchy, and church dominion.[24] It should not be surprising, then, that Herrera's historicist critique from the pulpit raised the "national question" in Peru at about the same time that, as Elías Palti notes, Alamán did in Mexico, and fully 40 years before Ernest Renan in France and two decades before Lord Acton in England.[25] In the old viceregal centers of Spanish empire in the Americas, history's "national question" was raised first in part because "ancient" precolonial and modern colonial histories were subject to diverse and polemical interpretation, and in part because these interpretations had profound political consequences for the definition of the new nation and state, its political form, and the nature of its sovereignty.[26] For these reasons, postcolonial Spanish America's conservative "spiritual" critics of republican nationalism and popular sovereignty were well "ahead" of their European counterparts.

In effect, Herrera's sermon proceeded to reject each and every Creole republican argument to the effect that Spanish rule had been a tyranny. Peruvians, Herrera noted, had spontaneously obeyed and affirmed the Spanish monarchy. Spain's mercantilist system was also not tyranny but simply "error" since the same policy had been applied to the metropolis as to the colonies. Indeed, the monarchy was uniform in this regard, and Peru was not really a "colony" at all.[27] For confirmation of his thesis that Peru was not a colony, Herrera shrewdly cited the prestigious authority of Alexander von Humboldt (who was also much admired by Bolívar and the Bolivarian republicans): "the Kings of Spain have considered these distant possessions to be integral parts of the monarchy and provinces of Castile rather than colonies, in the sense that, since the fifteenth century, the commercial countries of Europe have assigned to that term." Herrera also rejected the republican refrain that Spain had tyrannized the American mind with an "inquisitorial" and backward rule. Was it not true, he asked, that Spain had "founded all of our universities?" Nor did the Creole republicans have any right to argue that Spain had tyrannized the Indians, for "they themselves have killed, robbed, and dispossessed

Indians with impunity, and then they call themselves their Liberators; meanwhile, they accuse the [Spanish] government of tyranny [when in fact that government] had surrounded Indians with special privileges and rights not enjoyed by any other of her subjects."

The central problem as Herrera saw it, then, was not Spanish rule or Peruvian independence per se but rather that Peruvian republicans had been "captivated by the ruinous preoccupations and impious and anti-social errors spread by the French Revolution, that is, [by] the horrible impiety of that devil of the eighteenth century, I mean to say Voltaire, and the silly idea [of popular sovereignty] that escaped the wasted talent of Rousseau." Herrera then made his point clear: "that sovereignty comes from God is a Catholic dogma. That other sovereignty that does not come from God but from the People is a heresy that should horrify people of faith."[28]

This was too much. The enraged responses of "good republicans and American patriots" crowded Lima's newspapers, and they brandished Bartolomé Herrera as an absolutist and a traitor who, they cried, secretly supported a monarchist conspiracy. Herrera calmly denied the attacks. His position was actually constitutionalist, that is, not in direct contradiction with the independent form of government or representation, only with its theoretical basis. In Herrera's view, kingly absolutism was also heretical since it usurped God's sovereignty. Indeed, the bookish curate was simply making an explicit, Catholic argument for what in effect was already the practice in republican Peru: constitutional rule by the enlightened elite, frequently interrupted by military dictators who acted like "little princes." In this regard, Herrera and the Bolivarians, constitutional authoritarians and historicists both, may be seen to differ only by degree and not in kind. Both sides sought the rule of wise patricians and strongmen albeit from distinct theoretical bases. Herrera's remarks were aimed mostly at the same radical republicans or "pure theorists" of Peru's generation of independence—Monteagudo, Luna Pizarro, Sánchez Carrión—that Laso had attacked. His "dogmatic" argument thus dovetailed with the historicist argument of the Bolivarians in that it identified the devil of independent Peru as "foreign influences" and "French doctrine."

Laso, of course, defended the concept of popular sovereignty, but in many ways the debate was academic since popular suffrage was at the time denied to the vast, illiterate majority of adult males in Peru. A decade later, however, that circumstance would change as the Liberal Revolution of 1854, led by, among others, Juan Espinoza, Pedro Gálvez, and Sebastián Lorente, made a serious effort to widen civic participation by delivering on the "promise" of Peru's first republican constitution. Tellingly, in the newspaper and university-staged debates on popular sovereignty that followed the delivery of Herrera's sermon no one seriously questioned his "integral vision of Peruvian history." Soon after the debate Herrera rightly concluded that his position had been vindicated. The crux of the problem for Herrera was that the doctrine of popular sovereignty "openly contradicts the right of freedom" as it was understood in Catholic doctrine, and this right was unshakeable. As we shall see, it would be Lorente's task to reconcile, in a unified philosophical history of Peru, Catholic notions of freedom with the revolutionary republican doctrine of popular sovereignty.

Postcolonial Inopia

Among the conservative historicist critiques of popular sovereignty, Pruvonena's *Memoirs and Documents for the History of the Independence of Peru, and the Causes of its Bad Result* (1858) was something of a lightning rod as well. The pen name of "Pruvonena" belonged to José Mariano de la Riva Agüero y Sánchez Boquete, Peru's first president. Riva Agüero was a patriotic aristocrat whose fall from political grace was as hard and sudden as his rise. He was appointed prefect of Lima by San Martín and as such was entrusted with the defense of the province surrounding the capital city. When San Martín left Lima to confer with Bolívar in Guayaquil, however, Riva Agüero was proclaimed president following a conservative revolt led by Andrés de Santa Cruz against the "radical" Peruvian Congress. Loyalist forces drove Riva Agüero out of Lima to the port of Callao, where he parlayed with the viceroy. When Bolívar's field marshal Antonio José de Sucre arrived in Lima with his forces, Riva Agüero was captured and tried for treason, and then sent into exile in Chile. Riva Agüero made a comeback in 1838 (once again under the sword of Santa Cruz), becoming president for a second time, only now of the short-lived "North Peruvian State" (*Estado Norperuano*), which included Lima, of the tri-state Peru-Bolivia Confederation (1835–39).

Notably, Riva Agüero's personal vindication or apology places the blame for all of Peru's postcolonial woes on the "Jacobinism" and history-blind "theory" of his political enemies. Strangely perhaps, he includes San Martín, Bolívar, Agustín Gamarra, and other supposed "anarchists" in this enemy group, all of whom are accused of imposing a "foreign system" (that is, "democracy" and "the republic") that Peru was not prepared for. The horrifying "bad result" of this democratic and republican imposition was anarchy, plunder, misery and, finally, "inopia." As "we have seen in our days" in the case of France's First Republic, observes Pruvonena, in kingless Peru "the peoples groan under a multitude of despots." Those few "virtuous citizens" who had sacrificed most for the revolution of independence (Riva Agüero himself is chief among them) were the most abused and ungratified. Politically defeated, he now wrote for posterity, for only history's "true and durable fame" could right the injustices of the moment and, in time, clear his name.

Pruvonena's historical arguments are strikingly similar to those wielded by Benito Laso in his defense of Bolívar and indeed are inspired by many of the same historical thinkers: Montesquieu, Voltaire, and Tacitus. "Democracy" required "virtuous citizens" and Solon's law, but both were lacking in Peru (if Solon's law had been applied in Peru, San Martín and all the other "bad-mannered drunks" would have been executed!). The other problem was the popular press: In ancient Athens this vile tool of demagogues and "ochlocracy" (mob rule) was unknown. But the worse thing was the "disastrous example of the theories of popular governments" which

> in Peru had been more prejudicial than *cólera morbus* [Asiatic cholera] since these [theories] are not of a limited duration like [normal] cholera but instead are characterized by perpetual attacks that wreak havoc. These [attacks] increase in proportion to the doses of order that are applied against the disorder of ochlocracy, which destroys and confuses everything. If in Europe these theories have produced such bad results how much worse are these results here in a Peru populated by slaves, a diversity of castes, and idiots.[29]

The "bad result" of Peru's republican independence was an anarchic state of clueless confusion and destruction, wrought by a handful of drunken radicals and adventurers, and born of the foreign theory or "cholera" of popular sovereignty. The patriotic nobles of Lima had been brutally swept aside by these foreign adventurers and theories, and as a result Peru's independence degenerated into postcolonial inopia. Although Riva Agüero's historicist critique of "mob rule" and popular sovereignty was surely less palatable than Herrera's, it did nevertheless score some points. The foreign invaders—men like Monteagudo, San Martin, or Bolívar, and the radical theories they supposedly brought with them—and the idiotic and mixed-race mobs that followed them had destroyed the true aristocracy and social order that Peru needed to achieve a prosperous and dignified national independence. Once again, conservative historicists raised the national question in antirepublican, postcolonial ways: The independent nation was stillborn because popular sovereignty was foreign to Peru's historical nature and so could produce only inopia.

As we shall see, Lorente's historicist narrative of Peru's soul would respond to this antidemocratic complaint in decisive ways. However, first it was necessary that the Old Guard republicans of the revolution of independence respond to their conservative critics.

Old Guard Republicans Remember

Although not published until the 1850s and 1860s, the more notable writings of the revolutionary veterans Juan Espinosa (1807–1871), Santiago Távara (1790–1874), and Francisco Paula Vigil (1792–1875) represented the retrospective, historical voice of the founding generation of revolutionary republicans in Peru. Their partisan historical writings are characterized by dark or Black Legend views of Spanish rule as colonial despotism or tyranny, and they often depict the precolonial Inca order in more favorable if not utopian terms. They defended the triumphs and achievements of the republican revolution and the founding political principles of popular sovereignty and patriotism. Nevertheless, it was the polemical occasion of Herrera's critique that stimulated this writing, and as such these pieces are retrospective defenses of the revolution, not "expositions." These defenses were now buoyed by the achievements of the Revolution of 1854. In a word, that revolution provided the historical ammunition these old veterans needed to fire back at Herrera.

Juan Espinosa had first responded to Herrera prior to the revolution when in 1852 he published a collection of articles under the title *La herencia española de los americanos* (The Spanish Legacy of the Americans). Espinosa lamented the sorry state of the Peruvian Republic, which, as he saw it, was still wholly dependent on foreign powers and economies "because we don't know how to make anything." Because of the sorry "heritage" of Spanish misrule, "our industry is so retarded . . . that the typeset of this book . . . and the paper on which I wrote the original manuscript, and even the pen, are all imported!" exclaimed Espinosa. And now "conservatives" like Herrera celebrated "the Spanish heritage" and dreamed of bringing back the rule of Spain! What, Espinosa asked, was this "great heritage" that Peruvians had received from the Spaniards? It amounted to nothing more than "slothfulness, error, and brainless pride," as well as "the vanity of adorning oneself with lace and feathers, insignia and condecorations, which are most abundant among those with the least merit." The origins of "bad government" in America were to be found in Spain, the "most poorly governed country" in the world.

Espinosa's views would mature, however, with the advent of the Revolution of 1854, in which he played a notable role. This revolution would assume its place in the history books by declaring the abolition of "Negro" slavery and of the "tribute" paid by Indians. For Espinosa and Távara, this second revolution represented the chance to deliver on the unkept "promise" of the first. In his remarkable *Diccionario para el pueblo* (1855), Espinosa wages a prolonged war of words.[30] Citizens must now "arm themselves with a new lexicon" so that they might seize their role in history, he argues. Only in this way can the "promise" of independence truly bear fruit. Like Monteagudo, Espinosa will purge the old words or redefine them "for the People." In the *Dictionary*, Espinosa writes that the concept of *conquista* (conquest) that Spain used to legitimate its rule in America is no longer acceptable, since "commonsense and philosophy had condemned it" to death. The day will come, Espinosa prophesizes, "when the grand Conquistador will appear to be little more than a big bandit or thief." And what, Espinosa asks, is "conquest" anyway? It is nothing more than "robbing native sons of dominion over their own soil, and with it their national liberty," not to mention their "harvests, goods, and progeny." And no matter "how much philosophy and religion have civilized the Conquerors"—in a reference to the contemporary English and the French, Espinosa grants that the conquerors of his day are "no longer so despotic and brutish as they were in Antiquity or the Middle Ages"—they "will never cease being bandits who seek to usurp the goods of others. No matter how they try to dress up conquest, it will always be an abominable usurpation."[31]

Notably, however, Espinosa's republican attack on Spanish "conquest" is not a blanket condemnation of colonialism, which he takes pains to distinguish from conquest. In his entry under *colonias* (colonies), Espinosa reasons that "strong nations with superabundant populations, for example England and France, and who possess maritime power," can and should establish colonies outside their territory. Such colonies are "founded voluntarily by those who seek in them to better their social situation, stimulated by the establishment of property that is free or acquired at low cost." These legitimate settler colonies "take possession of uninhabited lands, either to establish factories or to find a place for criminals who should be separated from the breast of society." Espinosa's distinction between bad "conquest" and good "colonialism" was (and perhaps remains) typical of Latin American progressives. Similar views were held by many of Peru's leading twentieth-century thinkers, including Manuel González Prada, José Carlos Mariátegui, and Jorge Basadre, all of whom on this question followed the writings of the Cuban patriot and martyr José Martí. Martí held that the "pioneer" settler colonist in British North America had been just, virtuous, and progressive, while Spanish rule in the south had been unjust, despotic, and backward. Indeed, Karl Marx held this same position, albeit for different reasons. In short, for these thinkers, the "conquest" carried to America by Spain was bad because it was despotic and backward, while the "colonialism" of strong nations like England and France was good because it was carried out in "empty lands" and was liberating and progressive for the colonists and their home societies.

What had the Spaniards conquered, Espinosa asks? The "Peruvian was more civilized than his conquerors." The Peruvian Indian of Inca times was morally superior to the Spaniard, and his material achievements in "industry, botany, and engineering" are manifest "in the inimitable monuments that he has left to us," affirms Espinosa. With his medicinal and botanical knowledge, the Peruvian Indian "would have stunned the most learned Doctor of posh Oxford University."[32] The solar religion of the Peruvian Indian "was purer than that of the most fabled peoples." His was "more elevated and rational than the superstitious cults of the Egyptians and the Romans, the fantastic cults of the Greeks, the obscure beliefs of the Hindus and the Brahmins, and the sensual and materialistic cult of Mohammad." Those who "elevate their spirit to God in the presence of the spectacle of something so grand as the Sun are a much more rational people than those who worship a cow, a cat, or a stone idol . . . and more rational than the people who conquered her." The Peruvian Indian "was happy because, before ferocious men had corrupted his nature, and before the Old World's serpent of civilization had tempted his virginity and made him lose his paradise, he was good." The Incas "were not tyrants, but the fathers of their people." But, alas, the Indian of today had been degraded by Spanish despotism, and as a result he was now "more fanatic than the Spaniard about the religion of the crucified." Once again, the colonial discourse of the "certified simplicity" of the "miserable Indian" left its mark on republican rhetoric.

Espinosa now admitted that his archrival Herrera had been right. "American independence was initiated by proclaiming the restoration of the Empire of the Incas," he noted, and the defense of indigenous rights "was incessantly proclaimed"; indeed, "at every turn we invoked the names of Atahualpa, Montezuma, Manco Capac, and the rest, pretending that we—who, with our last names of Pizarro, Valdivia, or Cortés, had inherited their disdain for the indigenous race—were their descendents." These incessant proclamations of the campaign had been engraved in the national memory and were "made manifest in these verses, which we copy from a well-known song" of the period:

In his tomb the Inca stirs
In his bones an ardor revives as

He sees in his sons the renovation
Of the Patria's ancient splendor.

This song was precisely the one that was sung for the ceremonial entrance of Bolívar's effigy in Cuzco, which was literally carried to the tombs of Incas, as described in chapter 5. Nevertheless, "all of that now amounted to little more than the vilification of the noble sentiment of liberty, a mere pretext which, had it been the principle motive, should have been respected; but since it was made clear in subsequent manifestations that it was not, and was in fact a lie, it was a vile fraud to get the indigenous race to spill its blood for a liberty that it could not achieve on its own."[33] In short, Indians had not had their rights restored by independence but they were also incapable of winning those rights on their own. As a result, they are now "pariahs on their own soil." "We" taught them "to sing our cooked-up songs, in which the poor Peruvian Indian appears in the opening lines as lord of the land," but all he does is soak the soil with "blood and tears."

Why the sudden mea culpa? Herrera's claim that Peru's Creole republicans were not "Indians" or heirs to the "Inca empire" but instead the sons of Spanish conquistadors could now be admitted to be true, since in 1855 that admission served Espinosa as a rallying call to conscience and reform. That call was to make the democratic promise of republican independence a reality "for the oppressed indigenous race." If this promise were not fulfilled now, if the Indian was not liberated from his congenital oppressors by the revolutionaries, then he warned, "one day the Indians would produce a leader who would destroy the whites." Espinosa then turned satirical: "We" would of course win that battle by "killing thousands," and no doubt "the panegyric priests of conquest" would celebrate that too. "That," he added, "would be in keeping with our glorious origin in the Conquistadors." Tragically, Espinosa accurately predicted the future. In 1885 "thousands" of Indians were massacred in Ancash in the wake of the Atusparia Uprising, and the event was celebrated by conservatives in the opinion columns of Lima's newspapers, wherein that uprising was readily compared to Tupac Amaru's late-eighteenth-century "race war."[34]

Santiago Távara's *Historia de los partidos* (1862) appeared in serial form in the columns of Lima's leading liberal newspaper, *El Comercio*. Távara's historicist arguments reveal that, at least in retrospect, the founding republicans saw their mission as a progressive, democratic, and inclusive project that would redeem all of Peru's "races" in a multi-class alliance against "the King" and for

"Liberty." The enemies of that emancipatory project were rancid "aristocrats," foreign and reactionary "whites," "the King," and "the past."

In his *Historia de los partidos*, Távara outlined and defended the "two great problems" or challenges faced by the Revolution of Independence of 1821–24. The first involved "the political problem of expelling foreign authorities appointed by a foreign monarch" and "placing conditions on those immigrants who, upon arrival on our shores, constituted themselves as lords by virtue of being white." To achieve these things, "all that was necessary was valor and constancy—virtues which abounded in the epoch of our emancipation." The second big problem or necessity, Távara went on, "was to renounce and destroy the past." This "enterprise" of renouncing and destroying the colonial past "was arduous; it was the desert of the Promised Land through which we had to wander in order to purify ourselves if we were to leave to our successors and to our patria the Ark of Liberty established and venerated in Zion."[35]

Against Herrera, Távara now argues that when the colonial regime collapsed at the Battle of Ayacucho (1824), there was nothing left worth preserving. "What should we have preserved of the colonial edifice? The whip for the blacks? The whip and the corvée for the Indians? The Inquisition for nuns and monks? For religion, little donkeys and silver pendants pinned on the saints? The banality of the courts? The embezzlement of public funds? The monopoly on industry, and the prohibitions and restrictions on commerce? The ignorance and oppression of the people?" But now, after so much wandering in the desert in search of the Promised Land, the emancipatory path of renouncing the past "is opposed by the rancid leftovers of the old regime." This reaction against patriotic republicanism "is of recent invention," and it is the sinister work of "those 'decent' white people called conservatives." The "banner" of these white reactionaries "had no name until Doctor Herrera, like a good priest, baptized it with the name of authority."[36]

Against these new "white conservatives" Távara defends the revolutionary republicans who, rejecting the aristocratic and monarchist pretensions of San Martín "but respecting the great man," took control of the Congress in 1822–23 and established the republic on the sound constitutional principle of popular sovereignty. Why did they not go along with San Martín's design to establish an independent Peru with the support of a patriotic, merit-based aristocracy? Because the so-called aristocracy of Lima consisted of nothing more than the "idle rich." These rancid little *señoritos* had no political experience and no merits. Peru's first president, José Mariano de la Riva Agüero, had failed miserably in his brief attempt to consolidate a regime based on

the renovation of Lima's colonial aristocracy. Here Távara cites the same observations made by Humboldt to the effect that true aristocrats were rare in
the colonial Americas and, in any case, had more often based their spurious
claims to nobility on the "color of their skin."[37] San Martín, notes Távara, had
searched in vain for a legitimate Inca heir (the Spaniards had taken care of
that by exterminating any claimants to the royal line after the Tupac Amaru
II insurrection in the 1780s), and so the general had turned to Europe in
search of a deserving monarch for independent Peru. Given the impasse of
the aristocrats, true republicans opted for a "democratic fusion" of "Indians,
Cholos, Blacks, Mulattos, Pardos, Whites, and Mestizos." Had the "theorists"
and representatives to the first Constitutional Congress not agreed to this
democratic fusion, Távara exclaimed, "they would have been expunged from
their seats" by the people.[38]

In response to the criticism (recall Laso and Herrera) that the founders of
the republic were mere "theorists" who had slavishly "imitated" the slogans
of the French Revolution, Távara now notes that there is nothing wrong with
imitating "a true idea, and communicating it to others," whence "society assumes control of it, uses it, and thereby bequeaths the idea to future generations." In any case, Távara writes, French books had been banned by the colonial regime. How could France have been the model of Peru's revolution? In
fact, the revolutionaries "imitated the examples of Greece and Rome, because
they knew no other literature."[39] In the end, however, the true inspiration for
the republican founding of popular sovereignty in Peru was not France or the
republics of the ancient world but "the blood" and "sacrifices of the people"
who had struggled for Peru's independence. For that sacrifice, the Peruvian
people "deserved the liberty that they sought for themselves." The "compensation" for this sacrifice was "the sincerity and reality of the promise" of liberty, whose "best guarantee" was the republic and democracy. Recalling that
struggle, Távara writes that the "people felt the torment of the whip, and out
of pain and instinct they hated the Government with that whip; he was called
the King; his antagonist was Democracy and the Republic. That was enough!
To arrive at this conclusion the people did not need complicated syllogisms,
nor studies of the revolutions of France."[40] Moreover, continues Távara, the
democratic republicans of 1822 had adhered to Bolívar's military dictatorship in 1823–24 only because "it was necessary to save the *patria*" and to seal
independence, for without Bolívar's Colombian army Peru surely would have
succumbed to "the King" yet again. However, once the *patria* was secured,
Peru's democrats rejected Bolívar's authoritarian pretensions (represented in

Congress by Benito Laso and others), thereby preserving for posterity the republican "promise of liberty."

As we shall see in the next chapter, Távara's democratic promise would become a key concept in Jorge Basadre's "Peruvian history of Peru." But in the near term it would be Sebastián Lorente who would write the long history of Peruvian civilization as the story of liberty and the people's "communal spirit." Unlike Távara's partisan history, however, Lorente's story of Peruvian liberty was not divisive and it was not just a "promise."

The critical republican response to Bartolomé Herrera's pulpit critique of popular sovereignty was by no means limited to secular figures. Numerous priests had actively participated in republican independence, including the future archbishop of Lima Francisco Xavier de Luna Pizarro, who had dominated the First Constitutional Congress of 1822–23, rallying the faithful to the people's cause of the republic. Francisco de Paula Gonzáles Vigil was a brilliant spokesman for the progressive Peruvian Catholic Church. A committed Lascasian who edited the works of that distinguished sixteenth-century Dominican defender of Indian rights Bartolomé de las Casas, Gonzáles Vigil led the nationalist movement to end the Peruvian Catholic Church's dependency on the Vatican. For him, republican patriotism meant a nation of families under a national church.

Gonzáles Vigil's *Catecismo patriótico para el uso de las escuelas municipales* (1859) consists of eight dialogues between a schoolboy and his mother and father. The appendix features entries on "patria" and "patriot" taken from the French *Encyclopedia*, and his little book closes with the lyrics to the Peruvian national anthem. In the first dialogue, the boy asks his mother what *patria* means. She responds: "The Patria is a great family or, rather, it is the sum of all the families of citizens within the territory of the Peruvian Nation." The second dialogue describes the nature of patriotic love, and the third provides "ancient examples of patriotism" drawn from the classical histories of Greece and Rome. Dialogues 4 through 6 explain the civic responsibilities and "reciprocal interests" or mutual benefits of patriotism for citizens. In the seventh dialogue, entitled "The Patria in Republic," the schoolboy wants to know the difference between "Patria under Monarchy" and "Patria in Republic." His father responds that in the republic only those inequalities "created by nature and law" are recognized; all others are rejected as false and superfluous. In modern republics, property is not hereditary but alienable so that "the scandal of men living in luxury and superficiality while other men have no bread with which to feed their children" is unknown. "The republican is

content with a good harvest," nothing more. In the eighth dialogue the boy's
wise republican mother speaks of "America and Humankind." Here the good
mother counsels her son that "the Patria unites us with the rest of the American states, called 'Patria' by their respective inhabitants, and which together
compose America." Moreover, "a large portion of America cannot help but
be especially beloved since it once and for a long time formed a single nation,
and still conserves many bonds that unite us, which should grow stronger:
the same language, the same religion, the same defects, virtues, and customs."
This old nation was, of course, colonial Spanish America. Finally, "my son,
there is one thing that is greater and more admirable than the Patria and
America: Humankind. . . . First comes man then the citizen."[41]

Gonzáles Vigil's *Opúsculos sociales y políticos, dedicados a la juventud americana*
(1862) consists of a series of vibrant defenses of the American republics and
the concept of popular sovereignty. He is driven by a sense of urgency before
posterity. The history of the American republics was being written by her
enemies (among them, Herrera and Riva Agüero), he notes. It was time for
veteran republicans to write their memoirs and set the record straight. He
slams Herrera's sermon as a restorationist defense of the "antique opinion of
Divine Right." The "teachings" of Herrera and his colleagues were "disloyal"
and "anti-republican"; Herrera's sermon, which "threw popular sovereignty
into the dust" and "glorified the Spanish conquistadors," was scandalously
"anti-patriotic," particularly since it was delivered, "from the pulpit," on the
silver anniversary of independence. This unpatriotic conduct should be "corrected" by the government, not tolerated in silence.[42] Gonzáles Vigil's historicist concept of nation is, like that of Laso, inconsistently ontogenical. Spanish America is infantile, he explains, while the "two first, and most advanced
nations of Europe," England and France, are over 1,000 years old but not for
that reason decrepit, since, for him, one year in the life of an individual is like a
century in the life of a nation. Nevertheless, the ontogenical notion that Peru
was "not yet" Europe was actually quite useful for Gonzáles Vigil's defense
of the Peruvian Republic against her monarchist European (and European-
izing) critics. "If we bother to examine the histories" of England and France,
he notes, we find "so much sweat, so many alternatives, so much blood, so
many crimes, and so many centuries" to arrive "at the culminating place in
which they now find themselves." Having taken so many centuries, "they now
throw in our faces, after so few years [of national life], the accusation that we
have learned and advanced so little in so many years! What were they at our
age? How much had they learned and advanced?"[43] Although it would likely
take centuries for "baby boys" like Peru to catch up, the accelerated speed

of change in the nineteenth century actually left room for optimism on that score. Moreover, Peru could learn from the crimes and errors of Europe, as well as from her "lights and lessons." Those errors and crimes now included the imperialist regimes of restorationist France and reactionary Spain.

In *Impugnación de un folleto que tiene por título "Examen comparativo de la monarquía y de la república"* (1867), Gonzáles Vigil continues the ardent defense of the republic against those critics who supported constitutional monarchy, then represented in South America by the Brazilian empire and in Europe by the imperialist alliance of the dynastic houses that ruled France, England, and Spain. The anonymous authors of the *folleto* or pamphlet in question argue that constitutional monarchy represents the perfect Christian balance of authority and liberty. In the same vein as Herrera, the pamphleteers argue that both the "democratic Republic" and "absolutist Monarchy" are "atheistic" because both "the People" and "the King" represent blasphemous usurpations of God's sovereignty. The pamphleteers argue further that in America, independence produced the abomination of the "moderate republic," that is, republics that are neither democratic nor orderly, the result of which is chaos and petty fiefdoms. In contrast, they argue, constitutional monarchy recognizes God as sovereign by balancing man's individual rights of liberty against the social need for authority. Only liberty governed by authority can produce true progress in the material and spiritual realms, argue the two authors.

Gonzáles Vigil rejects all of this as nonsense. When democratic republicans speak of "popular sovereignty," they are talking about man, not God, he points out. He adds that God has always been the divine sovereign, but He has in his wisdom granted man the natural freedom to govern his social life in accordance with the design of Providence. As in Vico, for Gonzáles Vigil that design is liberty. And it is precisely this design that animates Lorente's history of Peruvian civilization.

Mestizo Critique: The Void and Truth of the Republic

Moments of postcolonial anxiety produced grave historical diagnoses of the condition of the Peruvian Republic. In the mid-1860s, a small Spanish fleet seized nitrogen fertilizer shipments from Peru's lucrative *guano* islands, the republic's principal source of revenue. The crisis was of transatlantic proportions. The Mexican Republic had fallen to Napoleon III's French army, and the restored Mexican empire now received a Hapsburg monarch; the outcome of the Civil War in the United States was still unclear to observers from across the seas; an alliance between the monarchies of England, France, and

Spain had rolled back republicanism in Europe; the three imperial vultures now hovered over the weak American republics. French and Spanish imperialists now sought to reclaim "Latin America" as the estranged daughter of the "mother civilization" of the "Latin Race." The "democratic promise" of the republic and of America seemed to hang in the balance and with it the future of liberty.

Carlos Lisson's *La república en el Perú y la cuestión peruano-española* (1865) turned the "national question" of sovereignty and civilization back to its repeating historicist origins in the rule of an enduring despotism initiated by the Inca dynasts. The "cancer" of Peru and Europe was that, a la Rousseau, "civilization" had negated the pure, natural, and moral rights of man in the family. Lisson's "Peruvian-Spanish Question," then, emerges from an historicist awareness of the sickness of an impending death. Peru's national crisis leads Lisson on a quest for its causes, and these causes remit to origins:

> And you, my motherland, born onto the world with your temples triumphantly adorned with laurel; you, the keeper of the American glory of Ayacucho; you, forgetting such brilliant antecedents, have let yourself be led by the hand for forty years, until you have touched the edge of the abyss. . . . You consider yourself a Republic! You think you are a nation? You, my beloved homeland . . . Is there nothing that can save you from the death sentence that hangs over you? What is the origin of your plight?[44]

Lisson's "imagination turns to gaze retrospectively upon the past and, within that theatre, to jump from age to age, albeit without coming upon a single solid point at which to rest, before finally resting upon those unknown ages" of the primitive past. "So deep-rooted is the cancer that corrodes your entrails," he laments.[45] His dark gaze falls on "the state of the Indians under the Incas and the Colony." The deep cause of Peru's cancer is "the tyranny that [has] weighed her down since Inca times."[46] Nothing is left of the Inca empire but a poor "flock of men." The "degraded Indian of the Inca Empire" was "enslaved, exploited, brutalized, and terrorized in the colony" by the Spanish. While the republic "somewhat emancipated" the Indian, "its work is incomplete and it still conserves deep traces and bad habits of the absurd and ferocious regime under which the Indian has lived for three centuries."[47]

Despite itself, Lisson's gloomy diagnosis of Peru's cancerous history does betray one "point at which to rest." This is the point of mestizo critique. For Lisson, a "new American race" had emerged that "began with a Spanish base" but was a "confused mix of all the known races of the world." Still, this new race had "no rights of affiliation" to any one race. This "bastard, weak, and upstart race" was rejected by the Spanish with disdain and was equally detested by the Indian, who viewed the mestizo with disgust as the Spaniard's right-hand man. This new race with no place began to "think of the idea of the Patria," to seek "a place in this land where they had been born."[48] In short, it was this new American race without a place that had achieved independence and gained a *patria*.

Contrary to European opinion but in agreement with Távara, Lisson argues that the revolutions of independence of the American republics had nothing to do with the English or French revolutions. Instead, they were inspired by "pure truth." Blissfully abandoned by the metropolis, in British America the "pioneers" had harvested the fruits of their own labors. The "English revolution" was not an inspiration there either. In Spanish America enslaved men labored under the vigilant eye of a degrading despotism or "system." In Lima no one actually read the works of Voltaire, Rousseau, or the discourse of Mirabeau.[49] The only source of news was *La Gaceta de Madrid* (Royal Madrid Gazette). The French revolution had, in any case, consumed itself and been destroyed. What kind of "example" was that? "Old and new European liberalism" now claimed that American independence was indebted to these revolutions, but when South America declared its independence, this liberalism was nowhere to be found in Europe! The hypocritical model that European liberalism now offered was that "of sovereign kings restored to thrones in a 'Holy Alliance' against liberty and the republic, because these were synonymous with blood, destruction, sacrilege, and ruin." In their insurrection against the tyrannical "Goths," South Americans had needed no other inspiration than the whip, and if "from the conflagration the Republic arose, it was because nothing else could emerge from where nothing existed, since where nothing exists only truth may appear." In truth, America "owes nothing to Europe. She became independent because her sons became men; and she became republican because the Republic is truth."[50]

It was "undoubtedly true" that South Americans spoke European languages, adopted European laws, and practiced European religions, but of course that was to be expected "after such a long period of domination." None of that justified Europe's pretension to be the model of American civilization. America calls "her intelligent workers" to her shores, and "appropriates her steamboats and great discoveries, just as Europe has taken from antiquity Arabic figures and other inventions," but she "does not accept Europe's current civilization, born of the Roman Empire, the Papacy, Charlemagne, feudalism, and privilege.... Enough of that sly sermonizing about gratitude and recognition!"[51] France and Spain now preach: "You are of the Latin Race, we are relatives, the same blood flows in our veins; you are weak, watch out or the Anglo-Saxon Race will devour you! Take refuge by my side and I will protect you; at my side you will prosper and preserve your autonomy." But, Lisson asks, "what is this Latin Race? Such a race has never existed in the classifications of ethnologists." The "slavery that the Romans exercised 2,000 years ago" on "the Visigoths, the Arabs," and some other peoples: Did that now make us all family? Why would we adhere to that? So that we may "take orders from Isabel II, or Napoleon III? And, after them, from some Charles or Philip with their little cliques and dynastic villanies?" Men "belong to the land where they were born, whatever their lineage. The place where he first sees light, where he passes his infancy and grows up, where he receives sustenance and experiences love, happiness, and grief; that is his Patria."[52] France and Spain now preach to us that we became independent "before our time," that "we were not prepared for public life. We ask ourselves: And when will *you* be prepared? Until now, neither civilized France, nor retrograde Spain, may exercise freedom of the press because they are not prepared," notes Lisson. So, "what does it mean, to not be prepared?" That of every people and each man we require "that they dress like Europeans, have kings, aristocrats, proletarians, permanent armies, irresponsible Crowns, grand theatres, and a policeman in every house?" No! "All men and all people are and should be free from the time that their physical being permits them to defeat the forces of nature and defend their personality; they can and should govern themselves from the moment that they believe in God and understand moral law. The American Race . . . has grown up; he has proven it in classical ways on the battlefield, and he is proving it now in his struggle to overcome nature." In short, and despite or rather because of the "cancer" of Peru's history, for Lisson there is no European historicist *not yet* that can keep truth from appearing in the void. What matters in human history is not the genealogy of blood but the genealogy of country, that is, the experience of being born and growing up in one's "country," and then proving it on the battlefield and in the development of the economy.

In four decades, exclaims Lisson, the Peruvian Republic had achieved more than Spain did in 300 years of colonial rule. Despite this progress, Europe now argues that the republic is "an impossible form of Government." The republic is "unrealizable" because it "demands virtues that you do not possess, and which in any case are not proper to man, who is naturally inclined to vice. . . . The Republics of Greece, Rome, Florence, Genoa, and France have all disappeared, and the same fate is reserved for the Union of

Washington as well." In response to Europe's historicist critique of the republican form, Lisson argues that "Rome, Athens and Sparta were republics in name only." The same held for the Italian republics, "with their coats of arms, princes, slaves . . . and seigniorial privileges." The French Republic drowned "in a sea of blood," only to "fall into the incomprehensible laxity of an imperial despotism" until it finally arrived "at the farce of modern liberalism, which has been and always will be its last word."

Lisson concludes that "the Republic, in the proper sense of the term, is unrealizable in the entire continent of Asia and Europe," which consists of "very old societies formed under so many different dominations, such that they were always molded by the principles of authority, unity, and privilege." In contrast, "the true Republic demands a different and purer atmosphere, another world within which its beautiful panorama may be realized." This "atmosphere" could only be found in America, where there was no true feudal tradition, only supposed aristocrats and pretentious viceroys, "speculators who came to America without antecedents" and then "after lining their pockets" returned to Spain; in Peru there was only "a nobility without historical precedents of honor and glory, and as a consequence without prestige or influence, and as a result the principle of authority was vitiated." The postcolonial American republics, then, had no historical precedents and no models: "Colonialism had created Nothingness."[53] And only from colonial nothingness could "truth" emerge. As a result, the only example that might serve as an inspiration to the postcolonial republics of South America was "the land of Washington." For Lisson, Washington was a model because Europe had not educated her; "she had the good fortune of educating herself."[54]

In the particular case of Peru, national sovereignty was "a gift" from the patriot armies of San Martín and Bolívar. As the fortified and privileged center of Spanish empire in South America, and lacking a true nobility of its own, Peru was not in a position to win the war without aid from her South American neighbors. This fact was a double-edged sword, for on the one hand Peru's "sons and soil" were spared from the "crimes against humanity committed in other parts" of South America, but on the other hand, "the virtues, good works, and sacrifices that such a conflict demands could not purge the public and private customs" of the colonial regime. As a result, the work of founding a republic in Peru was postwar and postcolonial, and it arose from a "gift of national sovereignty" given in a colonial "void in history." This postwar work of purging the old colonial customs consisted in "destroying the [colonial] State and dispersing its usurping functions among all the citizens, so that the Republic could become a truth."[55]

However, this truth of the republic, wrought of the postwar destruction and dispersion of the functions of the colonial state, was subsequently corrupted by imported French ideas and by the statist intrigues of Peru's military *caudillos*. The people's "sovereignty" was captured by the centralized state anchored in Lima; it became the booty of *caudillos* and parasitic clerks. The true republic of the people had degenerated into a "State-Republic" wherein the president was a "despotic" military *caudillo* or a "Persian" who was little different than the old Spanish viceroy. Sovereignty "was reduced to exchanging one ruler for another of a different nationality."[56] The result was the "militarization of society," with everyone—soldiers and civilians—grubbing to get a piece of the fiscal pie. The Peruvian Republic was now "a leper" on the stinking deathbed of the state.

For Lisson the only solution was to return the Peruvian people to "its primitive state and give it back its rights." To achieve this, he proposed a return to a federalist state that, reunited with Bolivia, would feature a "social pact" between the "nation" and the "communities." Both the nation and the communities are based on the family, the natural state of man, where only "moral law" rules. The true nation is an aggregation of communities, and communities of families. Key to this Rousseauian, American federalist utopia is its critique of the concentration of sovereignty in a single head. In Lisson's view this sovereign head could be a king, a viceroy, a president, or a capital city. The King's sovereignty, invested in the Spanish viceroy in Lima, had merely been passed to the Peruvian presidency, also based in Lima. The republic failed because it had become nothing more than a statist "national sovereignty," that is, it concentrated sovereignty in the Lima-based state. Moreover, the big, sovereign, capital city was a "European idea" that clashed with American realities. In contrast, in the United States Washington was established as a point of reunion for citizens, not a European-style, sovereign city. For Lisson, "the sovereign has no visible head: it is the people and it is everywhere," and so the capital of the republic should be a central place where citizens could gather, nothing more. "Lima should not, and did not deserve to be, the capital" of the new federation of communities and families, since it was "vulnerable" to sea-based attack and, moreover, was "without political influence."[57] In the heat of Spanish naval aggression against Lima's port, Lisson thus recommended that the capital of Peru be removed to a central location in the Andean highlands.

In certain respects, Lisson's vision resembled Laso and Bolívar's view, since it was based in part on an ontogenical vision of sovereignty as the political expression of natural man in his native country. In addition, for Lisson history was a catalog of horrors, and he agreed with Távara that the republic sprang not from history but from a colonial "nothingness" or "void of truth" in history, and on the unprecedented "gift" of sovereignty. Like Jules Michelet, Lisson argued that the "pure truth" of the republic sprang from this void. In Lisson's view, the cancerous nature of the Peruvian past, combined with the despotic nature of Europe, meant that the American republics had to be founded on the pure truth of the acephalous colonial void, which in turn should be redistributed in the confederated sovereignty of the people. In this, Lisson's view differed from that of the Bolivarians, however, in that the result of Peru's history was that, because of the "gift" of sovereignty in the colonial void, the people could be returned, via a labor of oblivion, to a primitive condition of stateless republican happiness. All that mattered to form a republic was "truth," and all that was needed to return to a state of grace was that men go back to the "family" as God-knowing, moral beings organized in a nation or "community of families" and confederated in a decentralized republic.

Lisson's mestizo critique of the "Latin" imperialism of Napoleon III (France) and Isabel II (Spain) was launched from the position of the colonial void. This void was also the source of the "pure truth" of the republic. Notably, Lisson's critique and narrative of the Peruvian Republic neatly addressed the aporia or fundamental impasse at the heart of the political doctrine of the contemporary age. The aporia may be stated thus: How could a people be prepared for self-rule if self-rule (man's natural state) required the abolition of history? Only "revolution" or marginality could supply this abolition. But if revolution itself was historically contingent, and thus prone to fail, as it did in France, and if marginality was extremely rare—as examples of the latter, Lisson cited the unique cases of Switzerland and the United States—how could democracy become universal? The narrative of colonial "nothingness" combined with the "gift of sovereignty" neatly resolved this aporia for Peru, since these things—nothingness and sovereignty—had in fact been delivered by history to America in the form of a "void of truth." This history-given void could be the basis of a "true Republic" among the Peruvian people. In a word, the "truth" of the Peruvian Republic (and of Lisson's critique) sprang from a nothingness created by colonial history, and this truth could be "realized" in a postcolonial labor of forgetting and return.

In the end, Lisson's brilliant vision of the permanent crisis of history— understood as a cancer, and born either of Inca "despotism" or the European "principle of authority," the cure for which was to be found in the colonial nothingness or void that gave birth to the pure truth of the federal republic of families—was undoubtedly powerful as a postcolonial theory of sovereignty but limiting as a historical narrative for the Peruvian future. His mestizo theory or "American race" idea of independence would also inspire Cipriano Zegarra but it tended to exclude if not negate the numerous Indians, blacks, and Creoles who made up the majority of Peruvians at the time, who were a "cancer" to be removed. As a historical discourse for postcolonial Peru, then, it had obvious deficiencies, chief among them its "pessimism" vis-à-vis any national future that could reclaim and build upon a deep and positive native history, and in this regard too Lisson's discourse was like Rousseau's. Lorente would restore that native and national past but he would also keep some of the acute edge of Lisson's critique, including his postcolonial rejection of Europe's historicist pretensions to be the original source, model, and protector of "Latin American" societies.

Lisson's pessimism passed. Peru successfully defended its republic against the revanchist Spain of Isabel II; the Union won its war with the Confederate South; and the Mexican Republic drove out the French and sentenced the liberal Hapsburg monarch of Mexico to a modern death by firing squad. In the 1870s, less-pessimistic histories churned off Peruvian presses. Lorente's contemporary, Félix Cipriano Zegarra, raised Lisson's mestizo critique to more sophisticated historical levels. He then published an inspired historical essay on Indian resistance to colonial rule in which he inscribed that long history of resistance in the story of a national liberty that led inexorably to Peruvian independence. "Yo el Rey: Ensayo histórico" (I, the King: An Historical Essay) appeared in Mariano de Paz Soldán's historical review, *La Revista Peruana*, in 1879.[58] Zegarra's essay examines the historical contrast between British America and Spanish America, not to lament the lack of liberty in Spain's America (as had Espinosa and Lisson) but instead to specify the different colonial trajectories of liberty. The Inca empire was a proud state that had never known defeat prior to the arrival of the Spaniards. The Spanish period was inaugurated with a blood bath, but soon another exchange of bodily fluids would create the mestizo. In Peru, "after humiliating him, the soldier-colonizer approaches the vanquished and, along with riches and services, asks for family, and a mixed race is born." This mestizo race "was destined to form the nucleus of the future population of the land." The many mixtures and distinctions that followed were "completely unknown in the American colonies of the English." There "in the Anglo-Saxon establishments of America" the land was "colonized by families," and "the European and the

Indian declared a war of extermination." The Anglo-Saxon colonist "found his salvation and tranquility in the disappearance of the indigenous people; his favorite pastime . . . was fighting against them."[59]

In contrast, what held the diverse castes together in Peru was not fighting against Indians but instead "the relations of the Sovereign with the subject." These relations had inhibited progress during the viceregal period, and after 50 years of republican independence they "still adhered in our social constitution." Indian subjects were degraded under this system since despite "the humane laws of the King" they suffered "abuses and taunts" at the hands of colonial functionaries, and in the name of the sovereign. The politics of the functionaries toward the natives could be "reduced to two words: exploitation and tyranny," and as a result the natives "felt a deep resentment in their chest against the unfamiliar Sovereign." Indian resistance had commenced immediately and was answered with Viceroy Toledo's savage execution of "Manco Inca" (Tupac Amaru I) in 1572 and by his ruthless drive to exterminate the heirs to the Inca throne. But even this carnage did not put an end to Indian resistance. Many Indian uprisings had occurred during the colonial period, including Tupac Amaru II's attempt in 1780, the principal object of which was "the extermination of the Spaniards and the restoration of the Empire of the Incas." Had Tupac Amaru II succeeded however, the result would have been "an ephemeral, poor imitation of the ancient empire, since there is no doubt that its leader would have fallen victim to the very imperfect political and religious education he had acquired under the same Spaniards." Subsequent revolts in the early 1800s in Cuzco (those of Aguilar, Zela, and Pumacahua), in which "the idea of independence assumed its full importance," would pave the way to independence.[60]

Cipriano Zegarra sketched a strong and enduring narrative of Indian resistance to colonial rule as a precursor to independence, but Lorente anticipated him in this narrative. For Cipriano, the true idea of independence could only be grasped in Lima, where an "enlightenment had been propagated in certain circles." These enlightened men were not the "Godless, lawless, and anarchist bandits without conscience" that many outsiders and reactionaries took them for. Instead, these men—republicans such as Miguel Tafur and Francisco Javier Mariátegui y Tellería—were imbued with "the instinctive love of independence, the only basis upon which to educate the masses in the new ideas."[61] It was Lorente who would carry the lessons of the event of independence and "the new ideas" that informed it, into the history classroom and onto the bookshelves of Peru, and from there to the national imaginary at large. He was able to do so in part because his history granted an "instinctive love of independence" not only to the republican elite but more profoundly to the soul of the Peruvian people.

The History of the Soul

Lorente was a philosopher of the soul who wrote history. He authored Peru's first course in philosophy, the four-volume *Compendio* or *Curso de filosofía*.[62] Lorente's course on philosophy is antipositivist and "antisystem" and it informs all of his histories. Indeed, what most clearly distinguishes Lorente from most of his Peruvian peers is his explicit and clear command of the modern philosophical discourse of "Universal History" and his ability to communicate that discourse to a wide readership. What was latent, implied, or half-developed in most nineteenth-century Peruvian history writing was both explicitly enunciated and deftly emplotted in Lorente's texts. Following Leibniz and Kant, Lorente defined the object of philosophical and historical meditation to be the "soul" and "spirit" of the world:

> Socrates wished to do battle with the Sophists and thus humanize a philosophy that lost itself in the material and in chaos. . . . Descartes placed himself at the forefront of a philosophical crusade against a Scholasticism that had declared to Reason: "you shall not pass this line"; and so he adopted as his motto the famous I THINK. In recent times, Kant has wrapped himself in his own thought in order to transcend a sensualist epoch, and today no one doubts that all who would propose solid bases for social doctrines, and who would lift themselves up toward God, must depart from the phenomena of the soul.[63]

In general terms, for Lorente philosophy was "the science of the human spirit." After Vico, Lorente admits that this science "does not embrace all spiritual developments" since only God exercises full dominion over the natural world. Philosophy is thus positioned "at the head of all the other sciences" that are concerned with "the moral world, such as History, Politics, Jurisprudence, and Economics." The "method" of modern philosophy is nevertheless "rational-empirical," since without "observations" and "experiences" it becomes nothing more than "interesting fictions" that "distance us from Humanity and Nature, thereby robbing us of the precious time demanded by science and virtue." Still, to remain at the empirical level or to be content with the mere description of the facts is to fall into grave error. For, if "we do not wish to leave the scene of facts or events we will be lost in their incessant variety, in their indefinite multitude and apparent incoherence," and the result will be "a subtle and tired statistics, impossible to comprehend; a dead letter from which nothing clear can be taken."[64]

Psychology, then, is philosophy's point of departure since it is the science of soulful thought itself. The word "psychology" has "two Greek roots," notes Lorente: "*Psiquis* signifies soul, and *logos* translates as 'treatise' or 'discourse' [*tratado*]; thus in its literal sense it means 'treatise' or 'science of the soul.'" Lorente defines psychology further as "the science of the faculties of the soul or, more precisely, the science of thought," adding these words of Descartes: "'by the word *thought* I understand all those things that transpire within us so that we may perceive that which is immediately before us.' Thus, 'thought' [*pensamiento*] does not only refer to understanding, wanting, or imagining, but also [to] feeling."[65] In short, man's thought is the multiple sensibility of his soul to other men, to nature, and to God.

On the question of language, Lorente follows Leibniz. Although language "is not absolutely indispensable for thought, there is no doubt that it assists thought marvelously." Signs are "any exterior object that reminds us of the idea of another; the palpitations of the heart that remind us of life, and the stripes that makes us think of military rank are among these. They always excite two ideas: that of itself and that of the signified object." What is important here for Lorente's historical method is the presupposition that the signified object "may never be a new idea but must necessarily be a memory, because he who has no knowledge of the signified cannot understand the sign."[66] Ultimately, the search for the origins of language "will lead us to the cradle of humanity and the primitive perfection of tongues . . . in Asia," but its final origin is "divine." Writing "amplifies and eternalizes" the word. And history writing is "the word itself triumphing in space and time."

> In writing there are no distances. A man ensconced in some corner of the globe conceives an idea and makes a sign on a brittle leaf of paper; the man dies unknown; the wind scatters his ashes before his ignored tomb is discovered. But still his idea circles the globe and is preserved intact despite the torrent of the centuries, among the revolutions of empires, in the catastrophes that sink the palaces of monarchs . . . and the thought of the unknown mortal is preserved . . . his spirit dominates the earth . . . and humanity will hear it in future centuries.[67]

Thus, although the soul of man is the means of his sensibility, it is also the good object of philosophical contemplation since it manifests itself across the ages of the written history of civilization. In this way, man's soul is "marvelously assisted" by the word and eternalized in writing, converting it into history itself, at once the subject and the object of man's soul. The soulful historian of the soul should "contemplate man across the ages and phases of civilization and tell us if, in the ignorance of the child or the savage, among the errors of mature generations and of barbarous peoples, or in the midst of the vacillating old age of nations led astray by social refinements, you find robust intelligences, so that in each case humanity may proceed with certainty toward its perfection."[68] As in Leibniz, Lorente's notion of the perfection of humanity's soul is historicist in the sense that it is perpetual. In *Principles of Nature and of Grace* (1718), Leibniz had argued that "our happiness will never consist, and ought not to consist, in a full enjoyment, in which there is nothing more to desire, and which would make our mind dull, but in a perpetual progress to new pleasures and new perfections."[69] Progress in this life was without "full enjoyment" as the life of the soul moved, certainly but ever so slowly, toward its unreachably perfect creator.

The perpetual motion of the soul followed from the notion that the life of the soul was necessarily ruled by an incomplete logic. Only God has a "complete idea" of the things of the natural world. The only "not yet" in the historicism of Leibniz and Lorente, then, is that which perpetually separates men from God:

> A complete idea is that which leaves nothing to be known, while the incomplete idea always leaves something to be desired. All of God's ideas are complete; but ours are necessarily incomplete in reference to real objects; since all beings in the universe are linked together, to comprehend a grain of sand it would be necessary to know the creator and all of creation; we may only aspire to have complete ideas of those ideal beings that, since they are the creation of our own understanding, include nothing but the properties that we have wished to unite in them.[70]

Echoing Vico, Lorente asserts that man may comprehend fully only his own creations; natural phenomena are the work of God; and, as a link in the chain of being, humans may never have full knowledge of such things. Lorente thus distinguished (as the Neokantians did in Germany) between the two kinds of history he taught in Peru: natural history and the history of civilizations. The latter could be fully grasped as an incomplete and ideal creation of man within a grand, providential, but ultimately unknowable chain. Consequently, ideas were not true or false, only clear or confused. A "clear idea is one that presents to us an object in such a way that it may be distinguished from any other, e.g., the idea of the sun on a cloudless day." Likewise, "clarity in language presupposes the clarity of ideas: a thing that is not distinctly conceived may only be expressed in a confused manner; when it is well conceived, means of expression abound. Those who say, 'I understand the subject well, but I can't explain it,' do not know what they say and do not understand what they think they understand." That is, "since every idea proceeds from a judgment and leads to other judgments, one may call true those that envelope true judgments and false those that envelope false judgments; thus, ideas do not possess truth or falsity in themselves, but rather by virtue of the judgments that accompany them." This is a key notion, since what the historian must thereby do is pass judgments on the events of history, the result of which is clarity in the prose. In effect, there is no other way to distinguish between what is true and what is false in history.

In the second part of his philosophy textbook on logic, Lorente addresses broader questions of "synthetic" logic. Here the schoolmaster reflects on the everyday republican art of study. Study is a meditative art that "requires no special rules." One need only familiarize oneself with the "laws" of logic and the great books. To make that study bear fruit, one need only withdraw from mundane distractions and "let the intellect roam freely in all directions around a question." Soon the mind will grasp the proverbial kernel of truth and, "like Archimedes, exclaim, 'I found it, I found it!'"[71] Although, as we have seen, clarity in language presupposes clarity of ideas, and to this Archimedean point of clarity the student arrives via meditation, the didactic fact is that in practice clarity is achieved only in writing. It is not sufficient to voice brilliant ideas; they must be cleanly written. Writing then is the vital art of the philosopher, and the soul of history is both his means and object. Since "logic is the science of truth, it is evident that its importance is not limited, for, as Cicero said, it inundates all regions of wisdom," including, of course, history.[72] Logic comes to the rescue of all professions and all thought, ensuring the perpetual progress of humanity. Likewise, logic triumphs in all things of the world because its force is unlimited. Like thought, if a politics or a civilization is not true it will disappear from the face of the earth.

> There is nothing durable in the world that is not logical. All the blind force in the world cannot impede the fall of a regime nor prolong a situation that is contrary to the science of truth. But that which is logical, that which is based on the laws of knowledge, if it has not yet come to pass will come to pass, and it will obtain a stable triumph against all deceptions and against all the brute forces in the world. The excellence of Logic is confirmed in the testimony of all the ages: Indostan, the cradle

of lights, beamed with its laws; Greece, mother of true philosophy, cultivated Logic with care and—an admirable thing!—since Aristotle presented it in rigorous, scientific form.[73]

In *Filosofía moral* (1860), Lorente accentuates the utility and universality of a Kantian "science of life" or "customs." "Just as Logic, observing the march of understanding, discovers means to arrive at the truth, so does Moral Philosophy study our will to walk the path that leads to virtue and happiness."[74] Moral Philosophy is everywhere. "All of the speculative sciences involve Moral Philosophy, because all contribute to our knowledge of man and his relations with nature and God, indispensable knowledge that guides us toward the good."[75] What's more, the science of the moral is universal among men, even among those who deny it. "The savant, the idiot, the writer of frivolities and the gravest of historians may not cite Moral Philosophy by name, but nevertheless they incessantly invoke moral principles, and in their language they demonstrate clearly their faith in the science of customs."[76] And despite the "variable determinations [of history] . . . it is of little importance which way the wind blows, softly or with violence . . . for we may study its eternal results."[77] Moreover, the historical study of "eternal results" is of great contemporary utility as a weapon against the "anti-social doctrines" of positivism:

> The study of the eternal will undoubtedly serve us well now that partisan clashes inspired by passions lead some to lose faith in virtue; as an ignoble positivism of sensuality threatens us with the new idolatry of the golden calf, when the cynicism of art and the propagation of antisocial and impious doctrines that rehabilitate the flesh as an apology for its crimes, and conspire in the tempestuous days of our youth to make us forget the eternal laws of the moral world.[78]

Yet the most important element of Moral Philosophy for the writing of history is the notion that said science "would be in vain if it limited itself to the enrichment of our understanding with speculative truths that leave our hearts cold." That is why moral philosophers of all the ages "have made beautiful the sacred ideas of the good, presenting virtue as the magnum opus of genius, dressing the repugnant nudity of abstract reason with all the productions of the fine arts."[79] These aesthetic principles of Moral Philosophy extend, to greater or lesser degrees, to the writing of books of all kinds, from poetry to the novel and, with certain limitations, to history as well. "Good books are professorships of the moral, in which the wisdom of all countries and all ages are reunited . . . her instruction is for all men . . . And although

History limits itself to sketching a portrait of the march of nations, the reading of events . . . is never entirely removed from our moral direction."[80] Lorente, then, was a moral aesthete; he authored a textbook on aesthetics and he taught the subject in Peru.

Lorente's metaphysics are also inspired by Leibniz. Metaphysics, notes Lorente, concerns what is "beyond nature" and it may be defined as the "general science" or the "first science." Its object of study is multiple, from "being" (*el ser*) and its "properties" and "relations" with "the material world," to "the language of God" in which it encounters definitive light and the limit of human knowledge.

> Leibniz has said: 'facts and events [*los hechos*] are the language of God, opinions the language of men'; we may add that Metaphysics is the divine science without which we would never hear the language of God, only the incessant noise of human chatter. Its principles are immutable as eternity, and even if the universe obeyed other laws, and all its creatures disappeared these would subsist and impose their order on all creation. . . . Here we touch the limits of knowledge, beyond which we fall into the abyss, into an ocean of doubts and shadows. But we are no less great for having discovered the outer limits of intelligence. . . . Upon reaching these limits of science the metaphysician can say that my understanding does not go further because there is nothing more to know. . . . The greatest men of all the ages have savored the contemplation of this mystery.[81]

This passage is notable because in Leibniz we find that the limit of knowledge, that is the abyss, is touchable for the metaphysician. He does not recoil from the abyss, but contemplates its mystery. Lorente's thought, both deeply religious and logical, sensed this abyss, and in part for this reason he militated against the positivists of his age.

Lorente's contemplative and historicist concept of the soul of man is central to an understanding of his history, since in effect the soul is both the object and the subject of history. In general Lorente's notion of the soul is, perhaps, and like Kant's, more head than heart, for logic rules in history. At the same time, however, and following Descartes, Lorente understood thought as the feeling and imagination of that which is directly before us. Moreover, the soul is "marvelously assisted" by the word and made eternally available to others in writing; that writing must therefore also be a lively letter, so that others may read and feel that soul in distant times and places. Like Leibniz's monad, the soul also appears to be singular, although it must be added that

Leibniz's notion of the monad, which he took from the lexicon of the Neo-Platonists, is that it is a mirror of the entire universe, a microcosm of the godhead, a multiplicity of the One. Like Leibniz's monad, Lorente's "seed" or "name" also undergoes changes, although its "preformed" essence or singular soul remains, and this soul always registers universal qualities.[82]

It was this philosophical appreciation of the life of the soul that allowed Lorente to write a "Peruvian history of Peruvian civilization" that in effect disarmed the pressing "national question" of the republic. By historicizing Peru's "Ark of Liberty" not as a "gift" or prize to be won in the desert in the "arduous task" of forgetting the past, and not as a civilizing goal that might take decades or centuries to reach, and not as a truth that can only emerge in a colonial "void of history," but, rather, as the inherent, primitively formed "soul" of Peru's "national development," Lorente effectively Peruvianized the divisive concept of popular sovereignty.

The Name of Progress

In Lorente's narrative, the colonial history of Peruvian civilization "under" dynastic imperial rule from abroad began when the "ancient history of Peru" (discussed in chapter 5) suddenly encountered the "vanguard of Europe." The universal result of the destructive but ultimately creative event of Spanish conquest was the birth of the "Modern Age." "Modern history" in Peru, however, was marked by a "colonial subjection that incurred the loss of its sense of national existence. Since central power was deposited on the other side of the seas it was not possible for the Nation to have a clear idea of its necessities or resources."[83] Although the "Nation's clear idea" was obscured, that did not mean that its "primitive name" had been erased. The palimpsest of "Providence, which never erases names from the book of life except to write new ones," would see to that, for "when the Empire of the Incas disappeared the seeds of a new nation began to germinate."[84] Indeed, "the same principles produced the independence of the colony," for "no force on earth was sufficient to swamp the seeds of progress." The providential name or seed of "the new nation" was sown in the "imperishable richness of the country" and in the "culture of the Incas." This new nation amalgamated Christianity, Spanish influences, and Inca culture to "repair the ravages" of conquest. Not only was there "progress" in modern colonial Peru, "the Viceroyalty gave Peruvians a more extensive and more glorious domination than that of the Incas." Moreover "beneath the uniform appearance of immobility there were diverse signs of progress."[85] Under Lima's influence, culture flourished throughout Peru, and "the bases of seven new republics were established."[86] Beneath it all, the primitive name of Peruvian civilization was still there, like Leibniz's Neo-Platonist monad.[87] For Lorente, then, "progress" is the renewal of "the primitive name" of Peru in "the new nation" seeded by colonialism after conquest.

Lorente distanced himself from the nativist, anti-Hispanic Black Legend view of Spanish colonialism more characteristic of Peru's republicans during the immediate postindependence period, rejecting the view that the colonial period was merely a "retrograde and lethargic parenthesis" in the national development of Peru.[88] His philosophical view of the historical development of Peruvian civilization could never admit such a "superficial" and "cynical" denial of the universal history of the modern age, and of the longer history of the name or seed of the Peruvian people's primitive civilization. Although critical of colonial rule, it was obvious to Lorente that a "new Peruvian nationality" had emerged under Spain's rule in the form of a colonial modernity. Moreover, under colonial rule Peru "enjoyed her own existence, since the Metropolis treated her with the distinction she deserved as a vast land of indestructible grandeur and glorious past."[89] The Christian religion provided a "common mode of thinking" that traversed the "heterogeneous castes" of colonial society, and a gradual process of race mixing anticipated a "national fusion" of conquerors and conquered.[90] In short, although the three centuries of colonial rule "impeded rapid progress," its "slow movement" actually had the positive—indeed providential—effect of establishing a "new nationality" with "deep roots in the land." The new nationality of the old civilization was "more solid" than it had been under the "fragile" order of the Incas. Peru's "glorious past" was thus "transformed, without losing its value."[91] Peru kept its name.

Lorente's history of republican and independent Peru formed part of the world history of the contemporary age initiated by the French Revolution. "Since 1789," he wrote, "we live in the Age of Revolutions . . . in which the domination of the multitudinous is felt more and more; if not all is done by the People, then we may surely say that all is done for the People."[92] Despite the political convulsions in Peru, the Age of Revolutions was characterized by "the predominance of democracy, the increasing solidarity of peoples, and rapid progress" in all human endeavors.[93] Indeed, "there was nothing comparable either in ancient or modern times with the grandeur of nineteenth-century civilization."[94] And despite the waves of reaction in Europe—from the antirepublican Holy Alliance to the caesarism of the 1860s—popular or republican liberalism, which was "the fundament of all contemporary revolutions," was moving forward both in Europe and the Americas, and signs of progress were evident in the "despotic states" of colonial Africa and Asia as well. In this regard, Lorente noted that progress was being made in India under British colonial rule: "Calcutta and other great centers of culture boasted handsome educational and social establishments." However, he added, "the despotism of Company rule had made things intolerable."[95] The Mutiny of 1857 checked the worst abuses of the Company, but the rebellion failed because of religious divisions and the monarchist clamoring of the mogulists. The queen's rule promised economic reforms and justice.[96] It was only a question of time before India too would achieve republican independence.

The revolutions in Spanish America were long in coming, for Peruvians were well-prepared by history. There is no "not yet" in Lorente's long evolutionary narrative of Peru's preparedness for independence. Indeed, the greatness and resources of the colonies had always far outstripped the metropolis, and "the ancient glory of the Peruvian and Mexican Empires responded for the future of powerful states." Under colonial rule, numerous "tentative movements for emancipation" had been made; they "only awaited the right moment to achieve complete victory."[97] The abuses of a "degrading tutelage" were everywhere manifest; "absurd and ruinous restrictions" imposed on the "civilizing movement" of commerce and ideas could not be sustained. The Spanish American Enlightenment of the eighteenth century (here Lorente has figures like Unanue in mind) provided the philosophical lights for the germination of liberty. At about the same time, the success of the United States emboldened Creoles, while the ravages of the Haitian slave uprising weakened their resolve. However, the French Revolution, despite the terror, "revealed the rights, advantages, and aspirations that condemned colonialism to death."[98] Breaking with those who had declared that a recalcitrant Peru had been dragged into independence, Lorente argued that in South America the first cries for independence were actually heard in Peru in 1804 with the "Aguilar and Ugalde conspiracy in Cuzco." It was only later that the incursions of the British in Buenos Aires were repulsed and patriotism bloomed there. Movements for independence quickly spread across the Americas after 1808, since Spain's own war of independence against Napoleonic France provided the opportune moment for the colonies to break free. The liberal military coup of 1820 in Spain brought an end to the absolutist reaction of Ferdinand VII, thus aiding the cause of American liberty.[99]

In Lima, San Martín's liberating army was warmly welcomed; had it not been for the Argentine general's constitutional monarchist sympathies, the republican revolution for independence, alive in Lima, could have avoided much bloodshed. The wavering of San Martín and the maneuvering of the last viceroy La Serna set the stage for the necessary and definitive military and political intervention of Bolívar, whose forces finally triumphed in Ayacucho in 1824.[100] Bolívar was thus the man of the hour, the "eagle-eyed and eloquent" personification of independence, the "audacious and indefatigable" republican "enemy of the name of kings." His "sublime aspirations and vast intelligence" best characterized South American independence.[101] Peru and South America now had an epic republican culture-hero, a brilliant founder of its contemporary age of revolutions. Nevertheless, in Peru and other South American republics, an undemocratic militarism was the most conspicuous legacy of independence. But was this not also the legacy in Europe, where generals vied with rancid monarchs for power? Moreover, not all military *caudillos* in the Americas were "opposed to the national interest," nor were they necessarily "destitute of an enlightened zeal to see the prosperity of the homeland." Peru's Ramón Castilla was the clear example. Castilla had taken command of the Revolution of 1854, which abolished slavery, liberated Indians from tribute, ended capital punishment, abolished tithes, broadened suffrage, organized liberal education, and put Peru on the path to economic prosperity.[102] The ongoing liberal revolution of the republic was, despite militarism, keeping its promises and moving forward. The present situation of the 1870s in Peru was relatively stable under the civilian president Manuel Pardo, although reactionary intrigues and fiscal problems presented "a very grave situation, full of danger and suffering." Nevertheless, "the great progress of Peru in a half-century of independent life was unquestionable," asserted Lorente. Now, as in the past, "the traditional greatness, privileged soil, and national spirit . . . announced a glorious future for the Republic."[103]

Historians may assign both Lorente's historicist faith in the Peruvian "name of progress" and the ready reception of his historical narrative of Peruvian civilization's "national development" to the prosperous material conditions of the period in which he was productive. Between the Revolution of 1854 and the War of the Pacific with Chile, which began in 1879, Peru experienced unprecedented economic growth and relative political stability largely thanks, in Lorente's words, to the "providential wealth" derived from that fabulous natural resource of coastal Peru called *guano*. In Lorente's view, the postcolonial dismantling of Spain's "absurd" colonial mercantilism had allowed Peru to reap the full economic and civilizing potential of this ancient national resource.[104] Indeed, on the wings of commerce, Peru's caked seabird droppings came to the rescue not only of Europe's nutrient-exhausted and plague-ridden potato and corn fields (earlier "Peruvian gifts to the Old World") but to Europe's poor peasants as well, and so Peru contributed once again to the material progress of liberty in the world. Ramón Castilla's wise administration was "the happiest period in the history of independent Peru," asserts Lorente, and, despite a series of reactionary putsches, the civilian presidency of Manuel Pardo now provided greater stability than in the militarist, *caudillo*-ridden past of the pre-1854 period.[105] Both of these remarkable, progress-minded presidents patronized Lorente. However, Peru's devastating defeat and occupation by Chile in the War of the Pacific (1879–1884) brought an abrupt and violent end to the Age of Lorente. His crowning synthesis and last book, *Historia de la civilización peruana* was published on the eve of Chilean invasion. After the war, Lorente was soon forgotten.

The Invisible Presence of the Lorentine Narrative

Lorente's tiny garden crypt is located in one of the nondescript and crumbling public mausoleums of Lima's old cemetery. Frugal and unattended, it is in many ways a fitting vault for a republican schoolmaster. On the face of the vault is a simple, white marble frieze of the man's profile still visible under the cracked glass that precariously protects it from vandals and the elements. That cracked glass and the abandoned crypt are metaphors, perhaps, for Lorente's place in the graveyard of Peruvian historiography. Lorente's republican history of Peruvian civilization was unmatched in nineteenth-century Peru, both for its philosophical and political coherence and for its narrative commitment to a popular pedagogy that he saw through to fruition; however, his achievement has been muted, his place in the history of Peruvian history eclipsed. Given this neglect, my emphasis on Lorente's philosophical history would seem to require an explanation. Why has Lorente been forsaken?

Peru's twentieth-century professional historians have tended to hold a dim view of Lorente. The origins of this view may be traced to Lorente's contemporary rivals who, from the opinion columns of the periodicals, launched xenophobic, ad hominem attacks on his work and person. Most notable among the pseudonymous aggressors was Manuel Atanasio Fuentes.[106] But it became disciplinary dogma in Peru largely it seems as a consequence of the summary judgments passed by the young José de la Riva-Agüero and Víctor Andrés Belaúnde. Riva-Agüero is often taken to be the "father of the academic discipline of history" in Peru.[107] Belaúnde is often given credit (and he credited himself) for introducing Peruvian readers to modern sociology (although that title belongs more properly to Carlos Lisson) and for inventing the idea of *peruanidad* (Peruvianness). Perhaps more by default than intent, subsequent generations of left-leaning social historians seem to have largely concurred with these summary judgments, in part (but only in part), one suspects, because few bothered to read Sebastián Lorente, who was for a long time out of print and out of style.[108] Among Peru's better-known twentieth-century historians, only Raúl Porras Barrenechea seems to have read Lorente closely enough to recognize the great significance of his work.[109]

Lorente's fate was perhaps symbolic of the republic's. The devastating War of the Pacific tore Peru apart. Lima was occupied by a Chilean command that used the National Library to house troops and to administer the city. Expeditionary campaigns pursued the Peruvian resistance throughout the Andean highlands, and, to make things worse, civil war between those who sought to end the war swiftly by making peace with Chile (the blues), and those who regarded any such peace as dishonorable to the *patria* (the reds), extended the conflict beyond the withdrawal of Chilean troops in 1884. Peru lost valuable territory on its southern border with Chile (from Arica to Antofagasta) and was obliged to compensate the winner as well. State finances collapsed as foreign bondholders took over the national debt at great profit, and, as a result of the bloody civil war, political, class, and ethnic tensions ran high. Peru returned to military rule, albeit under the compromised regime of the patriotic hero of the "red" national resistance, Andrés Avelino Cáceres. In the postwar dust, several of Lima's more notable intellectuals launched harsh criticisms of the dissolved republican order. The nation was nonexistent, they cried. The republic and its progress were illusions.[110]

In his review of the history of Peruvian historiography, Pablo Macera— regarded as one the founders of social history in Peru—dismissed Lorente's work as mere "elementary school textbooks."[111] Alberto Flores Galindo's brilliant reflections on the history of nineteenth-century Peruvian history, written in the 1980s, echo Macera's misguided views on this point.[112] Macera's dismissal became dogma in large part because he and his followers understood historicist thought—and in this they were anticipated by Basadre—to be progressive, nationalist, self-conscious, and collectivist. In Peru these progressive things were supposedly not present prior to the twentieth century, or so the profession wished. As will be seen in the next chapter, in the twentieth century the supposed absence of national historicism in the nineteenth century was routinely assumed to have been a primary reason for Peru's "failure" as a nation.[113] Jorge Basadre appears to show somewhat more respect for Lorente, noting in his encyclopedic *History of the Republic of Peru* that he had "founded university-level historiography in Peru" and also that "Lorente appears to have been the only historian . . . who has attempted to write a total study of the national historical experience in a format distinct from that of the textbook." But Basadre's notes on Lorente were insincere and derivative, based almost entirely on the more serious and valuable reading of his colleague Porras Barrenechea. As we shall see in the next chapter, Basadre and his postwar generation systematically ignored Lorente and his prewar generation; Basadre also derisively characterized Lorente's first writings (*Pensamientos sobre el Perú*) in Atanasio Fuente's derogatory terms, calling the work, in a whimsical phrase, "a lite testimony of a deep land."[114]

In ignoring Lorente, both Basadre and Macera followed the precedent of José de la Riva-Agüero. In his influential doctoral thesis on the history of Peruvian historiography, *La historia en el Perú* (1910), Riva-Agüero excluded serious discussion of Lorente on nativist or Creole patriotic grounds: after all, Lorente was not "born in Peru."[115] Grudgingly, and perhaps feeling the tug of his alma mater, where Lorente had been the founding dean of letters, Riva-Agüero was obliged, most likely by his thesis committee, to append two pages of commentary at the very end of his thesis. In these meager and hastily written pages he grants Lorente "the title of Vulgarizer." His histories, Riva-Agüero now claimed, were "neither scholarly nor synthetic." Lorente was little more than a "simple narrator, agreeable but superficial." In short, Lorente was, to use Hayden White's term, a mere "figurative historicist" (i.e., a simple narrator of history who fails to reflect on the philosophical and linguistic foundations of historical discourse) without brain power or research skills.[116] Lorente was "the perfect antithesis" of the "tedious and ponderous" Manuel Mendiburu and Mariano Paz Soldán—the only nineteenth-century Peruvian historians whom Riva-Agüero finds worthy of serious study, albeit as "historical sources" and not as writers or interpreters of history. But a deeper reason for Riva-Agüero's patriotic excision of Lorente may be found in the unsettling suspicion that the historical discourse of the "Vulgarizer" was in many ways quite close to his own. If we remove the scholarly apparatus and jargon of positivist sociology, we may appreciate no significant difference between Riva-Agüero's "critical method" and Lorente's "critical history." Both relied on the simple comparative tests of what was then called *crítica histórica* (historical critique), combined with ample doses of *sentido común* (common sense).[117] Both wrote "political history" and the "history of civilization." The indissoluble bond between patriotism and history was an article of faith for both historians, traceable in every work they wrote.[118] Both authors also revindicated, albeit with critical reservations, the legacy of Inca Garcilaso de la Vega. On the question of the legacy for Peru of the Inca state their positions were also similar. Both historians subscribed to greater or lesser degrees to William Prescott's liberal-Protestant critique of Inca despotism, although, tellingly, the neopositivist and later conservative Riva-Agüero is closer to Prescott than was the republican and liberal Lorente. Prescott had argued that the Incas were a "superior race" of Oriental despots whose rule stifled the "individual energies" of their inferior and docile native subjects.[119] In Riva-Agüero's words, Inca despotism was "thus responsible in large measure for the vices that still afflict modern Peru."[120] Despite Riva-Agüero's inclination toward positivistic methods and "more modern" citation procedures, both historians strove to write animated "philosophical histories" that synthesized the broad trends and lessons of Peru's long and storied past. Considered as narrative discourse, their histories were remarkably similar, and it is quite reasonable to conclude that on these grounds Riva-Agüero did not surpass or even come close to Lorente's achievement.

Belaúnde's doctoral thesis in jurisprudence, *Ancient Peru and the Modern Sociologists* (1908), dismissed Lorente's corpus in even less generous terms. Judging by his comments, however, readers of Lorente have strong reason to doubt that Belaúnde ever read his works in anything but a superficial or perhaps even secondhand manner. Belaúnde wrote: "señor Lorente, a superficial and diluted historian, followed Prescott, and his criteria were informed by Buckle's history of the civilization of England. His opus, principally descriptive, and without ideas of the whole, is inferior to Prescott's."[121] In truth, Lorente parted with Prescott on key issues, and he was very critical of Buckle's positivist history of England. Lorente's notion of the history of civilization was informed by a very different kind of historicist understanding: Leibniz, Kant, and Vico and not the positivists were his inspirations. Lorente was the only nineteenth-century historian of Peru to assemble in published prose a clear and unified "idea" of the essence and full scope of Peruvian history. His histories are not primarily "descriptive." They are informed on nearly every page by "emplotted" republican and liberal epistemologies of what was then called the "critical" (the comparison of discreet elements) or "philosophical" (attention to the underlying "logic" and "soul" of any historical development) history of civilizations. Lorente did read Buckle, but it is abundantly evident that the British positivist had no discernible influence on him. Indeed, Lorente attacks Buckle for an environmental determinism that condemned vast colonial populations to decay and he chastised the British historian for his "fatalism and sensualism."[122]

It is true that Prescott's work is informed by similar critical methods and liberal-republican prefigurations of history, but Lorente's philosophical history of civilization is more generous than Prescott's Yankee narrative of Spanish decline, studied by Richard Kagan in another context.[123] At other key points, Lorente wisely parts company with Prescott's dismissive judgments. Lorente admits that Inca civilization, in its "ideal or moral state," left much to be desired. It tended toward "the rule of one head" and thus immobility. Yet, from the perspective of *la crítica histórica*, that is, comparatively speaking, the Inca state was very admirable, first for raising the general welfare among its people to levels superior to those of feudal Europe, and second for uniting the great ethnic diversity of Andean peoples, thus "establishing the indestructible bases of Peruvian nationality."[124] Lorente's interpretation of Inca civilization is less damning and Orientalist than is Prescott's in part because Lorente's republican and patriotic philosophy of history was more sympathetic to Inca Garcilaso's sources, in part because Lorente searched for the ultimate origins of the Peruvian nation, whereas Prescott believed that any such quest lies "beyond the domain of history," and in part because Lorente was politically committed to a progressive, Lascasian project of Indian redemption.[125]

Unlike Prescott, and also unlike many of his Peruvian contemporaries, Lorente incessantly denied that the native people of contemporary Peru had been significantly and irredeemably degraded under Inca and Spanish dynastic rule. Although Lorente granted that the native people of Peru were imbued with an "Oriental spirit"—transmitted via the lost ur-languages of ancient populations that had migrated from Asia to America—this spirit (which had also brought light to Europe, and in particular to Germany) could nevertheless serve the providential design of ordered "progress," understood as the historicist renewal of the "name" or "seed" of "Peruvian civilization." All the "frigid declamations" about native Peruvians that present them as "stupid animals" characterized by "rudeness, ingratitude, sloth, indolence, incapacity and other more grave defects, which are supposed to be genetic and incurable," were nothing more than "the old calamity of the oppressing races against the oppressed races." And "even if this degradation had been consummated, there stood history ready to discount any supposed ineptitude with achievements that testify to their high level of culture."[126] Lorente's historicist defense of contemporary Indians anticipated the Peruvian indigenist positions of the 1920s and 1930s, but it also harkened back in certain ways to the "patriotic epistemology" of the eighteenth century. Patriotic epistemology tended to mark a sharp divide between a glorious and aristocratic native past and a miserable and common native present, however. As I have argued elsewhere, this same dystopian schism characterized much nineteenth-century historical discourse in Peru.[127] But in Lorente we see glimpses of its collapse. Indeed, Lorente's philosophical history tended to abolish the historical abyss between the glorious past and the miserable present, and it could not subscribe to the *not yet* of the Bolivarians, who had argued that Indians were political "infants" who were not yet ready to be republican citizens. In contrast, Lorente argued that it was "not necessary to evoke the past to dispel any doubt about the beautiful traits that characterize the native people of Peru."[128] These admirable traits "reveal themselves in serene valor on the battle field; they shine in higher education, in the press, on the bench, and in books." Natives "have given the Church saints and the Patria heroes." They have given examples of "sublime abnegation." The "sweetness" of Peru's native people "has rarely been denied," and their "docility, which has been exploited by alien ambitions, may now root the most perfect social order." They are denied any access to education and denounced for their lack of abilities; they are endlessly exploited, and their "servility" is declared to be "natural." Their so-called indolence is the consequence of being poorly paid, for it is rapidly converted into industriousness when they are paid what they deserve.[129] It is true that for Lorente Indians did exhibit a "deteriorated body" and the "air of decrepit races," but all of that was "the crime of inhuman tutors." The deterioration of the condition of Peru's native people "is not the work of time, which one day will abolish the races, but the impious opus of men, whose lack of foresight makes no scruples of converting other men into simple instruments of personal enrichment and madness."[130]

Lorente's so-called *historia ligera* (according to Basadre) or *historia superficial* (according to Belaúnde and Riva-Agüero) actually became Peru's underlying narrative or *historia profunda* (deep history). It is so *profunda* that it now passes undetected as the taken-for-granted narrative or "figurative historicism" of contemporary Peruvian history. For it was neither Belaúnde[131] nor Basadre[132] but, rather, Lorente who founded the contemporary image of Peru as a unifying and dynamic Peruvian "soul" or *peruanidad*. Lorente both articulated and promulgated the discourse of *historia peruana* as the progressive evolution of "the name" and "communal spirit" of an ancient civilization based on communities that, solidified under modern colonial rule and liberated by postcolonial republican revolution, endured in everyday customs and "the national spirit." This historicist "spirit" and "soul" were the true sources of Peru's popular sovereignty. Without recognizing it, Basadre would assume the broad outlines of this genealogical narrative, although he would fill it with the twentieth century's philosophical concepts.

The excavation of Lorente's historical discourse, interred under the twentieth-century layers of professional neglect and disdain, may also hold a deconstructive, postcolonial critical lesson for the writing of history and nation in Peru. Lorente's "superficial" and now invisible history of deep Peru confirms that the ancient tombs of modern nations are, as Benedict Anderson has so persuasively argued, both new and readily forgotten, but not for that reason easily banished.[133] It has become fashionable among some Latin American critics to fault Anderson for his ignorance of the particularities of "our history."[134] Among these critics, several have argued, against Anderson's contention, that the Creole nations of the Americas were not pioneers of the new, asserting instead that in the Hispanic world "nation" was a deep, "ethnic" concept whose local meanings were forged much earlier during the imperial or colonial period.[135] But these neo-Smithian readings of Latin American nationhood—after the modular ideas of Anthony Smith, which in turn are imbued with older, historicist readings of the "primordial origins" of France and Germany—tend to confuse the conceptual events of narrative discourse with the narrative discourse pronounced in the course of events. As we saw in the previous chapter, Lorente's histories were an event of discourse that mimicked or, to use Peralta's baroque lexicon, "imitated" in the prose of history the political discourse or "speech acts" of the foundational events of independence. It was precisely to the aid of this historiographical repetition of foundational political discourse that Lorente summoned the philosophical or historicist concepts that would later inspire in one way or another both Anderson and Smith. Anderson's post-Indochina War, "antigenealogical" argument that nations are newly imagined political communities that emerge from the colonial cracks of empires, is profoundly indebted to Renan's post-Prussian War historicist concept of the nation as a spiritual community based upon the forgetting of old imperial conflicts.[136] Smith's more Eurocentric and "genealogical" notion of the "ethnic origins of nations" may be seen to be based not on any rigorous anthropological concept of ethnicity but instead on the mythopoetic repetition of the name of the nation (most notably, those of "France" and "Germany") in European historical discourse.[137] Lorente's discourse anticipates both Andersonian (or Renanian) and Smithian notions, since it plainly reveals that the name of ancient nations is always the contemporary name of the future of the imagined polity. Hitching a conceptual ride on Lorente's truck of discourse, we may be permitted to propose a subject-centered theory of nation: the nation is that imagined political subject whose name is "forever ours."

This theory has certain advantages, among them its potential to gloss the aporia inherent to the theory of popular sovereignty. As Palti notes, this aporia was acutely registered in the acts and discourse of independence and democracy in the postcolonial Americas.[138] The aporia in question may be formulated as follows. Popular sovereignty evokes a conceptual knot or impasse in that it demands that citizens are also subjects of their own sovereignty. That is, the citizens who derive their freedom from national membership in "the people" are at the same time deprived of that individual freedom by the (Rousseauian) "general will" of the people. This aporia lies at the heart of the ontogenic and historicist narratives of the nation and the people. How can newly freed citizens (in this case, Creole) yield their personal sovereignty to the general will of a historically tyrannized and therefore weak and ignorant people (in this case, the Indian majority)? And which comes first, the sovereignty of the citizen or the general will of the people, deposited in the same citizen? To be sure, the "mixed" forms of republican government and the severe limits on citizenship constitute the institutional or state response to this aporia. In the short term, however, these questions were reflected in the speech acts of independence, since "the nation" and "the people" could not exist as sovereign subjects until they were so named and declared in symbolic acts of speech (thus San Martín's political baptism of the "Peruvians") and legalized in constitutional assemblies. This founding *poder constituyente* was, of course, endowed with authority only to the extent that it was theoretically based on the delegated sovereignty of the people (in practice, the leading "citizens" of the towns of Peru). Consequently, "the nation" and "the people" had to be invented or prefigured and then summoned as sources of political legitimacy, and historicist discourse provided this "patriotic service" in the form of a genealogy or ontogeny, but also in the form, as we have seen, of such concepts as "the void of truth" and the postcolonial labor of forgetting. This genealogy or ontogeny, depending on the case, as well as the postcolonial labors of forgetting and filling the colonial void, were inevitably founded on the imperial dynastic discourse of the old regime, however, in part because that discourse provided an earlier history of national sovereignty and suffering, in effect confirming the historical existence and future promise of "the people." Among the postcolonial historicist narratives of Peru, Lorente's was the most effective and foundational since it united, under the sovereign magic of the proper name of Peru, the republic, the people, the nation, the realm, the dynasty, and the country. In his discourse all of these would become one time, one place, one theory, one subject: that of Peruvian history.

The profundity and longevity of Lorente's unifying narrative or figurative historicism lies precisely in its homologies or harmonies, and in particular in the political unisonance of "Peru" (*patria, país*) and "Peruvians" (people, nation). Indeed, for Lorente, the historian's task was to achieve this mimetic effect as a "mode of truth." For "what the historian of Peruvian culture should never lose sight of is the harmony among all of the civilizing elements; this organic whole that constitutes civilization itself should reappear in distinct form in the harmonious body of his history."[139] It was the "harmonious body of his history" that endured even if and perhaps because it was not recognized as such, precisely because it constitutes the underlying "soul" or theory of Peru as an ancient, sovereign, and contemporary nation.

For Lorente, Peruvian history was not a burden to bear and it was not an obstacle to progress, and one could say the same about the readability of his histories. They were both easy on the eyes and full of "practical" and "moral" lessons. Moreover, Lorente's histories were engaged not only with Peru's national political debates but also with the global language and desires of the Contemporary Age of Revolutions. But this language and its desires would rapidly shift in the wake of the devastation wrought by the War of the Pacific. That war would bury Lorente's name, his history, and his republic. What Michel de Certeau calls a new "labor of death and labor against death" would soon commence. But as in all such historical labors, the words of the dead would leave their rhetorical mark on those of the living.

7

The End of the Peruvian History of Peru

We need a Peruvian history of Peru. . . . By Peruvian history of Peru I mean a history that studies the past of this land from the point of view of the formation of Peru itself. . . . We must insist upon an authentic history 'of' Peru, that is, of Peru as an idea and entity that is born, grows, and develops. . . . The most important personage in Peruvian history is Peru.

Jorge Basadre, *Meditaciones sobre el destino histórico del Perú*

Although many gifted historians graced the stage of twentieth-century Peruvian letters, Jorge Basadre Grohmann (1903–1980) was clearly the dominant figure. Today Basadre is universally celebrated as the country's most sagacious and representative historian and he is commonly referred to as "our historian of the Republic." Libraries, avenues, and colleges are named after him. The year 2003 was "The Year of Basadre" in Peru, with nearly every major cultural institution in Lima organizing an event in his honor.[1] The National University of San Marcos published a handsome new edition of his first scholarly work, *La iniciación de la república* (The Initiation of the Republic), while Congress commissioned a new anthology of his more inspired essays under the title *Memoria y destino del Perú* (Memory and Destiny of Peru).[2] Not to be outdone, the executive rechristened in his honor a stately room in the Presidential Palace, while the Central Reserve Bank saw to it that Basadre's penetrating eyes should meet those of every Peruvian lucky enough to hold in her hands the 100 *nuevo sol* (new sun) bill. Basadre's aura extends far beyond the ordinary reach of state and cultural institutions, however. Many of the historian's key phrases and concepts, such as *Perú posible* (the possible

Peru), *Perú problema* (Peru as problem), *el país profundo* (the deep country or nation), *el país legal* (the official country or state), and *la promesa del Perú* (the promise of Peru), now circulate as proverbial wisdom vis-à-vis Peru's national problem and identity. Scholars, presidents, journalists, taxi drivers, pundits, pedants, and maids constantly fall back upon these memorable phrases and concepts. All are deeply historicist, and together they constitute something like a national creed.

My critical reading of Basadre's historicist thought is more than an academic exercise. Basadre's thought and language are the closest thing to a mental map of the twentieth-century Peruvian historical imagination that one can find. The current revival of his thought responds, once again, to a postwar desire to imagine a promising national future with an affirmative past. In this case, the crisis is proximate: In the 1980s and 1990s, Peruvian civil society was ripped apart by insurgency, counterinsurgency, and dictatorship, tens of thousands were murdered, and hundreds of thousands were displaced. This crisis both upset and reaffirmed the received historical discourses, including those of Peruvian Marxism, nativism, and historicism. The aftermath of this crisis is the occasion for the writing of this book.

Here I am primarily interested in the theoretical implications of Basadre's thought, understood as a postcolonial form of "finalist" historicism. Although Basadre's discourse and desire were founded on a profound affirmation of the subject named Peru, such that he insisted that "Peru," if it were to fulfill its "authentic destiny," must now have a "Peruvian history of Peru," I argue instead that the subject named "Peru" has always had such a history. Basadre's historicist call for a proper and reflexive history of, in, and for "Peru" actually announces the aporetic end of the "Peruvian history of Peru," not its beginning. This is so because Basadre's opus reveals that "Peru" is nothing more than a perpetual or quotidian wager on past wagers on the proper name. The "end" of Peru is not to end. In revealing this aporia of historicism, Basadre's thought actually brings "Peru" back to its origin: the abyss of history.

Basadre's Wager

Basadre's historicist thought was in many ways a Peruvian catachresis of two philosophical propositions or wagers. The first was the oft-cited truism of the Italian philosopher and historian Benedetto Croce (later revived by the unoriginal R. G. Collingwood, to whom it is sometimes mistakenly assigned), namely, that "the only true history is contemporary history."[3] The second was the seventeenth-century French polymath Blaise Pascal's famous wager that

although God's existence cannot be definitively proven, it is more advanta-
geous to wager for than against it, since the positive wager opens up an infinite number of possibilities for a happy existence whereas the wager against
God yields only finite possibilities. In early twentieth-century Peru, however,
Croce's freshly minted maxim was anything but a truism, and Pascal's wager
could easily have drawn ridicule. Peru was still ailing from a humiliating defeat at the hands of Chile in the War of the Pacific (1879–1884); notable Peruvian intellectuals of the period characterized Peru's postcolonial republican
history (1821–1878) as a disastrous national failure that was better forgotten. The future could not possibly be based on that past. Swimming against
the tide, Basadre boldly proposed a positive, philosophical, future-oriented
interpretation of Peru's contemporary history. This proposal, however, was
presupposed by a void of death or an abyss of history opened by the national
"disaster" of the War of the Pacific and which would come to separate Peru's
"new" twentieth century from her old and dead nineteenth. In short, Basadre's project required the rehabilitation of a "contemporary history" that was
at the time not contemporary for many Peruvians.

Croce's maxim (which served as the epigraph to Basadre's first history,
La iniciación de la república) had summed up the Italian philosopher's ironic
defense of the affirmative truth of human actions and words in history.[4] In
Croce's thought, "the historical" or indeed "history" is not only the exemplary humanist product of actions and words, it is *all* that there is.[5] Basadre's
Pascalian wager (*apuesta para el sí*) for the Peruvian implications of Croce's
proposition—that is, that Peru's contemporary or republican history must be
true in a reflexive sense, and so it would do no good to turn away from it—
became a trademark phrase that signaled a moral and critical affirmation of
the "promise" and "destiny" of contemporary Peru. Moreover, and as Basadre
insisted on several occasions, this wager was an all-or-nothing proposition,
since "history is all that we have in common."

The Crocean truism and the Pascalian wager were also moral affirmations
of Basadre's understanding of his own life and work. The historian's personal
history was emblematic of Peru's twentieth-century political and intellectual history. The son of a relatively well-connected Creole merchant and
an educated German mother, Jorge was born in 1903 to a comfortable and
enlightened home situated on the central plaza of Chilean-occupied Tacna.
Following Chile's victory in the War of the Pacific, Tacna—an oasis town of
merchants and smallholders in the southern coastal desert—resisted "Chil-
eanization," and "the Heroic City" was reincorporated to Peru in 1931. After
a prolonged wait that led to a frustrated plebiscite, the new national border

dividing the two South American republics was drawn just to Tacna's south but, to the great displeasure of Peruvians, north of the important former-Peruvian port of Arica. Basadre's patriotic father did not live to enjoy the long-awaited day of repatriation. Young Jorge left his occupied hometown in 1912 and with his mother moved to the Peruvian capital, where he would study in Lima's exclusive Deutsche Schule, later renamed Colegio Humboldt.

Despite the canonical status of Basadre today as guru of the republic and master builder of Peruvian historiography, his youthful experience in occupied Tacna and, by his own account, his initial marginality as a provincial migrant and student in metropolitan Lima, betray the ambivalent marks of displacement or internal exile. Under the duress and isolation of Chilean occupation, the young Basadre had (in retrospect, at least) conjured an "invisible *Patria*" related to him in stories and read about in books.[6] An aging Basadre later associated this literary and imaginary *patria* with the irrigated fields that surround Tacna and give way to the desert. Late in life, the historian reflected on his youthful experience:

> An important element of my early intellectual formation comes from my childhood in Tacna. It is the sensation of the "invisible Patria," the concept of Peru as a symbol. Since I was a boy, Peru was for me, as it was for many, the dreamed, the awaited, the deep; the nexus of loyalty between the native soil and the home that invaders wished to sever; the vague idea of a history marked by brilliant moments and numerous defeats, and of faith in a future of liberation. . . . We learned to love Peru by divining the nebulous horizons and by following the dusty roads of books.[7]

Basadre's dreamy and bookish experience of a nearly lost Tacna vaguely resembled Ernest Renan's late-nineteenth-century sense of the national dilemma for France (and Germany) of Alsace-Lorraine. Reflecting on this dilemma and responding to European racialist thinkers, Renan proposed that the nation was a "quotidian plebiscite" and a "spiritual principle" based on memory and forgetting. As we shall see, Renan was an important influence, and indeed Basadre's adult life and vocation as a historian may be read as a "quotidian plebiscite" on the question that arose, in retrospect, from his early experience of Tacna. Would Peru persist or was it only a bookish dream? Might the bookish dream be the basis of a firm national existence? Although borrowed from European historicist thought, many of Basadre's key historical concepts appear to reflect his retrospective experience of Tacna, now writ large across the canvas of Peru. That Tacna remained Peruvian and Arica became Chilean suggested to him that states could shape "nationalities" against the people's desire; in short, a state or *país legal* could impose schemes that did not correspond to the true historical aspirations of the nationality, or *país profundo*.

For a brief but decisive period (1917–18), Basadre attended Peru's premier public lyceum, the Colegio Guadalupe, whose liberal curriculum had been designed in the 1840s by Sebastián Lorente, the Spanish-born founder of contemporary historical studies in republican Peru. After delivering his first historical essay (on the sore but heroic subject of the defense and fall of Arica to Chilean arms) at Guadalupe's graduation ceremony, Basadre pursued the doctorate in letters at the University of San Marcos (1919–27), where, once again, Lorente as the founding dean of the College of Letters had founded the professional study of Peruvian history. Basadre quickly found a job as an assistant in the National Library, where he worked from 1919 to 1930 under the wing of Lorente's star pupil and fellow Tacneño, the historian Carlos Wiesse. Basadre soon became director of the library at San Marcos and, after studying library science in the United States on a Carnegie Foundation fellowship, ascended to the position of director of Peru's National Library. He traveled to interwar Germany and Spain in the 1930s and was subsequently awarded several fellowships and grants to study, write, and teach in the United States and France. These opportunities included fellowships from the Organization of American States to work in the Hispanic Collection of the Library of Congress; a Rockefeller Foundation fellowship to expand his *Historia de la República del Perú* to include the twentieth century; and a UNESCO grant in the mid-1950s to participate in a collective editorial project on nineteenth-century world history, which took Basadre to France, where he exchanged ideas with the Annals historians. In the intervals between his travels and studies, Basadre twice occupied the cabinet post of minister of education.[8]

In *La iniciación de la república*, Basadre summoned Croce's maxim to his immediate task, which was to draw the attention of forgetting Peruvians to the vital significance of the history of an epoch that at the time seemed altogether less admirable and less worthy of study than the "glorious Peru" of the Incas or the "regal Peru" of the Spanish viceroys. A postwar cloud of failure hung over the history of the Peruvian Republic, and Basadre's courageous pen would cut through it:

> There is a black legend that hangs over the republican epoch, inflated by the reactionary propaganda of [Manuel] González Prada against the men and methods responsible for the disaster of 1879. According to this legend, the Republic was a cave of bandits. But we should not judge

so quickly those disorders and errors that were never devoid of sincere acts of merit. We do not pay homage to our Republic by seeing her as a reproduction of Lilliput mixed with the vices of Sodom.[9]

The context of Basadre's revindication of the republic was the centennial commemoration of Peru's independence (1921–24) under the "New Patria" regime of Augusto Leguía (r. 1919–30). This multifaceted event erected scores of monuments to independence and it deeply marked Basadre's generation. Although the postwar "Generation of 1900" was the first to claim the modernist, twentieth-century mantle of "the new," Basadre's centennial generation consciously lived and wrote under that master sign.[10] Notably, the Peruvian "new" of both of these generations was a postwar "after" that entailed a crisis of reason, for many of Peru's intellectuals had lost faith in the republic and its founding principles. As we shall see, Basadre's historicism would restore the reason of republican Peru, albeit in a new "social" idiom.

Basadre's Hermeneutic Circle

It may be said that Peru's nineteenth century comes to a close with the "experience of disaster" of the War of the Pacific (1879–1884) and that her twentieth-century intellectual history begins with the postwar diagnosis of her "national failure" in the late 1880s. If such a reading is viable, then it was the fiery polemicist Manuel González Prada (1844–1918) who, crying out from the ashes of death and defeat, initiated Peru's new century of historical thought:

> Although Chile's brutal hand crushed our bones and butchered our flesh it was our own ignorance and our own servile spirit that were the real winners, the real weapons of the enemy. France with its free but undisciplined revolutionary masses marched to victory; but with our armies of disciplined and unfree Indians Peru will always march to defeat. If we have made a serf of him, what Patria should he defend? Like the serf of The Middle Ages, the Indian will fight for his feudal lord.[11]

However, for González Prada it was not only the hunchbacked Indian of the *sierra* who was a medieval serf. "We," that is, the "Creoles and Mestizos of the coast," also were serfs because in the war with Chile "we" blindly followed one or another Peruvian general rather than rally round "the nation." González Prada went on to declare that "the true Peru does not consist of groups of Creoles and foreigners on the Pacific coast; the nation is formed by the masses of Indians" who dwell in the Andean interior of the country.[12] Given the right resources, it was this "real nation" that would redeem Peru. The recipe was simple: Give every Peruvian Indian a shotgun and thereby remake him in the Jeffersonian image of José Martí's North American "yeoman pioneer."

González Prada was in many ways the centennial generation's intellectual point of reference, both admired and despised. What most clearly distinguishes, for example, the historical vision of Peru of the brilliant and polemical José Carlos Mariátegui (1894–1930) from that of Basadre is the socialist's ready embrace of González Prada's denunciatory tone, his hermeneutics of suspicion, and his narrative of national failure, combined with a defiant, neopositivist, and revolutionary spirit. In contrast, Basadre built his affirmative project against that tone, hermeneutics, narrative, and spirit, although he also understood its analytical value and political appeal.[13] In both cases, González Prada was indispensable, a dark and prophetic postwar figure of the "new Peru."

Following the proposals of Wilhelm Dilthey and Paul Ricoeur, González Prada's interpretive tone may be associated with "the hermeneutics of suspicion," and that of Basadre with "the hermeneutics of faith." As Ricoeur notes, the hermeneutics of suspicion is indispensable for unmasking the class interests and ideology of texts, but as a method of reading it stands impoverished without a hermeneutics of faith that at least momentarily suspends disbelief so that the text may become the world that the reader or interpreter inhabits.[14] Hans-Georg Gadamar argues further that all hermeneutic study begins with an initial suspicion about the world but that the only world and being that we can know and communicate with fluidity is language itself.[15] Basadre's historicism appears to register this insight of the "linguistic" and "hermeneutic" turns in twentieth-century philosophy, which owed much to Gadamar and his mentor, Martin Heidegger, whose writings exercised an influence on the late Basadre. Building upon Gadamar's insight and combining elements of Ricoeur's scheme, Basadre's historicism may be characterized as a hermeneutics of faithful suspicion, since its initial suspicion or critical inquiry is always already fully invested in an affirmation of the being or literary ontology named Peru. Conversely, González Prada's discourse avails itself of a hermeneutics of suspicious faith, since its trenchant critique is fully invested in the denunciation of a "leprous" Peru that requires faith in a radical cure.

On a deeper, figurative level, what united the historical discourses of González Prada, Mariátegui, and Basadre was the shared notion that the reason for the failure of the national subject named Peru was that it was divided.

Although, as we shall see, the national subject and its imagined divisions were configured in different ways (along geographical, racial, biomedical, or cultural historicist lines), it was the notion of the divided national subject that distinguished postwar Peruvian historicism from the nineteenth-century republican historicism of Lorente. This shift from "genealogical" and evolutionary to "antigenealogical" and dialectical historicism is also seen in the thought of French and German historicists of the period (for example, from Ernest Renan to Otto Bauer, that is, from the 1880s to the 1920s). In both the European and Peruvian cases, these shifts reflect postwar intellectual responses to national crises. And in both cases the genealogical or early historicist narratives of nation would, despite the "crisis of historicism," continue to inform and underwrite the antigenealogical or late historicist narratives of nation in the twentieth century.[16]

The indispensability of González Prada for the "new" generation of Peruvian intellectuals had to do not only with the polemical tone of his rhetoric but with the novel diagnostic language of sociology that now gained ascendency in Peruvian historical discourse. This language was constitutive of the postwar milieu of interpretation or, in Dilthey's terminology, the "hermeneutic circle" that Basadre's texts addressed and inhabited. A key concept of this new sociological language and milieu was "feudalism." In Peru, the idiom of "feudalism" provided an arsenal of critical European concepts that would conspire to displace Lorente's philosophical and genealogical history of "Peruvian civilization," wherein, as we saw in chapters 5 and 6, Peru had escaped the pitfalls and advantages of Europe's "Middle Ages" via a sudden passage from the "Ancient" to the colonial "Modern." Now, however, Peru was mired in an endless "Medieval" and dialectical "feudal spirit" that impeded her progress toward a modern national unity. In Europe, feudalism was theorized, on the one hand, as the proprietal basis of modern freedom, and on the other hand as a necessary "stage" that must be overcome on the road to capitalism and, from there, toward socialism. In Peru, the discourse of feudalism centered on the "feudal hacienda" or rural estate, which was inevitably linked to the discourse on "the Indian" or the "indigenous peasant community" or *ayllu*, which was widely understood to suffer marginalization and exploitation at the hands of wicked "feudal" landlords or *gamonales* (rural bosses). In most instances, a colonial feudalism of the landlords and a postcolonial "semi-feudalism" of the bosses were seen as severe obstacles to the formation of modern capitalism and nationalism in Peru. By the 1920s, the notion of an enduring feudalism, as well as its link to the condition of the Indian, became by consensus the central "social problem" and "national question" of Peru.

A notable contribution to the Peruvian definition of this "problem" was González Prada's brief polemic, "Nuestros indios" ("Our Indians"), written in 1904 but published for the first time for the 1924 centennial commemoration of the Battle of Ayacucho. In many ways, "Our Indians" was a typical Black Legend denunciation of Spanish misrule. It located Peru's ills in the immemorial servility and ignorance of Indians, most recently manifested, or so it seemed, during the War of the Pacific. Paraphrasing the remarks of the Peruvian literary genius Ricardo Palma, González Prada declared that for the servile and ignorant Indian the war with Chile had been "a civil war between General Peru and General Chile."[17] In 1904 González Prada's position was surely polemical, but even then it was not new and did not remain unchallenged. For example, similar positions were voiced by the influential essayist and newspaper editor Luís Carranza, whose texts circulated widely in the 1880s. Notably, Carranza's stance and similar positivist positions were readily attacked and rejected as unfounded in and around 1885, however, when the blood of the battlefield was still fresh. Writing in 1885 in the notable Peruvian journal *La Revista Social*, José Antonio Felices blasted such positivist and denunciatory views, as had Cipriano Zegarra and Sebastián Lorente before him (see chapter 6).[18] On the eve of the War of the Pacific, Lorente had insisted that all such "frigid declamations" about the stupidity or unpatriotic nature of contemporary indigenous Peruvians were nothing more than "the old calamity of the oppressing races against the oppressed races."[19] Citing earlier conflicts, Lorente argued that the true "traits" of Peru's Indians "reveal themselves in serene valor on the battlefield," where they had demonstrated "sublime abnegation" for the *patria*.[20] Some Peruvian writers sympathetic to the resistance campaign led by Andrés Avelino Cáceres knew first-hand that indigenous guerrillas had in fact fought ferociously and suffered huge losses against Chilean (and unpatriotic Peruvian) troops. It was clear to many critics that Peru had not lost the war because Indians lacked patriotic instincts, as the historical sociologists of "feudalism" would have it. By 1924 the fresh polemics of the War of the Pacific were becoming "history," however, and so González Prada's rather dubious essay found a new lease on life. Besides oblivion, the essay benefitted from its bold proposal for action, which broke with the philanthropic tone of earlier republican discourse on the Indian, represented most notably by Juan Bustamante's Sociedad Amiga de los Indios of the 1860s, for which Lorente had served as secretary and spokesperson. There were now only two ways that "the condition of the Indian could be improved: that the hearts of his oppressors feel his plight and recognize his rights, or that his animus acquire sufficient virility to teach his oppressors a lesson." The old "liberal solution" of "education" was now rejected. The actual militant patriotism of indigenous fighters was forgotten, as too was the activism of the Sociedad Amiga de los Indios. Now, a plot of land and a shotgun, *a la* Anglo America, would do the trick.[21]

In the wake of news from the Mexican and Russian revolutions, however, land and the gun would take on new meaning in the historical imagination of Peruvian intellectuals. In 1927 Mariátegui adopted González Prada's defiant stance but added to it a revolutionary socialism that found its "root and cause" in the *ayllu* or Andean peasant community, and in the "socialism" or "ancient law" of the Inca state. But it was Hildebrando Castro Pozo (1890–1945) who made Mariátegui's socialist dream ethnologically viable and economically practicable, or so it seemed. Indeed, Castro Pozo's *Nuestra comunidad indígena* (Our Indigenous Community), also published in that magical Bolivarian year of 1924, was "must reading" in centennial Peru. The intellectuals of the 1920s became more receptive to "Inca socialism" thanks in large part to Castro Pozo's sociological study of the ayllu. His study demonstrated that Peru was not only the home of an immobile, despotic and feudal oppression of the Indian "serf." A "practical" and defensive "agrarian communism" had survived in the Andean peasant communities of the republic. Castro Pozo's survey of contemporary community institutions was unassuming and descriptive, based on agricultural reports, anecdotal observations, and interviews, most of which concerned the central highlands where Lorente had written his *Pensamientos sobre el Perú* in the 1850s. Castro Pozo's modest, 500-page "essay" that, in the author's words, "merely clears a small patch in the virgin forest of our national sociology" now suggested that in many cases the kin-based community organization of land and labor was still a vital source of fraternity and livelihood.[22] Plots were distributed to families in usufruct, and access to commons was based on collective rights. Newlyweds, for example, were provided with a new home, built by community labor. Castro Pozo observed that "not even contemporary communism" had figured out how to do this.[23] The Andean communities had also solved the modern "problem of labor." Although plantation owners and "feudal" landlords considered the natives to be indolent and untrustworthy, Castro Pozo noted that when they labored in and for the community (*minga*) they were energetic and productive. This was because "the indigenous community preserves two great socioeconomic principles that modern sociological science and the empiricism of the great industrialists have been unable to satisfactorily resolve: the multiple contracting of labor and the realization of work, all with minimum physical exertion and in an environment of companionship, emulation, and enjoyment. Modern labor unions and big-time economists may find in this institution a lesson and an example to imitate."[24] According to Castro Pozo, these "principles" had been cultivated by the Inca empire, which had guided "social and religious festivities toward work." But it was the contemporary community that had "conserved" them.[25]

Castro Pozo's study built upon the earlier historical sociologies of Javier Prado and the Generation of 1900, in particular the doctoral thesis of Víctor Andrés Belaúnde. Belaúnde had "discovered" the ayllu via Carlos Weisse's German-style seminars at the University of San Marcos around the turn of the century. Weisse had read and disseminated the reflections on the ayllu of the German sociologist Alfred Cunow. However, it is clear that it was Weisse's mentor Lorente who anticipated the centrality and longevity of the primitive, kin-based Andean community in his *History of Peruvian Civilization* (1879). The antipositivist Lorente, however, had not taken a "sociological" approach to his subject; his historicist appreciation of "the communal spirit" of Peru's villages now appeared old-fashioned to the new generation.

Mariátegui took Castro Pozo's land and labor lesson and used it to critique Louis Baudin's influential book, *The Socialist Empire of the Incas*, as well as Augusto Aguirre Morales' popular historical novel, *El pueblo del sol (People of the Sun)*. As Robert Paris noted, Mariátegui criticized the "liberal and individualist precepts" of these authors and called instead for "a little historical relativism."[26] For Mariátegui, in contrast, Castro Pozo was "free of liberal preconceptions."

> This allows him to treat the problem of the "community" with an open mind. Not only does Castro Pozo discover that, despite the attacks of liberal formalism placed at the service of a feudal regime the community is still a living organism, but also that despite the hostile environment in which it vegetates, suffocated and deformed, it spontaneously manifests clear potential for evolution and development. Castro Pozo sustains that, after Conquest, 'the Ayllu or community preserved its natural idiosyncrasy as a quasi-familiar institution in which its principle constitutive elements continue to subsist.' On this point he is consistent with [Peruvian anthropologist Luís] Valcárcel, whose propositions with respect to the Ayllu appear to some to be excessively biased by virtue of his political commitment to indigenous revivalism.[27]

Drawing on Castro Pozo's descriptions of contemporary indigenous communities, Mariátegui argued that the so-called despotism of the Inca socialist state was not so for the community workers of the ayllus. "For the Indians,"

Mariátegui argued, "generalized slavery [under the Incas] could constitute the only possible form of liberty." In making this argument, Mariátegui had, apparently without being aware of it, simply reiterated Lorente's historicist critique of William Prescott's liberal bias (discussed in chapter 6). By stressing the Indian's "natural tendency to communism" and his "communist spirit," the founder of the Peruvian Socialist Party had echoed once again, albeit in another political register, the Lorentean historicist language and concept of the "communal spirit" of ancient and modern Peruvians.[28] Despite the onslaught of feudality—always under the cover of the republic's "formal liberalism"—the Indian had "defended his ancient law." This was so because liberal "individualism" had not found the necessary conditions to flourish in a countryside where "communism was the Indian's only defense" against "feudal bosses." Thus, and again citing Castro Pozo, Mariátegui notes that "even in the indigenous villages where the old patrimonial bonds of community labor have been extinguished there still subsists, robust and tenacious, habits of cooperation and solidarity that are the empirical expression of the communist spirit."[29]

Although Mariátegui's language was frequently historicist, nativist, and romantic, he always stressed the causality of underlying "socioeconomic processes" in history. Indeed, in his texts Mariátegui often identifies himself as a "socialist" (and never as a historian), and socialists, of course, were then in agreement that "in the last instance" all of Peru's historical and cultural "problems" were "socioeconomic" in nature. Like Lorente, however, the socialist understood that the practical "communist spirit" of the agrarian communities must be transformed and mobilized, and that would require a modern ideal or mobilizing "myth." In Lorente's case, that myth was "Liberty" and its vehicle was "the communal spirit"; in Mariátegui's case, the myth was "Socialism," and the means was an "indigenist" or nativist "ancient law." This myth could mobilize revolutionary Creoles and mestizos in a national project capable of leading victimized but potentially "new" Indians out of "feudality" and into that brave new world of universal communism whose vanguard was Europe, or so Mariátegui thought.[30]

Mariátegui's vision of the nation was historicist and dialectical. Peru was a "nationality in formation" because it had not yet resolved its historical dialectic born of the "original sin" of Spanish conquest. Peru consisted of not one but two "epochal" cultural "elements" that had failed to achieve synthesis under the republic because Peru had no true capitalist class. Her Creole elite was "colonialist" and feudal, the hapless instruments of foreign capital, and thus incapable of building a nation. In Mariátegui's scheme, the two epochal elements of Peru were the indigenous or Inca and the Spanish or colonial. Citing Luis Valcárcel, Mariátegui confirmed the nativist anthropologist's view that the "dualism of the Peruvian soul and of Peruvian history in our age is defined by a conflict between the historical form elaborated on the coast and the indigenous sentiment that survives in the Sierra, deeply rooted in nature."[31] Also, like Valcárcel, Mariátegui took historical Peru to be a "coastal formation"; the rest of Peru was natural, ahistorical, a mass waiting to become historical (González Prada's "true Peru"). In short, the "Peru" of Mariátegui was in essence a colonial mirror of Hegel's "Europe," which the German philosopher of dialectics had conceived as the potential synthesis of the historical, dynamic, "Germanic" and Protestant North and the ahistorical, stagnant, "Romanic" and Catholic South.[32]

The Peruvian Republic had failed in its promise to redeem the Indian, Mariátegui argued, because it was nothing more than an empty "liberal formalism" at the service of "feudality" or "feudal power."[33] As such, "Peru is a concept to be created," and this concept "cannot be created without the Indian." It was the Hegelian historical task of his "revolutionary" generation to make a "new Peru with the Indian" that would thereby unite the indigenous, ahistorical, and ancient sierra with the Creole, historical, and modern coast. In this revolutionary revindication of the Indian, wrote Mariátegui, "consists the defeat of colonialism, still alive in the form of feudalism and bossism, but defeated in spirit. The revolution has revindicated our most ancient tradition."[34] This imaginary "revolution" of nativism leads the Peruvian socialist to a historicist appreciation of the Indian as "root and cause, never as program." As "root," the native was "in part immutable," a "hunched" demographic mass. Liberal policies aimed at giving him property had failed to energize him "because the Indian is never less free than when he is alone." In contrast, in community the Indian finds collective defense against feudal landlords but as a consequence of his "hunched," defensive posture he is "melancholic and nostalgic" and thus uninclined to revolution. Unlike the dynamism of Western civilization,

in Asiatic societies—akin to if not consanguine with Inka society—one notes, in contrast, a certain quietism and ecstasy. There are epochs in which history seems to stand still. The same social form perdures, petrified, for many centuries. The hypothesis that the Indian has not changed in spirit for four centuries is thus not unreasonable. Servility has undoubtedly depressed his psyche and body. It has made him more melancholic, more nostalgic. Under the weight of four centuries he has hunched over, both physically and morally. But in the obscure depths of his soul he has not changed. In the high sierra and in the deep ravines where the white man's law has not reached, the Indian guards his ancestral law.[35]

Mariátegui's historicist and Orientalist language was not uncommon for the period and in many ways represents a regress from Lorente's hybrid, East-West narrative of the Incas and of the soul of Peru. Like Basadre, Mariátegui employed a phylogenetic rise-and-fall narrative to his subject, as may be seen in this passage:

> The economy had sprouted spontaneously and freely from the soil and from the Peruvian people. . . . Its collectivist organization, governed by the Incas, had enervated the individualist impulses of the Indians; but it had developed in them to an extraordinary degree, and to the benefit of the economic regime, the habit of a humble and religious obedience to their social duty. The Inkas milked this virtue of the people for the maximum social utility possible, adding value and extension to the vast territory of the Empire by constructing roads, canals, etc., and by submitting to their authority neighboring tribes. Collective labor, the common effort, was fruitfully employed to social ends. The Spanish Conquistadors destroyed this machine of production without being able to naturally replace it. The indigenous society and the Inkaic economy were decomposed and completely atomized by the blow of Conquest. With the bonds of unity broken, the nation dissolved in dispersed communities. Indigenous labor ceased to function in an organic and solidary mode. The Conquistadors merely distributed among themselves the lands and men, and disputed the booty of war, despoiling the temples and palaces of their treasures, without considering the future means and forces of production. . . . In this period [of the Viceroyalty] . . . the Spaniards began to cultivate the soil and exploit the mines. Upon the ruins and residues of a socialist economy they erected the bases of a feudal economy.[36]

Fundamental to Mariátegui's characterization of colonial Peru as "feudal" was his notion, shared with Juan Espinosa, José Martí, and González Prada, that the Spaniards had not truly "colonized" Peru as the British supposedly had New England (that was a good thing); rather, they had merely "conquered" and "enslaved" it. Spain was too weak to effectively colonize her empire, and

so it was merely "an ecclesiastical and military enterprise." Unlike in the promised land of New England, no "bands of pioneers" had "landed on Peruvian
shores." Only greedy "viceroys, courtesans, adventurers, clergy, doctors, and
soldiers" came to Peru, and the "population of Lima was composed of a petty
court, a bureaucracy, a few convents, inquisitors, merchants, dependents and
slaves." As a result there was no "true force of colonization" in Peru. The Spaniard was inept at "creating nuclei of work," for "rather than utilize Indian labor
he sought his extermination."

For Mariátegui, independence in Latin America was merely a byproduct
of the "necessities of the development of Western or, more precisely, Capitalist Civilization." Spain was a backward economy that could not compete
with the "Capitalist West," that is, with northwestern Europe and the United
States. After independence, the "Capitalist West" invested in the export sec-
tors of Brazil and Argentina, where a national capitalist class could establish
itself. But "in the rest of South America," this development was "impeded
by the tenacious and extensive residues of feudality," which persisted behind
the "formalist" façade of liberalism. This tenacious resistance was tempered
by the "period of guano and nitrates," however. With the revenues from
guano exports, Peru was able to attract British capital in the 1840s through
the 1870s, and it was during this period (the Age of Lorente) that a commercial bourgeoisie, "confused and interlinked in its origins and structures
with the aristocracy," emerged. The "government of Castilla marked the stage
of consolidation of a capitalist class" on the coast, and this class organized
itself politically under the banner of *civilismo* (the Civil Party led by Manuel
Pardo). But during this period British financiers took control of the Peruvian
economy, including its railroads, which would be paid by projected guano
and nitrate export earnings. Guano earnings were in decline, however, by the
time Peru lost the nitrate fields to Chile in the War of the Pacific. Although
there were signs that a new dominant class had emerged in Peru during this
period, all that was proven "false" by the war, in which "not even the compensation of having liquidated the past" was achieved. Since the Peruvian
(and Chilean) bourgeoisie had failed to destroy that feudal past, after the
war power reverted to the military leaders or *caudillos*. Despite the rise of
new industries and the recovery of mining, the Peruvian economy remained
primarily agrarian. Commerce, finance, and mining were in the hands of foreigners; the Peruvian agrarian economy was dominated by the *latifundio* or
great estate of the feudal landlords, not by the urban capitalist. As a result,
and contrary to "the cause of republican emancipation," in Peru "the creation

of a capitalist economy had been left to the feudal spirit—the antithesis and negation of the spirit of the bourgeoisie."[37] In Mariátegui's historicist narrative, then, the "feudal spirit" and its "colonialist" culture still ruled in Peru.

The entire "Indian problem" of Peru was to be explained in similar terms.[38] All attempts to solve this problem that "ignore or elude the socio-economic problem" were for the Peruvian Marxist "sterile theoretical exercises." Only "socialist critique could discover and clarify the roots of the problem, because it seeks its causes in the economy of the country," and the "roots of the problem lie in the property regime." It would be impossible to address that problem while the "feudalism of bosses" or *gamonales* persisted in Peru. Since feudal power was not broken, liberal reforms were merely "formal" and so had not taken hold. Under the republic, liberal reforms aimed at redistributing property only insured that Indian lands would fall into the hands of feudal landlords. Here Mariátegui echoed the critique of González Prada and other nativists. That the "Indian problem" could be "ethnic" or cultural was mere "imperialist" ideology. He also dismissed the liberal proposal that education would uplift the Indian. In any case, in Peru education was for the most part still "colonialist."[39]

These dramatic claims of the Peruvian socialist were soon challenged, however. Critics would argue that they were unsubstantiated by the existing historical literature and that they merely recycled the Black Legend narratives both of Spain's imperial rivals and, as we have seen, of Peru's early republican revolutionaries. It was well known that Spanish empire in Peru was premised on extensive colonization and the building of great cities and mining centers, and that in the countryside the colonial order was based on the reproduction of Indian labor in organized village "republics," where the collection of tribute in labor, goods, and species could be had. Mariátegui's sweeping narrative of colonial Peru as "feudal" and "slavish" swept aside all of this, making it possible for him to argue that the Spaniards were not true colonists and that as a result they were obliged to import slaves to work the plantations. Moreover, by upholding an idealized Anglo America as the model of "pioneer colonization," Mariátegui's polemical narrative ignored the place of slavery in the British colonies. Still more inconsistent was the fact that Mariátegui's own conquest narrative contradicted his claim that "colonialism equals feudalism." Mariátegui had consistently argued that Peru was a "conquest economy" of feudalism and slavery. Only later, and "little by little," did it become a "bourgeois economy," albeit "without ceasing to be, from a global perspective, a colonial economy." There was an obvious contradiction between the bad "conquest" and the good "colonialism" narratives in Mariátegui's writings, and this same contradiction is found in the writings of José Martí and Juan Espinosa (see chapter 6).

In *La realidad nacional* (1931), a more mature, post-positivist Víctor Andrés Belaúnde firmly rebutted Mariátegui's "interpretation of Peruvian reality."[40] Mariátegui had blasted Belaúnde as an academic "colonialist" and a "Hispanist" allied with the old aristocracy, and the "colonialist" now delivered a sharp nationalist riposte that, for some observers, made Mariátegui look out of date and poorly read. In his riposte Belaúnde presented himself as a partisan of "integral Christianism" as opposed to Mariátegui's "integral Socialism." Ideological affiliations aside, however, Belaúnde made two strong historical critiques of Mariátegui's characterization of Spanish rule as a "feudal" and "slavist" "conquest" rather than as true colonialism, noting that the young socialist had based his views almost exclusively upon the infamous but unofficial British publication of Jorge Juan and Antonio de Ulloa's eighteenth-century internal or secret report on colonial government in the Indies (today known as *Noticias secretas de América*). Mariátegui had his history backwards: the English had only colonized a strip of land along the Atlantic seaboard of North America; in contrast, the Spaniards had colonized the vast interior of an entire continent, from sea to sea, adopting a "policy of penetration, which was not only exploratory, but for the purposes of colonization and permanent settlement."[41] Thus, Belaúnde could dispense with Mariátegui's dualist vision of Peru as simply ignorant of history. In reality, Belaúnde now asserted, Peru was an old mestizo nation of intermediate racial aggregations arranged in myriad local geographies far more complex than any simple coast/sierra duality could suggest. Moreover, the mixed populations of these heterogeneous zones were nevertheless disposed toward a historically forged, unifying "national spirit." But perhaps the most serious blow was Belaúnde's historicist critique of what he called Mariátegui's "naturalist" vision of Peru. Belaúnde now enlisted Ernest Renan's argument that the nation was a spiritual community of memory forged in quotidian cohabitation and based on the forgetting of old conflicts:

> No one has penetrated more subtly into the complex and elusive concept of nation than Renan in his famous essay. After discarding the predominance of the geographical-social factor, he inclines toward what may be called the historical and spiritual factors. It appears that the constitutive element of any nationality is the community of memory and hope constructed in a long political cohabitation. That spiritual community has existed [in Peru] despite our lack of culture and our illiteracy, our

incoherencies and divisions, and upon occasion it has been awakened in clear and effective ways. There is no doubt that this community has, despite our psychological complex, united whites and mestizos, mountain and coastal dwellers; and it may be affirmed that this community has also permeated the indigenous strata. I simply cannot believe that the entire indigenous mass lacks the concept of nationality, or that it is easier for them to assume a retrospective racial consciousness than it is to form a national consciousness.[42]

For many Peruvian intellectuals, including Basadre, Belaúnde's invocation of Renan moved the postwar debate on "the Indian problem" and "the national question" beyond nativism and positivism to another, increasingly historicist plane.[43] Mariátegui's view of Peru as an ethnogeographic, colonial duality frozen by "feudality" but still inhabited by communist Indians now appeared excessively rigid, economistic, and "naturalist," and thus outdated. The idea that the Inca state was "socialist" would also come under attack from many quarters, most notably from historical sociology and anthropology.[44] Nevertheless, Mariátegui's discourse was not as "naturalist" as Belaúnde claimed. Indeed, it was in certain ways quite historicist. In part for this reason, the denunciatory tone and analytical precision of Mariátegui's biting critique of Peru's "colonial feudalism" would continue to haunt Peruvian historical and political discourse, and to his credit Basadre was well aware of that haunting appeal.

This haunting continued in part because Mariátegui and his contemporaries succeeded at establishing another, long-lived dualism in twentieth-century Peruvian discourse on the nation. "Indigenists" or nativists such as Mariátegui and Valcárcel, and to a certain extent "Indoamericanists" like Víctor Raúl Haya de la Torre, many of whom embraced a denunciatory rhetoric and a combative socialism and/or anti-imperialism, were now entrenched against those they slandered as "Hispanists" or "colonialists."[45] These included Belaúnde and José de la Riva-Agüero and, to a lesser extent, "Latinists" like Francisco García Calderón.[46] As Lorente had done a century before, it was now Basadre's turn to construct a philosophical and historicist bridge across the chasm that divided nativists (*indigenistas*) from Hispanists.

The Historical Essay as Wager for the Republic

Basadre's first two major works, *La iniciación de la república* and *La multitud, la ciudad, y el campo en la historia del Perú* (The Crowd, the City, and the

Country in the History of Peru), appeared toward the end of President Leguía's 11-year "New Patria" regime, and in many ways they constitute critiques
of that regime's authoritarian tendencies (many of Basadre's friends and colleagues, among them Castro Pozo and Mariátegui, were harassed, impris-
oned, or forced into exile during this period) and of what Basadre called its
shallow and decorative "pastime nationalism." *La iniciación* is an innovative
account of the key political and military events of independence, and it relies
upon the explanatory device of the sociological sketch of social classes and
political doctrines or ideologies conceived, for the most part, in critical yet
non-Marxist terms. Working against the dominant notion that this period
was marked by chaos, Basadre gave national and social meaning to the independence campaigns, the political debates, and the *caudillo*-led military
regimes that marked the tumultuous postindependence period. In Basadre's
new interpretation, it was during this period that "the nationality was con-
solidated." Basadre periodized Peru's early republican history in broad accordance with a historicist language in which the historical subject is configured
as an unfolding totality in space and time, that is, in which Peru emerges in a
series of struggles that are assigned meaning as formative moments in a process of realization. The sequencing of the periods speaks for itself, that is, the
characterization of periods provides the narrative structure of rise, crisis, fall,
and renewal that prefigures any analysis and interpretation. National meaning is also written into the characterizations of the social classes, ideologies,
and *caudillos*. Thus, the seemingly chaotic parade of *caudillos* or military rulers is now depicted in accordance with the criteria of "ample but questionable
Peruvianism," on the one hand, and "limited but authentic Peruvianism," on
the other. The first label glossed a "grand Peru" reminiscent of past glory (the
Inca empire and the Viceroyalty of Peru), while the diminished Peruvian Republic with its cramped postcolonial borders is depicted as "authentic" precisely because it came to pass—here we see both the Crocean maxim and the
Pascalian wager at work—that is, because it exists as a "becoming" (*devenir*)
and so has a wider future than the grand Peru, which no longer exists except
as the "pastime" fantasy of Hispanists and nativists.[47] Basadre's affirmative
historicism thus turns away from dreams of grandeur and nightmares of loss
and instead takes Peru as it exists as "promise" and "possibility."

Basadre extended what he called the psychological sense of the contemporary inherent in Croce's maxim to its spatiotemporal dimension as political
proximity. Unlike most men of the colonial period and probably all men of
the precolonial age of the Incas—here Basadre echoed Vico's apprehension of
the ancients as primitives far removed from modern Europeans—the Creole

founders of the republic were "like us," that is, like Basadre and his readers, in short, "contemporaries." Basadre's "history of and for us" was thus both more limited and immediate than Lorente's nineteenth-century genealogical "we," which had fully embraced "primitive" communities of "Peruvians" and "our Incas" as national founders, although Basadre was also fond of the long, genetic view of Peruvian history, albeit as a species of functional prehistory.[48] But the gesture amounted to the same thing: Create a contemporary genealogical "we," across an abyss of history, out of those who were not. Despite his call for a social history of "deep Peru" or *Perú profundo*, for the most part Basadre wrote the collective autobiography of a Creole national state and society struggling to fulfill the promise upon which the republic was founded. In this regard, Basadre's "we" could be more authentic and inspiring because reflexive, that is, its subject was its own political autobiography understood as an urgent moral commitment to Peru's full historical realization and as a wager on Peru's "promise" as a democratic republic. Notably, Basadre's more immediate, Creole historical "we" is formulated in relation to the "national problem" and the "social problem" or "question" that, taken together, problematized the Creole-dominated republic in new ways by contemplating the apparent aspirations of the lower orders. In Basadre's writings these lower orders appear as an anonymous and telluric *pueblo raíz* (a translation of the German historicist concept of *Grundvolk*) and as spontaneous masses or crowds (*la multitud*), whose intermittent and often misguided actions nevertheless raised the social issue to the level of national problem. Basadre's generation posed this social question—in their view unanswered by nineteenth-century republican liberals—as "our social problems." For the most part, these problems were conceived as an inheritance from the precolonial and colonial pasts, but since they were also judged to be universal, they linked Peru to the rest of the world.

In many ways *La iniciación* is Basadre's most thorough study of an epoch, its dominant personages, and its cyclical or spiral trajectory. Notably, the prosaic style and essay-like strategy of the book, based on his doctoral thesis, would, as Gustavo Montoya has keenly observed, remain constant throughout Basadre's long career, and indeed these elements characterize key passages in his best-known work, the monumental *Historia de la República del Perú*.[49] Basadre's preferred style and strategy would always be the problem-oriented conceptual or philosophical essay and the sociological sketch of conditions, doctrines, and personages. In general, Basadre did not write compelling stories, and his prose is only rarely elegant. Indeed, at first glance it would appear that the analytical and essay-prone Basadre did not write narrative discourse on a subject with a proper name in passage through time, that is, "proper history" in the sense outlined by Rancière.[50] But this is an illusion. The success of Basadre's essay-like mode of writing may be attributed to the fact that the master subject of nearly all of his historical and philosophical writing is that named Peru, which is always preconfigured in affirmative, phenomenological, and ontological terms and which always already marks his essays and histories as proper history and historicism. As we shall see in subsequent passages, in spite of Basadre's early claims, his landmark history of the republic is not really a "synthetic narrative history" at all but rather, as the author himself confessed, a university teaching manual. In response to its unexpected commercial success, this work evolved over six editions and the addition of a dozen more volumes to become a massive biography of the republic, an encyclopedic pastiche of annals, sketches, essay fragments, notes, and figures compiled under the unifying, periodic framework first introduced in *La iniciación* and which preconfigured any meaningful reading of the contents as a massive and multiple process of "Peruvianization." Although a critical reading of the *Historia de la República del Perú* will reveal a great deal about Basadre's career and mode of writing history, the fundamentals of his philosophical historicism are more openly displayed in his essays.

Basadre's first major essay was delivered as the annual address at the University of San Marcos, then routinely attended by Peru's leading public figures. Inspired in part by Oswald Spengler's Goethean critique of Western civilization, *Decline of the West*, Basadre's *La multitud* makes a Fichtean and Hegelian reading of Peru's historical process. The essay outlines a critical vision of a Peru in crisis and decline that dramatizes, in historicist terms, modern urban man's alienation from his agrarian roots. Sounding the nativist themes and Hegelian dialectics of Mariátegui and Valcárcel, Basadre describes the emergence of a "cultural dualism" in Peru where the coastal city, new home of the Spanish conquerors, is historically dynamic, while the primal indigenous past "took refuge" in the Andean countryside. Under the ancient agrarian socialism of the Incas—here Basadre follows Louis Baudin—there had existed a "natural relationship" between the country and the city.[51] However, Inca centers were not true "cities in the Greco-Roman sense" but, rather, tributary and ceremonial lodgings for the ethnic elites. The precolonial order could not produce "true patriotism," in Basadre's view, since its diverse castes were "juxtaposed" cogs in a theocratic social machine. In contrast, the Spaniards were individuals or historical agents endowed with a Fichtean national consciousness (see discussion following), and this social-historical fact explains their "easy" victory over the Incas. The conquest had destroyed the old tributary relationship between urban centers and the countryside in Peru. After conquest, "the past took refuge in the countryside. . . . The last Inca [rulers] disappeared . . . but the masses survived, no longer tranquil and isochronous but persecuted, frightened, [and] displaced" across the land.[52]

In Basadre's account, the European civilization brought to Peru by Spain had been forged both from the "Romanic" tradition of the city-state and the "Germanic" influence of the decentered, rural-based nation-state.[53] The Viceroyalty of Peru, ruled from the new coastal capital of the conquerors, exploited the "semifeudal" countryside, where certain aspects of Peru's ancient rural economic order had survived. As a result, the Republic of Peru had inherited grave structural contradictions between city and countryside. These contradictions mirrored those of Hegel's Europe. The Peruvian solution to this Hegelian problem was to reunite the country with the city via a federalist decentralization so that the "region" (that is, provincial centers) rather than Lima would become the "administrative and economic base of national unity."[54] In short, decentralization of the state would produce a new national synthesis.

Despite the schism between city and country, coast and sierra, the crowd had emerged here and there from its docile, "isochronous" state under the Incas and "persecuted and frightened" existence under the Spaniards to become a unifying, albeit intermittent, force in Peruvian history. The crowd spontaneously expressed the "true historical sense of the people," but this sense was rarely heeded by the state and its leaders. The crowd appeared at different moments and was at turns Creole, mestizo, Indian, plebeian, urban, or rural. Indeed, the urban Creole crowd was present at independence, but the real actors and victors were the military chiefs or *caudillos* and their armies, not the people. Indians were oblivious to independence. Under the republic, the old colonial order of cities dominating the countryside continued, while large rural estates or *haciendas* expanded at the expense of Indian peasant communities. However, "spontaneous" rural uprisings—from Tupac Amaru (1780) to Atusparia (1885) to the recent unrest in the southern highlands of the 1920s—registered an ongoing discontent with that process.

Basadre's methodological argument was that the crowd could be read as a "seismograph" of the deep, telluric tremors of the Peruvian people. The new social historian was akin to the seismologist, his ear to the ground. Basadre exhorted his listeners and readers to leave behind the superficial and vainglorious "pastime nationalism" of the day and to cultivate instead a bold new "problem nationalism." This call was an obvious attack on the Leguía regime's penchant for the monumental, its glorification of heroes, and its drawing-room nativism, and it no doubt made many of the "notables" present at the address—President Leguía was among them—uncomfortable. For Basadre, there were far too many historical problems to be resolved before Peru could claim true nationhood.

Restoring Peru's Historical Reason

In his second major collection of essays, entitled *Perú: Problema y posibilidad* (1931), Basadre painted a "panorama of the historical formation of Peru." Basadre's panorama was a Herderian "genetic history" of the epochal progression of the people and the land toward their destiny, from the primitive advent of pre-Inca civilization onward and, despite or rather because of the "social issue," upward toward the inevitable future of socialism. Basadre once again followed Baudin's characterization of Inca civilization as a "singular Empire, where man was a mere cog in a state machine and where, at the same time, his health and welfare was paternally protected . . . and any possibility of ambition, avarice, and the spirit of initiative was foreclosed. . . . Such an organization is only possible within a collectivity without thirst for liberty, power, or riches, and only with a numerous body of conscientious functionaries, armed with precise statistics."[55] He characterized the Spanish conquest as an "alluvium" that added a new layer to the "fertile soil cultivated by the Incas," and in that alluvium lay "the first sowings [*el comienzo de la siembra*] of the Peruvian nationality." The "harvest" follows but is not concluded during the colony, and independence sows new seeds of liberty and democracy. "Peruvian history," Basadre concluded, "loses its significance if the Inca period is not seen to be only the soil, the Conquest the sowing, and subsequent epochs the harvest and also the beginning of new sowings, which will one day germinate."[56] Independence was largely an urban, Creole phenomenon and therefore was only a "promise" and not the fulfillment of national aspirations. Basadre now proposed, after Mariátegui, that fulfillment would come in the future form of a European-inspired socialism by virtue of which Peru would definitively embrace world and regional or Latin American history and so resolve its social issue and national problem. The young Basadre closed with these words: "the exhausting historical formation of Peru is bound to culminate in socialism."[57]

Although Basadre's vision here was broadly social democratic or evolutionary socialist rather than revolutionary socialist, it was the only time that he let his historicism lead him down the path of the Marxian destiny. Notably, Basadre's path had crossed Mariátegui's because both men understood Marxism in national and historicist terms. After Mariátegui's premature death, however, Basadre turned away from Peruvian Marxism mainly because it took a rigid Stalinist turn. With Mariátegui gone, Peruvian Marxism was no longer sufficiently nationalist and historicist for him. Significantly, for Basadre this turn represented a regress to the "antihistorical" and "abstract" thinking of the nineteenth century.

In 1943 Basadre wrote that "the tragedy of our epoch lies in that the theoretical bases [of nineteenth-century thought] are now in crisis."[58] Despite his labors to restore the Peruvian Republic to respectability, Basadre deplored what he considered to be the antihistorical character of nineteenth-century thought. In ways similar to Dilthey's "critique of historical reason" and to Edmund Husserl's critical reflections on "the crisis of European science," Basadre characterized nineteenth-century thought in South America as antihistorical abstractions that had created "ideal" and thus false images of the nation and of man. For Basadre, nineteenth-century South Americans were "idealists" who viewed man as "a rational entity above history." For them, "history was an odious burden."[59] Basadre's historicist attack on nineteenth-century thought is often indignant, directed at "pessimists" and "Europe-worshippers." As in the preface to *La iniciación*, González Prada's "propaganda" is once again the primary target: His "positivist sociologism generally coincided with abstract progressivism in its submission to European fashions and, if it surpassed the old abstractions in its critical view of national reality, it also committed the sins of pessimism and fatalism."[60]

Basadre's critique of nineteenth-century Peruvian thought was also inspired by European fashions, however, and in particular by contemporary German, Italian, and Spanish historicist critiques of French neoclassicism, rationalism, and positivism. Moreover, his sweeping dismissal of nineteenth-century thought was clearly exaggerated and it wrought considerable collateral damage. In effect, Basadre leapt from the independence-era classical republicanism or so-called abstract progressivism of the founders (what Basadre took to be "idealism" or "rationalism") to the "positivist sociologism" of González Prada's generation (what Basadre took to be "materialism" or "naturalism"), thereby bypassing the more practical republican historicism of the 1850s–70s, including most importantly the historicist thought of Lorente, who in many ways had anticipated Basadre's "Peruvian history of Peru."[61] In short, Basadre's historicist critique was enabled by a space-clearing gesture that deposited Peru's pioneering postcolonial historicist tradition in the dustbin of "nineteenth-century thought."

In a critical passage, Basadre reviews the underlying world-historical causes of the crisis of reason and the consequent revision of the idea of progress. Notably, however, this crisis and revision do not translate into a crisis of the reason of Peru since for Basadre as a name, idea, entity, and being Peru was more enduring than was the crisis of ideas or the disenchanting innovations of positive science. Basadre now argued that "the promise of Peru" made at independence had become "an essential and permanent element of the national persona" and as such could not be denied. Paradoxically, Basadre's historicism now came to the rescue of Peru's ahistorical or abstract reason, for it was reason that had made the republican promise of equality and prosperity. What was important was not so much the founding reason but instead the historicist or ontological fact that, as a consequence of that reason, promissorial Peru existed as a mode of becoming. In the same gesture, Basadre's "problem nationalism" or historicist notion of the social issue came to the rescue of the nation's future, since that future was now conceived as a unifying commitment to the fulfillment of "the promise of prosperity and equality among Peruvians." Given the fundamental importance of this passage for any understanding of Basadre's historicist thought, I quote it at some length:

Over the last eighty years, the rationalist and idealist bases of [nineteenth-century thought] have been contradicted. The prodigious development of the biological, sociological, anthropological, and historical sciences, as well as infant psychology, the sociology of the masses, and psychiatry, has dispelled the idea of "rational man" erected as archetype in the early nineteenth century. The idea of the individual as an atomic unity, as a sovereign person, has also been dispelled, because man's life is inseparable from his social environment, and because if he has discharged his human inheritance and does not belong to a community, he is like an errant animal. The idea of progress also suffers an essential revision. Progress understood as human dominion over external nature exists, without any doubt, and is increasing. . . . But what once appeared absurd has now been realized: the new and prodigious instruments of science and industry have been placed at the service of war. The future is no longer "the sun that never sets" [*el sol sin occidente*]. In spite of his amenities and machines, man is not any happier or better off. At times the excesses of rationalism in the form of an excess of culture or refinement have led man into decadence, rendering him sterile, skeptical, antisocial. Nevertheless, something remains of abstract progressivism, such as it was understood in our America. We should not forget that it coincided with the process of Independence, which encouraged the growth of the concepts of sovereignty and national liberty . . . This concept of sovereignty and liberty is deeper than the pendulum motion of ideologies, and deeper than the changes produced by the contributions of the sciences. These remain as permanent and essential elements of the national persona, which it is necessary to defend and affirm. But the legacy is not limited to these aspects. It is not just an affirmation, but also a promise. Why did we achieve our independence? To develop to the maximum the potential of this soil, and to give the best possible life to Peruvian man.[62]

Notably, Basadre's historicist rescue and defense of national reason rest on an affirmation of the collective, albeit divided, "sovereign person" named Peru and on a rejection of the rational, sovereign individual, which he associates with early nineteenth-century thought. This social transposition of liberal notions of progress followed in part from the European devastation of the Great War. The critique of nineteenth-century ideas associated with the Enlightenment, German Idealism and classical historicism, as well as with positivism and the natural sciences, was especially acute in the interwar period when Basadre visited Germany and Spain. Edmund Husserl and his student Martin Heidegger, as well as the Spanish philosopher José Ortega y Gasset, were among the more acute critics, and Basadre read them all. The crisis was brought on in part by the human and ideological casualties of the Great War, among which was the boundless liberal faith in the Hegelian pageant of European civilization. Spengler's *Decline of the West* was an emblematic if shrill example of the new historicist critique of progress. As a result, many Latin American intellectuals who had previously worshipped European civilization (in Basadre's case, Germany in particular) now turned inward. Now, Basadre quipped, "we wish that we were even further away from Europe than we are."[63]

We should, however, put emphasis on the "wish," for Basadre's Hegelian reading of Peruvian history turned Peru into a not-so-distant mirror of Europe, and his historicist critique of nineteenth-century "reason" actually restored the reason of Peru, albeit in the form of a sovereign but divided persona whose historical mode of becoming was driven by the pursuit of an "abstract" promise that had become "essential and permanent."

Back to the Promise of the *Not Yet*

The imaginary turn away from Europe meant a turning inward toward a Germanic "deep Peru" and its promise. Like so many others of his generation, Basadre recommitted himself to the project of "true nationalism," to the embrace of *lo nuestro*, to the "Peruvian history of Peru," and to the social pedagogy of a real and vital national history that would serve as an inner wellspring of strength against unhealthy "international forces." The 1943 essay "La promesa de la vida peruana," or "The Promise of Peruvian Life," reappeared as the lead piece in *Meditaciones sobre el destino histórico del Perú* (Meditations on the Historical Destiny of Peru), published in 1947. The same essay was republished in 1958, along with two additional essays, as a bestselling book by the same title. In this key essay Basadre transformed the "abstract progressivism" or reason of Peru's contemporary democratic promise into a collective ontology, an affirmative call. No longer merely an abstract idea, Peru's promise became in Basadre's hands a binding force that gathered up the already-lived in the existence of the present. In short, Basadre gave Peru a new historical reason that could not be denied without denying Peru itself.

The stated purpose of *Meditaciones* is "to seek the historical reason of Peru, the sum of the epochs, her fourth dimension." An inspired Basadre writes for a "public of youthful readers of all age groups . . . nuclei of serious people, desiring to think with dignity." He addresses this Peruvian readership in a universal key, drawing upon and appealing to the history of peoples: "Those peoples that are deserving of their name always guard spiritual and moral reserves, an unsuspected aptitude of fertility, a beautiful potential for a nobility of conscience, of dreams, and of enterprises." Basadre continues, characteristically, that "in spite of everything, in Peru it is necessary to write not only the history of servility, of disloyalty, of frustration, and of collective disillusion." It was also necessary to write an affirmative history of Peru "in her most fertile aspects, in her will to go forward [*voluntad de camino*], in her mission, and in her hope." In short, Basadre's *Meditaciones* are "an act of faith and, at the same time, of destiny."[64]

In "The Promise of Peruvian Life," Basadre explains in clear and persuasive prose the motivation behind his first history. Here Basadre poses historicism's foundational but repeating question, this time in relation not to Peru but to the republic that Peru has become. "Why was the Republic founded?" he asks rhetorically. "To fulfill the promise that it symbolized!"[65] Like the "collective impulse" (a translation of Dilthey's concept of *Trieb*, or unifying historical force) that had named Peru in "the abyss" of Spanish conquest, the promise of 1821 is itself a historical force or reason, for "without being aware of it, the promise gathered certain elements from the past, transforming them." These elements included the Incas, "who made the tribes whom they sought to aggregate under the Empire see the advantages of a more ordered and prosperous life," and then later, "once Peru was incorporated in Western culture," the fact that "her name resonated as a fascinating announcement of riches and well-being." Finally, states Basadre, "upon the foundation of Independence emerged the yearning for concert and community: 'For Union, Firm and Happy' says the motto on the coin . . . An additional element resided in the republican promise . . . the fervor for equality . . . that finds its maximum expression in the national anthem: 'We are free.'"[66] Basadre's promise was now an authentic call that had gathered the functional elements of Peru's past; not to hear that call was tantamount to denying both the possibilities of the past and the truth that all history was contemporary history. Once again, Pascal's wager and Croce's maxim were manifest.

Basadre's concept of the promise of the Peruvian Republic may be traced to Santiago Távara's *Historia de los partidos* in which, as we saw in chapter 6, the author had argued that the "promise of liberty" was the great "compensation" for the sacrifices of the people who founded independence. That compensation, given in a "historical void," could only be realized by means of a violent forgetting or negation of the colonial past, however. This was the necessary, destructive task of the generation of independence, and Távara likened it to the flight of the Jewish people from Egypt.[67] In Peru after the War of the Pacific, Basadre would reclaim that promise not as forgetting but as a memory with a future. Basadre would have Peruvian eyes turn away from the lost "paradise of the past, be it ahistorical (Adam and Eve) or historical (Incas)." Thus, Basadre rejected both the nostalgia of Peru's Hispanists and the socialist utopia of the Incas cultivated by the nativists.[68] Peruvians should turn "toward the future, toward the dream of a paradise not lost but yet to be found." For, the "dream of a future paradise for all arose together with the contemporary age. . . . Independence was made with an immense promise of a prosperous, strong, and happy life. And the tremendous thing is that here, after 120 years, that promise has not been fully realized."[69] For Basadre, then, the unrealized promise is not a colonial sign of underdevelopment vis-à-vis Europe but, instead, a tremendous thing, a stirring call to the collective labor of making a fully democratic future. Writing the republican basis for a future Peruvian utopia, or *uchronia*, then, would be the "true nationalist" task of his monumental *Historia de la república*.[70] That bookish monument to the republic would chart the many reasons why Peru's democratic "promise" had lived on because it had *not yet* been fulfilled, thereby contributing to its authentic realization in the future. In short, the twentieth century presented to Peru a second chance to get things right in a spectacular, utopian fashion; this "social fact" was a true gift of history, and it inspired Basadre and his generation.

Basadre's 1941 essay on the *país profundo* or "deep country," appended to the second edition of *La multitud* (1947), historicized the "problem of the very existence of Peru as a state [*país legal*] and as a nationality [*país profundo*]." In "Colofón sobre el país profundo" (Colophon on the Deep Country), Basadre argues that "the drama of Peruvian life emerges from the fact that the State would not seem to fit very well within the Nation."[71] This diagnosis leads to the conclusion that Peru would have two histories, one corresponding to the state, the other to the nation or nationality. This too had been a central theme of German historicist thought.[72] Unfortunately, writes Basadre, until now Peruvian history had been written only as the history of the state. Although he does not offer a fully worked-out example of an alternative, Basadre looks forward to the day when Peruvian history would be written not in relation to the state but "in relation to Peruvian nature."[73] By "history of Peruvian nature" Basadre does not mean natural history, however. Instead, he has in mind the "functional history" of the nationality as a "cultural aspiration."

Basadre rejected "naturalist" understandings of the nation and of history (such as those associated with the thought of Prado, González Prada, Mariátegui, or García Calderón). Nationality is not race or language or geography; it is not just the people and the land. Although Basadre's concept of Peru's *pueblo raíz* or original people was surely telluric and for the most part was consistent with German historicism's romantic notion of the *Grundvolk*, in his view the "history of Peruvian nature" lay at the dynamic or "functional" intersection of "the multitude" and its "leaders." Peru's historical multitude, in the form of the crowd, "manifests itself via a series of frequently confused urgencies and aspirations, in mutilated possibilities and necessities, in latent enterprises and hopes." As a result, the nation requires leaders if it will make its mark on the world. The historical role of these leaders is to articulate ideals or visions that are in harmony with but also exceed the aspirations of the multitude. Historically, Basadre now lamented, Peru had lacked such leaders.[74]

The functional relationship between the people and its leaders extends to the past and the present, and so serves as an ideal model for national history. "True nationality," Basadre argues, emerges spontaneously in the functional historical confluence of past and future, which is nothing but the merging of the primal "original people" with the more historical multitudes (Spanish, Creole, mestizo) under the guidance of wise leaders who sense the people's and the crowd's true historical interests. Uniting the people and leaders in a new "natural history" of the nationality would be the basis for a holistic history of Peru's historical reason. This history would unite the past with the imaginable future but exceed both.

> Only that which has a future may possess a fecund past. For the Patria—totality in space and continuity in time, community of destiny and cohabitation in the present—yesterday is useful only to the extent that it resonates here and now, and only if those resonances are prolonged into a future far beyond the place to which our own perishable lives will reach. History is not just the relation of events. History is also the search for what remains after the passage of events.[75]

Basadre's primary inspiration here is the Spanish philosopher Manuel García Morente. García Morente had combined Renan's famous notion of the nation as a spiritual commitment to collective memory (or more precisely, as Palti argues, a quotidian commitment to the active forgetting of the violent conflicts upon which nations are founded) with Ortega y Gasset's idea that the nation is a possibility that consists in the collective "adherence" to a shared vision of the future.[76] García Morente found that Ortega y Gasset and Renan had agreed on a fundamental point, namely, that the nation is a "quotidian plebiscite" on the question of the relationship between a past and a future. García Morente now brought the insights of these two European philosophers of nation together to offer a third view. He proposed that the nationality is the sum of the past and the future, but that it also exceeds this historical sum. He concluded that the essence of a nationality is "style." As a "style of collective life," the nationality cannot be defined or observed because it is not an idea or a thing but a "mode." It can only be imagined or configured as an archetype or ideal figure modeled after "the national man." In the case of Spain, this archetypal figure is "the Christian gentleman" whom "all Spaniards desire to be" but whom "no one has, is, or ever will be."[77] Basadre quotes García Morente as follows:

> "Neither race nor blood, territory nor language is sufficient to elucidate the being of a nation. The nation is both a futural enterprise and an adherence to a past of glories and regrets. That to which we adhere is neither past historical reality nor present historical reality nor a concrete project of the future, however, but instead what these three moments share, that which links us to a unity that lies above the plurality of instants in time."[78]

García Morente's political subtext is that the nation will come to reject any project that is incongruent with its style. Since Spain's style is guided by the heroic as well as humorous figure of the *caballero cristiano* (an ideal somewhere between the mythical El Cid, the fictional Don Quixote, and the legendary conquistador), international communism was obviously not for Spain. García Morente's theory of the nation was not at odds with Franco's national project, but Basadre—whose politics were always, in Peruvian terms at least, left-of-center social democratic—appears not to have associated that theory with a conservative political ideology (the same goes for his reading of Heidegger, whose thought clearly influenced García Morente), in part because Basadre shared his historicist concept of a "national man." If socialism were to take root in Spain (or in Peru), it would have to do so in a manner consistent with the nation's historical reason and style (that is, with the formation of the national man).

Although Basadre does not appear to have enlisted the word "style," he did adopt García Morente's general theoretical point that nationality exists beyond the natural and the ideal, and that it is everywhere "functional," in the sense that it unifies and exceeds history. Basadre's genetic concept of national formation, along with his reading of the Spanish historicist tradition, led him to conclude that nations like Spain were of ancient or medieval origin. Such nations could harbor diverse, cohabitating populations as long as these groups identified with a unifying style forged in a shared history and in a land with particular natural characteristics. In this regard, Spain's heterogeneous history offered some hope to Peru. Since, as we shall see, Basadre located the true birth of the Peruvian nation at or shortly after conquest (in the "abyss of history" and "baptism" subsequently confirmed by the "collective impulse" whose name was "Peru"), his ontogenetical language and theory of nationhood tended to the conclusion that the Peruvian nationality was, despite the ancient origins of the "original" or "root people," relatively young. As a result, Peru had not yet reached the zenith or full expression of her style.[79] However, the sources of that style undoubtedly existed in the study of the past and in the adherence to the promise of Peru. In short, if "Peruvian man" were to reach his destiny and in the process acquire a unifying national style, he would need a push from history.

Pedagogy for a Divided Subject

History as national pedagogy was hardly a new idea in Peru. It could be said that Pedro de Peralta Barnuevo's eighteenth-century dynastic history had

anticipated that notion and that, for Lorente, republican history *for* the people was the true cause of the contemporary age. Since José de la Riva-Agüero
and his Generation of 1900, however, the notion of history as national pedagogy in Peru had been increasingly modeled on the national historicisms
cultivated in German and Italian universities. Riva-Agüero had argued that
the study of history in Lima's university should emulate "those Germanic
and Italian universities" which in the nineteenth century had been "ardent
centers of patriotism and valorous partners in the renovation of their respective nationalities."[80] Peruvian history was hardly unique in this regard. The
Prussian model of historical research and the university-based seminar was
emulated in France, the United Kingdom, and the United States, and German
historicism (and philosophy) became the universal standard of the discipline.
Although Riva-Agüero's patriotic charge was anticipated by Lorente's call for
a "history of and for the people," in postwar Peru the task of national history
took on a graver, more urgent and pedantic tone. That Peru's "national soul"
lives in the "mysterious community of the centuries" had been established
by Lorente, but Riva-Agüero's Enlightenment metaphors of sleep and light
suggested that the "national soul" had been overshadowed, and it was the
pedagogical task of university-based *historia patria* to revive self consciousness of that soul:

> Much has been said and is said, with laudable purpose, about *forming
> the national soul.* At bottom this must mean, first and foremost, and if
> it is not a vain phrase, the fomentation and popularization of *historia
> patria,* depository and mistress of the tradition of the country and true
> creator of the collective consciousness. The national soul is not impro-
> vised, it does not surge suddenly out of nothing at the conjuring of an
> individual or a generation but lives in the mysterious community of the
> centuries: it is the sum of the best in us, our highest and most generous
> aspirations, added to those of our fathers and ancestors and all of those
> who have proceeded us in these lands, and whose configuration and
> influences determine, as everywhere else in the world, peculiar interests
> and private manners of feeling, and are translated in a persistent ideal,
> more or less concrete, at times served and at other times abandoned by
> volition, dormant or active in accordance with the times. One does not
> speak, therefore, of *creating* the national soul because that soul exists,
> even if lethargic or somniac; and if it did not exist, our patria would not
> have a reason for being. One speaks instead of the necessity of lifting

her out of the shadows in which she unconsciously sleeps and dreams, to bring her to the regions of light, to make her feel and know her own life so that, in a word, she acquire clear and full consciousness of herself. Only by virtue of this task, in which History, properly understood, should play the most principal part, will our patriotism . . . rise to that firm and decisive step that distinguishes the nations that know their destines and are resolved to conquer them.[81]

Here we have in a nutshell the entire pedagogical program of twentieth-century Peruvian historicism. Now, the true task of national history was to stimulate Peru's acquisition of "a clear and full consciousness of herself" as a *patria* and a nationality, so that she might defend herself and fulfill her "destiny." It was Basadre's destiny to shoulder this task.

In the essay "El sentido de la historia peruana" (The Meaning of Peruvian History), which opens the collection entitled *Perú: Problema y posibilidad*, Basadre proposes a program of national history education that closely follows the programmatic ideas of Johann Gottleib Fichte, announced in his *Addresses to the German Nation* (1807–1808). Basadre's pedagogical reflections on history as a means toward raising national consciousness are more than academic here, since as Peru's minister of education he promoted Fichte's "New Education" in the schools, albeit with mixed success. Basadre's gloss reads as follows.

The New Education asks: What is historical knowledge and teaching good for? In the old days it was thought that History was the mistress of life, the forger of good conduct, the source of patriotism. But that was an all-too-naïve intellectualist conceit, since it follows that historians would thereby be the monopolists of heroism, civility, and virtue. . . . It is presently believed that History is the instrument of a jealous and aggressive nationalism . . . and that "from this to that bank of the Rhine the truth changes." But the bellicose error is passing as the world internationalizes more and more.[82]

Why then learn and divulge history? "The specialist responds in the name of the search for truth. . . . But what of the citizen in general?" The New Education "takes these citizens into account when it says that History serves to yank children and adults outside of themselves (*sacar de si mismo*), that is, to place them in a conscious relation to the world in which they live, so that they may consider themselves to be actors and authors in a great drama that began before they were born and that opens up perspectives that transcend in importance any personal interest." This "placing in conscious relation" is "the true end of history."[83]

This new pedagogical task for national history was, of course, based on the Fichtean and Hegelian proposition that the people are not true historical agents until they gain consciousness of themselves in the world. The people must be "yanked out of themselves" and into historical consciousness if the nation's potential is to be realized in a more accelerated fashion. As Palti notes in his study of European historical thought on the nation, this was precisely the point that had troubled Otto Bauer and the one that in interwar Europe raised the specter of a divided and incomplete subject within the nation. The fear not only of this specter but also of the possibilities it raised appears to have played a significant role in the rapid rise of the violent, mass myth-making projects of German and Italian fascism as well as Soviet communism.[84] Having turned away from Europe, in Basadre's Peru the nation-making task of historicism might be achieved gradually and peacefully by "creating historical consciousness of self" through education rather than mass propaganda. "For all these reasons," Basadre explains, "nationalism—which in other places is either not necessary or, ominously, superseded—is urgent here. In other places nationalism is something destructive, but here it should be constructive. Constructive of consciousness and constructive of solutions. In other parts it is offensive; here it must be defensive. Defensive against absenteeism and defensive against foreign pressures, and material and mental absorption."[85] Moreover, that nationalist task provides a fecund historical reason for those "knowing" subjects or "leaders" who would guide the process. In short, by raising historical consciousness, national history in the Fichtean, New Education mode would turn the preexisting, ahistorical heterogeneity of preconscious nationals into a collective and defensive "intentional desire" (*querer intencional*) to which all Peruvians could adhere.

Notable here is Basadre's rejection of the Ciceronian topos of *Historia magistra vitae*. As we have seen, that topos had long guided Peruvian historical thought, from the colonial dynastic histories of Inca Garcilaso and Peralta through the republican history of civilization of Lorente. "The light of truth" was no longer the ingenious product of the *artes historicae*, that is, of the artful writing and philosophical contemplation of luminous or dangerous *examplae* drawn from the genealogical past of the historical subject. That old concept of historical truth was nothing more than "the intellectual conceit" of court historians; it was now displaced by the bold new concept of "historical consciousness." As Koselleck noted for Fichte's historicist Germany, this shift followed in part from the elevation of history to the status of a reflexive science.[86] Basadre now argued that "historical consciousness is the search for the authentic, collective 'I,' that is, what 'is' and what 'should be' in the midst of what is present and vanishing."[87] Echoing Riva-Agüero, Basadre insisted that "for the duration of the nineteenth century Peru lacked historical consciousness" precisely because Peruvians lacked a conscious sense of their "collective 'I.'" Indeed, for Basadre this is why the historical study of the "distinct realities" of the national community is itself "true nationalism," for that study is the only basis for the achievement of authentic historical consciousness. Basadre now argued that

> men have lived not in a universal community but rather conditioned by geography, economy, sociology, etc., and within the framework of states and nations. True nationalism is the study of these distinct realities. This has palpable significance before the spurious and blind implantation of typically exotic conceptions. It is also significant from the perspective of History, because in Peru History is the only thing that we possess in common; all that does not emanate from the historical is, in Peru, radically heterogeneous.[88]

For Basadre, history's new pedagogical task of national subject formation was thus grounded in the historicist notion that "the historical" is by definition a unifying force that both creates and is created by historically conscious agents, albeit within the framework of states and nations. In short, if reflexive the historical is unifying and national, and as such it will shield "Peruvian man" from "the implantation of those typically exotic conceptions" that produce "defeatism." Basadre exclaimed, finally, that if history is not a conscious and thus unifying national force then it should be abandoned altogether and not be taught at all in the schools of Peru.

Foundational for Basadre's Fichtean pedagogy of subject formation via historical consciousness-raising is the concept of "memory." Without memory, the individual self has no continuity; similarly, without collective memory, peoples and nations go astray. This is because, following García Morente, "a country is a combination of tradition and destiny. By tradition we mean continuity. And continuity necessarily implies memory."[89] The total loss of memory necessarily produced insanity, and insanity is the loss of one's name.

> Memory . . . is not only the conservation of the past in the present: it is also (and this is the important thing) the collaboration of the already lived in the actuality of existence. . . . If we take away an individual's

memory he falls into insanity, into the unconscious, into the daily learning of the most essential things, into the endless beginning. Insane asylums and graveyards are full of human bodies that do not know their name, who do not know what they were, or what they have done. An analogous thing occurs with peoples. Collective memory fortifies and accentuates in them their own personality. What bonds of union would Peru—a land of geographical contrasts and diverse populations—have if not for the bonds of a common tradition and destiny?[90]

The bond of tradition with destiny resided in the historicist concept of the participation of the "already lived in the actuality of existence" (here Basadre borrows Dilthey's concept of *Erlebnis*, translated as *vivencia*).[91] This combination of living cultural patrimony and memory is profound and futural, for it carries the seed for the "realization of Peru."[92] Adherence to the promise of Peru as *Erlebnis* required not only the New Education, however; it also needed a scholarly factory so that Peru's true beginnings as a collective subject or self would not be lost among "the endless beginnings."

The Airborne Factory of Consciousness and Desire

In an essay fragment included in *Meditations* entitled "Theory of Peru" (1937), Basadre poses that quintessential national-historicist question: "When was Peru born?" The possible answers, he notes, are several. "The geologist," Basadre writes, "will provide information about the precise moments in the life of the earth that correspond to the distinct strata of the Peruvian soil." On the other hand, "the historian of Western civilization will say that Peru enters upon the stage when Francisco Pizarro lands at Tumbes." Still, "the student of political rights will respond by pointing to that scene in the Plaza of Lima and to that instant in which San Martín pronounced these words: 'From this moment . . . we are free.'" But "when one attempts to investigate the birth of Peruvian national consciousness, the answer may only be given after an inquiry." Basadre's inquiry leads him to another reckoning of Peru's date or event of birth:

> Peru as a name and as a social fact in which the Hispanic and the indigenous coexist does not appear modestly or imperceptibly. . . . It is a new society born of blood and tears in an abyss of history, with a loud crash that shook the world. . . . The name 'Peru' itself is the fruit of a collective impulse. . . . 'Peru' arose from an anonymous baptism, displacing the official name of 'New Castile.' . . . This new country found its expression

in a work which, far from being clandestine or ignored, would acquire universal fame. It was edited in Lisbon in 1609. Its title is the *Royal Commentaries*. . . . One may object that Inca Garcilaso feels less a Peruvian than, in the First Part [of his history], a descendent of a fallen empire or, in the Second, a Spaniard. Something of the mythological figure of the Centaur inhabited his eminent and bifurcated soul. . . . But this dualism was proper to the auroral hour to which he belonged. And in this dualism lies the stamp of unity. In binding the names of Manco [Capac] and [Francisco] Pizarro, Peru as a continuity in time becomes visible. And Peru as a totality in space emerges in those pages where we peer up at 'that inaccessible mountain range never set foot upon by man, beast, or bird. . . . ' The *Royal Commentaries* are the *cantar de gesta* of the nationality.[93]

In short, and as we saw in chapter 1, Basadre's inquiry into Peru's birth as national consciousness remits to Inca Garcilaso's founding *cantar de gesta*. Here Peru as a "continuity in time" is "seen" in the binding of Inca and Hispanic dynastic histories, that is, by uniting the name of the founding Inca Manco Capac with that of the founding captain and *adelantado* of Charles V, Don Francisco Pizarro, while Peru as a "totality in space" is glimpsed in the pages where the high Andes appear as that bookish "invisible Patria" yet to be climbed. Basadre now argues that since "Peru may not be considered to be a nation at its zenith," she "should at least have an intentional desire [*querer intencional*] that is the consequence of an irrevocable fact: Peru exists as a totality in space and as a totality in time":

> Totality in space, that is, the harmonious coexistence of mountain and altiplano, condor and albatross, quinoa and cotton, corn beer and brandy, sweet cream and hot sauce, the Inca stones in Cuzco and courtly life in Lima, the revolutions of heroic Tacna under Chilean occupation, forgotten after reincorporation, and Tumbes trapped by the greed and jealousy [of Ecuador]. Totality in time, that is, a long historical event where the Incaic is present only to the extent that it survives within Peruvianness [*peruanidad*], and only to the extent to which, and amount in which, it serves Peruvianness; and where the Hispanic is present only if it has adapted to, or rooted itself in, Peruvianness.[94]

Here Basadre performs that alchemist's leap which is made on the wings of the proper name, wistfully bridging the gap between the words of the *Comentarios reales* and the "irrefutable facts" and things of nature and culture.

These words and things are now bound by that figurative leap of "national consciousness" which imagines that Peru is a "totality in space and time." The means of this functional totality is "Peruvianness." In short, the purpose of Basadre's inquiry into the "birth" of Peruvian "national consciousness" is to pique Peru's "intentional desire" to fulfill her destiny as a "totality." This was precisely the task of Basadre's monumental *History of the Republic of Peru*: to compile a functional totality of words that would create, affirm, and sustain the bookish dream of a Peru that "exists as a totality in space and a totality in time."

History of the Republic grew in spurts, like those interminable buildings in Lima which always seem able to accommodate yet another floor. The ground floor of this interminable edifice of intentional desire was *The Initiation of the Republic*, while subsequent additions (that is, new editions) were built of historical material drawn from Basadre's essays and new investigations. Although Basadre characterized the first edition as a teaching manual and a "global and synthetic narrative history" with no pretension to be definitive, the *History of the Republic* was never a rounded narrative history, nor did it fully achieve a persuasive synthesis as an interpretation, even after six editions and the addition of a dozen or more tomes. Although by the fifth or sixth edition it defined "the totality" of the field by its sheer bulk and erudition, the work does not achieve definition in part because of the cumulative, patchwork, and notebook-like nature of the contents, and in part because it later became clear to Basadre that "definition" was not in the cards. More than a synthesis, the *History of the Republic* became an "airborne factory" (*fábrica aérea*) and a warehouse of knowledge that provided an ever-rising scholarly roof for Basadre's affirmative struggle to raise the historical consciousness of Peruvians.

As the author confesses in the preface to the fifth edition, *History of the Republic* is actually an interminable "essay in functional or 'relational' history." Basadre's concept of "functional" or "relational history" draws upon the holistic thought of García Morente. In a word, "functional history" contemplates the "natural history" of the nationality as a transcendent and unifying cultural aspiration forged in the presence of a Renanian past of "glories and regrets" and in the intentional desire for and Orteguian adherence to a collective future. Now parting with Dilthey, but following as ever the thought of Croce, Basadre explains that "authentic historical consciousness" requires that "we make the past precisely that: past" and thereby make "what is dead" available to consciousness and being as "experience" or "the patrimony of the present."

Croce has written that historiography should liberate us from [what is dead in history], in the sense that it places the past before us, reduces it to a mental problem, and resolves it as a proposition of truth that may serve as an ideal premise for a new life. Thus understood, historicism is not guilty of promoting fatalism, nor does it pretend to retrace the path of time and return to how things were. . . . To be sure, authentic historical thought does not cut off the relation with the past; but it also does not live submerged in it. It rises ideally above the past and transforms it into knowledge, carrying out its cathartic or purifying function, which is similar to the function of poetry when freed from servility to passion. In this case what is procured is an orientation in the world in which we live, and in which cohabit memories and traces of what has passed, latent forces that did not mature and new and original energies, which is where we should find and carry out our mission and duty. For all these reasons, as Croce says, authentic historical consciousness stimulates a true *vela de armas* which does not need narcotics or barbiturates, and instead of carrying out the functions of the warder opens up the gates of a prison within which we would otherwise remain jailed.[95]

Echoing points he made in the preface to *The Initiation of the Republic* and elsewhere, Basadre now confesses that the wider goal of the ponderous ten-volume "essay" is to stimulate "national maturation" by fomenting a *toma de conciencia histórica* vis-à-vis a republican past that was "as turbulent and lurid as it is Peruvian." Citing Boris Pasternak and George Barraclough, Basadre notes that "man does not die like a dog in a ditch. He lives in history. History is the 'sum of all the possibilities that have been realized,' it grants us the comforting sensation that we 'belong' to something, it tells us from whence we have come, who we are. It frequently offers an answer to the question of how things came to be the way they are, for what reasons the world is as we encounter it before our eyes."[96] *History of the Republic of Peru*, the author notes, seeks to achieve this cathartic effect of belonging in the reader by means of "understanding, objectivity, coordination, and ensemble."[97]

A second preface (a reworked version of a previously published essay) reviews trends in twentieth-century European historical thought.[98] Paraphrasing the English historian Sir Maurice Powicke, Basadre notes that historical science is never complete because "not all problems can be solved, since when they are, they only reveal new ones. The historian opens a road, he does not close it."[99] History is a sublime and liberating art and human science; its method is constructivist, and it remains vital as a critical mode of apprehending the world and our place in its Faustian unfolding.

> In our epoch, to be sure, there has been no dearth of egregious and vulgar voices that accuse History of lacking both solidity as a science and utility for life. Paul Valery, one of the greatest writers of the twentieth century, has said, in an oft-repeated phrase, that History is the most dangerous product ever elaborated by the chemistry of the intellect, since it makes people dream, it intoxicates them, it suggests false memories to them, and it torments them in their repose, leading them to the delirium of grandeur and so making nations unbearable and vain. Nevertheless, and despite these and other criticisms, History is still there, living as it has always lived as long as it was authentic: a science in its attachment to the possible truth; and an art in the aura of beauty that accompanies every evocation and affirmation of life. History is an airborne factory, impalpable, subtle, made of ideas and sentiments, although, in a certain sense, it is comparable to architecture since to endure it must ground itself in technical principles when selecting materials, but be inspired by aesthetic principles in the construction itself. However rich our epoch is in apparatuses, instruments, and appetites, in the end humanity is composed of more dead than living. Our epoch, so antitraditional, is inserted in an essentially historicist culture. The sacred books of Christianity are, in their own way, history books. Classical historiography was a creation of the Greco-Roman tradition. Our arts, our literature, our lives are themselves full of the echoes of the past. But there is something more: in the twentieth century History is a vital preoccupation, like science was in the nineteenth century, philosophy in the eighteenth century, and theology in earlier centuries. Today writers, philosophers, sociologists, and politicians come up against History. This characteristic has its roots in Hegel, in Marxism, and in Positivism, but it reaches greater plenitude in Dilthey, and is evidenced by the debate on being and time proposed by Heidegger, by Max Scheler's sociology of science, and in Karl Mannheim's sociology of knowledge.[100]

Basadre's assertion here that "authentic history" is the vital preoccupation of the twentieth century seems to run counter to conventional European wisdom, which holds that the long nineteenth century (in Germany at least) was the "century of history," the ultimate scenario and expression of historicist thought. This is a notable reading, since the debates and trends that Basadre cites here may be seen to represent precisely the "crisis of historicism" in

Europe or, at any rate, serious challenges there to what today is often called "classical historicism."[101] That Basadre connected these critical thinkers to an ancient Western historicist tradition suggests that he may not have accepted the extent to which some of those thinkers (Heidegger in particular) had begun to undermine those foundations.[102] In Peru, and perhaps in Latin America more generally, the "general crisis" in interwar Europe seems to have prompted an inward turn toward a more vital preoccupation with history as means to create a "true" or "deep" nationality.

In Basadre's case, this inward turn went to the epistemological and poetic core of history. The "greatness and servility of History," Basadre wrote, consists in the fact that "the historian creates his own object," and the veracity of this invented object of historical study can be said to exist only insofar as it pertains to the historicity of the historian as "the subject who knows." In short, Peruvian history is the invented object and "servant" of Basadre's own historicity, which in turn is, of course, also Peruvian. For Basadre, this realization means that "the knowing subject should seek, above all, to convince himself, in a centrifugal commitment, of the truth inherent in his own apprehension of the past, to distance his Self as much as possible from all the purely imaginary forms of representation, and to transmit that message with fidelity to his readers or listeners."[103] Basadre's "centrifugal commitment" evokes a sense of the knowing subject and of history as two forces, each of which flees from its axis or center. History always flees from that knowing subject that creates it as an object of study, and so knowledge is always insufficient, the labor of the historian interminable. The knowing subject or the historian also flees from "the purely imaginary forms of representation," however, so as to "transmit a message of fidelity" to readers. The historian, then, is also a servant of readers or, rather, of a certain "fidelity to readers," and history is the elusive servant of the historian or, rather, of "his apprehension of the past." The truth of history, then, is clearly both "great" and "servile."

The Aporetic End of Basadre's Historicism

Basadre built an airborne factory against the real threats posed by neighboring states and the imaginary ones posed by "foreign doctrines" from Europe, but his historicist thought and historiographical production were also anxious bulwarks against the divisive threat of radical heterogeneity within Peru, against the nightmare of endless beginnings born of forgetting. In his intentional desire to write and realize an all-encompassing Peruvian history of Peru, that is, a history of Peru that was homologous with Peru's own formation, Basadre's historicism located all that was "heterogeneous in Peru" in the constitutive inside, or the ahistorical. This was so because "in Peru history is the only thing that we possess in common; all that does not emanate from the historical is, in Peru, radically heterogeneous."[104] At the same time, Basadre's wager and poetic project *for* Peru was meaningless without that heterogeneous inside, without the *not yet* that the divided subject of Peru presented not as the antechamber of underdevelopment but as a "tremendous thing." In this sense, his statement that the historical is "all we have in common" is surely aporetic, for it is the ahistorical and the heterogeneous that, in this line of historicist thought, provide the historical and knowing subject with its raw poetic material, and so it too is "held in common." If history is to be truly homologous with its subject, then Basadre's "Peruvian history of Peru" would have to admit not only the radically heterogeneous or ahistorical as its founding unreason, but also the antihistorical (condensed in the figure of "abstract nineteenth-century thought" and more particularly González Prada) as its necessary intellectual predecessor and opponent.

It may now be seen that the enabling impasse or poetic aporia in Basadre's historicism lies in the figure of an ambivalent subject that is at once ahistorical (and so heterogeneous, forgetful, nameless, and inert) and historical (and thus unified, knowing, named, and dynamic) and where the ahistorical is aided by antihistorical intellectual forces that must be combated. Both the ahistorical and the historical are subsumed under the name of a master historical subject: the idea, entity, and being named "Peru." In short, since Peru is a "totality in space and time" and thus draws all into its field, it is necessarily a radically heterogeneous subject that is never fully historicized, since "the historical" is merely its conscious and authentic mode of becoming as an adherence to a memory with a future. The historical dimension of Peru is the unified future that cannot become without its prior ahistorical being, but the ahistorical dimension of being also exists as a present thing and, assisted by negative antihistorical forces, it everywhere threatens to become the future and thus destroy the historical. What unites this precarious historical subject is "the name of Peru," understood as that which transcends or "remains after the passage of events." This is so because Peru exceeds history. Peru is the holistic unity of all significant points past, present, and future. The name of Peru had abruptly emerged in "an abyss of history" and was propelled into the historical by an impulse and an anonymous baptism, and it was later renewed at independence as the "promise" of a happy and prosperous life for "Peruvian man." In Basadre's thought, then, history or historicism becomes the internal battleground of the historical against the ahistorical and the antihistorical, and this contest is both transcended and made possible by an appeal to the "totality" marked by the proper name or signature. Historicism's internal battleground is a life-or-death affair or, rather, a life-and-death affair, an aporia beyond which history becomes unthinkable and unnecessary, for if either opponent suddenly retreats from the field, the game is up. In other words, without a means (that is, the ahistorical) for apprehending the truth of his own historicity, the historicist or knowing subject cannot configure an affirmative object of study and so cannot "serve" anything "great" that would explain or reveal his own historicity to himself.

Drawing on the insights of Partha Chatterjee and Ranajit Guha on Indian historiography, Dipesh Chakrabarty has suggested that, in the colonial world, history configured its subjects in developmental or evolutionary narratives that typically traced a gradual trajectory toward unification and modernity, on the model of European history. Indian history (or the history of any other postcolonial national subject) might begin with an ancient, glorious past but it moved through dark ages and a Renaissance steadily toward a future national plenitude, albeit via what Chatterjee called a "miserable present" marked by "lack" and "lag."[105] The referent of all such histories, Chakrabarty argues, was and is a hyperreal Europe. This is so because "Europe" was made coterminous in the modern historical imagination with reason, modernity, and (since Marx) capital, understood as universal historical categories that can explain everything, everywhere, at all times. As a consequence, historicism is a colonial discourse that denies the "radical heterogeneity" and now-ness of the historical subject. Although Basadre's historicism often recycles dialectical and developmentalist themes and language that may indeed be traced to European discourse, his notion and emplotment of the historical is not evolutionary in a naturalist sense but is instead an affirmative wager for a future that is itself the consequence or destiny of affirmative past wagers (the impulse, the promise). Moreover, these wagers propel Peru toward a future whose "historical reason" must be distinct from that of modern Europe, since that reason is the product of Peru's own historical mode of becoming that which at independence "Peru" itself proposed it become. The name of this intentional becoming, configured as the historical and the social, was born in the "abyss of history" of conquest but it is clear that this abyss—understood as the radical heterogeneity of "all that is not historical in Peru"—continued to exist in Basadre's Peru, and indeed was the founding unreason for his historicist project, the "truth" of his apprehension of the past.[106]

What is notable here is that the historical subject named Peru does not depart—as Chakrabarty and Chatterjee's readings of historicism might suggest and as indeed is the case in certain European historicist narratives—from a lost historical utopia (for example, the socialist empire of the Incas, or the primitive communism of the ayllu) and it does not move "naturally" toward the future fulfillment of a plenitudinous modernity derived from evolutionary, European models of progress (although, to be sure, Aristotelian and Neo-Platonist notions of continuity, gradation, and plenitude do lurk in the background).[107] Rather, Peru as a "name and social fact" is a necessarily divided and self-perpetuating subject born in that "abyss of history" which is also the historian's or knowing subject's abyss.

Basadre's "Peruvian history *of* Peru" is, above all, a poetic history *for* Peru since his writing strives to create, against the abyss of the heterogeneous and the ahistorical, the conditions for its own future reception and realization among those who would adhere to Peru's collective becoming. Given the great popularity in Peru of Basadre's historicist concepts, there is little doubt that "our historian of the Republic" has been a good servant of history. Indeed, for Basadre the authentic adherence to the historical by reading citizens is history, and the practice of writing history is "true nationalism." Both on the Left and the Right, this Basadrean faith in the transformative efficacy of true historical knowledge continues to inspire historical research and writing in Peru today. As a space-time totality and holistic cultural aspiration, "Peru" itself is an all-encompassing theory of "authentic becoming," and the writing of "Peruvian history" is nothing short of an act of faith or adherence to this becoming. In short, Basadre's historicism is not just about creating a historical sense of belonging and commitment to a project of national development. It is, more profoundly, about that ultimate goal of all philosophical pursuits, from Heraclitus to Heidegger: the authentic form of existence.

Basadre's historicist pursuit of the authentic form of existence is both troubled and enabled by Peru's radical heterogeneity, understood as "all that is not historical" or, more wishfully, "not yet historical." Since the ahistorical and the *not yet* historical are inscribed in the idea (or entity, being, or becoming) that is "the totality of Peru," Peru is a divided subject whose becoming may only be understood and narrated as a struggle with itself on a path toward the fulfillment of the nation's "intentional desire." Still, any cathartic arrival at that fulfillment would bring Peru to its extinction as a mode of becoming and it would also obviate the need for historicism and history. In this sense, Basadre's wager is a Faustian wager "for Peruvian life," that is, an endless and "tremendous" struggle against "endless beginnings," or, as Palti asserts in his reading of Badiou's theory of the subject, a "second-order wager" or "a wager for the wager."[108] This is why Basadre's opus reaches no definition. Instead, his opus is an "airborne factory" of memory against the endless beginnings of forgetting. But the factory of memory has no historical reason without the endless forgetting that threatens it and spurs it on. And so Basadre's "Peruvian history *of* Peru" moves not toward an evolutionary destination but instead toward that destiny which is none other than the aporia or "centrifugal commitment" of the knowing subject's life. The vehicle of this movement toward a centrifugal destiny is the finite historian's wager for the infinite future of the memory named Peru, a wager moreover that confirms "the inherent truth of his apprehension of the past," where that truth is nothing if not a wager on "the most important personage in Peruvian history," that is, "Peru." It is only in this sense that Basadre's Peruvian history of Peru is homologous with Peru's own formation, for "Peru" is not "an idea and . . . entity that is born, grows, and develops" but instead a series of prosaic wagers on, and centrifugal commitments to, that name which was born in an abyss of history.

Epilogue

Peru is made in history, that is, by means of the passage in time of
Peruvians and, at the same time, what presupposes that history is
Peru.

Jorge Basadre, "La enseñanza de la historia del Perú"

Following the insights of Jorge Basadre and his Peruvian predecessors, in this epilogue I consider the several ways in which Peruvian
historical discourse on "Peru" may be read as a theory of history.[1] In what
does this theory consist? And what are its implications for history and historicism at large?

The meaning of the epigraph to this epilogue may appear at first glance
to be straightforward. But what Basadre means here by "history" is actually
rather ambiguous. He appears to be talking about the passage or cumulative succession of events outside the text, that is, in the world at large, where
Geschichte (the historical succession of events) apparently happens or, as it
were, makes things happen; however, if we read more of Basadre—as we did
in chapter 7—we soon realize that any such passage of events and time has
no "historical" existence outside the "impulse" and "promise" of "the name
of Peru." In effect, we may faithfully transliterate Basadre's phrase as follows:
"Peru is made in the writing of history, that is, by means of the passage, in the
world of the text so named, of the proper name of Peruvians and, at the same
time, what presupposes that writing is the proper name of Peru."

Basadre's "Peru" actually consists in the effects and desires of the unisonance and homology of the name, wherein writing the passage of the name
is consonant with living the passage of events. As we saw in chapters 5 and
6, it was actually Lorente and not Basadre who firmly established this mimetic prosaic method and style as the underlying "figurative historicism" or

mythopoetics of contemporary Peruvian history. Lorente invented the contemporary variant of the "Peruvian history of Peru." Before Lorente, however,
and as we saw in chapter 1, it was Inca Garcilaso who inaugurated the "Peruvian history of Peru." In Basadre, the mimetic effect established by Lorente is
further realized by emplotting "Peruvians" in the text as subjects who undergo
Peruvian passages, that is, by prefiguring or designing the entire narrative as
the unfolding story of the realization of the collective, master historical subject named Peru. As we saw in chapter 7, the "means of the passage in time of
Peruvians" is none other than the architectural design of Basadre's "airborne
factory" of historiography, whose "true nationalist" wings—borne by the
name or signature of Peru—are at the service of "historical consciousness."

    The historicizing effects of the text's architecture follow too from Basadre's
"experimental" and dialogic engagement with the processed fragments of the
Peruvian past assembled in the opus. Basadre insisted on a "dialogue with
the past [carried out] in a serene tone so that the small voice of history not
be silenced by the subjective tumult [of the historian engaged only in the
present]."[2] In part because of this serene, self-referential engagement with its
own archive or assemblage, Basadre's "Peruvian history of Peru" gets to the
heart of the matter of historicism. This is so since, in spite of its "intentional
desire" to affirm a phenomenological and ontological Peru outside the text,
his thought calmly touches the necessarily invented and predictive or poetic
nature of the historical subject—a subject that is enunciated and created as a
vessel of collective life and an object of study. It is at this finalist and aporetic
point that Basadre's historicism requires a second-order Pascalian wager on
the name of Peru, for there is no point from which "Peruvian history" may
be told that is not, as Basadre put it, "presupposed by Peru." But what is "presupposed by Peru" is a divided subject consisting of ahistorical, antihistorical, and historical elements, such that the historical "Peru" remits to its own
founding abyss in "all that is heterogeneous" or ahistorical, that is, to the utter
precariousness of its existence outside the "invisible Patria" and "intentional
desire" that drives the historian to write his text and live his "national" life.
This founding abyss, then, is the poetic *Abgrund* of Basadre's historics.

    Basadre's key concept of "the promise" is a good example of the aporetic
and poetic nature of his historical wager on the abyss of history named
"Peru." As we saw in chapter 7, Basadre's "promise" was a Diltheyan "historical force" that, "without being aware of it, gathered certain elements from the
past, transforming them." The powerful "promise" names itself, writes its own
history, and creates its own "functional" genealogy. But it does so via a poetic

appeal to potential "Peruvian" historical agents who are thereby annexed to its project: To write its own formation as a historical "totality." To "exist" as a collective singular unity, the means named Peru requires "Peruvian" subjects, since they are its only means to a future. These "Peruvians" would be the true or real "anchor" of "Peru" except that these subjects, too, are effects of the name. This is so since in Basadre's thought the "Peruvian" means to a means named Peru consists not only in the heroic and patriotic efforts of knowing subjects whose actions and words fight against forgetting, but also, and more fundamentally, in the living pedagogical objects (or potential subjects) who are the original sources of forgetting and thus the true poetic means of "the historical." On the one hand, these objects—the ahistorical and antihistorical "Peruvians" who have "not yet" become "true" historical subjects—are the source of the denunciations and "pessimism" which, for Basadre, undermine the affirmative historicity of the collective singular subject as a mode of becoming; on the other hand, there is no historical "Peru" and no "tremendous thing" without them. Consequently, "Peru" boils down to the protagonism of a proper name in the domain of the so-named but *not yet* (the ahistorical Peruvians) that must be overcome.

As Reinhart Koselleck argued in another context, this omnivorous desire for unity and totality in a conscious mode of becoming corresponds precisely to the all-encompassing semantic reach of the modern concept of history. According to Koselleck, it was only in the last third of the eighteenth century that "history" (*Geschichte*) attained this vast reach, in the process becoming the dominant concept of the "new" or "modern" age—at least as that age was understood by intellectuals in Germanic or northwestern Europe.[3] By absorbing the semantic domain of the Germanized version of the Latin term *historia* (*Historie*), the term *Geschichte* became a "collective singular noun" or "name" that collapses the notion of the succession of events and subjects with the science and writing of those events and subjects. The result of this semantic collapse—whose rule we still live under today—was a single, seamless, universal concept that both produced in fact and characterized in consciousness the temporal and human condition of modernity. "History" could now proceed "along its own course" in accordance not only with the historical consciousness of the knowing subjects who made and wrote history, but more significantly and ominously in accordance with "history itself," that is, in accordance with its own protagonism as a temporal subject or cumulative force that moved time in a forward direction. Displacing and absorbing the venerable topos of Divine Providence, "history" would now come to mean not only the whole course and destiny of "the world" and of "man," within which all of the particular "national histories" could advance along their respective paths; "history" now came to name the sovereign agent or subject of all human destiny and social progress. "History" not only explained everything; it was everything past, present, and future. This is the collective singular concept of history of the enormously influential "German tradition," a tradition that includes not only historicism and the philosophy of history but also professional history proper, that is, such founding figures as Herder, Hegel, and Ranke.[4]

In Basadre, the name of Peru performs the same modern alchemy as does the collective singular name of history, but it does so in revealing or deconstructive ways that point to the abysmal foundation not only of the totality of "Peru" but of that of modern "history" at large. The semantic domain or "totality" of "Peru" in Basadre is necessarily divided into historical, ahistorical, and antihistorical elements that although when taken together may suggest a certain Peruvian repertoire and "style" of becoming, are in fact and theory in perpetual war with one another. This war is fought most acutely perhaps in the anxious soul of the philosophical historicist, whose "centrifugal commitment" to his own wager for the historical (Peru's unified and authentic becoming) and so against the ahistorical ("all that is heterogeneous in Peru") confirms the truth of his own historicity as a knowing and writing national subject.

Thus confirmed, however, the historicist's knowing self must admit that his soul is dangerously plural since it is "made in Peru." That is, and like Peru itself, the knowing Peruvian subject's soul is also inhabited by the unhistoricizable or *not yet* historicized signs of the ahistorical, and by the audible but dangerous voices of the antihistorical (the cant of "defeatists" and "Europeworshippers" for whom "history is a burden" and Peru a "cancer"). Basadre's historicism appears to be a philosophical bulwark against these signs and voices, that is, against the entropic cacophony that postcolonial "Peru" could readily be imagined and experienced to be. The anxious impulse of Basadre's opus follows in part from the historian's reading of his own life experience, which suggested to him that "Peru" was a beautiful but fragile thing, an "invisible homeland" of desire under constant siege by the ignorant forces of forgetting and division. This Peru might not survive the errors of the nineteenth and twentieth centuries.

To be sure, Basadre's lexicon embraced the conventional evolutionary (historical Peru is a cumulative development) and phenomenological (Peru is an entity and being with a historical mode of becoming) languages of classical (Vico, Herder, Ranke) and late or finalist (Droysen, Dilthey, Meinecke, Croce) German and Italian philosophical historicism. Moreover, and like Croce, Basadre argued that the "theory" as well as the "lesson of history" was "relativist humanism" (*humanismo relativista*).[5] But, both in the beginning and in the end, his relativist humanism or historicism comes down to a reflexive or philosophical wager on the promise and possibility of past, present, and future wagers on the name of Peru. This is not "relativist humanism." To give the totality named Peru a historicist mode of intentional becoming, Basadre was obliged to configure his "Peru" not only as "the historical" but also as the ahistorical and the antihistorical, since these last two elements provide the founding unreason or raw material for the historical. That is, the unified national subject of consciousness-in-becoming named Peru is by definition historical, and the task of historicism or "true nationalism" is to further the making of that unified national subject by raising the consciousness of Peru's ahistorical and antihistorical elements, that is to say, of Peru's founding historical unreason, albeit from the "perspective" of the reflexive historicity of the knowing and writing subject. Consequently, the reason for being of historicism and of the national subject named Peru is not ahistorical unreason but historical unreason, that is to say, the poetics of the abyss of the name, without which there is no negative means for "becoming" and no "destiny." This is why, for Basadre, Peru's *not yet* is not something to lament but instead a "tremendous thing," a stirring call to the writing and the making of history, whose purpose is to make historicist or historical subjects. Basadre's late philosophical reflections betray that there can be no end to this means, for that would entail the end of history and the end of Peru. This is why Basadre's historicism is, like "Peru" itself, without closure and without any "secure anchor" other than the name itself.[6]

Basadre's historicist thought on the divided subject of Peru thus constantly comes up against, and then leaps across, its own nominational and self-referential limits. These limits reveal not only the self-affirmative, reflexive effects of the Crocean truism (all history is contemporary history, history is all there is) and the Pascalian wager (the expansive probabilities of the positive wager for the existence of God, that is, for the master or sovereign subject who created all from nothing) on the name of Peru but also the always threatening but poetic abyss of oblivion and heterogeneity that lies just behind or in the name. In short, Basadre's configuration of Peru deflates the modern certainty that "history is everything." History is not everything. History is at once "more and less" than everything. This "more and less" is a consequence of the fact that history cannot help but be a poetic discourse on that subject which presupposes it. Peralta would have been pleased with Basadre.

Who Is (Not Yet) History?

Gilles Deleuze has proposed that Friedrich Nietzsche's critical method of "active philology" and "genealogy" provides means to a new theory and method of history. This new theory follows from the proposition that the first question of historical inquiry is not Plato's "what is?" but instead, "who speaks, who names" what is?[7] For Nietzsche, the "who speaks, who names" question makes the "soul" or subject of history a dangerous "plurality" of competing names and repeating voices.[8] Given this cacophonic plurality of the soul or subject of history, the ultimate "ground" of history and being was never "what is" or "that which exists" (historics), nor was it any transcendent essence prior to the historical existence of "what is" (for God is dead); instead, the ground of history was "the abyss" or the ungrounded (*der Abgrund*). This founding unreason or abyss is pregnant with multiple possibilities for becoming however, albeit in the sense of overcoming "what is."[9]

The question for history, then, is not "What is history?" but "Who is history?" That is, who and what is the ungrounded subject of history that may overcome "what is"? As Rancière noted, the answer to this question is always the same: the proper name.

Although Basadre's historicism firmly committed itself to making something desirable out of the "historics" or historical "what is" of Peru, in thinking through the historical process of Peru's "becoming" he recognized that the "what is" was simply insufficient. More important was "that which remained after the passage of events," which was always more than "what is." For Basadre this excess was a holistic, living, future-oriented "historical force" born of the affirmative wagers "for Peru" of past "Peruvians." These past wagers had made "Peru" itself into the "protagonist" of its own history. The answer to the "Who is history?" question was, therefore, clear for Basadre: "Peru" was "the who" (the subject) and "the what" (the object) of history.[10]

In *Provincializing Europe*, Dipesh Chakrabarty argues that "historicism—and even the modern, European idea of history—one might say, came to non-European peoples in the nineteenth century as somebody's way of saying 'not yet' to somebody else."[11] The discourse of European historicism applied brakes to decolonizing desires for independence, in effect assigning Indian subjects to the "antechamber of modernity." This may be true for India but it does not hold for Peru and the Spanish Americas. It does not hold because of historical differences, that is, because of the greater antiquity of colonial and postcolonial historical discourse in the Americas and because early Spanish empire was in certain ways quite unlike late British empire.

The historical differences are critical. As Roberto Dainotto has argued, it is critical to note that Chakrabarty's modular "Europe" and its developmentalist "historicism" were largely inventions of the late-eighteenth- and nineteenth-century French and German historical imaginations, that is, an invention that corresponds to Koselleck's *Sattelzeit* or "saddle period" (ca. 1750–ca.1850).[12] During this period, the European south (Portugal, Spain, Italy, Greece) was effectively marginalized, orientalized, or exiled from "new" or "modern Europe." On the one hand, the southern reaches of the continent were reconfigured as Europe's "old" or premodern past; on the other hand, those regions became a borderlands contaminated by Asian and African climatic, racial, and cultural "influences."[13] In the colonial and postcolonial worlds of the "new" or late northwestern European empires, historicism could now appear as a colonial discourse of development that said "*not yet* to somebody else" in large part because that discourse had already said *not yet* to contemporary southern Europe.[14]

In response to this *arribiste* northern verdict, historical discourse and historicist thought in southern Europe and its colonial worlds found reason to distinguish itself and its origins from those of the north and its colonial worlds. As Jorge Cañizares-Esguerra has demonstrated, eighteenth-century Spanish and Spanish American historical thought engaged in an innovative, academic war against the condescending views and provincial theories of northwestern European historians. In certain limited ways, Cañizares-Esguerra suggests, this Ibero-American defense anticipated the postcolonial critique of European theories of history. In any case, it questioned the master narratives of modernity produced in the north. The Spanish American critique of "armchair" European theory and "philosophical history" was duly informed by a "patriotic epistemology" which sought to ground its critique in an intimate Creole access to native sources. As we saw in chapters 3 and 4, Peralta and Unanue's histories were in one way or another inspired by these polemics and intimacies. An essential element of these eighteenth-century southern European and Spanish American critiques was the "Arabist thesis," which held that the modern history of civilization and "genius" had passed from the ancient Roman empire via the Arab world to southern Spain and Italy, and from there north to "Europe." Another element of Spanish (and Italian) defense was a positive appreciation of the influences of the ancient

civilization of Egypt and also of "the African clime," on northern Mediterranean civilization and on the "character" of her inhabitants.

As Peralta had argued, Spain's rise to world empire was due in part to the favorable "influences" visited upon her inhabitants by her privileged geographical situation at the crossroads of Africa and Europe, the Mediterranean Sea,
and the Atlantic Ocean. Similarly, Unanue would argue that Asian, African,
and Iberian elements of "genius" had crossed the Atlantic to Peru, where they
had merged, under the burning sun and exquisite climatic diversity of circumequatorial America, with the "national genius" of the Incas, in effect making "Peru" the most universal land on the face of the earth. Unanue's historicist critique of Europe followed in part from Peru's colonial position within
an Orientalized and Africanized Iberian world that, since the eighteenth century, had served as the subaltern, constitutive inside of a Francocentric and
Germanocentric "Europe" that was increasingly conceived from the north as
the modern site and end of history. However, Peruvian historical discourse
was also positioned in the subaltern constitutive inside of Spain. This layered,
inside-outside position made it possible for "Peruvian" historians to stand in
a critical but "universal" position vis-à-vis both "Spain" (as in Inca Garcilaso
and Peralta) and "Europe" (as in Unanue, Lorente, and Basadre).

The deprovincializing critical concept of the universality and modernity
of Peru as a historical subject ran deep. Inca Garcilaso's foundational Peruvian history of Peru is the universalizing consequence of a Divine Revelation
visited upon Tawantinsuyu by the preternatural messengers of God (archangels and the Virgin Mary). These messengers guide and protect the mundane
forces or "invincible arms" (the Spaniards) of the Pope and Holy Roman Emperor Charles V. It was not that the primitive religion of the "ancient Peruvians" was less pure or monotheistic than that of the primitive Christians—here
again Peru exceeded the Old World, for the faith of "primitive Peruvians" was
purer than that of the old Christians—but simply that the written Word had
not been revealed unto them. The authority of Inca Garcilaso's logocentric
writing was derived from its retrospective and phonocentric inscription of
speech as the native oracular source of a universal truth.[15] Since pre-Revela-
tion "Peru" had no writing, no history, no written annals, and thus no true access to the universal history to which it had long belonged without knowing
it, it was the revelatory task of the historian Inca Garcilaso to add the missing
Old World element called "culture." The "Peruvians," of course, were more
than "ready to receive the seed of the Word," since the "Inca Kings of Peru
that were" had "prepared the soil." In accordance with Neo-Platonist precepts
about the verisimilar relation between the original ideas inscribed in spoken

words and the essence of the things they named, the authentic history of the Inca kings was made available to the multilingual Inca Garcilaso. This access enabled the writing of a retrospectively "proper" dynastic history of a sovereign Peru.

In certain ways repeating Inca Garcilaso's ambivalent gesture of Indian or colonial "commentary," Peralta's ostensibly apologetic history of Spain was actually a critical colonial mirror for Spain written not from the perspective of Andalusian exile but instead from the new Peruvian center, Lima. Peralta's Lima was the "Political Phoenix" of its own modern empire, a new "seat" of historical knowledge that now aspired to be a center of historical poetics. Peralta freed "History" from "the Prince" so that Peruvian history could become the poetic product of its own making, that is, a sovereign domain of critique and prognosis that would "guide Peru" into that future "which was its own inheritance." Peralta's colonial historical poetics achieved something similar to what the discourse of German history accomplished in another idiom several decades later. Writing in the 1720s and 1730s, Peralta turned the "history" (*historia*) of the dynastic Book of Kings tradition into a "collective singular" or sovereign concept of prognosis manifested in the career of Lima, albeit via poetic means and by working within the Latin and Hispanic semantic field of the name *historia*.[16] Peralta's poetic reflections on dynastic history registered the old Aristotelian polemic of "historics" (what is) versus "poetics" (what should be).[17] Like Aristotle, Peralta assigns poetics a higher value since it is more universal than historics. Poetics is superior to or more "majestic" than historics because it encompasses the conditions of the possible, that is, the "should be" and not merely the "what is" of "rustic annals." Poetics is prognostic and expansive and not merely descriptive of what has been, and this is why the poet Virgil is Peralta's model historian. Peralta's colonial gesture is to make historics poetic, and the means to this end—which is not an end, per se, but a means to a future—is to turn the sovereign figure of "the Prince" into the sovereign figure of a "History" whose locus of enunciation is Lima. Thus freed from the prince, the poetic copy named history would become available to the Peruvian imagination as the sovereign subject and force of its own future, as the maker of its own "inheritance."

Although Peruvian historical thought on a decolonizing political separation and independence from the Spanish monarchy may be characterized as broadly historicist, none of Peru's leading philosophical historicists (Peralta, Unanue, Lorente, Basadre) assigned Peru as a whole to the antechamber of modernity. To the contrary, and as we have seen, all suggested that Peru was well-prepared for a modern or contemporary independence of her own making. They did so in large part because the discourse of "Peruvian history" itself was, since Inca Garcilaso, founded on the premise that "Peru" was a sovereign historical subject. Basadre, who by European standards was the most self-consciously historicist of these Peruvian historians, was very clear on this point. Echoing Lorente and an earlier generation of Peruvian historical thinkers, albeit without citing them, Basadre argued that the commonly held view that Peru's independence was a consequence of the importation of European ideas "paints Peruvian history as a mere reflection of European history." Instead, Basadre argued, Peruvian independence registered a preexisting, eighteenth-century "consciousness of self" (*conciencia de si*) evident in the "pre-revolutionary nationalism" of the likes of Unanue. Moreover, and again per Lorente, Peru's revolution formed part of a hemispheric or American movement to end "the first European colonialism" or "old colonialism" and was thus a "very important episode" in the worldwide "democratic revolution."[18] From Peralta to Basadre, "Peru" is not *not yet*.

Instead, in Basadre the *not yet* is internal to the master subject named Peru. The *not yet* historical is the malleable (and therefore poetic) substance of the ahistorical, that is, "all that is heterogeneous in Peru." With the aid of Inca Garcilaso's founding exegesis, however, we may see that the originary name of this *not yet* historical subject is "Beru." In chapter 1 we saw that "Beru" is the proper name of the barbarian "Indian," that is, of those native colonial subjects who dwell "at the ends of the earth." We also saw that Inca Garcilaso makes Beru's utterance of his own proper name available to universal history. The "Inca Indian" historian does so by inserting his erudite commentary in the time and verisimilar truth of Beru's barbaric speech at "the moment of discovery." It is anxiety or fear and expectation—as we saw in chapter 1 made understandable to European readers via the tale of the shipwrecked Pedro Serrano—that, in Inca Garcilaso's text, drives Beru to utter his name. And it is precisely this anxious colonial utterance that names "Peru" for empire and history. In this subaltern speech act, interpolated from an imperial future that already is, Beru becomes the Founding *cholo* or ex-Indian of Peruvian history.

Peru's genealogy is thus double. On the one hand, and as Inca Garcilaso's Neo-Platonic exegesis of the Inca dynasty makes clear, Peru's origin as a sovereign subject remits to the exemplary founding king or Inca Manco Capac, "the cornerstone of the edifice" of "Peruvian history"; on the other hand, Manco Capac's (and Inca Garcilaso's) "reason" was none other than the founding barbarian, who gives his name to "the country" and so contributes to her proper making as a *patria*. Moreover, "Peru" is Beru's posterity, Beru's gift, sent via the pen of Inca Garcilaso, to all future "Peruvians." "Peru," we might say, was "born in an abyss of history," but not as Basadre's affirmative "collective impulse," "promise," or "intentional desire." Instead, "Peru" was (and is) a subject-effect of the anxious requirements of empire (later, nation) and history-writing. Both polity and history (and historicism) require a sovereign past, that is, a retrospectively imagined sovereign subject—in this case, "the Inca Kings of Peru that were" and, later, simply Peru—but also a limitless future, embodied not in the "promise" but in the subaltern subject who is the necessary colonial and postcolonial object or *not yet* subject (the "Indian" whose proper name is "Beru" and, later, simply, "Peruvian") of the civilizing and historicizing "impulse."

One may make different critical readings of this historicist impulse. Chakrabarty's critique of historicism or "history of" is largely content-driven. His reading makes a strong critique of the "developmentalist" and colonialist message of historicism but it tends to underplay the poetic dimensions of retrospective narrative discourse, which nearly always exceed the referential function of language. In contrast, my reading of the history of Peruvian history and historicism is informed by White's insight that history "is never only history of [but] always also history for . . . not only in the sense of being written with some ideological aim in view [as Mannheim argued], but . . . in the sense of being written for a specific social group or public." I add to White's insight the notion that this "specific social group" for which history is written is a projection of the proper name. That is, the "Peruvian history of Peru" is always already a "Peruvian history for Peru," that is, a history that is generative of a Peruvian future.

White adds that the "purpose and direction of historical representation is indicated in the very language which the historian uses to characterize his data prior to any formal technique of analysis or explication that he may bring to bear upon them so as to disclose what they 'really are' or what they 'truly mean.'"[19] I have noted that this "very language" is, as Rancière argues, constituted and configured first by the proper names and topoi that both mark an absence and govern what Jean-François Lyotard calls "the world of names" of historiography, or, in Barthes' more structuralist idiom, the "units of historical discourse." These names and units of discourse underwrite and compose any history and every historicism as a self-referential and literary "mythology" for the future; moreover, this mythology has legitimate claims to scientific and political standing.[20]

Provocatively drawing upon the reflections on history of Claude Lévi-Strauss, White argued that "to historicize is to mythologize." To mythologize or historicize is not to falsify or mislead but instead to enlist the poetic faculty of language for history. To historicize is to preconfigure, often unconsciously, not only the nature of the subject to be narrated and in so doing to define the objects of cognition that populate the "historical field" of inquiry for the reading subject, but to preconfigure the means of that subject's future in discourse. Consequently, the supposed distinction between "historicism" and "history" proper—an assumption that still informs professional historical discourse—is ill-conceived. This disciplinary convention, argues White, followed from the foundational but in many ways unfortunate, post-Rankean separation of "philosophy of history" from "historiography." Instead, White argues that historicism, or more precisely "philosophical historicism," flows from the same narrative or rhetorical imperatives as does history or historiography. This is why "history proper" or professional historiography is, for White, better understood as "figurative historicism," that is to say, as a kind of antiphilosophical convention that prefers not to draw attention to the ways in which its language or form prefigures the meaning or content of its prose, since these are simply "given" by the established protocols of the discipline. Again, this antiphilosophical stance, ostensibly taken in the defense of objectivity and science, simply masks history's dangerous and creative powers.

As Rancière notes, these powers are literary, political, and scientific. As an inquiring, retrospective narrative discourse directed toward posterity, history's science is to uncover and reveal the living presence or effects of a lost or invisible past whose future or posterity, as it were, already is, or at least already is visible to the historian as an imaginable desire. As the critical art of the possible and the desired, history is always political in this potent sense. More: History's political nature is pronounced because, when compared to most fiction or "literature," the poetic license of historians to name subjects, and then narrate the series of events that happens to those subjects, is constrained by past and present usage and the protocols of research, and for that reason is both more familiar and more dangerous. Literature, Rancière notes, "lives only by the separation of words in relation to any body that might incarnate their power," whereas history has long lived by their union.

Obliged by protocols of evidence and rules of mimetic representation to write credible stories based primarily on eyewitness accounts and archives, the narratives of historians more often than not follow upon the damaging and deathly ones of conquest, destruction, and conversion enacted by the captains, emissaries, and priests of empire, who name colonial subjects so that they may be taken possession of, ruled, and redeemed. After empire, no less foundational for the writing of history are those seductive and violent calls of the architects and agitators of nations or postcolonial states who, in the name of "the people," seduce and implore subjects to assume their "historical destiny" as proper patriots, as forgetting citizens, or as vengeful proletarians of the revolution. Before history, empires and nations live long and kill many by the proprietary power of naming, commanding, calling, forgetting, and seducing. And yet, if history's bloody and beloved names heave a more explicit, political, and scientific burden on the shoulders and shelves of historians, this is surely so not because the annals of historiography guard, and with patience reveal, secret truths (the "royal-empiricist" conceit, notes Rancière, both of court and modern scientific historians) otherwise beyond the reach of the literary and popular imaginations, but precisely because history (or historiography) and literature (or fiction) have far too much in common. In literature, as in history, "it is not by describing that words acquire their power: it is by naming, by calling, by commanding, by intriguing, by seducing that they slice into the naturalness of existences, set humans on their path, separate them and unite them into communities."[21]

History's wordy union with the political body is "made flesh and spirit" not only because the Christian ethos sundered the cosmos into two imaginary domains but because the body of the sovereign subject of mundane history was generally conceived as double. Historically—speaking both for the Mediterranean and the Atlantic worlds—the "chronicling tradition" and the Ciceronian *artes historicae* of the early modern period were primarily addressed to and concerned with the "two bodies" of the sovereign, that is, both the person of the king or prince to be informed and educated, and also the imagined "head and eyes" of the body politic, that is to say, "the King" and "the Prince" understood as universal concepts of divinely sanctioned rule by oversight.[22] After the republican revolution in history, that is, under the sway of democratic-republican forms of postdynastic rule, the sovereign subject would become the "body" or political community itself, that is, "the people" or "the nation" (or some fragment thereof), of and for some manner of which most "contemporary history" has been written.[23]

Friedrich Meinecke's influential study of the genesis of *Historismus* has for a long time ruled as the classic statement or measure of what historicism or historism is, but it may tell us more about what German historicism was *for*. Following Wilhelm Dilthey, Meinecke associated "historicism" with the progressive achievement of "full historical consciousness" as such. For Dilthey, as for Basadre, such an "awareness of the finitude of all historical phenomena ... is the final step toward the liberation of man."[24] Meinecke's study was a Neokantian defense of German thought written after Germany's humiliating defeat in the Great War, and it is itself a perfect example of the historicist poetics and method it so ably describes. This method and poetics generally require that the writing subject inscribe him- or herself in the domain and genealogy of the master subject of his or her history (in this case, the historian of historicism is himself heir to the master name or idea of *Historismus*), which in turn is the true protagonist of the story that the book tells. In this book Meinecke traces the emergence of a self-consciously historical mode of thought that combined elements of "natural law, Neo-Platonism, Christianity, Protestantism, Pietism, natural science, a curiosity in the voyages of the XVII century, the first sprouts of national sentiment and the liberty of peoples, and finally and no less important, the flowering of poetry."

For Meinecke, the new historicist or historical view of the world—which he took to be a singular achievement in the universal history of ideas—crystallized in "the great German movement, from Leibniz to the death of Goethe," and this movement produced an enduring reference or "founding father" figure for history and anthropology in Johann Gottfried Herder. Finally, this "great German movement" led to the professional historiography of Meinecke's professor, Leopold von Ranke, to whom the faithful student devotes a long and somewhat tedious script, judiciously reserved for the appendix. Although historicist thought drew upon many currents, including Neo-Platonism, pre-Romantic (British) vitalism, and the genetic or botanical notions of natural evolution more proper to the French and Dutch Enlightenments, for Meinecke historicism was essentially a German movement that had sought to counter the antihistorical French system and its "universal history of man in general."[25]

In polemical contrast to an idealized, antihistorical opponent named "French system" or the universal philosophical history of "man in general," Meinecke argued that historicism posited as its point of departure and key concept the dynamic individuality or singularity of the historical subject. The singular subject of historicism since Herder and Goethe had been the "individual human" in all of his and her dimensions, spiritual and material, and, at the same time, "those ideal or real formations of the collectivity which only manifest themselves in their evolution."[26] That is, the language of historicism was "made flesh" in individual subjects and "made spirit" in collective subjects. As Koselleck has noted, Herder's concept of historicism was deeply Pietist. Its epistemological roots may be traced to the theological conviction that the historical Jesus incarnated or "made flesh" the revealed Word of God and that the truth of this divine revelation of the word is continually revealed in natural and human history.[27] Meinecke does not subject this Pietist tradition to rhetorical or formal analysis, but those "ideal or real formations of the collectivity" (nations, peoples, civilizations) of the historicist imagination were nearly always configured in a phylogenetic language of spiritual gardening, which is ultimately of Biblical origin. This language, as Cañizares-Esguerra has demonstrated, was widely disseminated throughout the colonial Americas.[28] This language inundated Leibniz's influential, Neo-Platonist theory of monads, which were conceived as singular but infinitely multifaceted "seeds" or "souls" that potentially contain or reflect "the world as a whole," which, in Herder's famous phrase, was a "great garden in which the peoples grew like plants."[29] Leibniz's monad, which informed Lorente's concept of Peru's "communal spirit" as the seed or name of "progress" and "national development," was based on the notion of a preformed *evolutio* or "genetic program" that, since it is a microcosmic mirror or "soul" of the god-head, already contains everything that it will ever become. This monad or soul is singular in a universal way, since it mirrors from its own vantage point the cosmos as a whole. Likewise, for Herder the great earthly garden of history is an isomorphic mirror of the universe (planets are likened to peoples) as it was then understood.[30]

If we trace the history of historicism or historism beyond Meinecke's "history for" of "the great German movement," however, we soon encounter a more ambiguous conceptual history. The critical readings of Maurice Mandelbaum and Chakrabarty notwithstanding, the wide semantic field of historicism is not easily reduced to "the idea of development." Noting Nietzsche's aphorism that "all concepts that summarize semiotically an entire process escape definition; only that which has no history is definable," Elías Palti argues that the history of the usage of "historicism" suggests that the concept has always eluded precise definition. This is so in part because the semantic domain of historicism cannot be readily distinguished from that of modern history itself.[31]

In Koselleck's brief sketch of the emergence of the term, "historicism" appears as a conscious or philosophical elaboration of the significance for the history of thought of what had already taken place in historical discourse at large: the resignification of "history" as the universal and "final instance" of a self-referential truth that was both objective and subjective in nature. As noted above, in the German discourse of the last third of the eighteenth century, the German term *Geschichte* (from *geschehen*, denoting an occurrence, happening, or event) had overtaken and merged with the Germanized Latin term *Historie* (denoting the science and writing of events, or what today is often called historiography) to become a collective singular noun or name.

"History" did not just refer to any particular succession of events or any writing of such events. Instead, "history" in the collective singular became the universal "protagonist of human destiny and social progress." This "threshold" concept, Koselleck notes, emerged just prior to what would, thanks to the rapid circulation of the new collective singular concept of history, come to be known as The Revolution (that is, the French Revolution).[32]

Although, and following Meinecke's antinomies, Isaiah Berlin has insightfully read the eighteenth-century historicist tradition, represented by the thought of Vico, Leibniz, Herder, and Johann Georg Hamann, as the "Counter-Enlightenment," there are strong reasons to think that this counter tradition shared fundamental concepts and practical goals with its polemical opposite, now known as the Enlightenment proper, and that, as a result, it contributed to the dialectical formation of a theory of Europe as the modern stage, end, and tribunal both of universal history and national historicist thought.[33] As Koselleck has pointed out, the generic notion of universal history (history as a collective singular noun) went hand-in-hand with the development of the notion of national history, which was always subordinated to the former.[34] And as Palti has recently argued, the debate between the elder Kant and the younger Herder—sometimes misread as an illustration of the difference between rational/enlightened and romantic/historicist thought—reveals that the two men actually shared foundational assumptions about universal history as a "progressive and cumulative process destined to reach the full realization of the potentiality of the species," and that historical rhetoric and pedagogy could and should serve as the "guiding thread" to that realization.[35]

In many ways these notions of universal history as realization and guiding thread echoed Saint Augustine's Neo-Platonist notion of history as "the education of the human race."[36] In short, Enlightenment philosophical history of "man in general" (for example, Voltaire or Kant) and the so-called Counter-Enlightenment historicism of particular collectivities (for example, Vico or Herder) were not necessarily at odds when it came to "the ends of history" (universal enlightenment), in part because these two discourses shared idioms and concepts that conspired in a modern theory of history that configured "Europe" (that is, France and Germany) as the privileged place or stage of a totalizing modernity. In some versions of this universal and totalizing history of modernity, including those of Montesquieu and Hegel, which were highly influential, northern or "Germanic" Europe became the destiny or "end of history."[37] But not in all versions.

As Koselleck argued, *Historismus* appears to have been coined in that revolutionary Age of Isms by the Neo-Platonist poet, philosopher, and "prophet of romanticism" whose pen name was Novalis (Georg Philipp Friedrich Freiherr von Hardenberg). It was not long, however, before Ludwig Andreas von Feuerbach attacked the *ism* (in the 1840s), associating it with falsity and mysticism, while at about the same time Christlieb Julius Braniss used the same word in a positive sense to designate a new, future-oriented philosophy of history. By 1852 Felix Dahn had defined "true historicism" as "the history of the world as a whole, understood as a unitary and necessary evolutionary process, in accordance with the laws of reason," an approach based in part on the philosophies of Gotthold Ephraim Lessing and Immanuel Kant.[38] In his 1881 study of the work of Giambattista Vico, Karl Werner also used the term in memorable and rather different ways, referring to the Neapolitan's *New Science* as a bold new "philosophical historicism."[39] Although in each of these cases, "preformist" and Neo-Platonist notions of "evolution" and "development" are at work, Vico's linguistic approach to the history of human "civil institutions" is readily distinguished from the ontological visions of Herder and Kant, and it exercised a strong influence on White's reformulation of the theory of tropes. But the most momentous break with "preformist" or genetic and organic historicism, which informed Lorente's histories, comes in the late nineteenth and early twentieth centuries, when the Neokantian phenomenological approaches of the "late" philosophical historicists (such as Droysen, Dilthey, Meinecke, and Croce) take a "finalist" turn.[40] As Croce noted, history no longer consisted in the writing and imitation of Ciceronian or humanist aphorisms; humanist history was now historicism, that is, the conscious understanding that history was everything.[41] Historicism now becomes associated with the realization that "history is all there is," that the condition of humans is entirely self-made and, consequently, liberating or damning. This finalist turn clearly informs Basadre's "relativist humanism."

Chakrabarty's critique appears to ignore this "late" or finalist turn in historicist thought. He argues that "the idea of development" is the central concept of historicism, but this is not the case with finalist, twentieth-century historicism.[42] "Historicism," he argues, "tells us that in order to understand the nature of anything in this world we must see it as an historically developing entity, that is, first, as an individual and unique whole—as some kind of unity at least in potential—and second, as something that develops over time. . . . The idea of development and the assumption that a certain amount of time elapses in the very process of development are critical to this understanding." As a result, says Chakrabarty, "much history writing still remains deeply historicist. That is to say, it still takes its subject to be internally unified and sees it as something developing over time. This is particularly true—for all their differences with classical historicism—of historical narratives underpinned by Marxist or liberal views of the world and is what underlies descriptions/explanations in the genre *history of*—capitalism, industrialization, nationalism, and so on."[43]

In search of a history that is not historicist in this developmentalist, *history of* sense, Chakrabarty proposes a *history in*. In this *history in*, the historical subject is configured not as a developing entity but instead along the lines of Heidegger's proposals. To reduce an exceedingly complex and idiosyncratic language to its bare essentials, Heidegger's notion appears to be that the *noch nicht* or *not yet* aspect of becoming is an always already existing but not necessarily "present" dimension inherent to being, such that the *not yet* denotes not the future yet to be but "the futures that already are." In such a notion of the historical subject, it would be inconsistent to argue that any being has "not yet" become its full self, or that the individual or collective subject could only be apprehended, as Meinecke had argued in the 1930s, "in its evolution." In Heidegger's formulation, the historical subject is always fragmentary or *not-one*, and as a result its future may suddenly appear as the past of what it has now just become as presence. History, in short, is nothing other than the succession of *nows* of the subject that is always *not-one*.

Notably, Heidegger's thinking on the *not yet* dimension of being draws upon Nietzsche's notion of "eternal return," albeit now posed as a "resolute repetition" (*Wiederholung*) of *Dasein* (a dense concept that implies both "Being-there-now" and "Being-toward-death"), understood as a "going back into the possibilities of the *Dasein*-that-has-been-there." Heidegger envisioned a critical method for *history in* that would write the possibilities of past *nows* as present futures, that is, as *not yets* that already are. In Heidegger's words, "resolute repetition makes a reciprocate rejoinder to the possibility of that existence which always has-been-there. But when such a rejoinder is made to this possibility in a resolution, it is made in a moment of vision; and as such it is at the same time a disavowal of that which in the 'today' is working itself out as the 'past.'"[44] It is this disavowal of today's past in favor of a future that already is that makes *history in* a radical possibility. Chakrabarty concludes:

> To critique historicism in all its varieties is to unlearn to think of history as a developmental process in which that which is possible becomes actual by tending to a future that is singular. . . . To think of the "not yet," of the "now," as a form of "unrealized actual" would be to remain trapped entirely within historicism. For a possibility to be neither that

which is waiting to become actual nor that which is merely incomplete, the possible has to be thought of as that which already actually is but is present only as the "not yet" of the actual. In other words, it is what makes not-being-a-totality a constitutional characteristic of the "now." It is in this radical sense of never being a totality that the "now" is "constantly fragmentary" and not-one.[45]

The proposal for a *history in* of fragments is a stirring call for experimentation in the writing of history. Still, the poetics of history of a Heideggerian *history in* may not be so radically different from the poetics of history that, at times in spite of itself, appears to underwrite Basadre's late historicist "Peruvian history of Peru." This is so not only because Basadre's Peru is a divided and at times dialectical subject but because retrospective narrative discourse is always already founded, as Croce noted, on a future that already is, that is, on *history for* an imagined or desired state of being. In other words, any "past" exists for the world of names of history only to the extent that its future or "posterity" has become a present in which its trace may be apprehended and written. This is simply a longwinded version of Croce's maxim: All history is contemporary history. By way of an elaboration, we simply add that what makes it "contemporary" is the future it makes possible as its own posterity. In short, and notwithstanding the Heideggerian critique, a more ecumenical history of history need not reject historicism or *history of* as hopelessly colonizing and inevitably developmentalist. However, such a history would first require that we stop thinking of historicism as a European "idea of development" which then spread, via late or second-wave colonialism, to the "Third World." We should also stop thinking of historicism as something distinct or separable from history or historical discourse in general.

Peruvian history was thought and written in a universal key before Chakrabarty's "Europe" was imaginable as such, and when that "Europe" and its historicism emerged in the late eighteenth century, Spanish and Spanish American history was frequently written against it.[46] In the Peruvian case, at least, this writing against was possible in part because the philosophical and rhetorical roots of its historical discourse may be traced to an earlier, colonial Renaissance and Baroque *artes historicae* of classical Mediterranean origins. Finally, if postcolonial Peruvian historical writing selected, imitated, detoured, and at turns exceeded the conventions of European historiography and historicist thought it was because the history of the proper name of "Peru" itself constituted a theory of history. That theory has stood and stands both inside and beyond "Europe."

Notes

Chapter 1. The Founding Abyss

1. Jacques Rancière, *The Names of History: On the Poetics of Knowledge*, trans. Hassan Melehy (Minneapolis: University of Minnesota Press, 1994), 5.

2. Michel de Certeau, *The Writing of History*, trans. Tom Conley (New York: Columbia University Press, 1988), 5.

3. Hayden White and Erlend Rogne, "The Aim of Interpretation Is to Create Perplexity in the Face of the Real: Hayden White in Conversation with Erlend Rogne," *History and Theory* 48 (Feb. 2009): 64.

4. Roland Barthes, "The Discourse of History," *Comparative Criticism* 3 (1981): 7. Drawing on E.G. Collingwood, who in turn drew upon Benedetto Croce, Donald R. Kelley makes a similar hermeneutical point: "Herodotus, Thucydides, and their successors wrote for posterity—and for the time being we *are* this posterity." See Kelley, *Faces of History: Historical Inquiry from Herodotus to Herder* (New Haven: Yale University Press, 1998), x.

5. The classic statement on the distinction between historics and poetics is found in Aristotle's *Poetics*. There Aristotle notes that historics is particular and descriptive of what is and has been, whereas poetics is universal and predictive of what should be. For this reason poetics is more philosophical and, therefore, superior to historics. As we shall see, the more philosophical or poetic Peruvian historians, including Peralta, Lorente, and Basadre, would have agreed with Aristotle.

6. Rancière, *Names of History*, 63.

7. Jorge Basadre, *Meditaciones sobre el destino histórico del Perú* (Lima: Huascarán, 1947), 104–105.

8. Basadre, *Meditaciones*, 104–107.

9. Edmundo O'Gorman's writing belongs to the middle decades of the twentieth century.

10. For a more detailed and trenchant critique of Rankean "historical science," see O'Gorman's *Crisis y porvenir de la ciencia histórica* (Mexico City: Imprenta Universitaria, 1947).

11. The semantic domain of the Spanish term *hecho histórico* is wide and may include the English notions of both historical fact and historical event.

12. O'Gorman, *La idea del descubrimiento: Historia de esa interpretación y crítica de sus fundamentos* (Mexico City: Centro de Estudios Filosóficos, 1951) 379–80.

13. O'Gorman always uses the term "man" (*hombre*) and never "people," and in most cases it is clear that by "man" he means European or Western man; that is, here "man" signifies not a primitive or natural state but a certain civilizational and/or creative state of being and becoming that is the consequence of a history of civilization. O' Gorman, *La invención de América: Investigación acerca de la estructura histórica del nuevo mundo y del sentido de su devenir* (Mexico City: Fondo de Cultura Económica, 1995), 152.

14. O'Gorman, *La invención de América*, 57.

15. Giorgio Agamben traces the negative notion of the subject as void back through the traditions of negative philosophy (Hegel, Heidegger) and theology to Aristotle. See Agamben, *El lenguaje y la muerte: Un seminario sobre el lugar de la negatividad* (Valencia: Pre-Textos, 2002).

16. See Alain Badiou, *Being and Event* (London and New York: Continuum, 2005), particularly parts 1 and 5. My reading here draws on Elías José Palti, "Poststructuralist Marxism and the 'Experience of Disaster': On Alain Badiou's Theory of the (Non-) Subject," *European Legacy* 8, no. 4 (2003): 459–80.

17. Elías Palti, *Verdades y saberes del marxismo: Reacciones de una tradición política ante su crisis* (Buenos Aires: Fondo de Cultura Económica, 2005).

18. Basadre, *La promesa de la vida peruana y otros ensayos* (Lima: Mejía Baca, 1958), 17.

19. Inca Garcilaso de la Vega, *Segunda parte de los comentarios reales de los incas o historia general del Perú* (Cordova, 1617), bk. 1, chap. 38, fol. 31.

20. My reference here is of course to the unforgettable image that Walter Benjamin conjures in his reflections on Paul Klee's 1921 drawing. Benjamin's European angel of history is hurled backwards into the future by the storm of progress that gathers in her wings, and so she can only look back over the wreckage that progress has wrought. In colonial history this wreckage is often reckoned not as progress but pillage. In colonial history progress—or, rather, providence—exerts any compensatory effects not in the material but in the spiritual or soulful domain.

21. Inca Garcilaso de la Vega was baptized Gómez Suárez de Figueroa after his great-grandfather. He was the son of the Spanish captain Sebastián Garcilaso de la Vega y Vargas and of the niece of the Inca Guayna Capac, baptized Isabel Suárez Chimpu Ocllo. Since Crown policy prohibited interracial marriage, Sebastián later married the Spanish woman Luisa Martel and arranged for Chimpu Ocllo to be joined with the Spanish commoner Juan del Pedroche. Gómez Suárez de Figueroa sailed to Spain in 1560, adopting his father's surname and the titular "El Inca" in 1563. Some scholars have suggested that Gómez Suárez favored his father's surname for its literary association with Garcilaso de la Vega (1503–1536), a celebrated Golden Age poet-soldier.

22. Roberto J. González-Casanovas, *Imperial Histories from Alonso X to Inca Garcilaso: Revisionist Myths of Reconquest and Conquest* (Potomac: Scripta Humanistica, 1997), 114.

23. See Jean-François Lyotard's reading of Freud's theory of mourning in Lyotard,

"Universal History and Cultural Differences," in *The Lyotard Reader*, ed. Andrew Benjamin (Oxford, U.K.: Basil Blackwell, 1991), 316.

24. The foundational account is Francisco de Xerez, *Verdadera relación de la conquista del Perú y de la provincia del Cuzco llamada la Nueva Castilla* (Seville: Casa de Bartholome Pérez, 1534). Consulted in the John Carter Brown Library, at Brown University.

25. Inca Garcilaso de la Vega, *Primera parte de los comentarios reales de los incas* (Lisbon, 1609), bk. 1, chaps. 4–5.

26. On the life of Blas Valera, see Sabine Hyland, *The Jesuit and the Incas: The Extraordinary Life of Padre Blas Valera* (Ann Arbor: University of Michigan Press, 2003).

27. This is Inca Garcilaso's contention, but other contemporary accounts of first contact place the mythical river of "Viru" or "Veru" or "Pelu" closer to Panama, where Yunga was not spoken. The Inca's version has become the accepted truth.

28. Inca Garcilaso, *Primera parte*, bk. 1, chap. 4, fol. 4.

29. Crown grants, or *capitulaciones*, named New Castile and New Toledo, of 200 leagues each but later extended by 60 leagues, were granted, respectively, to the *adelantados* Francisco Pizarro and Diego de Almagro.

30. Inca Garcilaso, *Primera parte*, bk. 1, chap. 4.

31. Inca Garcilaso, *Primera parte*, bk. 1, chaps. 4–5.

32. See Raoul Mortley, *The Idea of Universal History from Hellenistic Philosophy to Early Christian Historiography* (Lampeter, U.K.: Edwin Mellen, 1996).

33. It is not clear whether "proper names" or surnames existed as such in "Peru" prior to the arrival of the rite of Christian baptismal. I do not take "Beru" to be anything more than Inca Garcilaso's retrospective baptismal name for the anonymous Yunga native, and I take that anonymous native to be a hermeneutical necessity and a historical truth.

34. Thomas Cummins, "La fábula y el retrato: Imágenes tempranas del Inca," in Thomas Cummins et al., *Los incas, reyes del Perú* (Lima: Banco del Crédito, 2005), 1–41.

35. Margarita Zamora notes that Inca Garcilaso's exegesis of the name of Peru is more than a mere "linguistic curiosity" and serves instead as an opening demonstration of his method and mode of argumentation. See Zamora, *Language, Authority, and Indigenous History in the "Comentarios reales de los Incas"* (Cambridge, U.K.: Cambridge University Press, 1988), 165.

36. Perhaps the most lucid discussion of this requirement is found in Rancière, *Names of History*, passim.

37. José de Acosta, *Historia natural y moral de las Indias* (Seville: 1590; Madrid: Dastin, 2003), 92–93. Citations are to the Dastin edition.

38. Acosta, *Historia natural*, 91.

39. Pedro de Peralta Barnuevo, *Historia de España vindicada* (Lima: Francisco Sobrino, 1730), s/n. Held in the John Carter Brown Library, at Brown University.

40. Cited in Sabine MacCormack, *On the Wings of Time: Rome, the Incas, Spain, and Peru* (Princeton: Princeton University Press, 2006), 192–93.

41. Pace MacCormack, *On the Wings of Time*, 193.

42. Barthes, "Discourse of History," 7 (see chap. 1, n. 4).

43. Zamora, *Language, Authority, and Indigenous History*, 39.

44. Roberto González Echevarría, *Myth and Archive: A Theory of Latin American Narrative* (Durham: Duke University Press, 1998).

45. Inca Garcilaso, *Primera parte*, bk. 1, chap. 15.

46. Inca Garcilaso, *Segunda parte*, bk. 1, chap. 36, fol. 28.

47. de Certeau, *Writing of History*, 45–47.

48. Zamora, *Language, Authority, and Indigenous History*, 61–62.

49. On the sly civility of the colonial subject, see Homi Bhabha, *The Location of Culture* (London and New York: Routledge, 1994), 85–101.

50. See Patricia Seed, "'Failing to Marvel': Atahualpa's Encounter with the Word," *Latin American Research Review* 26, no. 1 (1991): 7–32.

51. Zamora, *Language, Authority, and Indigenous History*, 165.

Chapter 2. The Arts of History and the Arts of Rule

1. Cited in Donald R. Kelley, *Faces of History*, 136 (see chap. 1, n. 4).

2. *The Education of a Christian Prince*, which Erasmus dedicated to the young Hapsburg prince who would become Charles V, and Niccolò Machiavelli's *The Prince*, the printed edition of which was addressed to Lorenzo de' Medici, were among other things, composed to gain employment as court historians, in 1516 and 1513, respectively. Early modern dedications to princes in the prologues to Spanish and Spanish American histories often reiterated the aphorisms of Erasmus, as for example in Pedro de Peralta Barnuevo's *Historia de España vindicada*, discussed in chapter 3. See Desiderius Erasmus, *The Education of a Christian Prince*, trans. Lisa Jardine (Cambridge, U.K.: Cambridge University Press, 1997).

3. See Richard Kagan, *Clio and the Crown: The Politics of History in Medieval and Early Modern Spain* (Baltimore: Johns Hopkins University Press, 2009), 18–22.

4. David A. Lupher, *Romans in a New World: Classical Models in Sixteenth-century Spanish America* (Ann Arbor: University of Michigan Press, 2003), 43–50.

5. Roberto González-Casanovas, *Imperial Histories* (see chap. 1, n. 21).

6. Thomas Cummins, "La fábula y el retrato," 8–9 (see chap. 1, n. 34).

7. The Requirement (in Spanish or Latin) was to be read to those "lords" whom the Spaniards encountered in lands granted by the Pope to the kings of Castile. The text demanded that the subject lord pledge allegiance to "the King of kings" and to the papacy. If the pagan lord did not submit, he could face "just war" and "enslavement." According to most early accounts, "Atabaliba" (Atahualpa) had tossed to the ground the Bible that was presented him by Father Valverde, who also read the Requirement, at which time the Spaniards, shouting "Santiago," fell on him and his royal guards.

8. The foundational account is Francisco de Xerez, *Verdadera relación de la conquista del Perú* (1534) (see chap. 1, n. 24).

9. François Hartog, *The Mirror of Herodotus: The Representation of the Other in the Writing of History* (Berkeley: University of California Press, 1988), 200.

10. The anthropological notion of the kingly origins of "barbarian nations" may be traced to Tacitus. This notion is developed into a theory in Vico's *New Science*. See Kelley, *Faces of History*, 62.

11. Xerez, *Verdadera relación*, cols. 1–2, fol. Biii–Bv.

12. A number of ecclesiastical historians vigorously objected to elements of Xerez's account. The loudest voice among these was that of the ex-*encomendero* (recipient of an Indian labor grant), later Dominican monk and eventual bishop of Chiapas, Bartolomé de las Casas. Las Casas wrote several critical histories of the Indies, but one short manifesto would secure his fame: *Brevísima relación de la destrucción de las Indias* (A Short Account of the Destruction of the Indies), published in 1542. Making use of Xerez's account but adding to it the condemnatory statements of a supposed eyewitness (the Franciscan monk Marcos de Niza), Las Casas portrays Pizarro as a ruthless and greedy "tyrant" who mercilessly slaughtered innocent and peaceful Indians. Pizarro, decried Las Casas, had "burned Atabaliba" so as to get rich at the expense of the emperor, thus jeopardizing the preservation of his realm. Indeed, Las Casas makes a general denunciation of nearly all nonclerical Spaniards in the Indies. But his central thesis is that the Indians are the purest and most innocent souls imaginable. The *Brevísima relación* is addressed to the prince and his circle of advisors, and its creation coincided with the founding of the Viceroyalty of Peru, but the book did not see public circulation for another decade. When published it spread like wildfire among Spain's imperial rivals, who sought, with considerable success, to peddle the so-called Black Legend of Spanish tyranny in the New World. However, Las Casas' account of the events of conquest was providential, dynastic, and imperialist, and it exercised a notable influence on Inca Garcilaso.

13. See MacCormack, *On the Wings of Time* (see chap. 1, n. 40).

14. MacCormack, *On the Wings of Time*, 57.

15. Cummins, "La fábula y el retrato," 17.

16. See Martín de Murúa, *Historia del origen y genealogía real de los reyes incas del Perú* (Madrid: Testimonio, 2004); Felipe Guamán Poma de Ayala, *Primer nueva corónica i buen gobierno* (Mexico: Siglo Veintiuno, 1980).

17. On Antonio de Herrera, see Kagan, *Clio and the Crown*, chap. 5.

18. Inca Garcilaso, *Primera parte*, bk. 1, chap. 15 (see chap. 1, n. 25).

19. Ibid., bk. 2, chap. 20, fol. 37.

20. Zamora, *Language, Authority, and Indigenous History*, 158 (see chap. 1, n. 35). Eusebius's *Praeparatio evangelica* integrated the founding figures of Plato and Moses, paganism and Judeo-Christianity, in a Hellenistic universal history of human culture. See Mortley, *Idea of Universal History*, 196–99 (see chap. 1, n. 32).

21. Michel Foucault, *The Order of Things: An Archaeology of the Human Sciences* (New York: Pantheon, 1970).

22. Inca Garcilaso's theory of language presupposes that the royal names tell a verisimilar truth about the nature of the rulers and their reigns, for names in the original

language (not in an ultimate sense but in the sense of being the original and "general" language of the Inca, that is, before translation and corruption into Spanish) are vehicles of ideas—that is, they are inscribed with the essence of the original idea. Since most Spanish chroniclers did not have access to this original truth, their accounts often fell into error. See Zamora, *Language, Authority, and Indigenous History*, 81–84.

23. Zamora, *Language, Authority, and Indigenous History*, 14.

24. Inca Garcilaso, *Primera parte*, bk. 1, chap. 11.

25. Zamora, *Language, Authority, and Indigenous History*, 141.

26. Zamora, *Language, Authority, and Indigenous History*, 148.

27. MacCormack, *On the Wings of Time*, 60.

28. Mortley, *Idea of Universal History*.

29. González-Casanovas, *Imperial Histories*; Marie Tanner, *The Last Descendent of Aeneas: The Hapsburgs and the Mythic Image of the Emperor* (New Haven: Yale University Press, 1993).

30. On the Inca precolonial dynastic tradition, see Catherine Julien, *Reading Inca History* (Iowa City: University of Iowa Press, 2000).

31. Lupher, *Romans in a New World*.

32. Inca Garcilaso, *Primera parte*, bk. 9, chap. 39, fols. 262v–263.

33. Inca Garcilaso, *Segunda parte*, bk. 8, chap. 21 (see chap. 1, n. 19).

34. See MacCormack, *On the Wings of Time*, 177–201.

35. See Roger Rees, *Diocletian and the Tetrachy* (Edinburgh: Edinburgh University Press, 2004).

36. Inca Garcilaso, *Segunda parte*, bk. 1, chap. 40, fol. 32.

37. MacCormack, *On the Wings of Time*, 72–75.

38. The *Primera parte* of Inca Garcilaso's history, published in Lisbon in 1609, was duly dedicated to the Queen Regent of Portugal. The second edition of the *Primera parte* (Madrid, 1723) adds a dedication to King Philip V by Nicolás Rodrigues.

39. Inca Garcilaso, *Segunda parte*, prologue, fols. 2v–3.

40. The father of Gómez Suarez (Inca Garcilaso de la Vega's baptismal name) was one of these Spanish soldiers of conquest.

41. As Zamora notes, "Amerindian culture all but fades out of the picture when [Inca] Garcilaso begins the narration of postconquest history." Zamora, *Language, Authority, and Indigenous History*, 10–11.

42. Inca Garcilaso, *Segunda parte*, prologue.

43. José Eusebio Llano Zapata, *Memorias histórico, físicas, crítico, apologéticas de la América Meridional* (Lima: IFEA, UNMSM, PUCP, 2005 [1757]), and *Epítome cronológico o idea general del Perú: Crónica inédita de 1776* (Madrid: Mapfre, 2005 [1776]).

44. Basadre, *Meditaciones*, 104–107 (see chap. 1, n. 7).

45. On this point, see José de la Riva-Agüero, *La historia en el Perú* (Lima: Pontificia Universidad Católica del Perú, 1965), 180–87.

46. Inca Garcilaso, *Primera parte*, bk. 1, chap. 9.

47. Ibid., chap. 10.

48. Ibid., chap. 15.

49. Ibid., chap. 12.

50. Ibid., chap. 21.

51. Ibid., chap. 25.

52. Inca Garcilaso, *Primera parte,* bk. 2, chap. 2, f. 27.

53. Alejandro Cañeque, *The King's Living Image: The Culture and Politics of Viceregal Power in Mexico* (New York: Routledge, 2004).

54. Jorge Cañizares-Esguerra, *Nature, Empire, and Nation: Explorations of the History of Science in the Iberian World* (Stanford: Stanford University Press, 2005), 84–85. See Juan Solórzano y Pereyra, *Política indiana* (Madrid and Buenos Aires: Ibero-Americana, [1647] 1930), bk. 2, chap. 6, paras. 32–33, and chap. 25, paras. 8–9.

55. Inca Garcilaso, *Segunda parte,* dedication.

56. Ibid., prologue.

57. Ibid.

Chapter 3. The *As If* of the Book of Kings

1. Jean Bodin, *Method for the Easy Comprehension of History* (New York: Norton, 1969).

2. Roberto González Echevarría, *Myth and Archive,* 55 (see chap. 1, n. 44).

3. José de la Riva-Agüero, *La historia en el Perú* (see chap. 2, n. 45).

4. Jerry Williams, introduction to Pedro de Peralta Barnuevo, *Historia de España vindicada* (Newark, Del.: Juan de la Cuesta Hispanic Monographs, 2003 [1730]), xi–lii. Williams' critical edition is a welcome recovery of Peralta's history, which had been out of print for some 273 years. My reading notes and citations are based on the 1730 Lima imprint held in the John Carter Brown Library, at Brown University. In that imprint, the dedication to the prince of Calderón y Cevallos and Peralta's prologue are unnumbered. The body of the text is numbered by columns. Therefore, some of my references to the text lack page numbers.

5. The second part of Peralta's *History of Spain Vindicated* has not been found and appears not to have been completed, most likely because of lack of funds and the author's waning health. See Williams, introduction to Peralta Barnuevo, *Historia de España vindicada,* xi–lii.

6. González Echevarría, *Myth and Archive,* 3–8.

7. Calderon y Cevallos, dedication, in Peralta Barnuevo, *Historia de España vindicada* (Lima: Francisco Sobrino, 1730), s/n.

8. On the intellectual siege of Spain and Spanish America, see Jorge Cañizares-Esguerra, *How to Write the History of the New World: Histories, Epistemologies, and Identities in the Eighteenth-century Atlantic World* (Stanford: Stanford University Press, 2001).

9. "Concolorcorvo" was the alias of the compiler Don Calixto Bustamante Carlos Inca. The text presents itself as the travel diary of colonial official Alonso Carrió de la Vandera.

10. Williams, introduction to Peralta Barnuevo, *Historia de España vindicada,* xliv.

11. Riva-Agüero, *La historia en el Perú*, 273.

12. Ibid.

13. Ibid., 292.

14. Ibid., 293.

15. David Brading, *The First America: The Spanish Monarchy, Creole Patriots, and the Liberal State, 1492–1867* (Cambridge, U.K.: Cambridge University Press, 1991), 393–99.

16. Riva-Agüero, *La historia en el Perú*, 288.

17. Peralta, *Historia de España*, s/n.

18. Giambattista Vico was for a time a provincial vassal of the composite Spanish monarchy via the Aragonese principality of Naples under Charles VII (r. 1735–1759). Charles VII of Aragon named Vico "Historian of the King" late in life; the same Charles was proclaimed Charles III, Emperor of Spain and the Indies, in 1759.

19. On mythic genealogical history under Charles V and Philip II, see Marie Tanner, *Last Descendent of Aeneas* (see chap. 2, n. 29).

20. Peralta, *Historia de España*, chap. 1, cols. 3–4.

21. Ibid., col. 104.

22. Ibid., col. 105.

23. See Anthony Grafton, *What Was History? The Art of History in Early Modern Europe* (Cambridge, U.K.: Cambridge University Press, 2007), 167–73; Kelley, *Faces of History*, 75–92 (see chap. 1, n. 4); and Tanner, *Last Descendant of Aeneas*, 150–51.

24. On "history" as "homonymy," see Jacques Rancière, *The Names of History* (see chap. 1, n. 1).

25. Patrick Geary, *The Myth of Nations: The Medieval Origins of Europe* (Cambridge, U.K.: Cambridge University Press, 2001).

26. François Hartog, *The Mirror of Herodotus*, 200 (see chap. 2, n. 9).

27. Peralta, *Historia de España*, chap. 1, cols. 1–4.

28. See Cañizares-Esguerra, *How to Write*. Peralta patriotically turns the tables on Creole "patriotic epistemology."

29. On the *maskaypacha* in colonial Peru, see Carolyn Dean, *Inka Bodies and the Body of Christ* (Durham: Duke University Press, 1999).

30. Pedro de Peralta Barnuevo, *Lima fundada o conquista del Perú* (Lima: Francisco Sobrino, 1732), s/n.

31. Jorge Juan and Antonio de Ulloa, *Relación histórica del viaje a la América meridional* (Madrid, 1748).

32. Prince Ferdinand (proclaimed Ferdinand VI) was the hope of Spanish reformists, including the leading and most controversial Spanish philosopher of the time, Benito Jerónimo Feijoo, with whom Peralta had corresponded. Notably, Feijoo's student and for a short time official chronicler of the Indies Martín Sarmiento had also sought the prince's favor for his design of a palatial façade at the Bourbon Palacio Real, in Madrid. Sarmiento's design included allegorical columns of Atahualpa (the "Peruvian emperor") and Montezuma (the "Mexican emperor") as "trunks" that symbolically fed into or sup-

ported the vast royal genealogy of the Spanish throne. See Martín Sarmiento, *Sistema de adornos del Palacio Real de Madrid* (Madrid: Sociedad Estatal, 2002).

33. Alejandro Cañeque, *The King's Living Image* (see chap. 2, n. 53); Alejandra B. Osorio, *Inventing Lima: Baroque Modernity in Peru's South Sea Metropolis* (New York: Palgrave Macmillan, 2008).

34. The image of Lima as the union of the two dynastic histories of Inca and Spanish "Monarchs of Peru" was performed in royal ceremonies or *fiestas reales* in the plazas of Lima, described by Peralta himself in 1723. Notably, Peralta appended to his description of the celebrations a historical summary of the Inca dynasty that anticipated Ulloa's "Resumen histórico" of 1748. See Peralta Barnuevo, *Jubileo de Lima y fiestas reales* (Lima: Luna y Bahorques, 1723).

35. On Alonso de la Cueva's and other Peruvian images of the Inca and Spanish kings, see Natalia Majluf, "De la rebelión al museo: Genealogías y retratos de los incas, 1781–1900," in Thomas Cummins et al., *Los incas, reyes del Perú*, 253–327 (see chap. 1, n. 34).

Chapter 4. The Proper Name of *El País de los Incas*

1. Arthur O. Lovejoy, *The Great Chain of Being: A Study of the History of an Idea* (Cambridge, Mass.: Harvard University Press, 1978 [1936]), chaps. 6–9.

2. Jorge Cañizares-Esguerra, *Nature, Empire, and Nation*, 64–78 (see chap. 2, n. 54).

3. Note, however, that for Calancha the name of Peru was a curse. Misreading Inca Garcilaso's account and confusing that reading with others, Calancha forgot about "Beru" and insisted that the river was farther north and named "Verú." His proof, however, was astrological. "Verú" was the name of a comet "very long and slender, like a sword without a sheath, it roams near the Sun, and is horrible and frightening; its nature is a mixture of Saturn and Mercury; it corrupts the fruits of the land, and it means the death of Kings and nobles, Princes, great lords, and rich men … for Pizarro this land of Verú presented the same conditions of the comet, long and not too wide, and his entry into it caused the deaths of the Inca Kings, the noble Caciques, the principal Kurakas, and even his own disaster." Antonio de la Calancha, *Crónica moralizada* (Lima: Universidad Nacional Mayor de San Marcos, 1974), 76–77, 134–37.

4. Jorge Cañizares-Esguerra, *Puritan Conquistadors: Iberianizing the Atlantic* (Stanford: Stanford University Press, 2006). For another revisionist, transatlantic reading of the emergence of Humboldt's scientific romanticism, see Mary Louise Pratt, *Imperial Eyes: Travel Writing and Transculturation* (New York: Routledge, 1992).

5. Cañizares-Esguerra, *Nature, Empire, and Nation*, 112–28.

6. In *How to Write the History of the New World* (see chap. 3, n. 8), Cañizares-Esguerra argues that patriotic epistemologists often praised Manco Capac as the most sagacious of "legislators" precisely because his "laws" were well adapted to the "enervating" climate and "indolent" customs of tropical South America. Such arguments were deployed by colonial elites to justify the maintenance of tributary forms of compulsory labor. Without such benevolent systems of coercion, officials argued, indolent and stupid

native commoners would lapse into their natural state of barbarism. Nevertheless, the alleged necessity of compulsory production was not the only reason for heaping praise on Manco Capac. The original Inca culture-hero was an icon of *patria* in the ongoing historiographical battle over origins.

7. On "microcosmic narratives," see Cañizares-Esguerra, *Nature, Empire, and Nation*, 112–28. Cañizares-Esguerra's discussion emphasizes the microcosmic natural attributes of the Spanish American "kingdoms." As will be seen in subsequent notes for this chapter, what is notable about Unanue's discourse is that this microcosmic diversity extends to "races" (which, moreover, do not conform to European classifications) and so outstrips any "country" in Europe.

8. Cañizares-Esguerra, *How to Write*.

9. Among the Peruvian scholars who defended American nature and civilization, José Eusebio Llano Zapata (1721–1780) is worthy of mention. Llano Zapata compiled a three-volume treatise on the three kingdoms in Peru and presented it before the court in Madrid in 1758. Although the work labors "under the shadow" of León Pinelo's *El paraíso en el Nuevo Mundo* (Llano Zapata carried Pinelo's manuscript from Buenos Aires to Madrid, where he presented it to Secretary of the Indies José de Galvez for deposit in the Biblioteca Real), Llano Zapata's treatise was praised by the Spanish Royal Academy of History, which at the time favored "practical" and scientific approaches to history. Because of poor relations between the academy and the court, however, Llano Zapata's manuscript failed to gain royal permission to publish. Like Inca Garcilaso, Llano Zapata had left Peru for Andalusia; unlike Garcilaso, most of his work did not see the royal light of day, and so his chance of influencing Peruvian posterity was correspondingly diminished. The first of the three volumes of Llano Zapata's treatise was recovered and published in Lima by Ricardo Palma in 1903, but the other two volumes remained in the archives of the Palacio Real in Madrid and were not published until 2005. Llano Zapata's dynastic history of Peru was also thought to have been lost until Víctor Peralta Ruíz recently identified it under another title in the archives of Madrid's Real Academia de la Historia. It too was published for the first time in 2005. See Antonio Garrido Aranda, "La larga sombra de León Pinelo en las memorias de Llano Zapata," in José Eusebio Llano Zapata, *Memorias histórico, físicas, crítico, apologéticas de la América meridional* (Lima: IFEA/PUCP/UNMSM, 2005), 93–132.

10. The name of the journal would appeal to subsequent generations of Peruvians, who read it as an intimate, epithetic flag of national identity and so a "precursor." Mercurio or Mercury was a common name for French publications that, since the seventeenth century, aspired to be that messenger of the gods who delivers true words to the universe of men. Indeed, *El Mercurio Peruano* thus acknowledged not only its debt to *Le Mercure Français* but also to the official *El Mercurio de España*. There is also a difference, for the Peruvian journal was not merely the "*Mercurio* del Perú" (that is, the local version of the Spanish official gazette) but a Mercury who spoke from the subject position of the epithetic adjective "Peruvian." See Jean-Pierre Clément, *El Mercurio Peruano, 1790–1795*, vol. 1, *Estudio* (Madrid and Frankfurt: Iberoamericano/Vervuert, 1997), 52–59.

11. In 1791 *El Mercurio Peruano* was the voice of an academic society initially called La Sociedad Académica de Amantes de Lima. The society's name was later changed to Amantes del País.

12. *El Mercurio Peruano*, 2 Jan. 1791.

13. Juan Pablo Viscardo y Guzmán, *Obras completas* (Lima, 1988), 206.

14. *El Mercurio Peruano*, 2 Jan. 1791.

15. Ibid.

16. Jorge Juan y Antonio de Ulloa, "Resumen histórico," en *Relación histórica del viaje a la América meridional*, iii (see chap. 3, n. 31). My translation.

17. Ibid., clxiii.

18. For a discussion of this colonial discourse, see Cañeque, *The King's Living Image*.

19. Unanue's postcolonial status as "Peruvian" was threatened when, as a consequence of the War of the Pacific, the province of Arica became part of Chile. This threat was answered with a cultural offensive to enshrine Unanue as the principal figure of the "Peruvian Enlightenment."

20. Llano Zapato had made earlier incursions in this domain, but as noted his work remained unpublished.

21. Notably, Unanue does not partake of the Black Legend view of conquest. It was Gonzalo Pizarro (Francisco Pizarro's brother) and his band of traitors to the Crown who pillaged Inca tombs, not the noble servants of the Crown. The first emissary and viceroy Pedro de la Gasca upheld the honorable name of Spain.

22. José Hipólito Unanue, "Idea general de los monumentos del antiguo Perú, e introducción a su estudio," *El Mercurio Peruano*, 17 Mar. 1791.

23. Ibid.

24. Ibid.

25. Ibid.

26. Unanue, "Geografía física del Perú."

27. Ibid.

28. On the Neo-Platonist and Aristotelian concepts of gradation, diversity, and plenitude, see Lovejoy, *Great Chain of Being*.

29. Giambattista Vico, *New Science*, trans. David Marsh (New York: Penguin, 2001).

30. Alexander von Humboldt, *Researches Concerning the Institutions and Monuments of the Ancient Inhabitants of America, with Descriptions and Views of Some of the Most Striking Scenes in the Cordilleras!*, trans. Helen Maria Williams (London: Longman, 1814), 29–33.

31. Alexander von Humboldt, *Researches*, 28–33.

32. But this is only partly true. Humboldt set "Oriental" Aztecs in romantic "views" or landscapes with Greco-Roman mythological figures. The Orientalist imagination was always about images, critiques, and projections of European culture. Humboldt was no exception in this regard.

33. "Descendents of some navigators from Europe or the Canary Islands, tossed by a storm on the coast of Brazil." Abbé Guillaume Raynal, *Histoire philosophique et politique*

des établissements et du commerce des Européens dans les Deux Indes (Geneva, 1783), 19–20.

34. For a blistering political critique of Humboldt's Orientalist view of Peruvian Indians, see Manuel Olaguer Feliú, "Discurso del Señor Feliú en que hace la apología de los indios contra las imputaciones del Baron de Humboldt," in *Noticias del Perú* (1811) 8: 83.

35. José Hipólito Unanue, *Observaciones sobre el clima de Lima y sus influencias en los seres organizados, en especial el hombre* (Lima, 1805), 97–98.

36. Unanue, *Observaciones sobre el clima*, 87.

37. Ibid., 87–89.

38. Ibid., 90–91.

39. Ibid., 91–92.

40. Ibid., 93.

41. Ibid.

42. Ibid.

43. Cañizares-Esguerra, *How to Write*, 157.

44. See Roberto M. Dainotto, *Europe (in Theory)* (Durham: Duke University Press, 2007).

45. Mariano Eduardo de Rivero and Juan Diego de Tschudi, *Antigüedades peruanas* (Vienna: Imprenta Imperial, 1851), 1: 256–57.

46. Rivero and Tschudi, *Antigüedades peruanas,* 1: 210. See also Charles-Marie de La Condamine, *Relation abrégée d'un voyage fait dans l'intérieur de l'Amérique méridionale* (Paris, 1745).

47. Rivero's examination of "Peruvian antiquities" found its first published expression in the thin *Antigüedades peruanas, parte primera* (Lima: Imprenta de José Masias, 1841). This first, inexpensive Peruvian imprint includes a desperate plea for funds to cover the costs of the printing of plates. The text of the Peruvian imprint is close to the definitive version that would appear in the first volume of the 1851 Vienna imprint.

48. Alexander von Humboldt, *Vue des Cordilleres* (Paris, 1803), 199.

49. Baalbec or Heliopolis was an ancient Phoenician city.

50. In 1830 d'Orbigny traveled overland to the newly named city of La Paz in the newly named country of Bolivia from the Peruvian port of Arica and from there reconnoitered the site at Tiahuanaco in 1833. Based on his reading of the usual colonial chronicles and supported by his observations at the site, d'Orbigny concluded that the original Inca Manco Capac was probably from the Tiahuanaco area, and that the ancient city's monuments had been built by the "Aymara nation." Said nation was more ancient than Inca civilization. Indeed, the monolithic Sungate at Tiahuanaco suggested that the Inca's solar cult had originated here as well. For his services to the new nation, none other than Andrés de Santa Cruz, president of the republic, inducted Monsieur d'Orbigny into the Bolivian Academy of Sciences. The new nation invented by Bolívar could now boast European confirmation of its most ancient "Aymara" origins. Two years later, Santa Cruz would reunite Bolivia and Peru; his ancient Peru-Bolivia Confederation lasted four years

(1835–1839). See Alcide d'Orbigny, *La relación du voyage dans l'Amérique méridionale,* vol. 3 (Paris: Chez P. Bertrand; Strasbourg: Chez V. Levrault, 1844), 347.

51. W. Golden Mortimer, *Peru: History of Coca "the Divine Plant" of the Incas* (New York: J. H. Vail, 1901), 29–33.

52. José María de Córdova y Urrutia, *Las tres épocas del Perú o compendio de su historia* (Lima, 1844), 1–3.

53. Also see Mark Thurner, "Peruvian Genealogies of History and Nation," in Mark Thurner and Andrés Guerrero, eds., *After Spanish Rule: Postcolonial Predicaments of the Americas* (Durham: Duke University Press, 2003), 141–75.

54. See Sara Badía, Carmen María Pérez-Montes, y Leoncio López-Ocón, "Una galería iconográfica," in Leoncio López-Ocón and Carmen María Pérez-Montes, eds., *Marcos Jiménez de la Espada (1831–1898): Tras la senda de un explorador* (Madrid: Consejo Superior de Investigaciones Científicas), figs. 52–53, p. 149.

55. See *Boletín de la Sociedad Geográfica de Lima* 1, nos. 10–12 (31 Mar. 1892): 444–48. Crisóstomos Nieto's field report was reprinted from *El Peruano,* vol. 10, n. 28.

56. Samuel G. Morton, *Crania Americana* (Philadelphia, 1838–39), 63.

57. Ibid., 83

58. Ibid., 97.

59. Pentland, "Report of the Fourth Meeting of the British Association for the Advancement of Science," 624. Morton also cites "Additional Reports, which were published in Waldie's Journal of Belles-Lettres, 1834."

60. Morton, *Crania Americana,* 101.

61. Ibid., 113–15.

62. Ibid., 120. Morton's "patriotic epistemology" or empirical defense of native American civilization was not unusual among Anglo American antiquarians, and it suggests that Cañizares-Esguerra's thesis may apply beyond the Spanish American sphere.

63. Von Tschudi also capitalized on the fact that the "Inca or Modern Peruvian" skulls that Morton diagrams and discusses in *Crania Americana* were actually taken from "cemeteries" at Arica, Atacama, Chimu, and Pachacamac, that is, from the coast and not from the altiplano region around Tiahuanaco. These skulls had been presented to Morton not by Mr. Pentland but "by my friend Dr. Ruschenberger, M.D. of the United States Navy, and author of *Three Years in the Pacific* and *A Voyage 'Round the World.'*"

64. Mortimer, *Peru: History of Coca,* 32–33.

65. Rivero and Tschudi, *Antigüedades peruanas,* 1: 17–19. Perhaps not so curiously, the pages in *Antigüedades peruanas* where Rivero makes these unpatriotic claims have been torn out of the Peruvian National Library's only copy. To read these passages it was necessary to consult the complete copy held in the John Carter Brown Library, at Brown University.

66. Rivero and Tschudi, *Antigüedades peruanas,* 1: 19.

67. Ibid., 1: 63.

68. John Ranking, *Historical Researches on the Conquest of Peru, Mexico, Bogota, Natchez, and Talomeco, in the Thirteenth Century by the Monguls, Accompanied with*

Elephants, and the Local Agreement of History and Tradition, with the Remains of Elephants and Mastodontes, Found in the New World (London: Longman, 1827).

69. Rivero and Tschudi, *Antigüedades peruanas*, 1: 63.

70. Strictly speaking Rivero and Tschudi were not co-authors. Tschudi wrote two technical chapters on skeletal materials and native languages, and Rivero wrote the rest. Rivero is the sole author of the text's national and republican message. Tschudi's addition gave the publication scientific catchet and, more importantly, sponsorship by the Imperial Academy of Science in Vienna to produce the expensive lithographic plates at the Imperial Press.

71. Rivero and Tschudi, *Antigüedades peruanas*, 1: 286–87.

72. Ibid., 1: i.

73. Ibid., 2: iii.

74. On the logoization of ruins in the national imagination, see Benedict Anderson, *Imagined Communities: Reflections on the Origin and Spread of Nationalism, rev. ed.* (London: Verso, 1991), 182. The Sungate at Tiahuanaco become the most celebrated logo of Peruvian civilization in Peru. It was not until the mid-twentieth century that the image of the ruins at Machu Picchu displaced the Sungate as Peru's logo.

75. On ephemeral colonial arches as mirrors of the prince or the viceroy in colonial Spanish America, see Alejandro Cañeque, *The King's Living Image* (see chap. 2, n. 53), and Alejandra Osorio, *Inventing Lima* (see chap. 3, n. 33).

76. Strong arguments against foreign origins were made throughout the nineteenth century by a few foreign intellectuals as well. Among these, perhaps the English gentleman and explorer Sir Clements Markham was the most forceful. His arguments were not republican but imperial and patriarchal. See his *Travels in Peru and India* (London, 1862) and *History of Peru* (1895).

77. William H. Prescott, *History of the Conquest of Peru* (Philadelphia, 1874 [1847]), 1: 20.

78. Ibid., 1: 14.

79. Sebastián Lorente, in evident reference to Prescott's remark, writes: "It might be inferred . . . that the dimly lit and fabulous ancient age of Peru lies outside the domain of history. . . . But we cannot renounce such an interesting and instructive history." (*Historia antigua del Perú*, Paris and Lima: Masias, 1860), 15–16.

80. Ibid., 130–33.

81. Ibid.

82. Ibid.

83. Rancière, *Names of History*, 66.

Chapter 5. The Postcolonial Death of the Book of Kings

1. Sebastián Lorente, *Compendio de historia contemporánea para los colegios del Perú* (Lima: Benito Gil, 1876), 26. On the significance of the death of the king in French historiography, see Jacques Rancière, *Names of History* (see chap. 1, n. 1).

2. Bernardo Monteagudo, *Exposición de las tareas administrativas del gobierno desde*

su instalación hasta el 15 de julio de 1822 (Lima: Imprenta de D. Manuel del Río, 1822), 30.

3. Santiago Távara, *Historia de los partidos* (Lima: Huascarán, 1951), 85–86.

4. Sebastián Lorente, *Historia del Perú desde la Proclamación de la Independencia,* vol. 1, *1821–1827* (Lima: Gil, 1876), 3–4.

5. Rancière, *Names of History,* 11.

6. See Linda Orr, *Headless History: Nineteenth-century French Historiography of the Revolution* (Ithaca: Cornell University Press, 1990).

7. On the king as simulacrum in Spanish Peru, see Alejandra Osorio, "The King in Lima: Ritual, Rule and Simulacra in Seventeenth-century Peru," *Hispanic American Historical Review* 84, no. 3 (Aug. 2004): 447–74.

8. See Nicolas Shumway, *The Invention of Argentina* (Berkeley: University of California Press, 1991).

9. Decree of 17 July 1821, Latin American Manuscripts-Peru, Mendel Collection, box 9, May 1818–Aug. 1821, Lilly Library, Indiana University.

10. There is disagreement in the scholarship on the question of the meaning of Lima's title as "City of Kings." Some historians hold that it refers to the Feast of the Magi, the supposed day of Lima's founding by Francisco Pizarro, while others contend that its name honored the Spanish kings. Peralta Barnuevo's *Lima fundada o la conquista del Perú* (1732) suggests that by the eighteenth century the titular "City of Kings" could evoke images of Inca and Spanish kings (see chap. 3, n. 30).

11. Luís Antonio Eguiguren, *Las calles de Lima miscelánea* (Lima, 1948).

12. Neither the name of "City of the Free" for Lima nor that of "Peruvians" for Indians would stick, however. On the postcolonial vicissitudes of the term "Peruvian," see Mark Thurner, *From Two Republics to One Divided: Contradictions of Postcolonial Nationmaking in Andean Peru* (Durham: Duke University Press, 1997).

13. This was so because although the restored king Ferdinand VII had annulled the Constitution of 1812, that constitution had been restored in a liberal military coup in Spain in 1820. Thus the urgency of San Martín's 1821 intervention.

14. Jacques Derrida, *On the Name,* trans. David Wood (Stanford: Stanford University Press, 1995), xi–xiv.

15. Bartolomé Herrera, *Sermón pronunciado el día 28 de julio de 1846, aniversario de la independencia del Perú* (Lima, 1846), 9.

16. Jorge Basadre, *Historia de la República del Perú, 1822–1933,* 6th ed. (Lima: San Marcos, 1968), 240.

17. Monteagudo, *Exposición de las tareas,* 15.

18. Ibid., 11.

19. Personal communication, Juan Carlos Callirgos.

20. Mónica Quijada, "De la colonia a la republica: Inclusión, exclusión y memoria histórica en el Perú," *Histórica* 18, no. 2 (Dec. 1994): 365–83.

21. Part of the reason for this support may be traced to earlier events. The violent repression of the Andean insurrections of the 1740s–80s by royalist forces and loyal Indians had resulted in the consolidation of loyalism among many of the surviving

highland nobility. Led by a faction of "neo-Inca" chiefs and tradesmen who assumed or made genealogical claims to royal Inca ancestors—most notable among them, Juan Santos Atahualpa, José Gabriel Condorcanqui Túpac Amaru, and Túpac and Tomas Katari, in Alto Perú—the insurrections had opened old wounds between rival Andean communities and native and mestizo chiefs or governors, leaving as many as 80,000 casualties and widespread destruction of property and the disruption of trade and taxation. In response, a system of forts was built, the Creole officer corps was expanded, and a primitive standing army came into being. In short, militarization and heightened loyalism provided momentary means for the survival of Viceroy La Serna's campaign, in much the same way as it had served Crown interests when faced by the revolts of the 1800s and 1810s. In addition, La Serna played to the loyalty of certain Andean elites and at one point advertised his intention to enthrone a loyal "Inca" in the event that the Creole forces of independence, led by San Martín, did the same. These Incaist ploys may not have resonated strongly at the base of Andean communities, however, for the same insurrections and repression had both responded to and produced a decapitation and democratization of many rural communities. See Thurner, *From Two Republics*, and Scarlett O'Phelan Godoy, *Kurakas sin sucesiones: Del cacique al alcalde de indios* (Cuzco: Centro de Estudios Andinos Bartolomé de las Casas, 1997).

22. *El Sol del Cuzco*, no. 7, 12 Feb. 1825.

23. Decree of 4 July 1825, in Cuzco.

24. Benito Laso, *Exposición que hace Benito Laso diputado al Congreso por la provincia de Puno* (Lima: Imprenta del Estado, 1826), 9–10.

25. The Spanish Viceroyalty of Peru had restructured and renamed the far-flung Andean tributary realm claimed by Cuzco's Inca dynasty (called Tawantinsuyu, in Quechua), and it was even larger and more powerful than its fabled predecessor, since "Peru" formed part of the composite crown of the universal Spanish monarchy. The Viceroyalty of Peru was subsequently dismembered for administrative purposes during the Bourbon-ruled eighteenth century and then further fragmented during and following the independence wars, so that seven South American republics (Colombia, Ecuador, Peru, Bolivia, Chile, Paraguay, and Argentina) could, if and when they cared to, claim some manner of "descent" from the old realm of "Peru." Since in early colonial Spanish historical and political discourse the name "Peru" or "Peruvian empire" (Inca Garcilaso de la Vega had famously called it the *Peruano Imperio*) became the accepted name for "the empire of the Incas" (*el imperio de los incas*), that name now conjured two referents: the imperial dynastic realm of the Incas and that of the Spanish viceroyalty or "Kingdoms and Provinces of Peru," whose sovereigns were the kings of Castile. By the late eighteenth century, the overlapping dominions of the successive sovereign dynastic realms had been naturalized in Creole historical discourse—and exoticized in European travel writing—as "the land of the Incas" (*el país de los incas*). "The Land of the Incas" did and does still today serve as the most widely and readily recognized poetic sign, both in Peru and in the world, for the Peruvian Republic. In short, the dead dynastic realm was entombed in natural geography, and the gold of national history (and global

tourism) was born of history's poetic alchemy: "the country of the Incas." As a result, Peru's republican history would consist of the poetic "harmonization" and genealogical alignment of a new political fragment with the previous and much more extensive dynastic realms and it would be made eternal or at least "geological" by virtue of the territorialization of political time in the pages of history.

26. Indeed, this resurgence of the towns and provinces, represented by local *juntas* or town councils, had made the transfer of sovereignty from "the King" possible. Initially, Peruvian independence was declared by San Martín in the name of the "pueblos y provincias del Perú" and not "the people." This was because the pueblos or towns were the ultimate sources of the king's sovereignty in medieval Spanish jurisprudence. Sovereignty was reassumed by many town councils during the Napoleonic crisis of 1808–1813, but Ferdinand VII had restored absolute rule in Peru and elsewhere in the empire by 1814. However, after independence, the new Peruvian Republic would adopt a unified notion of the popular sovereignty of "the people" or "the nation of Peruvians." Although this unified notion of the people's sovereignty was achieved in theory by 1828, the de facto sovereignty of the towns and provinces remained characteristic of the postindependence period.

27. Juan Espinosa, *Diccionario para el pueblo: Republicano, democrático, moral, político y filosófico* (Lima: Imprenta Liberal, 1855), 134–36. Consulted in the National Library of Peru.

28. Lorente, *Historia antigua del Perú* (Paris and Lima: Masias, 1860), 7–9.

29. More so since Lorente's language stuck while much of San Martín and Bolívar's did not.

30. Mónica Quijada, "Los 'incas arios': Historia, lengua y raza en la construcción nacional hispanoamericana del siglo XIX," *Histórica* (Lima) 10, no. 2 (Dec. 1996): 246–47.

31. See Rancière, *Names of History*.

32. It is worth remembering that in 1813 Spanish America and Spain were constitutionally united as one "nation" of "Spaniards." Literalists would have to grant that at the time of his birth, Lorente's nation included Peru since Peruvians were then Spaniards.

33. See Gabriel Ramón, "La historia del Perú según Sebastián Lorente," paper presented to the fifth Coloquio de Estudiantes de Historia en el Perú, held in Lima, 1994.

34. On lending their "pens": Lorente was editor in chief of *La Voz del Pueblo,* the newsprint voice of the revolution.

35. Paul Gootenberg, *Between Silver and Guano: Commercial Policy and the State in Post-Independence Peru* (Princeton: Princeton University Press, 1989).

36. A near-complete list of Lorente's published works is compiled in Alberto Rubio Fataccioli, *Sebastián Lorente y la educación en el Perú* (Lima: Allamanda, 1990), 249–51.

37. Carlos Lisson, *Memoria del decano de la Facultad de Letras,* 1884, in *Anales universitarios,* vol. 13 (Lima: Universidad Nacional Mayor de San Marcos, 1887), 446–47; cited in Rubio Fataccioli, *Sebastián Lorente,* 142.

38. Fataccioli, *Sebastián Lorente*, 76.

39. Raúl Porras Barrenechea, *Fuentes históricas peruanas* (Lima, 1963), 489.

40. José de Riva-Agüero correctly recognized the poverty of Mendiburu and Paz Soldán's writing, noting that in these authors there was a "lack of philosophical criteria and synthetic vision, colorless and dense style, and total absence of animation and grace in the narrative." Riva-Agüero, *La historia en el Perú*, 331 (see chap. 2, n. 45). In addition to his self-confessed lack of literary skills, Paz Soldán was severely inhibited by his narrow conception of history, which required that he separate "narration" from "philosophy" and that "style be sacrificed on the altar of documents." See his prefatory remarks in Mariano Felipe Paz Soldán, *Historia del Perú independiente, primer período, 1819–1822* (Lima, 1868), i–v. By the term Rankean I do not wish to imply that Ranke did not write stylish prose. Instead, by "Rankean" I refer to the positivist and empiricist reception of Ranke.

41. See Ricardo Palma, *Tradiciones peruanas completas* (Madrid: Aguilar, 1964).

42. Friedrich Meinecke, *El historicismo y su génesis*, trans., José Mingano y San Martín and Tomas Muñoz Molina (Mexico: Fondo de Cultura Económica, 1943). The original German edition appeared in 1937.

43. Sebastián Lorente, *Compendio de la historia antigua de Oriente para los colegios del Perú* (Lima: Benito Gil, 1876), 4.

44. Ibid., 6.

45. On "generalizing spirits": Sebastián Lorente, *Compendio de la historia moderna para los colegios del Perú* (Lima: Benito Gil, 1875), 354.

46. Lorente, *Compendio de la historia antigua de Oriente*, 6.

47. Ibid.

48. Ibid.

49. See Cañizares-Esguerra, *How to Write the History of the New World: Histories, Epistemologies, and Identities in the Eighteenth-century Atlantic World* (Stanford: Stanford University Press, 2001).

50. Sebastián Lorente, *Historia de la civilización peruana* (Lima: Benito Gil, 1879), 21.

51. Ibid.

52. On Michelet, Ranke, and the historicist turn away from the ironic mode or trope of the Enlightenment, see Hayden White, *Metahistory: The Historical Imagination in Nineteenth-century Europe* (Baltimore: Johns Hopkins University Press, 1973). Nevertheless, White's reading of Voltaire is, as Karen O'Brien notes, rather one-dimensional. Many aspects of Voltaire's universal history have parallels in Lorente's, and although Voltaire has his satirical moments, he is, as Meinecke notes, also a serious historicist. On Voltaire, see Karen O'Brien, *Narratives of Enlightenment: Cosmopolitan History from Voltaire to Gibbon* (Cambridge, U.K.: Cambridge University Press, 1997).

53. Lorente, *Historia antigua del Perú*, 20.

54. On "explanation by emplotment" in nineteenth-century European history writing, see White, *Metahistory*, 7–11.

55. Lorente, *Historia de la civilización peruana*, 20.

56. Ibid.

57. Lorente, *Historia antigua del Perú*, 9–10.

58. Lorente, *Historia de la civilización peruana*, 21.

59. Lorente, *Compendio de la historia antigua de Oriente*, 7.

60. Thomas Abercrombie, "Mothers and Mistresses of the Urban Bolivian Public Sphere: Postcolonial Predicament and National Imaginary in Oruro's Carnival," in Mark Thurner and Andrés Guerrero, eds., *After Spanish Rule: Postcolonial Predicaments of the Americas* (Durham: Duke University Press, 2003), 210.

61. Lorente, *Historia del Perú compendiada*, 23.

62. Lorente, *Historia antigua del Perú*, 130–33.

63. See Unanue, *Observaciones sobre el clima* (see chap. 4, n. 35).

64. Justo Apu Sahuaraura Inca penned a dynastic annal in 1836–38, although the book was not published until 1850 (in Paris). A doctor in theology and a Cuzco churchman, Apu Sahuaraura Inca claimed to be an eighth-generation descendent of Túpac Inca Yupanqui. He also appears to have aided the cause of independence and to have been condecorated by Bolívar himself. Apu Sahuaraura Inca declares that his purpose is to "reconcile some confusions of our Inca Garcilaso concerning the succession of Sovereigns of the royal line down to our day, which is 1836." The self-serving genealogy argues that the legitimate line descends through the Tito Atauchis who married with the Apu Sahuaraura Incas. The curious doctor is none other than the last Inca. See Justo Apu Sahuaraura Inca, *Recuerdos de la monarquía peruana* (Paris: Librería Rosa y Bouret, 1850).

65. Córdova y Urrutia apparently joined San Martín's patriot ranks in 1821 and was made secretary to the first Peruvian Congress in 1823. Afterwards he held various secretarial posts in the courts and in Lima's Prefecture, whence he authored a statistical portrait of the province of Lima. *Las tres épocas del Perú o compendio de su historia* (Lima, 1844) linked Inca Garcilaso de la Vega's foundational dynastic history of the Incas with Antonio de Ulloa's Inca-Spanish dynastic annals and added to these the list of Creole liberators and republican heads of state. The founding epoch, named Foundation of the Empire of the Incas, was followed by the second epoch of the Dynasty from Abroad (*dinastía ultramarina*) followed by the third epoch, named Independent Peru. The three epochs of Peruvian history were linked by the unbroken "chain" of sovereign heads of state, beginning with the original "Peruvian Emperor" Manco Capac, followed by 13 successive Incas ending in Atahualpa, continuing through the "dynasty from abroad," starting with Charles V and here identified, as in Juan and Ulloa's eighteenth-century imperial history and plate, as "XV Emperor of Peru" and under whose name is listed all the colonial viceroys of Peru who served under his reign, and so on for each of the subsequent "Peruvian Emperors" of the "dynasty from abroad" down to independence. The dynasts and viceroys are followed by the independence-era heads of state, starting with "Don José de San Martín, Protector of Peru" followed by "Simón Bolívar, Dictator of Peru," and finally a list of all the presidents of the Republic of Peru down to the present (in 1845 Ramón Castilla was serving his first term as president). Córdova y Urrutia's

annal expressed that ingenious move, begun in the late colonial period, by which the Spanish viceroys sent to govern the "Kingdoms and Provinces of Peru" were naturalized as "Peruvian rulers" in Creole historiography. Indeed, Córdova y Urrutia's neodynastic annal approximates, albeit from the perspective of Lima's political history, the imagery of an altered, post-independence copy in cloth of Juan and Ulloa's poster, possibly produced to commemorate Bolívar's entry into Cuzco, and which depicts Bolívar in the central medallion occupied in the original by Ferdinand VI. See Teresa Gisbert, *Iconografía y mitos indígenas en el arte* (La Paz: Gisbert, 1980).

66. Lorente, *Compendio de la historia antigua de Oriente*, 8–10.

67. Ibid., 22.

68. Ibid., 24.

69. Edward Said, *Orientalism* (New York: Signet, 1979).

70. Lorente, *Compendio de la historia antigua de Oriente*, 22–24.

71. Lorente, *Historia del Perú compendiada*, 3.

72. The outline of *Historia de la civilización peruana* (see note 50) is evident in Lorente's popular handbook of Peruvian history, published in 1876 under the title *Historia del Perú compendiada*.

73. Lorente, *Historia de la civilización peruana*, 4.

74. Lorente, *Historia del Perú compendiada*, 23.

75. Lorente, *Historia de la civilización peruana*, 4.

76. Still, the communities in their traditional form could not be the basis of the new nation of contemporary Peru. This was because the extended web of kinship that internally structured the communities had the effect of "violating the human heart." The kin-based community's "communist sentiments" inhibited the development of "intimacy" in the family, equality between the sexes, and "self-abnegation" in the civic realm. Since the true or nuclear family was the fraternal basis of the well-built nation, the extended family or kinship structure of the community represented an obstacle to the full realization of fraternity and liberty. However, this kinship structure was not all that was involved in Peru's "community spirit." Positive aspects of that spirit would survive and serve as the building blocks of the future democratic nation. Lorente had observed and written poetically about that productive communal spirit in Peru's Mantaro Valley in the 1850s and so he thought he understood firsthand both its limits and potential. See Lorente, *Historia de la civilización peruana*, 153–54.

Chapter 6. Popular Sovereignty and the History of the Soul

1. On the advent of the "national question" among historians in Europe and Mexico, see Elías Palti, *La nación como problema: Los historiadores y la "cuestión nacional"* (Buenos Aires: Fondo de Cultura Economica, 2003), 138–46.

2. The phrase "Creole pioneers" is from Benedict Anderson, *Imagined Communities* (see chap. 4, n. 74).

3. Palti, *La nación como problema*.

4. See Dipesh Chakrabarty, *Provincializing Europe: Postcolonial Thought and Historical Difference* (Princeton: Princeton University Press, 2000), 8.

5. Laso's historicist defense of Bolívar was also clearly motivated by his desire to see the territories of "Bolivia" and "Peru" united, as they had been under Inca and Spanish rule. Indeed, Laso proposed that only Bolívar could unite all of the Andean republics against the looming monarchist threat represented in South America by Brazil. Laso hinted that even now Bolívar's general Antonio José de Sucre was preparing to march east in response to the stirrings of monarchist plots.

6. Laso, *Exposición* (see chap. 5, n. 24). For an English translation of the text of Bolívar's constitution for Bolivia, see Simón Bolívar, *El Libertador: Writings of Simón Bolívar*, trans. Frederick H. Fornoff, ed. David Bushnell (Oxford, U.K.: Oxford University Press, 2003), 54–85.

7. On these reforms, see Mark Thurner, *From Two Republics to One Divided* (see chap. 5, n. 12).

8. Laso, *Exposición*, 7.

9. See Thurner, *From Two Republics*.

10. Laso, *Exposición*, 11–12.

11. Ibid., 18.

12. Ibid., 27–28.

13. Ibid., 20.

14. Ibid., 14.

15. Ibid., 18.

16. Ibid., 17.

17. Bartolomé Herrera claimed that he would distribute 1000 copies of his sermon in the provinces.

18. Jorge Basadre, "En torno a los escritos y discursos de Bartolomé Herrera," in Bartolomé Herrera, *Escritos y discursos*, vol. 2 (Lima, 1934), lxxxi.

19. Bartolomé Herrera, *Sermón pronunciado el dia 28 de julio de 1846* (see chap. 5, n. 15).

20. Ibid.

21. This predicament of needing and desiring to forgive and forget so as to stake historical claims to a republican beginning was made more acute in the realm of political discourse after 1812, when all the free inhabitants of Spanish America, that is, everyone but the slaves of African descent, were constitutionally declared "Spaniards." The Spanish Imperial Constitution of 1812 had presented a knot for the patriots. Many "Indians" and "Indian governors" who were now "Spaniards" declared that they preferred to be "Indians"—not because they felt some deep "belonging" to the "Indies" but because as tribute-paying "Indians" they enjoyed certain privileges—namely, access to resources and legal representation as collectivities before royal courts ruled by the early colonial Laws of the Indies. These privileges were now being swept aside as Indian tribute was abolished and the Indian and Spanish "nations" united in the name of "equality" under empire, as declared in the Constitution of 1812. The old, pre-1812 order would find allies in the tribute-paying Indian communities, which were willing to adopt the new

constitution only if their "Indian rights" under the Laws of the Indies were upheld. The question was debated, and the Royal Tribunal in Lima decided that the Constitution of 1812 did not derogate the Laws of the Indies. Herein lay only some of the irony and political meaning of San Martín's 1821 secular baptismal of "Indians" as "Peruvians." Officially, "Indians" no longer existed in Peru; since 1812 they had been "Spaniards." Still, many of these new Spaniards or ex-Indians had demanded that their "rights" as "Indians" be restored, and these were indeed for the most part restored, with the modification that, since the name of "Indian tributary" was deemed "degrading," they should be recognized as "indigenous contributors." And so "Indians" in Peru became, for a brief interlude, "indigenous Spaniards." This enlightened colonial fiscal identity as "indigenous" would, after Bolívar and now minus the "Spaniard," be institutionalized under the republic as the "true" name of the ex-Indian population, and for the most part the term remains dreamily and politically correct today. Despite the name change, the Peruvian Republic would frequently have to accommodate the "Indian" because his rights were inscribed in the colonial Laws of the Indies, and these were still recognized. For further discussion, see Thurner, *From Two Republics*.

22. Bartolomé Herrera, *Sermón 28 de julio de 1846*, 18–20.

23. Ibid., 17.

24. In light of the comparison, Alamán's position might be rethought. Historians often explain Alamán's position as being a critique of the crisis of Mexican dissolution brought on by liberalism, but it seems just as likely that it followed from a Spanish genealogy of sovereignty in America, which Bartolomé Herrera and many others shared regardless of the political situation. The radical liberals in Peru were discredited after José de La Mar's disastrous war with Gran Colombia in the 1820s, and so more authoritarian *caudillos* took the stage. The Peru-Bolivia Confederation (1935–39) that had been championed by one of Bolívar's young generals, the liberal *caudillo* and president of Bolivia Andrés de Santa Cruz, had been defeated with the backing of conservative forces in Lima who, in turn, were backed by the Chilean army commanded by General Bulnes, and as a result Peru was smaller.

25. Palti, *La nación como problema*, 50. Palti's critical intellectual history of the "antigenealogical" critique of nationalism is most useful, yet it remits to the starting point of its critique, that is, to Anderson's "imagined political community" and to the "Creole pioneers" of the Americas. After tracing genealogical nationalism to its antigenealogical critique in interwar Europe, Palti concludes that "the national question" had already been formulated in the Americas 80 years before, that is, in the 1840s. Likewise, his critique comes to rest upon the conclusion, understood in early republican Peru, Mexico, or Argentina, that nationalism and its critique are always "political." Thus, rather than transcend Anderson's "antigenealogical" critique, he traces a circle back to his "imagined political community."

26. In this regard Anderson was quite right: Creoles were "pioneers" precisely because the invention of new nations from the disintegrating fragments of empire was from the start a political and military decision fraught with impending social dangers. These had to be actively forgotten. Those decisions and dangers thus took on forgetful

republican lives after independence. The regular raising of the "national question" became the "national pastime" because Creoles in Peru or Mexico forgot to remember what they had forgotten at independence (the colonial order of conflict), if for no other reason than to justify a military coup, the repression of an Indian uprising, or the rewriting of the constitution, or indeed to rally popular support around revolutionary armed movements or strikes. That is, and as Palti makes clear in his reading of Renan, nations must strategically remember what they forgot when they founded themselves as independent states. This was precisely Basadre's project: the critical recovery of the founding promise (republican harmony) was the necessary memory (historicism) of what "we" had forgotten (due to the postwar Black Legend of the early republic being little more than "a cave of bandits") about what "we" forgot (the colonial order of conflict) at independence. For Renan the memory of what "we actively forgot" had particular historical meaning for the "national question" in Alsace-Lorraine following the Franco-Prussian War; as we shall see, for Basadre its meaning was informed by a similar "plebiscite" on national identity held in the Tacna-Arica border region.

27. Bartolomé Herrera anticipated by a century and a half Jaime E. Rodríguez's argument in *The Independence of Spanish America* (Cambridge, U.K.: Cambridge University Press, 1998).

28. Bartolomé Herrera, *Sermón 28 de julio de 1846*.

29. P. Pruvonena [José Mariano de la Riva Agüero], *Memorias y documentos para la historia de la independencia del Perú y causas del mal éxito que ha tenido ésta* (Paris: Librería de Garnier, 1858), 5.

30. Juan Espinosa, *Diccionario para el pueblo: Republicano, democrático, moral, político y filosófico* (Lima: Imprenta Liberal, 1855). Subsequent references to Espinosa's *Diccionario* are to the 1855 edition. Espinosa's dictionary has recently been republished and edited with an introduction by Carmen McEvoy; see Espinosa, *Diccionario para el pueblo* (Lima: Pontificia Universidad Católica del Perú/University of the South-Sewanee, 2001). The original production of Espinosa's dictionary was funded by Domingo Elías (who was also Lorente's patron), and it coincided perfectly with the project of the Liberal Revolution of 1854.

31. Espinosa, *Diccionario*, 164–65.

32. Ibid., 614–15.

33. Ibid., 620–21.

34. See Thurner, *From Two Republics*.

35. Santiago Távara, *Historia de los partidos*, 6 (see chap. 5, n. 3).

36. Ibid., 6–7.

37. Ibid., 14–17.

38. Ibid., 14.

39. Ibid., 11.

40. Ibid., 85–86.

41. Francisco de Paula Vigil, *Catecismo patriótica para el uso de las escuelas municipales* (Callao, 1859).

42. Francisco de Paula Vigil, *Opúsculos sociales y políticos, dedicados a la juventud americana* (Lima, 1862), 317.

43. Vigil, *Opúsculos sociales y políticos*, 283–85.

44. Carlos Lisson, *La república en el Perú y la cuestión peruano-española* (Lima, 1865), 2–3.

45. Ibid., 3.

46. Ibid., 111.

47. Ibid., 4.

48. Ibid., 6–8.

49. But, of course, Lisson did read Rousseau. His argument that the new mestizo was the historical vehicle of independence is harnessed to the Rousseauian narrative of the pure truth of the natural state of man, a narrative which had also inspired Michelet's restoration-era history of the French Revolution as "pure truth." This narrative provides the philosophical grounds for Lisson's critique and so undermines his claim that French political thought had nothing to do with American independence.

50. Lisson, *La república*, 14–16.

51. Ibid., 16–18

52. Ibid., 19–20.

53. Ibid., 29–30.

54. Ibid., 113.

55. Ibid., 36–38.

56. Ibid., 45–46.

57. Ibid., 124.

58. Félix Cipriano Zegarra, "Yo el Rey: Ensayo histórico," *La Revista Peruana* (Lima, 1879).

59. Ibid., 51–52.

60. Ibid., 195–204.

61. Ibid., 203.

62. Lorente published a four-volume *Curso de filosofía para los colegios del Perú* (Ayacucho: Imprenta Liberal, 1853–54) and also a *Compendio de filosofía para los colegios de América* (Paris: Librería de Rosa y Bouret, 1860). The texts of these editions are nearly identical.

63. Sebastián Lorente, *Curso elemental de filosofía para los colegios del Perú: Sicología,* (Ayacucho, 1853), 10–11.

64. Lorente, *Curso de filosofía para los colegios del Perú: Sicología* (Ayacucho: Imprenta Liberal, 1853), 5–6. Subsequent references to Lorente's *Sicología* are to the 1853 Ayacucho edition.

65. Ibid., 9–10.

66. Lorente, *Compendio de filosofía para los colegios de America: Lógica* (Paris: Librería Rosa y Bouret, 1860), 29. Subsequent references to Lorente's *Lógica* are to the 1860 Paris edition.

67. Lorente, *Sicología*, 118–21.

68. Ibid., 18.

69. Cited in Lovejoy, *Great Chain of Being*, 248 (see chap. 4, n. 1).

70. Lorente, *Lógica*, 17–18.

71. Ibid., 224–25.

72. Ibid., 1–3.

73. Ibid., 4.

74. Sebastián Lorente, *Compendio de filosofía para los colegios de América: Filosofía moral* (Paris: Librería Rosa y Bouret, 1860), 1–2. Subsequent references to Lorente's *Filosofía moral* are to the 1860 Paris edition.

75. Ibid., 8.

76. Ibid., 3.

77. Ibid., 4

78. Ibid., 6–7.

79. Ibid., 9–10.

80. Ibid., 205–206.

81. Lorente, *Curso elemental de filosofía para los colegios del Perú: Metafísica* (Ayacucho: Imprenta Liberal, 1853), 1–5. Subsequent references to Lorente's *Metafísica* are to the 1853 Ayacucho edition.

82. Wilhelm Gottfried Leibniz, *Monadología*, trans. Antonio Zozaya (Madrid, 1889).

83. Lorente, *Historia de la conquista del Perú*, (Lima: Masías, 1861), 494.

84. Ibid., 494.

85. Ibid., 498.

86. Lorente, *Historia de la civilización peruana*, 4–5 (see chap. 5, n. 50).

87. Lorente, *Historia de la conquista del Perú*, 494–95.

88. Lorente, *Historia de la civilización peruana*, 5.

89. Sebastián Lorente, *Historia del Perú bajo la dinastía austriaca, 1542–1598* (Lima: Benito Gil, 1863), 382.

90. Ibid., 382.

91. Ibid., 382–83.

92. Sebastián Lorente, *Compendio de historia contemporánea*, iv–v (see chap. 5, n. 1).

93. Ibid.

94. Ibid.

95. Ibid., 184.

96. Ibid., 185–86.

97. Ibid., 204

98. Ibid., 205

99. Ibid., 204–206; also Lorente, *Historia del Perú bajo la dinastía austriaca*, 382–83.

100. Lorente, *Compendio de historia contemporánea*, 204–206

101. Ibid., 221.

102. Ibid., 278.

103. Ibid., 238–39.

104. Ibid., 239.

105. Ibid.

106. See, for example, "Tres preguntas al Señor Lorente," reprinted in Manuel A. Fuentes, *Aletazos del murciélago* (Lima, 1866), 1: 164. Also see the diatribe signed "Los Peruanos" in the 7 Aug. 1867 edition of *El Comercio,* Lima's leading newspaper. These rival "Peruvians" objected to Lorente's having landed a government contract to edit the *Memorias de los Virreyes.* Fuentes sought the same contract and later edited several volumes of the *Memorias.* In a series of comments that appeared in *El Comercio,* Fuentes, satirically signing as "a biped," questioned Lorente's mental (and bipedal) faculties. Fuentes dismissed Lorente as a thoughtless narrator who described such "impudent and immoral customs" as the Andean bullfight.

107. See Peter Kaulicke, ed., *Aportes y vigencia de Johann Jakob von Tschudi (1818–1889)* (Lima: Pontificia Universidad Católica del Perú, 2001), 78.

108. Thanks to the University of San Marcos press, Lorente is no longer out of print. See Mark Thurner, ed., *Sebastián Lorente: Escritos fundacionales de historia peruana* (Lima: Fondo Editorial de la Universidad Nacional Mayor San Marcos, 2005).

109. In his 1945 university course packet on sources for Peruvian history, published in book form 18 years later as *Fuentes históricas peruanas* (Lima: Instituto Raul Porras Barrenechea, 1963), Porras Barrenechea criticized Riva-Agüero's dismissal of Lorente. Porras calls Lorente "one of the greatest pioneers of Peruvian history" (256). Moreover, he adds that "as an historian preoccupied with the social revolution and with the genesis of the nationality, Lorente occupies a much higher place than other historians who were absorbed in data or in the informative function of history" (258–59). Only one other significant figure in the history of Peruvian thought appears to have read Lorente with profit: Pedro Zulen.

110. On the war and its postwar blues, see Efraín Kristal, *The Andes Viewed from the City: Literary and Political Discourse on the Indian, 1848–1930* (New York: Peter Lang, 1987); Nelson Manrique, *Campesinado y nación: Las guerrillas indígenas en la guerra con Chile* (Lima: Pontificia Universidad Católica del Peru, 1981); Florencia Mallon, *Peasant and Nation: The Making of Postcolonial Mexico and Peru* (Berkeley: University of California Press, 1995); and Thurner, *From Two Republics.* Manuel González Prada, Luís Carranza, and Ricardo Palma were among the many critical voices who found an echo in subsequent historical discourse.

111. Dismissing nineteenth-century history in Peru as nothing more than textbooks and compilations, Pablo Macera argues that it was the generation of Riva-Agüero and Belaúnde that constituted Peru's "first historicism." Macera places this "first" or "traditional" historicism in the period between the War of the Pacific and World War I and he specifically cites Riva-Agüero and Belaúnde as examples of it. See Macera's essays "Historia e ideología" and "El historiador y su oficio," which are collected in volume 1 of his four-volume *Trabajos de historia* (Lima, 1988 [1977]), 5–7, 129–30.

112. Alberto Flores Galindo, "La imagen y el espejo," *Márgenes* 2, no. 4 (Lima, 1986), 4.

113. Sadly this wishful thinking continues. In a recent review of Basadre's work, the young historian Gustavo Montoya repeats Macera's dubious claim that no historian

before Basadre had "produced a synthesis of the Peruvian historical process." See Montoya, "Jorge Basadre: El ensayo como estrategia," in Jorge Basadre, *La iniciacion de la república* (Lima: Fondo Editorial de la Universidad Nacional Mayor de San Marcos, 2002), 18.

114. Jorge Basadre, *Historia de la República* (see chap. 5, n. 16); also see Basadre, *Perú: Problema y posibilidad, ensayo de una síntesis de la evolución histórica del Perú* (Lima: Mejía Baca, 1958).

115. In the introduction to his thesis, Riva-Agüero states that he proposes to study "las cualidades que para la historia ha revelado el ingenio peruano" (the Peruvian talent for history) but he applies the native-born criterion only to secular historians (he includes comparative discussion of Spanish-born ecclesiastical historians). The doctoral thesis cast a long shadow over twentieth-century Peruvian historiography. Unanimously acclaimed as a masterwork, it is frequently cited as the founding text of "modern historiography" in Peru. In his prologue to the third edition of *History in Peru*, Basadre boasted that it was the world's first "history of history" and that it counted among the masterpieces of Hispanic prose. The prose is often moving, but one of the primary effects of the text appears to have been to discourage Peruvian historians from investigating the history of Peruvian history. In any case, and despite Basadre's strained efforts to applaud the work, *History in Peru* is not a history of historical thought in Peru. The thesis takes "history" to be about what actually happened in the past and who did it, and is about what the author reasons, in the light of more recent and international scholarship, to be reasonable about what previous historians "born in Peru" had written about Peru's past. The claims of Peru's historians are judged on this basis—that is, they are judged as false or true, hyperbolic or duly reserved, frivolous or serious. It is an exercise in deciding what is true and useful and what is not. There is no explicit approach to the material, no discussion of method, and the conclusions amount to a lamentation on the sad state of history in Peru. That history, concluded Riva-Agüero, had amounted to little more than a few chronicles of dubious value. Peruvian historians "have always lacked a philosophical and synthetic spirit, and in most cases profundity and the arts of composition." As a result the thesis often is, like its subject, "tedious and heavy."

116. On "figurative" versus "philosophical" historicism, see Hayden White, "Historicism, History, and the Figurative Imagination," in *Tropics of Discourse: Essays in Cultural Criticism* (Baltimore: Johns Hopkins University Press, 1978).

117. See, for example, José de la Riva-Agüero, *La historia en el Perú* (Lima: Pontificia Universidad Catolica del Peru/Instituto Riva-Agüero, 1965), 140–43. Page citations correspond to the published and revised third edition, which corresponds to volume 4 of his *Obras completas*. My reading is also based on the original thesis of 1910, held in the Instituto Riva-Agüero library in Lima. The published third edition was censored and annotated by Riva-Agüero himself, who then wished to purge any "impious phrases" in the original. The author publicly retracted his "errors" in 1932 and returned to the fold of the Peruvian Catholic Church.

118. Riva-Agüero, *La historia en el Perú*, 504–505.

119. See William Prescott, *History of the Conquest of Peru* (Philadelphia: Lippencott, 1874 [1847]).

120. Riva-Agüero, *La historia en el Perú*, 179–80.

121. Víctor Andrés Belaúnde, *El Perú antiguo y los modernos sociólogos: Introducción a un ensayo de sociología jurídica peruana* (Lima: Universidad de San Marcos, 1908), 32.

122. Lorente, *Historia de la civilización peruana*, 8–9.

123. See Richard Kagan, "Prescott's Paradigm: American Historical Scholarship and the Decline of Spain," *American Historical Review* 101 (Apr. 1996), 423–46. Prescott applied a similar narrative to the Aztec and Inca civilizations, as well as to the Spanish empire in the Americas.

124. Lorente, *Historia de la civilización peruana*, 146–47.

125. After Bartolomé de las Casas, the sixteenth-century Dominican bishop of Chiapas. Lorente was an active and founding member of the Society of Friends of the Indians, which championed the legal defense of Indians against abuse by landlords and corrupt officials. The Society of Friends professed a Lascasian ideology and published editions of Las Casas' writings in defense of Indians.

126. Lorente, *Historia de la civilización peruana*, 38–39.

127. See Mark Thurner, "Peruvian Genealogies of History and Nation," 141–75 (see chap. 4, n. 53).

128. Lorente, *Historia de la civilización peruana*, 39.

129. Ibid.

130. Ibid.

131. On *peruanidad*, see Víctor Andrés Belaúnde, *La realidad nacional* (Paris, 1931), and *Peruanidad* (Lima, 1957). Karen Sander's recent *Nación y tradición: Cinco discursos en torno a la nación peruana, 1885–1930* (Lima: Instituto Riva-Agüero, 1997) continues in the postwar national tradition of ignoring nineteenth-century precedents.

132. Basadre's trademark was his integral view of deep Peru as "a totality in space and continuity in time." This view is doctrinal in Peru today. But it is clearly anticipated by Lorente.

133. Anderson, *Imagined Communities*.

134. See, for example, my review of *Beyond Imagined Communities: Reading and Writing the Nation in Nineteenth-century Latin America*, by John Chasteen and Sara Castro-Klaren, eds., in the *American Historical Review* 109, no. 5: 1606–608.

135. See, for differing examples of this neo-Smithian line of interpretation, applied to the cases of Mexico and Peru, respectively: Claudio Lomnitz, *Deep Mexico, Silent Mexico: An Anthropology of Nationalism* (Minneapolis: University of Minnesota Press, 2001), and Jesús Díaz-Caballero, "Nación y patria: Las lecturas de los *Comentarios reales* y el patriotismo criollo emancipador," *Revista de Crítica Literaria Latinoamericana* 59 (2004): 81–107.

136. On Anderson's debt to Renan and on "antigenealogical" and "genealogical" concepts of the nation, see Elías Palti, *La nación como problema* (see chap. 6, n. 1). Palti's contention is that Renan is a bridge between nineteenth-century "genealogical" views and twentieth-century "antigenealogical" critiques of nation. To the extent that

Anderson revives Renan's concepts, however, his view also remains a bridge between more bluntly antigenealogical views, such as those of Ernst Gellner, and the genealogical ones embedded in Smith's primordial approach. This connection arises, in part, because in Anderson's reading, although nations write their own autobiographies or genealogies, such histories are in part derived from the fact that as heirs to colonial administrative fragments, nations "nationalize" functional elements of the "cultural systems" previously managed from remote centers by "dynastic realms" and "sacred" or ecumenical religious communities. Anderson notes that his reflections on the origins of nations began with his attempt to make sense of the bloody war between two postcolonial Marxist regimes in Southeast Asia: Cambodia and Vietnam.

137. In *The Ethnic Origins of Nations* (Oxford, U.K.: Blackwell, 1986), author Anthony Smith defines the nation as "a named community of history and culture, possessing a unified territory, economy, mass education system and common legal rights" (334). This definition is obviously anachronistic and cumulative, since we may easily find "named communities of history and culture" without "unified territory" and the rest (these are precisely the pitfalls that Anderson's theory avoids), but the point is that Smith's theory remits to the nominational origins of community, at which point his ancient "ethnicities" recede into the thick air of discourse and what Peralta called (see chapter 3) "generative political genealogy." For a summary critique of the ethnic mythologies that inform national discourses of origin in Europe, see Patrick Geary, *The Myth of Nations* (see chap. 3, n. 25).

138. Elías Palti, *Aporias: Tiempo, modernidad, historia, sujeto, nacion, ley* (Buenos Aires: Alianza, 2001), and *El tiempo de la política: El siglo XIX reconsiderado* (Buenos Aires: Siglo XXI, 2007).

139. Lorente, *Historia de la civilización peruana*, 21.

Chapter 7. The End of the Peruvian History of Peru

1. There is no systematic work on Basadre, but several Peruvian scholars have reflected upon aspects of his work, and the centennial celebration has prompted the publication of conference proceedings. See Pablo Macera, *Conversaciones con Basadre* (Lima: Mosca Azul, 1979); Alberto Flores Galindo, "Jorge Basadre o la voluntad de persistir," *Allpanchis* 14, no. 16 (1980): 3–8; Magdalena Chocano, "Ucronía y frustración en la conciencia histórica peruana," *Márgenes* 1, no. 2 (1987): 43–60; Fernando Iwasaki Cauti, *Nación peruana: Entelequia o utopía; Trayectoria de una falacia* (Lima: Centro Regional de Estudios Socio Económicos, 1988); Miguel Maticorena Estrada, *Nación e historicismo de Jorge Basadre* (Lima: Asociación de Docentes Pensionistas de la UNMSM, 2003); Scarlett O'Phelan Godoy and Mónica Ricketts, eds., *Homenaje a Jorge Basadre: El hombre, su obra y su tiempo* (Lima: Instituto Riva-Agüero, 2004); Manuel Pantigoso, ed., *Cátedra Basadre* (Lima: Editorial Hozlo, 2004); and the special issue of *Historia y Cultura* 25 (Lima, 2004).

2. Ernesto Yepes, ed., *Jorge Basadre: Memoria y destino del Perú* (Lima: Congreso de la República, 2003).

3. Jorge Basadre, *La iniciación de la república* (Lima: Fondo Editorial de la Universidad Nacional Mayor de San Marcos, 2002), 47.

4. Hayden White, *Metahistory: The Historical Imagination in Nineteenth-century Europe*, 375–425 (see chap. 5, n. 52).

5. David D. Roberts, *Benedetto Croce and the Uses of Historicism* (Berkeley: University of California Press, 1987). The German historicist notion of "the historical," or *Historik*, is developed in the philosophy of Wilhelm Dilthey and modified by Johann Gustav Droysen.

6. Manuel Pantigoso, "Basadre, el Perú y el libro: Lo visible de lo invisible," in Pantigoso, ed., *Cátedra Basadre*, 141–70.

7. Basadre, *La vida y la historia* (Lima: Industrial Gráfica, 1975), 110–11.

8. Basadre's revision of *Historia de la República del Perú* produced the fifth edition of that work. Posthumous editions have since appeared.

9. Basadre, *La iniciación de la república*, 51.

10. The Generation of 1900, or the centennial generation, included José de la Riva-Agüero, Víctor Andrés Belaúnde, and the Paris-based brothers Francisco and Ventura García Calderón.

11. Manuel González Prada, "Discurso en el politeama," *Pajinas libres* (Paris, 1894 [1888]), 72–73.

12. Ibid., 73.

13. This is why Basadre makes a clear distinction between the two. "Between [González] Prada and José Carlos Mariátegui there is a radical difference," wrote Basadre. "Prada embodies bourgeois thought in rebellion, in crisis; Mariátegui announces the presence of the proletarian writer. Prada was a man of questions and problems; Mariátegui, a man of answers and solutions." Basadre also did not consider Mariátegui to be a true intellectual but, rather, a "journalist" and an "agitator." Thus, he wrote: "Properly speaking, his position is not that of an intellectual: an intellectual, after all, senses the voluptousity of a problem, of the search in itself; he is a man of interrogations. The position of Mariátegui is that of an agitator, it is full of proselytism; one always knew where his reflections would lead, like those Yankee movies that always end in a wedding; it is the position of the man of answers. As a man of answers, he only studied Peruvian reality to find solutions." Basadre, *Perú: Problema y posibilidad*, 170, 197–98 (see chap. 6, n. 114).

14. See Paul Ricoeur, *Hermeneutics and the Human Sciences: Essays on Action, Language, and Interpretation* (Cambridge, U.K.: Cambridge University Press, 1981).

15. Hans-Georg Gadamer, "The Hermeneutics of Suspicion," *Man and World* 17 (1984): 313–23, and *El giro hermenéutico*, trans. Arturo Parada (Madrid: Catedra Teorema, 2001).

16. See Elías Palti, *La nación como problema* (see chap. 6, n. 1), and Donald R. Kelley, *Frontiers of History: Historical Inquiry in the Twentieth Century* (New Haven: Yale University Press, 2006).

17. Manuel González Prada, "Nuestros indios," *Obras* 2 (1985): 208.

18. See José Antonio Felices, "El soldado peruano," *La Revista Social,* 1 Aug. 1885, pp. 3–7.

19. Lorente, *Historia de la civilización peruana,* 38–39 (see chap. 5, n. 50).

20. Lorente, *Historia de la civilización peruana,* 39.

21. González Prada, "Nuestros indios," 209.

22. Hildebrando Castro Pozo, *Nuestra comunidad indígena* (Lima: El Lucero, 1924), 498.

23. Castro Pozo, *Nuestra comunidad,* 32.

24. Castro Pozo, *Nuestra comunidad,* 47–48.

25. Castro Pozo, *Nuestra comunidad,* 47.

26. See José Carlos Mariátegui, "El problema de la tierra," in Mariátegui, *Siete ensayos de interpretación de la realidad peruana* (Lima: Minerva, 1977 [1928]), 83; and Robert Paris, "José Carlos Mariátegui y el modelo del 'comunismo' inca," *Allpanchis* 14, no. 16 (Cuzco, 1980): 9–18.

27. Mariátegui, "El problema de la tierra," 80–82.

28. Mariátegui equates "Peru" and "Peruvian" with the indigenous and the precolonial, as well as the contemporary; the Lorentean genealogical lexicon is fully naturalized in his discourse. Much like Basadre, however, Mariátegui ignores Lorente, preferring instead to engage European thinkers.

29. Mariátegui, "El problema de la tierra," 82–83.

30. See Gerardo Leibner, *El mito del socialismo indígena en Mariátegui* (Lima: Fondo Editorial de la Pontificia Universidad Católica del Perú, 1999).

31. Mariátegui, *Siete ensayos,* 205.

32. On Hegel's dialectical theory of Europe, see Robert M. Dainotto, *Europe (in Theory)* (see chap. 4, n. 44).

33. José Carlos Mariátegui, "La tradición nacional," in Mariátegui, *Peruanicemos al Perú* (Lima: Minerva, 1975 [1925]), 122

34. Mariátegui, "La tradición nacional," 121.

35. Mariátegui, "El proceso de la literatura," in *Siete ensayos,* 336.

36. Mariátegui, "Esquema de la evolución económica," in Mariátegui, *Siete ensayos de interpretación de la realidad peruana* (Lima: Empresa Editorial Amauta, 1989 [1928]), 13–34.

37. Mariátegui, "Esquema de la evolución económica."

38. Mariátegui's writings on "the Indian problem" actually appeared in various fragments, one of them in the *Nation* (16 Jan. 1929) under the title "The New Peru." Notably, the piece entitled "El problema del indio" was not included in the first edition of *Siete ensayos.* It was the editors of Mariátegui's *Collected Works* who decided to include the essay in posthumous editions.

39. Mariátegui did recognize the value of the "liberal" efforts of Lorente and Pedro Gálvez to reform the Peruvian university system. After Lorente, however, the Peruvian educational system had lapsed back into a "colonialist spirit" reminiscent of the viceroyalty until the advent of the 1919 student movement for university reform, in which

Mariátegui participated. See Mariátegui, "El proceso de la instrucción pública," in *Siete ensayos*, 130–35.

40. This book was a collection of essays, many of which appeared in the 1910s in the periodicals *La Ilustración Peruana* and later in *El Mercurio Peruano*, then under Belaúnde's direction.

41. Victor Andres Belaúnde, *La realidad nacional* (Lima, 1931), 89–90.

42. Ibid., 91–92.

43. Basadre was very clear on this point: "The idea that a nation must have in its population a common race, blood, language, or economic interest corresponds to a moment when excessive importance was attributed to the natural sciences. The nation is a historical phenomenon and history is not a natural science. Soil, language, or blood form part of the body of the nation; but the explication of this phenomenon is not viable by way of natural things. The nation, says a savant of our times, is above all natural realities and all concrete things because the nation is an exclusively human creation. . . . The nation emerges as one of the human structures, the legitimate offspring of man." In another work, Basadre cites the Neokantian Heinrich Rickert, who "traced the division between the natural and cultural sciences and definitively proved that history is not a natural science, demolishing every determinist thesis that positivist sociology had encrusted in the historical process, so that it could elaborate fixed and inexorable laws, which is the basis of its pessimism and fatalism." Notable here is the concordance with Lorente's Kantian antipositivism. Basadre, *La multitud, la ciudad, y el campo en la historia del Perú* (Lima: Huascarán, 1947), 270, and *La promesa de la vida peruana*, 32–33 (see chap. 1, n. 18).

44. One of these quarters was historical or comparative sociology, the other ethnohistory, and both were inspired by developments abroad. Belaúnde himself was an early player. Belaúnde was inspired by the same new "social" or positivist sociological critique of "liberal" political history that had so influenced Mariátegui. Indeed, it was the young Belaúnde who had openly declared the twentieth-century triumph of "the social" over "the political" (latter being the master sign of the nineteenth century). Historical sociology in early twentieth-century Peru now defined itself against the supposed dogmas of nineteenth-century "liberal formalism" and its "political history." Belaúnde would study the "real social laws" of ancient Peru without regard for their "moral" content. To Peru's everlasting shame, Belaúnde declared, that real history had until now been written only by foreigners. These enlightened foreigners included Sir Clements Markham, Alfred Cunow, Guillaume De Greef, Max Uhle, Herbert Spencer, and the Bolivian sociologist Bautista Saavedra, whose book *El ayllu* (1903) was also indispensable bibliography for the new sociological study of "ancient Peruvian institutions." Belaúnde noted that the Peruvians Carlos Weisse and José de la Riva-Agüero had also made notable contributions, although this was because they had followed the insights of foreign scholars. Like Riva-Agüero, Belaúnde ignored Lorente's foundational contribution to the history of ancient Peru, as we saw in chapter 6, by wrongly and inconsistently associating Lorente with a "superficial" and merely "descriptive" political history. Rather than focus on the "Peruvian Monarchy" or the top of the state as the "liberal" historians supposedly had done in the nineteenth century, the "modern sociologist" of ancient Peru would turn

his scientific gaze to the true "constitutive elements" at the base: the ayllus. Cunow's hypothesis that "the Peruvian monarchy respected the organization of the ayllus, and the only thing it did was to systematize it" constituted "a true revolution in the manner in which the Inca Empire is considered. . . . To study Tawantinsuyu with certainty today, one need see the monarchy as a whole; instead we should study the small constitutive elements, the ayllus." But of course this revolution had been anticipated by Lorente in the 1870s, when he shifted the eyes of history away from the "monarchy" at the top to the "community spirit" of the "Peruvian civilization" of the indigenous communities "under" the Incas. For Belaúnde, the new sociological focus on the ayllu revealed that the Inca state had not been "socialist." Rather, that state was "simply the result of the union of small aggregations or Ayllus under the domination of the strongest tribe . . . the Quechua. The dream of Peruvian socialism has been dispelled. . . . Ancient Peru was not the archetype of the socialist state . . . it was simply an enormous agglomeration of Ayllus." See Víctor Belaúnde, *El Perú antiguo y los modernos sociologos*, 17–24 (see chap. 6, n. 120).

45. Haya de la Torre's anti-imperialist "Indoamericanism" saw the history of "Our America" as a series of "invasions"—Spanish "feudalism" and "mercantilism" followed by British and U.S. "industrial capitalism"—whose cumulative result was the subjugation and exploitation of "Indians." The "great problem of the Indian" was "eternal in America," and for this reason Haya names his master subject/object "Indoamerica." Rejecting the names "Hispano America" and "Latin America" as Europhile and following Waldo Frank, Haya de la Torre declared that "the European was becoming extinct or transformed in America, just as the Asian or Aryan [migrant had] in [ancient] Europe." In "Indoamerica" the European was consciously and subconsciously "Indianized," since it was "a historical law that the influences of conquerors are extinguished and transformed by conquered peoples." As a result, the "new revolution in our America will be a revolution of the Indian base, and its style will be Indian." Like his Peruvian peers, Haya argued that the best method for studying "our reality" was "the Hegelian method, that is, the dialectic," whose "ancestor was Heraclitus," who had said, "nothing is permanent, and all becomes." Still, continued Haya, Heraclitus was a "fatalist" because he ignored "liberty in the process of becoming." Marx had "applied this method to European societies," and it could now be fruitfully applied to American history. Spanish colonialism was the synthesis of the precolonial native thesis and the antithesis of conquest, but independence had failed to destroy "feudalism" and indeed had exacerbated it. Unlike the antifeudal French Revolution, the Spanish American revolutions had failed in this regard, and so it was the task of Haya de la Torre's generation to finally destroy feudalism and to produce a new, positive synthesis of "Indian" liberty. Real democracy did not yet exist in America, "because the reality was feudal." Haya thus emphasized the unifying, and anti-imperialist "racial" element of Indianness in America, while Mariátegui's revindication of the Indian was more class-based. Although Haya's vision was continental, both were nativists and nationalists, and their thought was revolutionary and historicist in the sense that it turned to the past only to transform the present. In the Peru of the 1920s and 1930s, that combination often translated into a nativist and neo-Hegelian

vanguardism broadly aligned with the notion that socialism and proletarian (and thus Indian) rule were both inevitable and historically authentic. See Víctor Raúl Haya de la Torre, *Indoamerica* (Lima: Ediciones Pueblo, 1961), 15–83.

46. Francisco García Calderón spent much of his productive life in Paris, where he became Peru's first "Latin Americanist." His histories, including *Le Pérou contemporain: Etude sociale* (Paris, 1907) and *Les démocraties latines de l'Amérique* (Paris, 1912), were obsessed with the "idea of race and culture," which the author took to be the "dominant question of contemporary politics." Although *Les démocraties latines* appeared in Gustavo Le Bon's series *Bibliotheque de philosophie scientifique*, it is clear that the Peruvian's ideas about "race" were more heterodox or Creole than the Frenchman's. García Calderón's depiction of the Incas is for the most part consistent with Prescott's, and like the positivist Javier Prado before him he relies upon Luis Carranza's influential ethnological notes on the "Peruvian indigenous race," which had argued that Peru's natives were condemned by the history of despotism and by Lamarckian biology to vegetate in servile roles.

47. Basadre, *La iniciación de la república*, 146.

48. Thurner, "Peruvian Genealogies of History and Nation," 141–75 (see chap. 4, n. 53).

49. Gustavo Montoya, "Jorge Basadre: El ensayo como estrategia," in Basadre, *La iniciación de la república*, 18–20 (see chap. 6, n. 113).

50. Basadre wrote only one book that came close to being a history of a subject in the round, narrative sense of the term. A well-written "life and times" book built around the viceroy Conde de Lemos, it is perhaps Basadre's best read.

51. Louis Baudin, *L'Empire socialiste des Inka* (Paris: Institut d'Ethnologie, 1928).

52. Basadre, *La multitud*, 58–59.

53. Ibid., 259.

54. Ibid., 261.

55. Basadre, *Perú: Problema*, 1–12.

56. Ibid., 4.

57. Ibid., 248–49.

58. Basadre, *La promesa de la vida peruana*, 27.

59. Ibid., 28.

60. Ibid., 31.

61. Thurner, "Una historia peruana para el pueblo peruano: De la geneología fundacional de Sebastián Lorente," in Thurner, ed., *Sebastián Lorente: Escritos fundacionales de historia peruana*, 15–76 (see chap. 6, n. 108).

62. Basadre, *La promesa de la vida peruana*, 29.

63. Ibid., 32.

64. Basadre, *Meditaciones*, ii–iii (see chap. 1, n. 7).

65. Basadre, *La promesa de la vida peruana*, 20.

66. Ibid., 17.

67. Santiago Távara, *Historia de los partidos* (see chap. 5, n. 3).

68. Basadre's usage of "ahistorical" and "historical" here is inconsistent with his earlier

usage, which had followed the Hegelian vision shared by Mariátegui. Here by "ahistorical" Basadre appears to mean a vision of the past that is false, that is, a nostalgic longing for something that never existed; "historical" is applied to the Incas here because for Basadre their socialist utopia did exist in the past but was no longer possible.

69. Basadre, *La promesa de la vida peruana*, 13–14.

70. As Koselleck notes, the historical notion of a utopia located in the future rather than in the past and that could be projected from the present as a possible *uchronia* emerged in France shortly before the revolution. Reinhart Koselleck, *The Practice of Conceptual History: Timing History, Spacing Concepts*, trans. Tom Samuel Presener and others (Stanford: Stanford University Press, 2002), 86–88.

71. Basadre, *La multitud*, 267–68.

72. Basadre attributed the phrase *país profundo* to the Frenchman Charles Péguy (1873–1914), but the notion was common among German historicists and was reflected in such concepts as *Kulturstaat* and *Machtstaat*, or *Kulturnation* and *Staatsnation* (found both in Fichte and Meinecke).

73. Basadre, *La multitud*, 269–70.

74. Basadre, *Perú: Problema*, 35–36.

75. Basadre, *La multitud*, 279–80.

76. Manuel García Morente, *Idea de la hispanidad* (Buenos Aires: Espasa-Calpe, 1938). See Palti, *La nación como problema* (see chap. 6, n. 1); on Ortega y Gasset's idea of possibility, see Luís Arista Montoya, "La razón histórica: Ortega y Gasset y Jorge Basadre," in Pantigoso, *Cátedra Basadre*, 37–68 (see chap. 7, n. 1).

77. García Morente, *Idea de la hispanidad*, 67.

78. Basadre, *La multitud*, 279–80.

79. Basadre, *La multitud*, 270–71.

80. José de la Riva-Agüero, *La historia en el Perú*, 509–510 (see chap. 2, n. 45).

81. Ibid., 506.

82. Basadre, *Perú: Problema*, 1–2.

83. Basadre, *Perú: Problema*, 2–3.

84. Palti, *La nación como problema*.

85. Basadre, *Perú: Problema*, 6–7.

86. Reinhart Koselleck, *Futures Past: On the Semantics of Historical Time*, trans. Keith Tribe (New York: Columbia University Press, 2004), 41.

87. Basadre, *Meditaciones*, 63–64.

88. Basadre, *Perú: Problema*, 2–3

89. Basadre, *Meditaciones*, 48.

90. Ibid., 49.

91. See Wilhelm Dilthey, *Das Erlebnis und die Dichtung: Lessing, Goethe, Novalis, Hölderin* (Leipzig: Teubner, 1910).

92. Basadre, *Meditaciones*, 49–50.

93. Ibid., 104–107.

94. Ibid., 94–95.

95. Jorge Basadre, "Nota preliminar a la quinta edición," in *Historia de la República del*

Perú, 1822–1933, 6th ed. (Lima: Editorial Universitaria, 1968), xxi–xxii. Basadre cites Spanish translations of Croce's *Teoria e storia della storiografia* and *Storia come pensiero e come azione*.

96. Basadre, "Nota preliminar," xlii.

97. Basadre, "Nota preliminar," xx–xxi.

98. Basadre, "A propósito de los puntos de vista de este libro: Reflexiones sobre la historiografía," in *Historia de la República del Perú*, xxxv–xlvi. This new preface follows the preface to the sixth edition (in which Basadre attempts to argue that the new edition sports a Braudelian design). Basadre's late attempt to give his masterwork a Braudelian design consisted of appending old material on the "geographic, economic, social, and cultural 'bases' of the Republic," and adding two new chapters on "the Church and the State," and "the idea of the Patria." Although Basadre shared Braudel's modernist vision of "total history" or "complete history," which would be produced in multidisciplinary workshops, he never undertook the history of capitalism or material life. Basadre left that task to the new generation, who eagerly responded to the call of the Annales.

99. Basadre, "A propósito," xliv.

100. Basadre, "A propósito," xxxv–xxxvi.

101. Charles R. Bambach, *Heidegger, Dilthey, and the Crisis of Historicism* (Ithaca: Cornell University Press, 1995).

102. Basadre's appreciation contradicts Popper's claim that "modern historicists" are ignorant of "the antiquity of their doctrine." In general, Popper's rationalist rejection of historicism as "superstition" could only be applied to Basadre with great injustice. His historicism did not cling to "immutable historical laws" nor was it "afraid of change." Karl Popper, *The Poverty of Historicism* (Boston: Beacon Press, 1957).

103. Basadre, "A propósito," xxxvii–xxxviii.

104. Basadre, *Perú: Problema*, 2–3.

105. Partha Chatterjee, *The Nation and Its Fragments: Colonial and Postcolonial Histories* (Princeton: Princeton University Press, 1993), 75–115.

106. Here I am indebted to Dipesh Chakrabarty's concept of "the subaltern past." See *Provincializing Europe*, 97–113 (see chap. 6, n. 4).

107. On the history of these notions, see Lovejoy, *Great Chain of Being* (see chap. 4, n. 1).

108. Elías Palti, "Poststructuralist Marxism and the 'Experience of Disaster,'" 459–80 (see chap. 1, n. 16).

Epilogue

1. Jorge Basadre, "En torno a la teoría de la historia," *Historia y Cultura* 1 (Lima, 1965), 9.

2. Ibid., 9.

3. Part of the problem with imposing the German "new" or "modern" age schemata on Peru and, indeed, on France, is that the Germans were latecomers to this epochal

name. In the Latin world, "modern" was the name of the period following the "discov⌐ of America," while "contemporary" became the name of the period opened by the "Age of Revolutions," which in unrevolutionary Germany was called "the modern."

4. Reinhart Koselleck, *historia/Historia*, trans. Gómez Ramos (Madrid: Editorial Trotta, 2004).

5. Basadre, "En torno a la teoría de la historia," 19.

6. Ibid., 8.

7. Gilles Deleuze, *Nietzsche y la filosofía*, trans. Carmen Artel (Barcelona: Editorial Anagrama, 1986), 106–113.

8. Leslie Paul Thiele, *Friedrich Nietzsche and the Politics of the Soul: A Study of Heroic Individualism* (Princeton: Princeton University Press, 1990).

9. Michael Allen Gillespie, *Hegel, Heidegger, and the Ground of History* (Chicago: University of Chicago Press, 1984), 120–21.

10. Another reason Basadre remains king of "Peruvian history" is that "Peru" has lost ground as the master name and subject under which professional historians now labor. Under the influence of ethnohistory, archaeology, and the French Annales school of historiography, the ethnogeographical concepts of "the Andes" and "Andean man" have since at least the 1980s begun to eclipse "Peru" and "Peruvian man" as the governing topoi of social scientific, cultural, and historical discourse. Young Peruvian social historians, some of the brightest of whom sought training in France or England, read and wrote history from an avowedly Marxist or at any rate "Mariáteguist" *idea crítica de la historia*. This "new generation" of historians committed itself to the task of writing the long history of capitalism and *mentalité* in Peru. Key themes in this "new critical history" were "modes of production" and "the transition" and "resistance" to capitalism, and in cultural history what came to be known later as "the Andean utopia." Studies of indigenous rebellion and particularly of the Túpac Amaru insurrection of the 1780s were the order of the day, in part because such studies allowed radical historians to transcend the traditional discourse of Peru's Lima-based Creole nationalism (or so it was thought) and instead embrace a regional, "Andean" history of resistance—a new "Andean" image of the past that could serve as a roadmap to a revolutionary future. Notably, by the late 1980s and early 1990s, this "new history" of the social "turned" back to political history, albeit via anthropological and cultural approaches to the political. The "new history" carried out the Annales project that Basadre had anticipated, setting up interdisciplinary workshops of rural or Andean social history, and reaching out, in some cases via Peruvian NGOs and in others via leftist political parties, to the "deep country." As Manuel Burga noted in his reflections on Peruvian historiography, however, one of the effects of the turn to "the Andean" was the rise of "multiculturalism" and the apparent decline of "national history." Nevertheless, it is tempting to think of "the Andes" as a contemporary gloss on the "Peru" of Inca Garcilaso, Peralta, Unanue, and Lorente. Unlike Basadre's national Peru (which both existed and was not yet), the "Peru" of these earlier Peruvian historians was the projection of a regional and universal desire, much like "the Andes" is imagined to be today. On the other hand, it was Basadre's "airborne factory" or toolbox

and repertoire of historiography that clearly guided the "new history" of the 1970s–90s. And when the new historians did write national history, they often did so under the cover of Basadrean topoi. See Manuel Burga, *La historia y los historiadores en el Peru* (Lima: Fondo Editorial de la Universidad Nacional Mayor de San Marcos, 2005).

11. Chakrabarty, *Provincializing Europe*, 8 (see chap. 6, n. 4).

12. Dainotto, *Europe (in Theory)*, 108–124 (see chap. 4, n. 44).

13. Dainotto, *Europe (in Theory)*.

14. In this regard, it is unsurprising that the inspiration for Subaltern Studies comes from the Italian discourse of national failure that permeated the historical vision and theoretical language of Antonio Gramsci's "Notes on Italian History." Before Gramsci, however, many of the historians of southern Europe never accepted this honor of being the failures of history. Instead, they "wrote back" against "Europe."

15. On logocentrism and phonocentrism, see Jacques Derrida, *Of Grammatology*, trans. Gayatri Spivak (Baltimore: Johns Hopkins University Press, 1988).

16. The modern romance languages have no term that is strictly equivalent to *Geschichte*, although by the eighteenth century it appears that *historia* had acquired many of the same connotations. *Historia* has long been the regnant term here, although in the early modern period "chronicle" and "relation" were also common. These latter terms, however, never exercised the full semantic reach of "history," which was reserved for more systematic annals and/or more elegant philosophical accounts, both of which were based on classical models. Moreover, it appears that since at least the early seventeenth century the Spanish use of *historia* could and did refer to the orderly succession of "events" or *hechos* (*res gestae*), as it does in Antonio de Herrera's official Tacitean anal of "the deeds" of Spaniards in the conquest of the New World. The Spanish *historia* awaits the writing of its conceptual history.

17. Koselleck, *historia/Historia*, 47–59.

18. Basadre, *La promesa de la vida peruana*, 95–107 (see chap. 1, n. 18).

19. Hayden White, "Historicism, History, and the Figurative Imagination," in *Tropics of Discourse: Essays in Cultural Criticism* (Baltimore: Johns Hopkins University Press, 1978), 104.

20. As Barthes notes, foundational historical discourse performs a poetic or "mytho-poetic" function since no matter how sober, scientific, or objective, it always assumes the form of the "of thee I sing" of the poets, only in this case the "I sing" (even when, in accordance with the protocols of the discipline, the "I" of the historian is cloaked in an authorizing "we") unites the future that already is with its enabling death or forgotten past by virtue of the genealogical or mythological "thee" that it reveals in prose as a presence or truth. See Barthes, "Discourse of History" (see chap. 1, n. 4); Lyotard, "Universal History and Cultural Differences" (see chap. 1, n. 22).

21. Jacques Rancière, *The Flesh of Words: The Politics of Writing* (Stanford: Stanford University Press, 1994), 3–5.

22. The classic study is Ernst Kantorowicz, *The King's Two Bodies: A Study in Mediaeval Political Theology* (Princeton: Princeton University Press, 1997).

23. Although the subjects or names of historical discourse today are frequently imagined to be more democratic, diverse, and scientific than were the imperial and national histories of monarchs and republics, there is no escape from the demands that subjects impose upon the writing of history. Indeed, and as Rancière argues, the subjects of historical writing today are notoriously elusive and thus more difficult to defend as true, but not for that reason avoidable. How can historians claim, as they do every day, that an ethnicity, a social class, a gender, a region, a germ, or a body of water "experiences" something, or "undergoes" some fundamental change? History's poetic answer remains the same: the proper name. Then, as now, history's truths "live" only by virtue of their retrospective and thus poetic incarnation in properly named bodies of power, the so-called agents of history.

24. Cited in Elías Palti, "What Is Historicism? The Erratic History of a Concept," paper presented to the panel "Historicism and Its Limits," American Historical Association Annual Meeting, Washington, D.C., Jan. 2008. Palti cites the quote in Pietro Rossi, "The Ideological Valences of Twentieth-century Historicism," *History and Theory* 14, no. 4, Beiheft 14 (1975): 108. Rossi in turn cites Wilhelm Dilthey, "Plan der Fortsetzung zum der Aufbau der geschichtlichen Welt in den Geisteswissenschaften," in *Gesammelte Schriften* 7, 290.

25. For another classic study of the "German tradition" and concept of history, see Georg Iggers, *The German Conception of History: The National Tradition of Historical Thought from Herder to the Present* (Middletown, Conn.: Wesleyan University Press, 1968).

26. Friedrich Meinecke, *El historicismo y su génesis*, 14–15 (see chap. 5, n. 42).

27. Koselleck, *historia/Historia*, 34.

28. Jorge Cañizares-Esguerra, *Puritan Conquistadors* (see chap. 4, n. 4).

29. Meinecke, *El historicismo*, 370.

30. On the "preformist" configuration of the subject in European historical discourse on the nation, see Elías Palti, *La nación como problema* (see chap. 6, n. 1).

31. Palti, "What Is Historicism?"

32. Koselleck, *historia/Historia*, 338–45.

33. See Joseph Mali and Robert Wokler, eds., *Isaiah Berlin's Counter-Enlightenment* (Philadelphia: American Philosophical Society, 2003), and Isaiah Berlin's *Three Critics of the Enlightenment: Vico, Hamann, Herder* (Princeton: Princeton University Press, 2000).

34. Koselleck, *historia/Historia*, 33–38.

35. Elías Palti, *Aporías: Tiempo, modernidad, historia, sujeto, nación, ley* (Buenos Aires: Alianza, 2001), 140.

36. See Kelley, *Faces of History*, 75–98 (see chap. 1, n. 4).

37. Enlightenment and Counter-Enlightenment histories shared a cosmopolitanism that recognized the validity of singular national histories as well as their universal and converging tendencies. On Enlightenment histories, see Karen O'Brien, *Narratives of Enlightenment* (see chap. 5, n. 52). On the "end of history" in Montesquieu as France, and then in Hegel as Germany, see Dainotto, *Europe (in Theory)*, 73–118, and passim.

38. Koselleck, *historia/Historia*, 134.

39. Karl Werner, *Giambattista Vico als Philosoph und gelehrter Forscher* (Vienna: Brau-müller, 1881).

40. Palti, "What Is Historicism?"

41. Benedetto Croce, *History as the Story of Liberty*, trans. Silvia Sprigge (New York: Norton, 1941), 315–20.

42. On this point Chakrabarty follows Maurice Mandelbaum, whose *History, Man, and Reason: A Study in Nineteenth-century Thought* (Baltimore: Johns Hopkins University Press, 1974) argues that development was the central idea of nineteenth-century European historicism.

43. Chakrabarty, *Provincializing Europe*, 23.

44. Martin Heidegger, *Being and Time* (Oxford, U.K.: Blackwell, 2004), 437–38. Emphasis in original.

45. Chakrabarty, *Provincializing Europe*, 249–50.

46. Dainotto, *Europe (in Theory)*, 108–124.

Index

2, 16, 75, 80, 142, 249